Sel
Sparrows

JUDY WRIGHT

What did I learn from you, grandpa?
What were the tales from your grave?
I learnt that to eat, you sold sparrows,
For which tuppence a dozen was paid.

Victims or Villains?
A true story of crime
in 19th-century Bedfordshire
and convict transportation to Australia

For the descendants of
George White and Thomas Dockerill
wherever they may be,
who are compassionate enough
to accept the weakness of humankind,
with apologies to those who are not.

First published October 2006
by
J.H.Wright
in association with
The Book Castle
12 Church Street
Dunstable
Bedfordshire LU5 4RU

ISBN 0 9553516 0 X
ISBN 978 0 9553516 0 0

Designed and typeset by Caroline and Roger Hillier
The Old Chapel Graphic Design

Printed in Great Britain by T J International Ltd, Padstow, Cornwall

CONTENTS

ACKNOWLEDGEMENTS

My grateful thanks to the following people without whose help and encouragement this book would not have been written:

U.K.
My family: Bryan Hill, Sarah Silverton, Lisette Abrahams, Marcus Brookes.
Lyn Scadding (Bedfordshire and Luton Archives and Records Service)
Kathy Scott, Joyce and Dennis Pearce

Australia
My family: Kath & Jack Simmons, Jessie & John Ruffle.
Jane and Jim King; Sue White; Barbara and Lloyd Hasleby

And to the following sources of reference:
National Archives, Kew
Bedfordshire and Luton Archives and Records Service, Bedford
British Library of Political and Economic Science, London
Haslemere Museum, Surrey
Guildford Institute of the University of Surrey, Guildford
States Record Office of Western Australia, Perth
Battye Library, Perth
Claremont Museum, Western Australia
Chiverton House Museum, Northampton, Western Australia

Illustration Acknowledgements
I give my grateful thanks for permission to reproduce illustrations as follows:
Haslemere Museum (from Illustrated London News) – pages 10, 16, 19, 20, 21, 22, 42, 49, 66, 93, 105, 106, 109, 142, 143, 145, 178, 193, 201, 202, 217, 225, 234, 235, 236, 237, 239, 249, 255, 279, 311, 349, 350, 351, 431; Bedfordshire and Luton Archives and Records Service – pages 23, 25, 29, 57, 59, 62, 65, 82, 85, 98, 103, 181; The National Archives – pages 177, 188, 189, 219, 227, 228, 229, 277, 297, 299, 332, 333, 341, 343, 345, 355, 368; The Guildford Institute of the University of Surrey (from Illustrated London News) – pages 13, 15, 46, 54, 67, 112, 158, 160, 161, 162, 218, 248, 250, 278, 287, 306, 346, 352; Bedford Central Library (from Illustrated London News) – pages 6, 26, 44, 51, 68, 69, 242, 244, 245, 252, 298, 315, 324, 427; Worthing Central Library (from Punch Magazine) – pages 34, 35, 37, 52, 131; Weymouth Reference Library – pages 231, 233, 240; Battye Library, Perth – cover, page 273, Accession 2816A/3; State Record Office of Western Australia – pages 241, 270, 318, 410; Northampton Historical Society, Inc. and George McDonald – pages 399, 400, 408; Bryan Hill – pages 87, 384, 406, 409, 412, 413, 414, 415; Jim King – page 407; Brian Mead – page 404

Trial Judge Mr. Baron Rolfe, appointed Lord Chancellor in 1852

The Accused

The small courtroom of the Bedford Crown Court was packed with curious observers on the morning of Saturday 10th March, 1849. It was the third day of the Lent session of the Bedford Assizes and, despite the bitter winter weather, a crowd had begun to form early in the morning, for there was little room inside for many spectators and those disappointed had little choice but to repair to a nearby public house to keep in touch with the events. As the doors opened they had pushed forward, jostling with their eager neighbours for a better view of the dock, already unpeeling the layers they had donned against the harsh conditions outside. Once inside, the air was warmed by the breath of these vociferous creatures and the increasing drone of their voices. Their cackling mouths were never at rest, vying with one another, as each know-all sought to outdo the other with the extent of his criminal knowledge. For each believed he was more conversant with the facts of the case than his neighbour, each seemed to have first-hand information, more intimate knowledge or knew a person who had. The noise got louder as they interrupted one another, eager to tell their tales, 'in confidence, of course'. And the facts became more distorted, being a better tale to tell. Then at once all became hushed as the magistrates entered.

In the judicial chair that day sat the right Honourable Mr. Baron Rolfe and nearby sat the body of 'esquires' whose austere presence composed the forbidding 'Grand Jury'. There too were their compatriots, for the day at least. Today these twelve lesser mortals had donned the mantle of superiority and were magnified in their self-importance, but after today they would lose their prestige, for these were the 'twelve good men and true' that composed the 'Petty Jury'.

The judge could look forward to a busy day, for he had four trials to direct and one man, convicted the previous day, to sentence. But for the most part, the first three trials were of little interest to the avid spectators, for that which was attracting such heightened curiosity was the fourth and main case of the day, that of three men local to the area who were charged with having, on the 25th January, 1849 at the parish of Stanbridge in Bedfordshire, unlawfully and maliciously wounded two police constables, James Parrott and William Clough with the intent to prevent their lawful apprehension.[1] Amongst the spectators in the courtroom sat the young wives, families and neighbours of the accused, apprehensively awaiting the start of the proceedings, for the most part oblivious of the curious stares and pointing fingers, insulated against them in their common bond. There too were the accusers, intent on revenge. But by far the majority of the crowd was made up of greedy onlookers hungry for sensationalism. For some, their interest carried sympathy and support for their fellow village folk, but most, if they were honest, were there for the scandal and excitement, for the crime of which the accused were charged could carry a severe sentence, possibly that of transportation.

Earlier that morning the barristers and judge for the session had gathered behind the scenes to prepare themselves for the day. As did the judge, one of the barristers, Mr. Prendergast, had a full caseload. He was prosecuting in two of the trials, and appearing for the defence in two more. Of the others, Mr. Tozer and Mr. Fitzpatrick were prosecuting and Mr. Burcham and Mr. Power were defending. Mr. Burcham was feeling somewhat indisposed that day, but elected to proceed with the task of defending his clients. Mr. Power stood by ready to assist him.

Meanwhile, in the cells of Bedford Gaol, the day dawned like any other since their remand for our three accused prisoners. Breakfast was the same as usual, just one pint of oatmeal gruel and eight ounces of bread.[2] But in every other respect, today was different. Today they had no stomach for their breakfast which, even though tasteless, would normally be consumed with relish. For two days now, since the start of the Assizes on the previous Thursday, the three men had been waiting with apprehension for their summons to appear. But now their agonizing wait was over and today would decide their fate. As the hour drew near for their appearance, the men were escorted from the holding cell to the dock of the Crown Court. The atmosphere was charged with emotion as they were led in, for it was the first time the men had been brought face to face with members of their families, and their accusers, since their various arrests and subsequent appearances at the Petty sessions.

All three men had been born and bred in Bedfordshire. The first was Thomas Dockerill from Stanbridge, believed to be the ringleader of the gang. Dockerill was much the tallest of the three men at nearly 6ft, and was the eldest at twenty-nine years. He had dark brown hair above an oval face, with fresh complexion, sharp nose and a small mouth.[3] His eyebrows and eyelashes were light brown and his eyes were light hazel, one of which, the left, had a scar beneath it which, along with his general air of resentment, gave him a somewhat unsavoury appearance. He also sported scars on his stomach and arm, bearing witness to the fact that he was no newcomer to a good scrap. There was a vaccination mark on his arm. Dockerill was married to Rebecca, the sister of our second accused, and they had three children, Ephraim who was ten years old, Joseph who was six, and Mary who was sixteen months. Dockerill alone had a further charge against him, that of shooting and wounding the aforesaid James Parrott.[4]

The second man, George White, was raised in the tiny hamlet of Thorn, but now resided in Houghton Regis. George was twenty-four years old, 5ft 7ins tall with a fresh complexion, round face, light brown hair and grey eyes.[5] He was of stocky or stout appearance and wore a light smock, common to agricultural labourers at this time, breeches, and leggings adorned with bright buttons. George had been married just over seventeen months to his second wife, Sarah, and they had a baby daughter, Eliza, just five months old, although court records stated he was unmarried.

The third man, William White, was from Chalk Hill, Dunstable, also known as Puddlehill, and was the youngest at twenty-two years and the shortest, standing 5ft 5ins tall and with light hair and blue eyes.[6] His normally pale complexion was heightened by his obvious nervousness of the proceedings. William was George's nephew though he was just three years younger, and was the son of George's eldest brother, John. William had been married to his young wife, Mary, for just two years and they were expecting their first child in the summer. All three men were agricultural labourers and both George and William were shown to have identification marks of scars on their thumbs caused by the tools of their trade.

At the start of the trial, which was to last nearly six hours, it was by no means certain that the prosecution, led by Mr. Prendergast and Mr. Tozer, had a strong enough case against George and William White to get a conviction. But the evidence against Thomas Dockerill was quite conclusive. The case against the Whites rested solely on the identification by the two police officers, one of whom could not be certain, especially in the case of William, that they had the right men. Witnesses both for the prosecution and for the Whites' defence sat eyeing each other, waiting to be called to give evidence. For Dockerill there was no witness.

At the end of the proceedings, when the verdict was pronounced it caused much excitement, with shouts from the accused, and William being carried from the dock in a dead faint.[7]

A court case in 1849 would attract a large crowd.

CHAPTER 1

Village Life – Thorn and Puddlehill

One might be forgiven for thinking that the tiny hamlet of Thorn, situated just north of Dunstable in Bedfordshire, was of little consequence.

There was nothing of a planned village there, the hamlet seemingly just evolving if not by accident, then as a by-product of the junction with the Turnpike Road which ran from London to the north of England. From here there was easy access to the farms along a rutted leafy lane which gently unfolded to reveal this rural retreat, the track probably beginning its life as a well-used path between the common fields, twisting and turning to avoid puddles and marshes through to its mother village of Houghton Regis. From here the cattle, fattened by their sojourn on the green commons, could be driven leisurely along the Turnpike to the market in Dunstable. Those errant roving herds, which were in no hurry to reach their fate, were a noisy grievance to the stagecoach traffic as they bottlenecked the toll-gate that once graced the roadside at Puddlehill, but had moved further north to Kate's Hill by 1826.

Thorn itself consisted of no more than a couple of farms with a handful of tiny farm labourers' cottages dotted around them, sixteen in all, calling themselves home for some ninety inhabitants. Continuing along the track, from Thorn Green towards Bidwell and Houghton Regis, was Bury Corner with another farm and worker's cottage, then Washbrook Corner with one more cottage, before Carcutt farm, and the turning which led to

Houghton Regis through Bidwell. These few dwellings swelled this small community to one hundred and six.[1] Everybody knew everybody else in Thorn and each knew the other's business. Every face was familiar and family secrets were common knowledge. The inhabitants were ignorant of learning, illiterate, but they had little need for the written word. They relied on one another from birth to death. It was a narrow existence.

There was not much else at Thorn. There was no village shop for the wives to exchange a yarn, no alehouse for the men to meet up with their contemporaries, although there was one not far away at Puddlehill. But in Thorn itself there were just the few tumbledown cottages, each crammed full of quarrelsome snotty nosed brats, their powerful discordant bellows heard day and night as they struggled for their place in the pecking order of the family nest. Then there were the farms, where the men spent their working day from daybreak to nightfall digging, planting and harvesting the crops, tending the cattle, repaying their debt of gratitude to the farmer in the sweat and toil of their labours for the privilege of earning a meagre existence. Once, there had been a small Baptist Church at Thorn, where worshippers travelled from afar to attend a service, but it was decided that it was too out of the way, too great a distance to travel in winter. And so the chapel was moved brick by brick to Houghton Regis just a couple of miles away in the early part of the nineteenth century.

But this little country lane through Thorn, a quagmire of mud in the winter rutted by the cart tracks and horses hoofs, was still well used. For those wagoners and carters coming from the North it was a convenient route from the Turnpike to Houghton Regis, and saved the journey through the notorious Puddlehill. There were the itinerants, the gypsies, fiddlers and entertainers, who would amble down the lane at fair time. There were the peddlers too, hoping to tempt the housewives with their goods. For those eager souls it was an opportunity for them to acquire much needed household items. For there was only so many times the frugal villagers could re-use items before they became worn out. An old piece of leather could mend a shoe, a nail could be straightened and

SPLITTING WOOD FOR BASKETS.—FROM A DRAWING BY G. H. THOMPSON.

Splitting wood for baskets.

used again, and old clothes had endless possibilities. But even if they could not afford his goods, the hawker provided a welcome chance for them to catch up with the gossip and news from outside their restricted community.

It was down this lane towards Thorn in the spring of 1837 that Thomas Dockerill, a gangling youth of only sixteen, but with a maturity beyond his years, would hurry from his native village of Stanbridge to meet a comely lass named Rebecca White. It was in Thorn that Rebecca, some two years senior to Thomas, lost her heart and her virginity to him, and later lost the baby she bore him. And it is Dockerill who is the first of our accused men.

It was in Thorn that George White, Rebecca's brother, was raised, and fought elders and babies alike for his recognition in the family nest. It was here that, as a lad of thirteen years, he first encountered Dockerill, who was to become his brother-in-law and friend. George, then, is the second of our accused men.

And it was in Thorn too that William White was born to Sally, the wife of John White, Rebecca and George's eldest brother. William is our third accused.

The tiny farm cottage in which George and his twelve living siblings were raised would have provided no more accommodation than a single room, or maybe two, on the lower storey with a lean-to scullery attached. It would have been the same upstairs also, with, for decency's sake, a curtain, made from an old counterpane or old clothes, hung across to divide the parents from the children. Those who would not fit in this small space, and who could not be crammed top to toe, arguing and kicking each other into the shared beds, would be relegated to the floor downstairs. In comparison, the comfort of the floor should not be underestimated, as the beds themselves probably consisted of no more than straw pallets. But this teeming nest provided a haven, presided over by its swollen matriarch, Lucy, whose fleshy arms were ever ready to comfort her endlessly increasing brood of children and grandchildren. The conditions in each in this cluster of cottages would not have varied

Water had to be carried from the well.

Washday was a monumental chore.

much, only by the number of its inhabitants. Sanitation was almost unheard of and water supply inadequate, although there was a communal pump on the farm where the gossips could tattle to their heart's content on washday, and thus relieve the strain of the monumental chore of laundering their clothes. The cottagers would have shared or fought for their turn in the privy, maybe only one closet between two or three cottages, or possibly even more, although sometimes there was not one at all.

Some of the cottages might have had their own pigsty close to the building, for the pig was an important beast, cherished by the whole family. For the adults, possession of a pig gave an anticipation of future mouth-watering enjoyment in the form of succulent meat and bacon, lard and savoury dripping on a chunk of bread, pork pies, the delicacy of his trotters and chitterlings, and then the porker's head boiled to provide brawn. For the children he was a pet, for awhile at least, until the dreadful day came when his sty was empty. But, in the meantime, the family's friend smiled contentedly as he chomped relentlessly on the snails and the dandelions that the children collected for him, blissfully ignorant of his crucial role in the family's investment for a hard winter. Apart from the smell of the beast himself, the most obvious sign of his presence within the family nest would be a 'pig tub' at the back door – a receptacle for all scraps and waste, left-overs, slops and even washing-up water. Of course, there was a stench from the beast's living quarters, but this was generally no more offensive than that from the human privy, which on a windy day could permeate the very soul of the little cottages.

Furnishings in the cottages would have been simple, bare walls, with mud or stone floors – some with bright rag rugs, a couple of wooden chairs and a table. An open fireplace, with maybe an oven beside it, would provide warmth for the occupants and play host to a few pots and pans. But for some of the larger, poorer families where the women were too disheartened to provide bright rugs or maybe a plant on the window-sill, their rooms remained soullessly bare and depressing with a few sticks of furniture and a pensioned off sack serving time once more as a rug.

Personal cleansing would have been nothing more than a quick dip by the back door, inside in winter, outside in summer, the children probably thankfully escaping with none.

Faced with the prospect of cooking on an open fire, or at best a primitive oven, and a lack of suitable cooking equipment, food would have been unimaginative, anything which could be boiled, bread and tea. Poorer workers would not have afforded meat, the lack of this being made up with more bread and potatoes.

But as a contrast to the labourers' existence, the farm where they toiled would have been practically self sufficient. Corn was gathered and threshed by flail, and later by machine. Cheese and butter were produced, the latter in a churn, really a barrel with a handle. Meat would be salted and the vegetables crops stock-piled for winter, potatoes, turnips, and beans. Candles too would be made on the farm. The farmer could be satisfied with his lot.

And for the thriftier of the housewives' families, there was a veritable harvest to be gathered from the hedgerows, a task doubtless attracting many volunteers amongst those youngsters who might be courting, thus given a plausible excuse to slip out into the privacy of the thickets with other more pleasurable things on their mind than picking berries. For those willing gatherers, there were cowslips and elderberries to be made into a good drop of wine, blackberries and plums to be made into jam, crab apples into jelly. There were hazel nuts and chestnuts, all to be hoarded for the harder times. For those harder times were aplenty.

With such a large family as the one that George was born into, it would have been impossible for all to sit round a table at mealtimes, the meal would have to have been taken in more than one sitting. Or maybe the children would sit on the floor in the corner of the room with their food in their hands, with the smaller ones out of sight under the table, and quiet too if they had any sense, in an effort to avoid an elder's boot.

As a contrast to the conditions inside, the front of the cottages would have presented an idyllic scene in summer, with an outward look and feel of comfort. The cheerful sociability of the housewives as they chatted to their neighbours at the front doors which abounded with honeysuckle, roses and hollyhocks, belying their meagre existence. It was a picturesque foreground against a backdrop of poverty and human squalor, for the cottages afforded little more than the basic requirements of shelter, warmth and a place to eat. But the humble villagers bore the inadequacies of their living arrangements with stalwart good humour, for they had experienced no different. Of course, they dreaded the damp because it brought on their rheumatics, and they might not like the draughts, which came from all directions and brought the smell from the pigs, and worse from the privy. And then there were frequent coughs and fevers too from the poor sanitation, but "mustn't grumble".

But without question they did recognise that there was another quality of life. They saw the opulence of the big houses, like Houghton Hall which dominated the Green in Houghton Regis. It was here that Squire Brandreth lived, from where he rode through the village in his carriage or across his estate with his hounds. But this was not for the likes of them. For 'The Squire' was an important man. He was a gentleman and, as such, afforded the deference of his lesser mortals. It was the natural disposition of things. It was an in-born right assumed by the upper classes, and never questioned by the lower. In the order of submission there was a higher echelon than that of the Squire, and

A veritable feast could be gathered from the hedgerows and trees.

that was the Duke of Bedford. The Duke was Aristocracy, and as such was at the top of the social scale. But at a local level, the Squire was the man who commanded the importance of his position. Because, socially, England was fettered by bonds of deference, each of the lower orders servile to their 'betters'. So the villagers stood to one side as he rode by, some doffed their caps, and some curtseyed. Others did neither, but looked on sullenly. For deference to their betters could split a family,

The squire was an important man.

The villagers stood to one side as the Squire rode by.

The stagecoaches had arduous journeys.

causing many arguments, some seeing them as persons to whom they should show respect and humility and obey unquestioningly, whilst other members of the same family would see this subservience as humiliation rather than humility.

From the cottages at Thorn, across the golden fields of Greenman Farm was a fine view of the notorious Puddlehill, which had been the cause of so much hardship for the stagecoach traffic, but was now tamed by the cutting that had been gouged through the chalk hill to lower the road as it snaked its way to the outskirts of Dunstable, the nearest market town. The excavated chalk now defaced the valley on the side of the ridge, but this was a necessary price to pay for progress, for the newly formed road was a tremendous improvement for the stagecoaches. But for the Puddlehill Trustees, who were responsible for the road improvement from Dunstable to Hockliffe, it was a short lived triumph, as the threat of steam became a reality. For the railway line which had been started from London reached Tring in 1837, and was completed

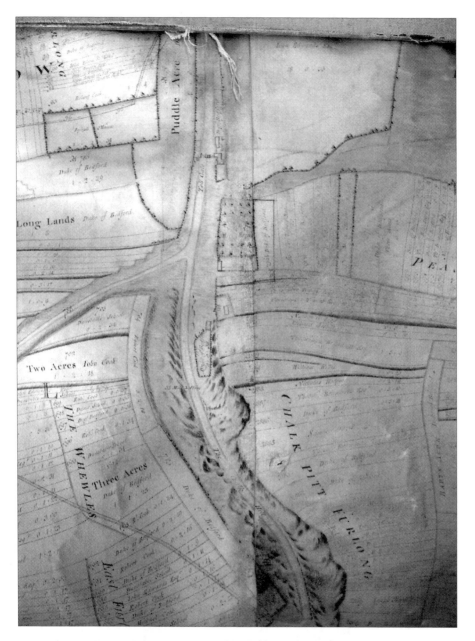

Map of Puddle Hill and Turnpike Road 1762 showing alternative road for stagecoaches and tollgate. The land is still farmed in strips. *B553*

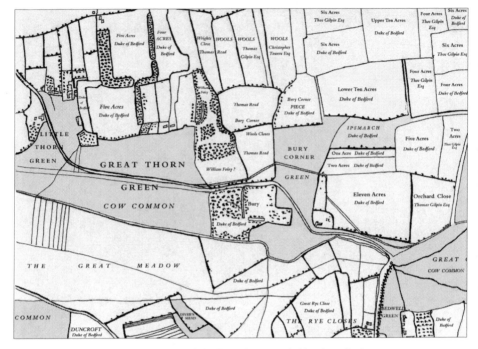

Map of Thorn and Bidwell, turning towards Houghton Regis.
Drawn by author from enclosure map MA84/2 1796 (enclosed 1802)

through to Birmingham in 1839, taking a great deal of the stagecoach traffic away. The stretch of road in 1835 brought in £2,770 in tolls; when the government made enquiries in 1840 after the opening of the London to Birmingham railway, this income had sunk to £1,030.[2]

Puddlehill had in its time played host to many villains. Highwaymen had found its terrain hospitable to their buccaneering ever since stagecoaches slowly edged their way along this treacherous stretch of road. But since the area was enclosed in the early part of the nineteenth century, it had become another small hamlet at the entrance to the chalk cutting. Puddlehill boasted twenty-six cottages housing some one hundred and eleven inhabitants and a public house called the Green Man.[3] There was a Wesleyan Methodist Chapel, which could hold a congregation of over eighty worshippers, backing onto a lane leading

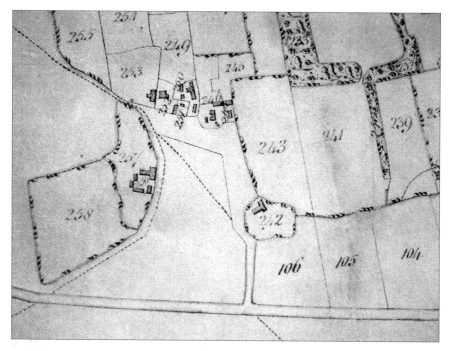

Detail from enclosure map showing the farms and labourers cottages at Thorn Green as they existed. *MA84/2*

to the small farming community of Sewell. Nearly all the cottages in this area were occupied by what was broadly termed as 'agricultural labourers'. For the menfolk, there was little other work to be found. These agricultural labourers might have been hard workers and skilled tradesmen, but they had no recognised social standing. They had no status or respect that their abilities should have commanded. And when there was no work, to put food on the table, they were faced with little choice. They sought to live off the land as their elders had done before them, and to put into practice skills which had been learned from them. But now, since enclosure, these skills went under another name and that was 'poaching'.

All hands were needed at harvest time.

CHAPTER 2

Facts of Life for Labourers

The process of agricultural reform had begun long before our three accused men sought to earn their living from the land. It was during the eighteenth century and early nineteenth century that England was undergoing great change in its agricultural system, fuelled by the search for improvement in farming methods which in its turn was encouraged by the urgent need to feed a fast growing population that had almost doubled during this time. The open field system as it had existed prompted communities to be self-supporting based on co-operation. Villagers worked their own allotted strips of land in common fields, one of which was usually sown with wheat or rye, another with barley, oats, beans and peas, and the third left fallow. The narrow strips of an acre or half-acre were divided by grass banks, or balks, and each villager had his allocation in each field. The two fields under cultivation were fenced off from the time they were sown to the time they were harvested, then the fences were removed and the cattle driven in to feed off the stubble. The same system applied to the meadow; it was fenced between Lady Day and Midsummer Day when the hay was cut, after which the cattle were put to graze. The common played host to pigs and cattle chomping lazily at the grass, and villagers foraging for what they could find from the hedgerows. All members of the community depended on agriculture; they were in tune with nature deriving all their needs from the countryside. The blacksmith shod horses and forged tools and agricultural implements; the carpenter would make field gates or coffins, and it was as easy for a wheelwright to make a wagon as a wheel. Corn was ground in the mills, and commodities such as butter and eggs could be exchanged at the market. Both farmers and labourers could turn their hand to making implements, feeding troughs and rattles for bird scaring.

But this method of farming was considered impractical by those who sought to improve farming methods. It was time wasting because the strips that each labourer worked were in different fields. It did not lend itself to experiment and neither did it produce enough food. However, it kept a great number of labourers usefully employed, and it encouraged an existence of co-operation and self support. And if within their immediate scope the labourers had enough food to eat and to feed their families, then why should they be convinced that the system should change?

This system too had always proved an obstacle to the introduction of experimental methods, because it was necessary for the whole village to agree to any changes.[1] So what was effected in the name of progress had to be done by Acts of Parliament, but gradually villages and common land were enclosed to become part of the bigger farms and estates.

Houghton Regis was the subject of enclosure in the late 1700s through the turn of the century, when the common ground which once played host to the cattle of the local labourers was re-distributed to the large land owners. Amongst these areas were Great Thorn Green and Little Thorn Green where Cow Common straddled the bridleway, and next to it the Great Meadow. So too was Carcutt Common and Great Crixsey Cow Common which was situated further along the road towards Bidwell Hill.

Early enclosure weighed heavily in favour of a few prominent men, Christopher Towers, Thoswihan Brandreth, Thomas Gilpin and Thomas Read to name a few. The later awards at the turn of the century mentioned others; John Hill; Edmund Thorn who was the owner of the Rye; Henry Brandreth, the Squire: Joseph Freeman – the land where the windmill stood; Daniel Parkins and Joseph Anstee; Edmund Wodley, the vicar,

127

Thomas Gilpin Esqr. Wm. Barton Tenant

A.R.P   A.R.P

Carcut Farm

Inclosures

196 Farm House Barns Stable Yard Garden Orchard Rights &c. Moats &c.		5·0·3
219 Prion Close Arable		13·0·20
220 Part of Wools Close		4·0·31
		22·1·14

In Bury Field, belonging to South Field Season

1557 Orchard Close four Acres	5·0·19
1561 One Acre next Ipsmarsh	1·0·25
1563 Two Acres, shooting North to little Bound Way	3·0·20
1565 Six Acres, shooting to Maynards Way Acre	5·1·29
1567 four Acres, shooting to Upper Bound Way	3·1·36
1568 four Acres, shooting to little Bound Way	3·1·26
1571 Six Acres, shooting to Butterwell	5·1·0
	27·0·3

Common Field Sward, or Lammas Ground

1570 Pound Close	
1579 Part of Carcut Green Part Ploughed	5·0·9

Awards to Thomas Gilpin Esq. *B554 1762*

were some of the names. But by far the majority of the land was allotted to the Duke of Bedford, already the main land owner in this area. The successive Dukes had always been observant for the acquisition of land, there ready to make a tempting offer to a needy small owner. By this method the Dukes of Bedford, the Russell family, added to their estate acre by acre until it seemed as if all Bedfordshire and even the surrounding counties belonged to them.[2]

The history of the Russell family shows their lives swaying between politics and agriculture, with the latter mostly winning.[3] Francis, the fifth Duke of Bedford, whilst still maintaining his place in the political sphere, must be counted amongst those agriculturally-minded landlords to whom England owed much for introducing both new crops and methods of farming. For enclosure alone did not automatically mean that the yield of crops improved. Planting a hedge around a field did not mean the corn in that field would grow. New crops, new methods of fertilizing, and new ways of tending those crops had to be tried. A model farm was established at Woburn, it being the first of its kind; and experiments were made to improve the soil. However, it was the breeding of sheep that held pride of place and all tenants and farmers around were encouraged to take active interest.[4] But Francis was not yet thirty-seven years old when in February, 1802, he complained of exhaustion and pain after a game of tennis.[5] He died on 2nd March of a strangulated hernia. Francis was succeeded by his brother, John, the sixth Duke of Bedford. Although John's main interest was in politics, the interest in agriculture at Woburn still continued.

Broadly speaking, taking the economic view and that of the upper classes, enclosures were a matter of necessity – England had to produce more food or face starvation.[6] Enclosure meant that crop rotation and mixed farming were improved and in the cycle of agriculture, more crops meant more food for cattle, more cattle meant more manure for crops, and more manure for crops meant better yields. Everybody would have more food, and everybody would be happy. Well, not quite.

If we take a more exclusive view and take into account the moral claims of the lower classes and the poor, then we are looking at a social disaster. Once agricultural labourers had their strips of land in common fields which they cultivated to provide for their families; now that land was enclosed and their rights to common access removed. Villages had commons, heath and woodland to which the villagers had rights

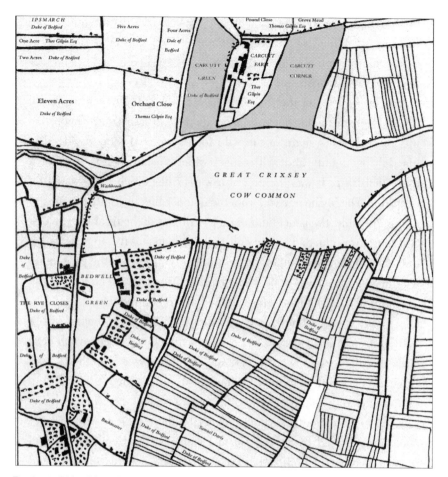

Turning to Bidwell from Thorn, showing commons and fields in strips prior to enclosure at the turn of the century. *Drawn by the author from enclosure map MA84/2 1796.*

of common, now the commons were enclosed and they no longer had the right to pasture animals there, to cut turf to smoke the bacon, or to gather wood and bracken for fuel from the thickets. They no longer had the right to the odd rabbit which taunted them from an enclosed field, a field which, bewilderingly, was once theirs to roam at will. Where once after the corn was harvested, it was a family affair to glean the fields, the women and children swarming over the stubble, their eyes alert, and nimble fingers ready to pounce on any ears of corn that the horse-rake had missed. When once there was the exciting prospect of a bushel or two of flour from their hard toils, now it was a crime to venture on that land and to pick up an ear of corn.

So, in the eyes of the labourer, he was robbed. He was robbed of his stake in the land, however inadequate this might have been. He was robbed of his share of the wild food supply. He was deprived of his right of dignity and self-respect which sustained him through a life of hardship. It was the end of a way of life which had existed for centuries. The joy he derived from the outdoor life, the daily blessing of the countryside, the peaceful quietude – all part of the rural life, though still there, was clouded by the constant battle to survive, to put food on the table, to stop cold and hungry children crying. But as the population continued to rise it was impossible to provide work for everyone. For the agricultural trade had absorbed all the labourers it required.

As with most Parliamentary operations, an enclosure began with a petition from a local person or persons setting out the inconveniences of the present system and the advantages to be gained from the change. Having received the petition, Parliament would give leave for a Bill to be introduced; it would be read a first and a second time, before being referred to a Committee. After considering those petitions against the enclosure referred by the House of Commons, the Committee would present its report. The Bill would then be passed, sent to the Lords, and receive the Royal Assent. Finally those Commissioners who had been named in the Bill would descend on the district and allocate the land.[7]

The petition was often from a big landowner, whose solitary signature was enough to set an enclosure process in motion, and prior to 1774 it was not even incumbent on this individual to advise his neighbours that he was asking Parliament for leave to redistribute their property. It was not uncommon therefore, for those whose land was due to be enclosed to know nothing about it until the transactions were virtually completed.[8] Then in 1774 the House of Commons made a Standing Order stating that, when land was due to be enclosed, a notice was to be affixed to the church door for three Sundays during the month of August or September, informing the parishioners of the forthcoming enclosure. But although this process publicised the enclosure application, it did not, in practice, give the villagers any say in their own future. Generally all plans were already in motion prior to the notice being displayed, and the applicant(s) were not bound to accept the opinion of any public meeting which might be forthcoming. In fact, proprietors of large estates had usually already agreed the measure amongst themselves.

But what could the common worker do when a notice appeared? Mostly, the people were left bewildered as to what it meant and what they could do about it. The parson was generally the only person who could read, but that parson sometimes had a vested interest in the enclosure himself and was afraid to tell the people exactly what the notice said. Some men ripped down the notices in anger, but most were unaware of just what the enclosures would mean to everyday life. It would be unjust to say that the general apathy that followed made the villagers in any way to blame for not receiving what little right they may have been entitled to. To find that before a specific time, they must submit to the parson, or to one of the magistrates whom they might have stood before on a little matter of poaching, or to their landlord's bailiff, a concise and correct statement in a legal form of their rights to claim their share of the allotment of land, when none of them could read or write, would have seemed an impossible ordeal. They had neither the courage nor the knowledge to present their case.[9]

They did not understand just what their claims were, nor did they know how to present them. And of the few who managed to fight their way through this tangled web of bureaucracy, some had their claims ignored because they were not presented correctly, or they were too late, or not in the correct form. It was little wonder that the villagers felt a sense of despair and a loss of self-respect. Whilst they were able to keep a cow, or farm a small patch, there had been a strong determination amongst them to refuse the refuge of the Poor Law. Now many of them had little choice.

There were the rich, better off by a great many acres.

There is no doubt that in a lot of places these enclosures caused great distress and hardship, and that it was a pitiable time in general for the agricultural worker, suffering from both unemployment and high prices. In some areas of the country this led to revolt, and in the villages of Bedfordshire too, they suffered their share. With enclosure

And there were the poor, the 'faceless class'.

came a re-organisation of classes. The squire and landowners were still there, generally the better off by a great many acres, the large farmers were still there closeted in an increased social standing, but below them, small farmers and farm workers, all had merged into the one faceless class of the 'agricultural labourer'.

Many were forced to become paupers and to claim relief from the parish under the Poor Law system, the distribution of which was generally in the hands of salaried guardians appointed by the justices out of a list of names submitted by the parishioners, although in some parishes application had to be made to unpaid overseers nominated by magistrates. Relief could be paid in two ways; outdoor, which was a weekly pension of a shilling or two at home, or indoor, which was admittance to a workhouse or poorhouse. In many areas the outdoor relief was the only form of payment, but in areas where there was a workhouse, if the applicant refused entry he forfeited his right to any relief at all, although his fate would depend on the parish officers. Workhouses were dreaded by the poor for the dirt and disease and devastating fevers which swept through them.[10] Under Gilbert's Act of 1782, the guardians were not to send able-bodied poor to the poorhouse, but to find work for them, or maintain them until work was found; the guardian was to take the wage and provide the labourer with maintenance. Thus was formed the roundsman system by which pauper labour was sold to the farmers, labourers being paid by the parish but sent 'on the rounds', going from one farmhouse to another looking for work. To make matters worse, the labourers were prevented from leaving their village to seek work elsewhere. In order to do so they must first obtain a certificate to leave their own parish, or be invited by another, running the risk of expulsion if they didn't. Because they were entitled to relief only from their own parish, none other was willing to settle outsiders, and in case they had the expense of bringing them back should they fail to find work, or fell ill, their own parish was unwilling to give them certificates to leave. The only ways for a villager to obtain settlement in another parish were either by paying taxes, by executing a public annual office, serving a year's apprenticeship, or by being hired for a year's service in the parish, but the latter applied only to those unmarried.[11]

To this end, great statute fairs, acting as primeval labour exchanges where lucky ones would be hired by an employer for the whole year, were held all over the country. In Dunstable, the statute fair was held every

THE AGRICULTURAL QUESTION SETTLED.

PRIME MINISTER.—"I'm very sorry, my good man, but I can do nothing for you."

The face of poverty ignored.

September. It was a colourful event, attended by jocular farmers seeking to hire their work force and labourers seeking employment. For the day at least, all would put aside their cares and woes in anticipation of a contract of work to be followed by a good time at the fair. It was a time to catch up with old friends and possibly exchange notes on prospective employers. For hiring was not all one-sided, there were the merits of the farmer to be taken into consideration, and those of his wife. To labourers seeking a live-in position great importance might be placed on being hired by those of a generous nature when it came to food. Workers would stand in their allotted batches, both men and women proudly displaying a symbol depicting their trade. There was the shepherd holding his crook, the carter with string tied round his hat or with a whip, the cowman with a wisp of straw, and the cook with her ladle. There were laundry maids and dairymaids, their bosoms might be more readily displayed than the symbol of their trade in the hope of catching the eye of a prospective employer. Or indeed that of some handsome and willing labourer who might fancy a bit of fun and perhaps buy them a jug of ale in return for a few favours in the hayfield when the serious business of the hiring was finished and the frolics of the fair began. Once hired, the young lads and maids received a shilling as a testimony of acceptance and stuck a ribbon in their cap or hair in honour of the bargain. That over, the pleasures could begin. Music and singing poured out of the alehouses, fights broke out and beer flowed freely. But for those not lucky enough to be hired their prospects were bleak.

Then in 1795 an increasing number of poor people in all parts of the country rose up from the abject pitiable state into which they had declined, and revolted. In Aylesbury, for the most part, it was women who started the revolt. They took possession of all the wheat the farmers brought to market, forcing them to accept prices fixed by the rioters. The uprising in general was orderly and well organised. They did not steal food from the shops as such, but they acquired it, distributed the sale of it at what they considered to be fair prices and then handed the money over to the owners of the shops.[12] At the same time, throughout the rest of the country similar uprisings were occurring.

As a result of these riots new systems were introduced. One system to be reformed was the Settlement Law. Now men could seek employment in other parishes without the need to obtain a certificate from their own, and as long as they could maintain themselves in work, without the need to seek aid, they would not be removed back to their original parish. But another was the despised 'Speenhamland' poor relief, whereby wages were supplemented from the parish rates with every family member receiving a certain sum when the price of a loaf rose to a shilling. This amount was to increase in accordance with the rise of the price of bread. But instead of increasing the income of the families, it had a demoralising effect on them, whilst lining the pockets of the wealthy. Instead, the large landowners and farmers were relieved of having to pay a living wage to their labourers, and often the labourers were forced to take part of their wages in bad corn and worse beer.[13] Other smaller farmers were forced to subsidise the larger landowners with their rate contribution. And the labourer was forced to become a pauper, even though he was in full time employment.[14] So the villagers continued to suffer. The end of the Napoleonic War brought the dismissal of thousands of soldiers and sailors with no jobs. It also brought the opening of the Baltic and German ports and an import of corn to a hungry England. The price of bread fell and farmers were forced to sell their crops at a loss. The answer for the government was simple; in 1815 they introduced the Corn Law forbidding the import of corn until the price of wheat fetched 80/- per quarter. What was simple for the government spelled further misfortune for the labourer. 80/- per quarter meant more hunger for the poor. As a result, his protests unheeded and faced with the prospect of a hungry family, the labourer had little choice. Poaching became commonplace countrywide, because now it was illegal for anybody except the owners of the estates or their heirs to kill game. The thrill of the night-time jaunts served to relieve the monotony of the labourers' humdrum lives, and was second only to the satisfaction of gaining the advantage over the bailiffs from the large estates, with the added bonus of a 'little for the pot' to feed the hungry mouths. Nobody ever considered that what they poached was not their just right. For who could tell these hungry men that what they snared were other men's rabbits?

In the early part of the nineteenth century in much of Bedfordshire, as elsewhere, the plight of the labourer had reached an all time low. It became the custom for those unemployed to line up on a Monday morning when the farmers would bid for their services. But as they returned home to their hungry families, the prospects for those not hired were grim because, with such a surplus of agricultural labourers in the local villages, many would only be hired during the harvesting season. In fact this was a time when the whole family, men, women, and children alike, could look forward to guaranteed work, for all hands were required on the farms at harvest time.

As the plight of the villagers increased, so did the rise in poaching, and who could blame them when the acquisition from a night's poaching was often more than wages earned over several weeks. In 1818 a Bedfordshire gang was reported to earn between £50 and £70 a week, a wealth which was short lived, for this gang was soon captured. The gentry became concerned to protect their property, and things became harder for those indulging in this questionable pursuit. There existed laws which made the act of poaching punishable by imprisonment with hard labour. Further still, the magistrates might sentence the offender to serve a spell in the army or navy. In 1816, a few years before our accused were born, this act was superseded by another which meant that if an offender was caught in the possession of nets and an offensive weapon he would to be tried at the Quarter Sessions, and if convicted, sentenced to transportation for seven years.[15] But in general, nobody took much interest in this law. Everybody in the villages seemed to be in on the questionable pursuits, one way or another, except the gamekeepers of course, with whom there was a continual war waged, although there were those that considered the gamekeepers the biggest poachers of all. The practice of poaching was thought by everybody else, even the constables and clergy, to be quite an innocent pursuit and a bit of agreeable sport, especially when the men would make sure there was a little for those who would look the other way.

Most years when there was no work in their villages, at haymaking time local men would gather in their numbers, say goodbye to their womenfolk, generally for a few months at a time, and trek off to the rich meadows of Middlesex. Here they could be sure of finding work for the short season, after which they would make their way home to Bedfordshire, doing odd jobs such as hoeing on the way.[16]

For those left working on the farms at home, life held few attractions for the labourer as he returned home after a hard day on the land. The cottage in which he lived was small, and cold and damp in winter, overcrowded and stifling in summer. It was crammed full of squabbling children, kicking each other as they lay side by side, end to end in their makeshift beds. If the weather was fine he could go and tend a few vegetables, but for the younger unmarried man this held little appeal. Much better to spend a few sociable hours in the alehouse, with a spot of poaching to liven the night.

Despite the unquestionable poverty of the labouring class throughout England at this time, it could be argued that in terms of opportunity for work, the populace of Dunstable and some of the surrounding villages were more fortunate than those in other areas of the country. For Dunstable was a thriving market town situated on the main highway between London and the North which brought a degree of prosperity in the form of the numerous stagecoaches which thundered through each day. Every stagecoach brought passengers requiring hostelry and a team of horses requiring changing and stabling. Inns sprang up on both the main and side roads, all vying for their share of the trade. The inns required food to feed their travellers and for this they looked to the farms and market gardens in the villages surrounding the town. For those opportunists who chose to dabble in a little light poaching there were customers in the form of the coachmen, who would stop surreptitiously outside the towns where poachers would lie in wait, away from the prying eyes of the town. Their business conducted, the coaches would

Much better to spend a few sociable hours in the alehouse.

once more thunder on their way, the coachman better off by a brace of game destined for the ready market to be found in London, at inns and at Leadenhall and Newgate markets. Nobody in London worried about where the game came from and nobody in the villages was thought worse of for supplying it.[17]

But also in the villages around the town of Dunstable, there was fast growing another trade by which women and children were able to supplement their husbands' income and thereby cushion the blows from their periodic lack of work, and that was straw-plaiting.

What did I learn from you mother, as I stood, just a child, at your knee?
Watching your fat bloated fingers as you taught skills of plaiting to me,
I thought I was just your helper, but my efforts to please you were vain.
I had sores round my mouth
From moistening the straw
And often would cry with the pain.
Oh, I learnt soon enough when my small fingers bled,
as I hastened to plait more and more,
Mine were only a pair of willing hands to avoid the hated poor law.

Women engaged in straw-plaiting.

CHAPTER 3

Facts of Life for Straw-plaiters and Children

The chalky area around Dunstable produced a fine white straw that was particularly sought after in the straw-hat trade for its superior quality and pliability for plaiting. The intricate plait of many beautiful designs could be coaxed into exquisite hats for ladies. Next door to the inns in Dunstable, hat manufacturers sprung up and, as the coaching industry declined with the advent of the railway, some of those inns converted their rooms for use by the straw-hat trade. Enterprising labourers now called themselves plait dealers, and in this new capacity bought their yards of plait from the women and children of the surrounding villages. Those busy womenfolk, their mouths always full of straw and the spittle with which they moistened it, spent their entire day plaiting, their nimble fingers constantly at work, never stopping. As soon as they were able, children, some as young as three years old, became apprenticed to their mothers' skilful fingers. The children tied the straw in bundles, both women and children split and plaited it and finally their handiwork was sold. Straws were split with the aid of a small splitter into four, six or even eight strands for the finer plait, and it was rolled flat in wooden roller plait mills which generally hung outside their back doors.

If you were to open the door of any labourer's cottage in this neighbourhood community you would find the same scene. All would be

STRAW BONNET.

The Straw Bonnets are of dark-coloured ground, ornamented with fine open straw-work.

The straw plait was turned into bonnets.

crammed full of straw, with women and children hard at work, plaiting. For whilst it was inevitable that the men were born and bred to become agricultural labourers, it was a woman's destiny to become a straw-plaiter. But straw-plaiting was not exclusively a female occupation. When the menfolk had no work in the fields they also turned to the craft. They bought straw from the farmers, scraped, cleaned and graded it. Men, too, after their day on the land, would sit well into the night plaiting straw as they chatted with their neighbours by the light of a solitary candle.

No social occasion for the women folk was complete unless they took along their straw-plait. A chat with the neighbours or going for a walk, their nimble fingers were never still as they split the straw and plaited the strands together. The straws would hang from their mouths as they kept them pliable, the art of chatting at the same time learnt at an early age. Experience had taught them how to manipulate the straw without cutting the side of their mouths; a few sores gained there soon ensured this skill.

Courting couples would be seen along the lanes, both of them with their fingers busy, building up their quantity of plait as quickly as possible, because there was always the chance their work would be checked by a waiting parent to make sure the couple had behaved circumspectly.

Everyone when engaged in plait making, carried a bunch of splints under the left arm, pushed close up to the armpit, the elbow having to be kept fairly close to the body to retain the bunch in place. The starting was a somewhat tricky business, but once fairly started, the experienced hands moved their fingers very rapidly, turning the splints in and out, over and under, with but a moment's pause now and again to 'set in' a new splint: this insertion was always spoken of in the singular number...whereas it should have been in the plural, for there were always a pair used when 'setting in', the rough or inner sides being face to face, the glazed or glossy sides being outward, so that in the plait itself, only the glazed side was seen....To ensure that the two splints were kept evenly together in the position just indicated, they were, when laced together, passed between the lips lengthways and lying flat, and so in this position drawn along close by the corners of the mouth, the saliva of which moistened them, and also caused a slight adhesion sufficient to keep the pair of splints in the even position required for the 'setting in'. This moistening trick had to be done with care, or a cut lip or tongue, or perhaps both, would be the result....I have known some children, whose lips and tongues received nasty cuts, when they were beginning to plait properly, but these cuts made them exercise care, and they soon learned the knack of moistening their splints with safety. Many women were accustomed to hold several splints in the mouth whilst working, and by the feel of the tongue and movement of the lips, would so twist, turn and manoeuvre them about, that a pair were always ready properly placed together glazed sides outward, when required for 'setting in';...I might here say that this obstruction in the mouth did not debar the women from talking, nor from the pleasure of joining in a little gossip, when friends met friends.

Grey, Cottage Life. 81–82

Each Wednesday in Dunstable a plait market was held. At 8am a hand bell heralded the start of the market. It meant a very early start from the outlying villages to be at the market ready to take their pitch, but it was worth it because here the housewives could bargain for more money instead of selling their plait to the local shop, or to dealers who called round the cottages. Here they would stand patiently, the looped plait slung over their outstretched aching arms, ready for the inspection of prospective buyers. The moment the bell was rung, the haggling would begin, the different types of twist fetching a variety of prices, the women standing firm to get the best price. Once they had made a sale they could buy their straw for the next week's plaiting.

Children were generally introduced to the craft of straw-plaiting at home, learning the basic skills from their mother and older members of the family. Boys were not exempt from this process; they had to learn as well as the girls. From the age of about three and a half or four years,

The straw-plait market in Luton.

some children were sent to a plait school. This was usually held in a
room of a local cottage, generally accommodating twice as many children
as the room could comfortably hold, being stifling in summer and with
no room to light a fire in winter. In actual fact these schools were little
more than a child-minding service, their main function being not to
teach the children the skill, but to make sure they produced as much
plait as possible. Those caught slacking could expect to be punished,
either caned or slapped. Around the year of 1836, some children earned
a penny a day, with the 'missus' supplying the straw and keeping the
plait. In 1867 the payment for the privilege of attending the school was
up to 2d per week for each child, and often the bundles of straw, split
and bleached, would be supplied by the parents, who had bought them
from the straw dealers or the village shop.[1] Younger children usually
worked between four and eight hours a day, being taught first with three
or four splints to twist them under and over to a little ditty and tune,

'under one and over two, pull it tight and that will do'.[2] Older children worked much longer hours, even from six in the morning until ten at night, and were expected to produce about thirty yards of plait a day, although some of the more skilled could even exceed this, especially when working the simpler patterns.[3] Those not reaching their required amount would be kept working until they did, their fingers sometimes sore and bleeding. The plait would be sold either at the weekly market at Dunstable or to dealers, but often it would be exchanged at the local shop for groceries. Apart from plaiting, the children's only scholastic instruction was to learn a hymn or verses from the Testament. Writing and arithmetic were not taught for the simple reason that the teachers could neither write nor do arithmetic themselves. Often they were not able to teach plaiting either.

These plaiting schools were the cause of some concern to the authorities. In 1864, an Assistant Commissioner visited the area to report on the matter of child labour. In Houghton Regis he found one child, aged between two and three years, engaged in the process of clipping plait which had been made by her sister.[4] And it was reported that in the villages of Tilsworth, Stanbridge and Eggington, there was no school in any of the villages, but there were seven straw-plait schools with eighty-five children under thirteen years old working in them. Other children were to be found plaiting in the lanes and at the doors of cottages.[5]

Later, after 1876, when the Education Act was passed making it compulsory for children to attend educational school until the age of ten, poor attendance was attributed to the fact that children still continued to work at the plait schools.[6] Generally, the additional income that they earned was crucial to the family survival, so it was almost impossible to carry out the Act. Often, when one of the authorities called at a plaiting school, the children would slip out the back door. It was only towards the end of the century, with the decline of the plait trade after cheap imports of plait flooded the market, that the plait schools diminished and children began to attend educational school.

But the children of Bedfordshire were not just required to do straw-

Truants from school.

plaiting; there were other tasks for them to do. It was the general practice for farmers looking to reduce the wages they paid out, to eke out their workforce with child labour. For even the lowest of wages paid to adult workers could be reduced if the adults were replaced by children. It was only at corn harvest time that every available hand was needed, adult and child, male and female. So a ragged motley of children, both boys and girls, could be found from early morning until late at night, working on the farms. February was the month that they picked up stones in

A young child employed to scare birds, whilst another looks after the younger children.

the fields, and set the beans and peas. March and April found them racing around, arms flaying as they waved their rattles in the thankless task of bird-scaring. They had little effect in scaring them off of course, but this was probably more fun for the children than weeding the corn which was their task in April and May. But as they crouched low at this back-breaking task, the birds would still be prevalent, mocking from their superior position. June was the month for haymaking, and for thinning out the turnips, their small backs hunched, arms tugging at the weeds, their hands chafed and sore. They slashed at the thistles in an indiscriminate attempt to eliminate those obstinate blotches in the patchwork of the fields, not seeming to worry much about one another, and who might be in the way. In August they assisted with the corn harvest, and the rest of the year was the endless round of bird scaring, watching sheep and pigs, and stone picking, muck spreading and ditching. They trudged through the woods gathering sticks and, of course, acorns had to be collected for the pigs. At the end of the day, the children would return to their various cottages, exhausted by their day's labour, fit only to fall into their makeshift beds, with the same to look forward to the following day.

As they progressed from child to adulthood, the boys were expected to work alongside their fathers, ten or twelve hours a day. But once adulthood was attained, they commanded an adult wage, so they too became members of that all encompassing band of 'agricultural labourers' with so many becoming unemployable.

A woodman.

CHAPTER 4

The Whites – Family Life 1800–1849

B y the time George White thrust his way into the world during the early part of 1824, his mother, Lucy, had already produced three sons and eight daughters. As number twelve of this festering brood, his birth would have been as welcome as the inhospitable winter day on which he was born, but at least he was a male and as such his place in the family was established, the majority being girls.

During the early 1800s, George's father, John White, was employed by the estate of the Duke of Bedford as a hedger and ditcher, to work on the area of the newly enclosed commons in the area of Houghton Regis. In fact, the majority of the quicksets which enclosed the fields of the local tenanted farms in Thorn, Bidwell and Houghton Regis were planted by John between the years of 1802 and 1809, and the ditches alongside the hedges were dug by him.

It is likely that he headed a small gang of workers, as some receipts for payments in the records show payments to "John White & Co." and would otherwise seem rather high amounts for one person.[1] Possibly the other workers could have been his brothers, but none of his family has been established.

If enclosure had its critics, particularly amongst those of the labouring class for whom it brought loss of self esteem and poverty, there were also those who welcomed it, and for whom it brought employment. So whatever John White's views might have been on the act of enclosure, there was no room in his life for protest and sentimentality, for he was

Bedfordshire County Records Office. Russell Rent Books

Reference	Date		£. s. d.
C.R.O R5/83/1	1802 Nov. 28	Paid John White for repairing & watching the Fences at Houghton Regis from 1 Nov to this day	3. 0. 0.
C.R.O R5/83/1	1802 Dec. 25	Paid John White for repairing & watching the Fences at Houghton Regis from 29 Nov to this day	3. 0. 0.
C.R.O R5/83/1	1803 Mar. 5	Paid John White for repairing Fences & Quicksets at Houghton Regis from 27 Dec to this day	7.10. 0.
C.R.O R5/83/2B	1803 Apr.16	To John White & Co. for digging a New Drain & planting Quicksets & fencing the same on J.Eames Jun. Farm at Houghton Regis from 7 March to this day	19.16.11.
C.R.O R5/83/2B	1803 June 11	To John White for repairing Fences on New Inclosures at Houghton Regis from 18 April to this day	7.11. 8.
C.R.O R5/83/2B	1803 July 9	To John White & Co. for weeding Quicks & repairing Fences at Houghton Rs. from 14 May to this day	8. 8.11.
C.R.O R5/83/2B	1803 Aug 13	To John White & Co. for weeding Quicks & repairing Guard fences at Houghton Rs. from 11 July to this day	6. 8. 3.
C.R.O R5/83/2B	1804 Feb 3	To John White & Co. for repairing Fences & scouring out Ditches at Houghton Rs. from 13 Aug last to this day	42.11. 8.
C.R.O R5/83/3	1804 Apr 28	To John White for planting Quicksets, scouring Ditches & repairing & setting down Fences at Houghton Regis from 26 Feb to 28 April ins.	37. 0. 0.
C.R.O R5/83/3	1804 Apr 28	To Ditto for Quicksets as bought by him & planted at Houghton Regis	7.16. 6.
C.R.O R5/83/3	1804 July 21	To John White for repairing Fences & weeding Quicks etc at Houghton Rs. from 28 April to 21 ins.	21.18.11.
C.R.O R5/83/3	1804 Dec 27	To John White for scouring out Brooks & Ditches & planting & weeding Quicks & repairing Fences at Houghton Rs. from 23 July to 22 ins.	56.13.7½

Russell Rent Books R5/83/2B 1802/3 showing payments from the Duke of Bedford's Estate to John White. *Beds & Luton Archives Service (Settled Estates Collection)*

one of those men to whom it certainly brought employment. For the land which was newly acquired by the larger landowners and those re-distributed fields had to be fenced, hedged and ditched.

The predominant material used to encompass the new boundaries was a live hedge and the favourite choice was hawthorn. Young plants would be planted in narrow banks against a temporary fence to protect them in the early stages of growth, and a ditch dug in front of them. In Bedfordshire the cost of this was estimated to be 10s 6d per pole of quickset hedge, although it varied in different counties[2], and was borne by the acquiring land-owner. In the case of the land on which John was working this was the Duke of Bedford. John also sold wood he had cut down on behalf of the Duke, passing the proceeds over to His Grace.

Those villages which had recently been enclosed tended to have a rise in population just after enclosure, as workers from outside the area were brought in by the landowners. It is probable that John was one of those men, for although no record has been found of where John came from, it is unlikely that he was from Houghton Regis as the 1841 census states that he was born outside the county.

John was also employed to watch these new boundaries, for in Bedfordshire, as indeed throughout the rest of the country, there was some opposition to the new land enclosures. It was a time of unrest and protest amongst the labouring population and it was quite likely that, if they were not watched, the hedges might be damaged in some way, either cut down or set alight. So, after working all day planting his hedges, he would have to tramp his boundaries to make sure that no protester destroyed his hard work.

At the height of the summer of 1804, on 6th August, John White took time off from his hedging and ditching to keep a date in the Parish Church of Houghton Regis, Bedfordshire where he exchanged vows with his young bride, Lucy Turner. Working from the ages on their death certificates, Lucy was just eighteen at the time of their marriage, although John was somewhat older, at twenty-nine.

The wedding over, there would have been little opportunity for celebration, as John would doubtless have had to return to his work. Records show that at this time, John was planting the hedges on the farm of John Eames Junior who leased Bidwell Farm from the Duke of Bedford.[3] Possibly the couple made their first home in one of the cottages there as the 1861 census shows that their eldest son, John, was born in Bidwell in 1805. But certainly very shortly after this they had moved to their cottage in the small hamlet of Thorn close by, where Lucy was to spend the rest of her life raising her brood of children. Maybe the couple actually lived there at the outset of their marriage, as sometimes records made no differentiation between Thorn and Bidwell.

John was a hale and hearty man with weather-beaten face common

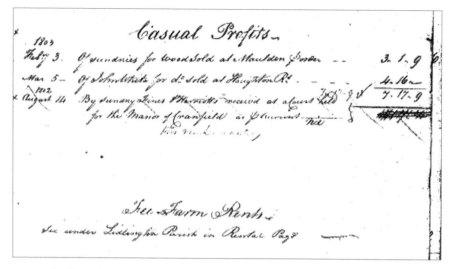

Bedfordshire C.R.O. Russell Rent Books R5/83/1 showing monies received from
John White for wood sold. *Beds & Luton Archives Service (Settled Estates Collection)*

to those who led an outdoor life. He and his young wife, Lucy, quickly
started to produce a very large family, which was to total fourteen children.
After George made his way into this overcrowded nest as number twelve,
another girl and a boy followed. Only one of the children, the daughter
born before George, died shortly after her birth, the rest of the brood
survived to adulthood and many into old age. The fact that only one of
John and Lucy's children died in infancy is quite incredible for those
days, when there was such a high mortality rate, particularly amongst
the children, from cholera, smallpox, consumption and fevers, mostly
as a result of contaminated water, because, through ignorance, people's
habits were unclean, and their lives surrounded by filth. There was no
sewerage or provision for the disposal of human excrement, and this
made the air foul and land rank. Their water came from wells generally
sunk beneath the sewage. Roads were just dirt tracks and therefore
uncleansed. As a result, mostly only the fittest babies survived, and
as thirteen of John and Lucy's children lived to adulthood, it is to their
credit that they must have produced a pretty healthy brood. But this

large healthy brood meant that there were a lot of hungry mouths to feed.

Baptism records of the children show John Senior's trade to be labourer. But the broad term 'labourer' encompassed so many facets of the trade, and in fact he was still employed by the Duke of Bedford's estate as a woodman, where he was to remain until his death in 1848.

In the years preceding George's birth, John was earning a weekly wage of 15/-[4] From this he had to support a wife and nine children, because by now his eldest child, John Junior, was able to contribute to the family income, and is shown to be employed along with his father on the Duke of Bedford's estate. This record shows the entry John White, Boy, 5/- per week, which rose to 6/- per week in 1821 and 7/- in 1822. In 1823 or 1824 (the record is not quite clear which) he earned 9/-, but at the same time, John Senior's wage had decreased to 14/-. During this latter time, younger brother James also joined his father and brother, earning 3/6d.

When he had just turned eighteen years old, the eldest son, John Junior, married his chosen bride, Sarah Ponter, or Sally[5] as she was known. The marriage took place on 24th April, 1823, at Houghton Regis Parish Church with friends William Fookes and Elizabeth Turner as witnesses. Their daughter, named Lucy after her grandmother, was born just a few weeks after the union. At the ripe old age of nearly twenty, Sally was a couple of years older than John's tender years, and came from Southgate in Middlesex, so it is possible that John Junior was one of those labourers who sought the richer pickings of Middlesex at harvest time and met his future bride there. Maybe after one such trip, when he was just seventeen years old, John returned home with his lass whose rounded swollen belly bore witness to the moments of passion she and John had shared amongst the hayricks that summer.

Doubtless John's mother would have welcomed Sally into the family, but Lucy was still grieving the loss of baby Charlotte the year before, and she was pregnant once more. Just a few months later George was born, a lusty howling replacement for the infant Charlotte, for fate had

JOHN WHITE (~1805 - 1865)

ELEANOR (ELLEN) WHITE (~1806 -)
bpd. 25 Dec 1806, Houghton Regis, Beds

ANN WHITE (1808 - 1857)
bpd. 14 Feb 1808, Houghton Regis, Beds

JAMES WHITE (1809 - 1857)
bpd. 3 Jun 1810, Houghton Regis, Beds

SARAH WHITE (1811 -)
bpd. 3 Feb 1811, Houghton Regis, Beds

LUCY WHITE (~1812 - 1852)
bpd. 6 Sep 1812, Houghton Regis, Beds

MARY WHITE (1814 -)
bpd. 22 May 1814, Houghton Regis, Beds

JOHN WHITE (~1775 - 1848)
& LUCY TURNER (~1786 - 1839)
bd. abt 1786, Houghton Regis, Beds

LEWIS WHITE (1816 - 1836)
bpd. 30 Jun 1816, Houghton Regis. Beds

REBECCA WHITE (1818 - 1888)
bpd. 1 Mar 1818, Houghton Regis, Beds

ELIZABETH WHITE (1820 -)
bpd. 23 Jan 1820, Houghton Regis, Beds

CHARLOTTE WHITE (1822 - 1822)
bpd. 12 May 1822, Houghton Regis, Beds

GEORGE WHITE (1824 - 1901)
bpd. 29 Feb 1824, Houghton Regis, Beds

HANNAH WHITE (1827 - 1868)
bpd. 7 Oct 1827, Houghton Regis, Beds

DAVID WHITE (1830 -)
bpd. 19 Dec 1830, Houghton Regis, Beds

volunteered this bare bawling innocent, at the first slap of his bloodied buttocks, to take on her abandoned persona and try and replace her in his mother's heart.

As were all his siblings, with the exception of the eldest brother John, George was christened at All Saints Church in Houghton Regis. This introduction to the Church fell on a winter's day on 29th February, 1824, and was performed by the vicar, Reverend Donne.

So, at the time of George's birth, just his brother John had married, and Charlotte had died, which still left twelve persons including the parents living at home, in what must have been very cramped conditions. However, it is quite likely that the little cottage was home to fourteen, as John and Sally may have been living with them too. Records show that the births of John and Sally's first children were at Thorn, so they either lived with the parents or in a cottage close by the family. Before long, the cottage had to stretch itself even more to include another two babies, George's sister Hannah, and William, a son for John and Sally, both babies born in 1827. The babies, William and his Aunt Hannah were christened together on 7th October, 1827. Circumstances of the overcrowded cottage probably meant that not only did Hannah and William share their christening, but that Hannah was moved over to make room for William in her crib, making aunt and nephew uneasy bedfellows at this tender age. Baby William was the first grandson for John Senior and Lucy and furthermore, being just 3 years younger, he

BAPTISMS solemnized in the Parish of *Houghton Regis* in the County of *Bedford* in the Year One Thousand Eight Hundred and Twenty-*four*.						
When Baptized.	Child's Christian Name.	Parents' Name.		Abode.	Quality, Trade, or Profession.	By whom the Ceremony was Performed.
		Christian.	Surname.			
Feb.y 29th No. 366.	George Son of	John + Lucy	White	Houghton Regis	Labourer	I. Doane Vicar

Baptism of George White.

All Saints Church, Houghton Regis.
Drawn by Marcus Brookes from an engraving by Thos. Fisher, 1812.

was a nephew and playmate for young George.

With so many children to support, any little bit of income would have been crucial to the family survival, and every member of the household, both adult and child, would be expected to contribute their share. And so the scene was set, a replica of that in any labourer's cottage in the area. Whilst John Senior, John Junior and young James were out on the land, for their part, Lucy and her daughters would sit from dawn until well into the night working at their straw-plaiting. There were so many inhabitants now in their small cottage that there was little room for the bundles of straw that stood ready to make the yards of plait. These would be hung around the walls ready for the plait dealer to call, or to be taken to market. Eleanor, Ann, Sarah, Lucy and Mary would assist their mother with the fine plaiting. Being the elder of the sisters, they had the most experience, were the most skilled and could earn the most money. Brother Lewis, and sister Rebecca, being younger, would be employed on coarser plaits, not in such high demand as the finer plait, but it still served a purpose in the learning process. The smaller children had to do their share, so George's apprenticeship would have begun at a very early age sitting on the floor alongside his sisters, as he and young Elizabeth industriously tied the plait into bundles.

The elder girls doubtless welcomed the opportunity to take their plait to the market in Dunstable whenever possible and whatever the weather. The few miles that they had to walk from Thorn, carrying their bundles of plait, presenting little deterrent, for such a trip had welcome bonuses. Whilst there, they had the opportunity to look around and meet friends, to delight in the hustle and bustle of the town after the quietness of the village. For the market was alive with both sellers and buyers, with carts of straw and carts of plait, the latter destined for the warehouses where they were eventually made into fine hats. There were shops to delight in, quite a rare treat for them, inns jostling with visitors, and hawkers plying their wares. And there was the added attraction of the many young men who might cast an eye upon them, and to whom they could simper.

James Greenwood 'On Tramp'

Dozens and dozens of them, little girls and big girls, buxom matrons and dames bent and grey, spick and span looking as the cotton print dresses and natty shoulder shawl, and twinkling earrings, and smoothed hair could make them; plaiting away, every one of them, as though their very lives depended on it, with hanks and loops of the manufactured outside festooning their neck, or worn sash-wise across their shoulders and with a sheaf of raw material at their side. They moved amongst the slipshod and tattered men and lads, laughing and larking, but never for a moment staying the movement of their nimble fingers.

Throughout the early years of his marriage, George's eldest brother, John Junior, worked with his father and lived at Thorn, but by the time their sixth child (another John) was born in 1832, John Junior and Sally had

Chalk Hill, showing John White's slaughterhouse.
The Moorings lived in the small terrace in front of the Baptist Church. *Z50/63/11*

moved to Puddle Hill, not far across the field from the Whites' cottage in
Thorn. Records show the rental of a cottage in Houghton Regis (which
encompassed Thorn and Puddle Hill) to John White from the Duke of
Bedford's estate during 1831 for the sum of £1.10s.0d.[6] Receipts at this
time also show that John White rented a "slipe" of land, which was 1
acre and 22 perches, in the area of Houghton Regis from the estate
of the Duke of Bedford.[7] A letter written at that time also states that
'the Duke has no objection to White having the nursery, but not the
spinney'. It is not clear whether these documents refer to John Junior
or John Senior, but, on moving to Puddle Hill, John Junior acquired or
built a slaughterhouse and established himself as a butcher. Thus the
Whites' butchers business which was to continue into the next century
was established.

John Junior & Sally had eight children in all, with two of the girls
dying young. Two sons, William and Charles, and George and his
younger sister Hannah, were all born within a few years of each other

and, living in such close proximity, the aunt and uncle and their nephews were probably inseparable playmates. Puddle Hill would no doubt have presented a much more exciting prospect for young George to bide his time than the cottage at Thorn, where he could have been called on at any time to help with numerous family chores. Whenever he could slip out, it was just a short distance to trudge across the field to his brother's house. On the way he could stop on the turnpike where once the toll-gate keeper stood guard ready to collect his fees, the toll-gate now moved to Kate's Hill further north. Here he could watch the exciting spectacle of the numerous stagecoaches beginning their arduous ascent of the steep chalk hill. First to appear to the small audience, through the fog or the chalk dust, would be the steaming, sweating horses snorting and tossing

A wonderful sight for a small boy.

their heads, muddy hoofs thundering along the road, a wonderful sight for a small child. Then the coach would appear, with the coachman, reins held tightly, shouting his orders to the horses, ever mindful of this treacherous part of the journey.

There was the 'Union' from London to Leicester which stopped at the Crown in Dunstable at 11.30 in the morning. Then there was the 'Tally-ho' from London to Birmingham calling at the Saracen's Head at mid-day. At approximately 2.30pm on alternate days, the

The exciting spectacle of a stagecoach.

'Defiance' travelling from Manchester would arrive at Puddle Hill on its way to London, stopping for refreshment at the Saracen's Head and the White Swan, followed soon after by the 'Star' from Liverpool at 3pm, the 'Tally-ho' from Birmingham at 4pm, both calling at the Saracen's Head, and the 'Union' taking its sojourn at the Crown at 4pm.

Often there would be a gentleman passenger on the roof, in winter muffled and wet through, but in summer, he too would be covered in the thick chalky dust. For the passengers inside, often fine ladies, the journey was not so exciting, being jolted along by force in a box, constantly exposed to any dangers that might present themselves, even to broken limbs.

Another attraction for the children at Puddle Hill was the road gang employed to dig out the chalk with the objective of lowering the turnpike in 1837. This gang of large, sweating navvies made short work of their task before shifting on to another job. Their skill lay in their sheer physical strength, large horny hands grasping picks tightly as they hoisted them effortlessly above their heads before smashing them into the crumbling chalk. There would have been many a yarn these giants of men could share with their fascinated audience when they threw down their tools and shared their rations at break time.

Then there were John's pigsties in which George and William could happily spend time with their squealing, fat friends, feeding them dandelions collected from the roadside, the innocence of youth not yet connecting these cheerful creatures with the lumps of flesh hanging around in John's slaughterhouse. They were the good years, those of ignorance, before the harsh realities of later years breached their lives and their friendship proved such a disaster for them. Because fate had

A village affair.

decreed that these two children were to become two of the accused in the dock of Bedford Crown Court some years later.

During these early years of George's childhood, five of his elder sisters and his brother James married. All the ceremonies, with the exception of Eleanor's, were held at Houghton Regis Parish Church.

George's siblings' marriages:

Eleanor & Henry Kingham
The next to tie the knot, after brother John, was Eleanor. The marriage, to one Henry Kingham, a labourer from Tebworth who was some years older than her, took place on 18th April, 1828 at Chalgrave Church in front of vicar, John Robinson. The witnesses at this union were her brother, John and Sally, and all parties signed with a cross. As Chalgrave was shown to be the parish for

Tying the knot.

both Henry and Eleanor, it is probable that Eleanor was living with Henry at the time of the marriage, or possibly they were both working on the same farm, he as a labourer and she as a house servant. The couple continued to live in Chalgrave, just a couple of miles away from Thorn at the start of their marriage, but by the birth of their second child in 1833, they had moved to Thorn, close to the family.

Ann & Abel Green Not quite a year after the wedding of Eleanor and Henry, Ann married Abel Green on 26th March, 1829. This time, parents, John Senior and Lucy, were the witnesses, with all parties again signing with a cross. It would appear that Abel came from Puddle Hill, and certainly this was where Ann and Abel made their home because James, their first son, was born there later that year. They lived in a cottage owned by Ezekiel Green, so it is probable that he was Abel's father, although no records have been found to confirm this.[8]

Sarah & Lawrence Emmerton Two years later, on 4th April, 1831, Sarah married Lawrence Emmerton, a labourer from Tebworth. The witnesses this time were Sarah's brother, James, and Hannah Emmerton, and Sarah was able to sign her own name in the register. Sarah and Lawrence set up home in a cottage at Thorn near her parents where their first son, also called James, was born later that same year.

Lucy & Thomas Hines The following year on 23rd September, 1832, the next to wed was Lucy who married Thomas Hines from Chalgrave. Again brother James stood as witness, the other being his future bride, Martha Thorogood. Lucy and Thomas moved to Chalgrave when they first married and where all their children were born, but sometime after 1846 they also moved to Puddle Hill.

James & Martha Thorogood James married Martha Thorogood on 27th May, 1833. The witnesses at James and Martha's marriage were his sister Mary and her future husband, Sam Poulton. Martha gave birth to their first son, Matthew, later that year in Thorn where they settled just two doors away from James' parents, and next door to his sister Eleanor.

Mary & Samuel Poulton The same year, Mary and Sam Poulton wed on 14th November, 1833. At this marriage friends, James Knight and Mary Hause, were the witnesses. Sam and Mary also moved to a cottage in Thorn next door to John and Lucy.

Records show that all the girls, except Eleanor, were expecting a child when they married, and it would seem it was customary in most parts of England at the time for couples not to wed until the female was pregnant. The predominantly middle class Victorian moralistic attitude of later years never did extend to the labouring classes, who did not have the same values. They were impervious to the dos and don'ts of upper society, ignorant of the rights and wrongs of procreation. They created their own values within the confines of their culture. The conditions in which they lived, mostly all sleeping in one room, gave an awareness and acceptance of sexual activity denounced by those who chose to be ignorant of the labouring class's situation. Because segregation of sleeping quarters was a luxury only extended to the upper classes, and immorality after all was only in the eye of the middle class beholder, protected from the world of the labouring class.

The Morning Chronicle 18th January 1850 states:
It really seems, in many places, to be taken as a matter of course that a young woman will be found with child before she is married. Many are married as soon as they become pregnant....Indeed, I have reason to believe that in an immense number of cases young people come to a distinct understanding with each other to cohabit illicitly, until the woman becomes pregnant, the man promising to 'make an honest woman of her' as soon as that takes place.

This they find more convenient than marrying at once, inasmuch as the girl may be of service for herself, and the man elsewhere employed all the time. They meet occasionally, and are thus relieved at least of the responsibilities of housekeeping, living better on their separate earnings than they could do in a house of their own. This practice of cohabitation before marriage is almost universal. It is not only a characteristic of low rural life; it is also so with the miners and fishermen.[9]

Within this closely-knit stream of children born to John and Lucy and then in turn to their sons and numerous daughters, it seems that each played an important part in the family spectrum. They all settled very near each other as they married, supported each other, and named their children after each other. At that time it was common practice, when one child died, to call another born after them by the deceased's name, but within the White family this was extended, with other family members also naming their next child by that name.

In 1836, when George was twelve, Hannah was nine, and young David was just six years old, the family was dealt a cruel blow with the death of his elder brother, Lewis, at the age of twenty. George was not born when his sister, Charlotte, had died, and even though there had been a number of deaths amongst the children of the family, it was the first time that his life was tainted by grief with the death of a sibling. Lewis was buried on 11th December in the churchyard at Houghton Regis Parish Church, where so many of the family were subsequently laid to rest. There is no stone to mark his grave and there would have been no flowers to be gathered from the hedgerows at that time of year. But death was a frequent visitor in those days and life for the family had to go on, especially the youth, impatient to dry its tears and move on.

By now, two more of George's sisters, Rebecca and Elizabeth, had begun to find their pleasures in the company of the local lads, and true to form, in the spring of 1837, Rebecca became pregnant.

Rebecca & Thomas Dockerill The father of the child was Thomas Dockerill, commonly known as 'Dock', and the name shown in the marriage register. Despite Thomas's tender years, the couple were wed on 8th October, 1837, by which time he had just reached seventeen years old, and Rebecca a couple of years older. The witnesses at their wedding were Elizabeth and her future husband, Joseph Mooring. Whether or not Thomas wanted to marry at such a young age, or was just made to 'do the decent thing', we shall never know, but if it was the latter, unfortunately he was trapped unnecessarily because the baby born to them, a girl, whom they named Ann, sadly died in December of that year and was buried in Houghton Regis Churchyard on 13th December. George would have been thirteen years old when Dockerill made his union with the family and, as such, would have been too young to form any bond of adult friendship with him. But he was probably at an impressionable age; he had not long lost an elder brother, and there could possibly have been a degree of hero-worship because there is no doubt that Dockerill was a colourful character. Dockerill was also to stand alongside George and William in the dock at Bedford Crown Court nearly twelve years later, suspected of being the ringleader of the gang.

Elizabeth & Joseph Mooring Elizabeth's turn came a few months later as she too became pregnant. She married Joseph Mooring on 8th April, 1838, with Thomas and Rebecca Dockerill returning the favour as witnesses; it would appear there was a special bond between these two sisters. Elizabeth and Joseph made their home in Chalk Hill, (Puddle Hill), near her brother John. At the time of his marriage, Joseph was employed as an agricultural labourer, but later he was to join John in his butchery business. Censuses show that the family lived in a small terrace of six cottages, built next door to the Wesleyan Chapel. These cottages were brick built with a slate roof, probably back to back, and each cottage had one room on the ground floor and one bedroom above. In later years these six cottages were converted into three larger ones. They were brick built with slated wood barns, and a closet behind. At the side of the cottages and adjoining the main road was a stable with a loft over. There was a large plot of ground at the rear, extending to the road leading to Sewell, and a yard with a brick and timber built slaughterhouse and piggeries.[10]

On 28th of January, 1839, in the throes of a long hard winter, when George was just fifteen, his mother, Lucy, gave up her struggle for life. The cause of her death was dropsy. She was fifty-three years old, and had spent twenty-six of those years producing children. As she neared her end, she was attended by a neighbour, Hannah Chapman, who was also the informant on her death certificate. Now that Lucy, the nucleus of the family, had gone, there was left a disjointed mismatch of her offspring. George's father, himself an old man now at sixty-six years, but still healthy and hearty, was destined to spend another nine years before he would join his wife in the churchyard. After the death of their mother, George and young David, who was now nine years old, continued to live with their father at Thorn next door to James and Martha, with Sam Poulton and Mary, and Eleanor and Henry Kingham close by.

But the rest of the family had begun gradually to move out of Thorn, most of them joining the others at Puddle Hill. All of the girls had now married, except young Hannah, who was just twelve years old. She was sent to live with her sister Sarah and her husband Lawrence Emmerton, next door to Abel and Ann Green, at Puddle Hill. By the 1841 census, four of the families were living there.

It would appear that the White family was not impoverished, and if there was an opportunity for advancement they took it. John had already started his butchers business, and in 1841, Ann's husband, Abel Green, purchased a piece of land at Puddle Hill from Frederick Schrader who had enclosed the land in 1824 'without molestation'. Abel sold it later that year to Job Chapman and on part of it Job built a cottage. The land was described as:

"all that piece or parcel of ground situate lying and being on the East side of Puddle Hill in the parish of Houghton Regis in the county of Bedford bounded on the West or front side thereof by

1841 CENSUS HO 107 / 5 / 17
Houghton Regis, Thorn Hamlet

John White	65	Agricultural Labourer	Not Born in County
George White	15	Agricultural Labourer	Born in County
David White	10		Born in County

1841 CENSUS HO 107 / 5 / 17
Houghton Regis, Chalk Hill

Joseph Mooring	20	Agricultural labourer	Born in County
Elizabeth Mooring	20	Straw plaiter	Born in County
Ann Mooring	2		Born in County
Ephraim Mooring	1		Born in County
John White	35	Butcher	Born in County
Sarah White	35	Straw plaiter	Not Born in County
Lucy White	15	Straw plaiter	Born in County
William White	14	Agricultural labourer	Born in County
Charles White	13	Agricultural labourer	Born in County
Joseph White	11		Born in County
John White	10		Born in County
Hannah White	7		Born in County
Lewis White	1		Born in County
Lawrence Emmerton	30	Agricultural labourer	Born in County
Sarah Emmerton	30	Straw plaiter	Born in County
James Emmerton	10		Born in County
Hannah White	10		Born in County
Abel Green	30	Agricultural labourer	Born in County
Ann Green	30	Straw plaiter	Born in County
James Green	10		Born in County
Ann Green	3		Born in County

the Highway leading from Puddle Hill to Hockliffe on the East or back side thereof by ground belonging to John Cook but now in the occupation of the said Job Chapman as Tenant thereof on the South side thereof by property formerly being other part of the said piece or parcel of ground so enclosed as aforesaid and lately conveyed by the said parties hereto of the first and second parts to the xxx Trustees of Mary Axtell of Houghton Regis aforesaid and bounded on the North side thereof by a Tenement or Cottage and premises occupied by the said Job Chapman and which said piece or parcel of ground contains in width on the West or front side thereof and on the East or back side thereof from the South to the North thirteen feet or thereabouts and from the front or the West side thereof to the back or the East side thereof Twenty three feet or thereabouts. . ."

This charming cottage still exists, as do others at Puddle Hill which were occupied by the family. After Abel's death, Ann is shown to be the owner of two cottages there, one of which she occupied herself.[11] The trustees of the estate of Ezekiel Green are also shown to own two houses.

By now George was seventeen years old and impatient with his desire to sample the fruits of life. As he grew older he cast his eye upon a lass named Emily Cherry, a friend of his young sister Hannah, who lived near her at Puddle Hill. George decided that Emily was to be his bride, and on 1st May, 1845, they took their vows of marriage in front of the Reverend John Donne at Houghton Regis Parish Church. The witnesses at this union were young Hannah, and Thomas Mooring. All parties signed their mark with a cross. By this time George was twenty-one but Emily was only seventeen years old, and it would be reasonable to assume that Emily might have been pregnant, but there has been no evidence found that there was a child born to them. Now he was married, George moved out of the cottage he had occupied with his father, and he and Emily set up home in Puddle Hill with Emily's family. It was around this time, too, that Rebecca and Dockerill moved there, and being in such close proximity their friendship could now reach a new level.

At the beginning of February, 1846, just nine months into George's marriage, and with the upturn in the relationship between George and Dockerill, there appears to be a downturn in their relationship with the law. Just what they were celebrating or commiserating, we shall never know, but on the 4th February, George, along with George Fensome, David Parrott and William Knight was arrested by the police for being drunk and disorderly. Again the time frame might suggest that Emily gave birth to a child. However, there was another George White living at Puddle Hill at the time, possibly a cousin, so it may have been him. But the trouble did not end there, for later that week Dockerill, too, had a brush with the law when he got into a fight with the police. It would seem that his battle with authority was beginning in earnest.

In any event, both men stood separately before Dr. Bland, Rev. W. McDougall, Rev. W.B. Wroth, and Levi Ames Esq., at the Petty Session on 16th February, 1846, on different charges. George, along with George Fensome, David Parrott and William Knight, all labourers, were brought up by the police, and charged with being drunk and disorderly on the fourth of that month at Houghton Regis. All the defendants were convicted and fined 5/-, which they paid. Dockerill appeared on a summons charged with assaulting one police-constable Attwood, at Houghton Regis, on 9th February. He was fined 20/-, and this too was paid.[12]

Unfortunately the troubles continued. The happiness of the newly-weds, George and Emily, was not to last. The summer of 1846 was hot and dry and it was followed in the autumn by a serious outbreak of typhoid throughout the country. Sadly, young Emily was taken ill and on 18th November she passed away at their home in Puddle Hill, just eighteen months after their marriage. The cause of her demise is shown on her death certificate as 'fever', so it is probable that she had typhoid, or enteric fever as it was then known. She was buried in Houghton Regis Cemetery on 22nd November, 1846. The informant on the certificate was Rebecca Pateman, a neighbour who was in attendance at her death.

Poor Emily was just eighteen years old.

If the sadness of young Emily's death could be made any worse, it was by the severe conditions that year. The hot dry summer of 1846 was followed by a long and bitter winter, causing much distress amongst the poor in Bedfordshire.

But, briefly at least, grieving was put aside and the bitter winter ignored for the celebration of the marriage of William, George's nephew who was now nineteen years old. On 4th February, 1847 at Houghton Regis Parish Church, William took for his bride seventeen-year-old Mary Tavener from Bidwell. William and Mary made their home in Chalk Hill, (Puddle Hill) near to William's father and mother, John and Sally. Next door to them lived William's aunt, Lucy, and her husband, Thomas Hines, and their five children who had now moved from Chalgrave.

The harsh winter which prevailed was followed by a cold and windy spring during 1847. In the middle of April it was reported that there had scarcely been a genial day to remind one that the spring quarter had arrived. Early flowers and vegetation struggled through in some guise or other, but the cutting winds by day, and nipping frost by night, stripped them of their beauty and scared them into a premature death. The fields were covered in the early mornings by a hoar frost and the ponds with a sheet of glass. If the temperature rose on the odd day to be what was commonly termed a 'growing day' then the sharp frost at night checked the vegetation. There was a smart fall of snow accompanied by cutting head-winds and adverse undercurrents. It was obvious that garden produce and crops would have a very late season that year.[13] People's hardship continued and brought about an increase in petty crime, mostly for stealing food.

Just a year and three weeks had passed since Dockerill's appearance in court for assaulting the police constable, when he was in trouble with the police once again, this time for stealing oats from a farm at Thorn.

It appears to be about the same time Dockerill was charged with this offence that the White family's long association with Thorn came to an end, and the rest of them moved away. This could suggest that the incident might have had something to do with it, but this can only be surmised. Possibly they fell out with the farmer after Dockerill stole the oats, or possibly Dockerill stole in retaliation for them falling out with the farmer. Whatever the reason, there were no longer any of the Whites left in Thorn.

John Senior and David, together with Sam Poulton, Mary and their children, moved into a cottage in Church Place, High Street, Houghton Regis. Here Sam Poulton is described in the 1851 census as a plaiting school master. However, as this is the only census to show him in this occupation, it would be reasonable to suppose that this was another window of opportunity which was grabbed, because other censuses show his occupation to be a labourer, both in 1841 when the family are living at Thorn, and in 1861 when they had moved to Beale Street, in Dunstable, (Upper Houghton Regis). At the same time, George's brother, James, rented a cottage and garden, in Drury Lane, Houghton Regis, and Henry and Eleanor Kingham moved to a cottage in Bidwell.

Whether he was grief stricken or not at Emily's passing, later that same year George took himself another wife just ten months after her death. This time the bride was Sarah Cook, the 19-year-old daughter of William and the late Elizabeth Cook who both came from Houghton Regis. Sarah's mother, Elizabeth, and George's mother, Lucy, were both born Turners, and although no connection has been established between the two, it is still very probable that they were related.

The marriage between George and Sarah took place on 30th September, 1847 in Houghton Regis Church, where George had also taken his vows with Emily a few short months before. This time they stood before the Reverend William Nelson, and, as before, young Hannah was a witness. The second witness was William Gregory, whom Hannah was later to marry. George and Sarah made their home in Houghton Regis in a cottage in Groom's Yard, next door to another young couple, John and Ruth King. John was just about the same age as George, and Ruth was three years older than Sarah. Evidence would suggest that the four were firm friends and were in the habit of talking to each other through the wall between the two cottages, it being so thin.

Throughout these years, John Senior continued to work for the estate of the Duke of Bedford. One day, during the winter of 1847/1848, on Thursday 10th February, still seemingly fit and looking hale and hearty, he called at the Crown Inn in Houghton Regis after work where he chatted to the landlady whilst he supped a pint of ale. Having finished his pint, he started to leave to go home for his dinner, but he did not get far. On reaching the threshold he suddenly collapsed. The landlady called for her husband who immediately went to John's assistance but was unable to revive him. The surgeon arrived five minutes later and tried to bleed him, but this had no effect. There was no doubt that John had died immediately after his collapse. As he had appeared so healthy, and the death was so unexpected, an inquest was held on Saturday 12th February. The jury returned a verdict of 'died from natural causes' and on the death certificate the coroner attributed his death to apoplexy. John was buried on Sunday 13th February, 1848, near his wife, Lucy, his son, Lewis, and his baby daughter, Charlotte in Houghton Regis cemetery.

From Bedford Times Saturday 19th February 1848:

EXTRAORDINARY CASE OF SUDDEN DEATH. –
A very remarkable instance of sudden death occurred at Houghton Regis on the 10th instant. A very hearty looking person, named John White, a woodman in the service of His Grace the Duke of Bedford, called at the Crown Inn and took a pint of ale. He conversed with the landlady, and appeared in very good health. Having finished his ale he was about to leave the public-house to go to his dinner, and suddenly fell down on the threshold. The landlady called her husband, who went to the assistance of the poor man immediately, but found he was quite insensible. A surgeon arrived in five minutes afterwards and tried to bleed the man, but without effect; there is no doubt he expired immediately

after he fell. An inquest was held on view of the body on Saturday, and the Jury returned a verdict of 'Died from natural causes'.

John was thankfully spared the events that would take place a year later.

Almost a year to the day after their marriage, on 29th September, 1848, George's wife, Sarah gave birth to a baby daughter whom they named Eliza after Sarah's mother. Baby Eliza was just over four months old when her father stood beside his nephew and brother-in-law in the dock at Bedford Crown Court.

The Village of Stanbridge 1820. *Z102/69*

CHAPTER 5

The Dockerills – A Pauper's Life in Stanbridge

What did I learn from you, grandpa?
What were the tales from your grave?
I learnt that to eat you sold sparrows,
For which tuppence a dozen was paid.

Although life could not be called easy for such a large family as the Whites, at least they had the relative security of their father, John, being in regular employment for the Duke of Bedford. But it was a different story for the Dockerills.

Thomas was one of a family of probably ten children, born in Stanbridge during the year of 1820 to John and Kingsmill Dockerill. Although the family was not quite as large as that of the Whites, life was very hard for the Dockerills. They were very poor.

Working from available records, Thomas's father, John, was himself the seventh and last child born around 1792 to Thomas and Sarah Dock, or Dockree which was the name signed on their marriage certificate. Thomas senior, after whom his grandson was named, was a pauper[1] and struggled to bring up his children on parish relief.

The problem of the poor and unemployment was national, but England lacked a central governing body to control the administration of the Poor Law. Therefore, it fell to the parish to perform this duty. Long before Thomas Dock found himself the recipient of parish relief, in fact some time in the sixteenth century or even earlier, the church became the arbiter of village affairs. For ecclesiastical purposes the parish was administered by the vestry meeting which was originally an assembly of all the parishioners, presided over by the priest. Gradually it became the practice at this annual meeting, held after Easter, to appoint an executive committee of one or two dozen members, generally the leading figures of the village, to conduct the day to day running of village affairs. This open vestry also selected the parochial officers, the most important of these being the churchwardens.[2] In 1601 the Poor Law Act charged these churchwardens with the care of the poor and appointed new officials, two or more substantial householders, called overseers, to assist them. The funds were provided by the taxation of every inhabitant, or occupier of land. Only the ratepayers had a voice at meetings. Some villages, such as Stanbridge, had a Select Vestry which comprised a more restricted membership and was generally dictated by a partnership between the squire and the parson.[3] To complete the administration of the village, along with the churchwardens and overseers of the poor, were the constables of whom there were normally two, who were paid only for expenses, and the Surveyor of the Highways.

The settlement law at this time restricted movement between villages, except in the event of residing in the parish for forty days after giving notice to the official, payment of the parish rate, or being bound in apprenticeship for a year. This in effect made the pauper a prisoner in his own parish. Harvest time was always an exception as all hands were needed. But even then it was compulsory for an outsider to carry a certificate from his native parish guaranteeing to take him back if he became chargeable to any parish. When travelling outside their home, the poor had to carry a similar type of certificate at all times in case they became chargeable on the rates and the churchwarden and overseer could apply for a removal order for any pauper entering the parish to remove him to his native village. One pitiful regulation to further demoralise the paupers required them all to wear the letter P on their

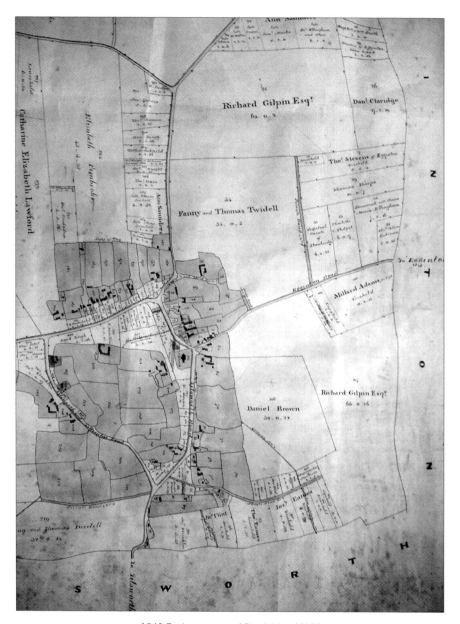

1840 Enclosure map of Stanbridge *MA60*

right shoulders, any non-compliance being severely punished.[4]

Village workhouses were becoming popular with authorities as they were less of a burden on the rates than out-relief payments. But where out-relief was given, systems used to employ the poor were open to abuse, especially in the apprenticeship of pauper children. After 1757, for these unfortunates, any legally stamped document would serve to replace indentures, even an entry in the parish records. Thereby village apprenticeship was often a fallacy, for impoverished children could be disposed of indiscriminately to any squire or farmer who wanted a drudge.[5]

Accounts for the parish were kept by both churchwardens and the overseers, and although strictly speaking the former dealt with church expenditure and incidental civil items, and the latter with poor relief, the two often ran in conjunction.[6]

Each parish elected two churchwardens, an office which was held on an annual basis. The position was unpaid, but expenses were fairly liberally awarded and they could look forward to a yearly dinner on release.[7] In Stanbridge, one of the churchwardens for the year of 1785/6 was John Oney (or Olney), chosen at the Vestry meeting at Easter, and confirmed in office at the Visitation at Leighton Buzzard. In those days such an appointment was no easy matter, their duties being many and varied. It was necessary at all times for them to keep accounts, and usually the first annual entry was for expenses incurred at the visitation of the archdeacon or of the bishop, to whom 'presentments' were made twice a year.[8] These presentments were reports on misconduct by parishioners, or even by the priest, and would include adultery, incest, drunkenness, swearing, hindering the Word of God, disturbing divine service, not communicating at Easter and not attending Church on Sundays or Holy Days. Typically, John Olney's expenses in 1785 for attending the Leighton Buzzard visitations were the first entry to be made and amounted to 3/6d.[9]

Duties of the churchwarden included maintaining the constitution of the Church. In this role he paid for bread and wine, and for washing

The Parish Church of St. John the Baptist, Stanbridge.

the surplice. For the former, the cost was 3/2d or similar, several times a year. Military and Naval victories were celebrated with a prayer, and the cost for a form of prayer was entered as 1/-, probably a perk to the person taking the service. This too was a regular cost. Mrs. Emerton appears to have been paid 1/- per wash for the surplice, and her husband, Joseph, was also paid, possibly on her behalf. Joseph Emerton also received a payment of 10/- in 1788 for what looks like 'being clerk'. In 1788, 6d was paid for a citation from the Bishop, and Mr. Wilson, the Vicar, was paid 10/6d on May 2nd, 1797, and again on 19th December of that year for his duties.

The maintenance also included the upkeep of the Church for which regular payments were made. In 1788, on 6th May, Mr. Franklin was paid £1. 1s. 7d., his bill for bricks, and on 7th, 6d for sand. At the same time, Goss received 8d for two Quarts of (?). On 23rd December, 1797, a payment of £1. 9s. 6d. was made to William Ellingham for wood and nails and his bill for work carried out. Interestingly, William Ellingham was also the churchwarden who drew up the accounts at this time. On a lighter side, on 29th December, 1797, Goss was paid 6/2d for 18 quarts and a pint of ale at the (?) churchyard, possibly supplied to the workers when work was carried out. The following year, Master Johnson was paid 4/3d. for work at the church. Mr. Hickman was paid £1. 0s. 0d. for work carried out, and 5/4d. for a Quartor (sic) of lime. Mr Cox received 7/3d for some 'cloath'(sic) and Joseph Emerton 1/- for making the pillar. Thos. Robard's bill for new wools was £4. 4s. 0d.[10] These expenses were paid from the Church Rate, which was fixed at the Vestry Meeting at Easter and was the duty of the Overseer to collect.

In addition to the administration of the church, the churchwarden had many civil duties to perform, including payment for the destruction of vermin. In 1785, 4d was paid for a 'polcat'(sic). By far the most entries are for sparrows, their capture seemingly occupying most of the village, both adults and children, paid at the rate of 2d per dozen by the churchwardens.

There are entries for both Thomas and his children for catching sparrows. From 1786 through to 1797 there are records of the payments in the Churchwardens' accounts,[11] the payment for the whole year of 1786 by the Churchwarden, John Olney, being:

17th April 1786   Paid Thomas Dock 1 doz sparows (sic)   £0. 0s. 2d.
17th April 1786   Paid Dock boy for 9 sparows(sic)   £0. 0s. 1½d

The Dock boy mentioned would have been their eldest son, Thomas. The next son, Joseph, had already died in 1785 at just a year old.

And then again the 1797/8 records of the Churchwarden, William Ellingham, show payments:

12th June 1797   Paid Dockrill Girl for 6 sparrows   £0. 0s. 1d.
10th July 1797   Paid Dockrill Boy for 9 sparows (sic)   £0. 0s. 1½d.
30th July 1798   Paid Dockrill Girl 1 D sparrows   £0. 0s. 2d.

The winter of 1801 was exceptionally bitter, the worst since 1740, with everything frozen for thirteen weeks. Thomas senior succumbed to the treacherous weather and died in January 1801. He was buried in Stanbridge graveyard on 19th January, when young John was just eight years old. Thomas's wife, Sarah, died three years later and was buried on 10th February, 1804. Their legacy was to leave a young family born into poverty. John's eldest sister, Elizabeth, had married during this time to William Shillingford in Leighton Buzzard on 20th October 1803, and they made their home in Stanbridge. It is probable that this young couple took on the burden of Elizabeth's young siblings. William and Elizabeth had one child, George, in 1807 before Elizabeth herself died. The next sister, Ann, married William's brother, John, in 1807 and in all probability continued to house young John Dockrill.

John was married at the age of twenty to Kingsmill Bignell in Stoke Hammond, Buckinghamshire on 2nd November, 1812 and the couple settled in Stanbridge along the Tilsworth Road near to, or with, the Shillingford family.

By this time, the Speenhamland system was in force and out-relief was liberally given to supplement wages. The amount paid was linked both to the price of bread at the time and to the size of a man's family. Thus a large family became a sensible investment with wages in the region of a shilling a day. The repercussions of this system were disastrous, encouraging early and prolific marriages and illegitimacy.[12] The population grew but no effort was made to house it, in fact cottages were being demolished in order to save the owners' rate liability. Illegitimacy was extensive, and although every effort was made to make the father responsible for the child, it otherwise fell upon the support of the parish. Forced marriages were also quite common, the duty of giving away the bride or acting as best man falling upon the churchwarden or overseer.[13]

As with his parents, fortunes did not improve for John and Kingsmill and their ten children. John himself seems not only to be dogged by unemployment, but by illness too. Both he and one daughter are listed in the parish records as being sick.

But they were not alone in their poverty. From the records of the Overseers of the Poor, it seems that life was very hard for a lot of Stanbridge families as there are so many paupers listed. It is apparent that the 'roundsman' system was in operation, the labourer being sent 'round' from one employer to another, working a week or two for each. A low rate was agreed and the poor rate added. Or the employer contracted with the parish of the man's labour and the parish paid the man, and maybe the employer was excused the payment of rates if he guaranteed to employ a certain number of pauper labourers.[14] Consequently, what the labourers were due in direct wages, they were obliged to receive in a patronising and degrading form.[15] And they were obliged to be reduced to a state of beggary and pauperism before anybody would employ them at all. When no work could be found for them, paupers were put to work on the roads, breaking stones into very small pieces so that their 'betters' might have a smoother ride in their carriages.

By this system too, the farmer, or rate-payer, was bound to employ, and pay at a certain rate, a certain number of labourers, whether he wanted them or not.[16] Or, indeed, whether he could afford them or not. The number could depend on his assessment to the poor rate, or to the number of acres he occupied.

For the lesser farmer, the burden of taxation at this time was overwhelming. Taxes were levied by both the central government and local authorities. The County Rate was fixed by the justices at Quarter Sessions and provided partly for the upkeep of the county bridges, and various expenses connected with justice and the police, including the constables who were paid only for expenses – there was no regular police force. The Highway rate was levied in each parish by the surveyor of highways and provided for the upkeep of the roads. The Church Rate was levied by the churchwardens for the maintenance of the church, and expenses of public worship. There was a Militia Rate which supplied the pay of militiamen who agreed to take the place of those men who had originally been chosen by lot.[17] Each man chosen was obliged to serve for three years or provide £10 for a substitute, but a small owner's liability was discharged by payment from the rates. And then finally there was the Poor Rate to assist the poor of the parish. In theory, the Poor Rate was assessable on the ratepayer's income, but the difficulty in determining this made the assessment almost entirely depend on land and property. And in fact, it was not levied on the owners of such properties who were generally the large land owners, but fell on the shoulders of the occupiers who were generally their tenants, the small farmers.

Consequently, some of smaller tenant taxpayers struggled to pay their dues, and applied to the Vestry Meeting to have their taxes abolished. Records of 1827 show: (sic)

The Ninth Select Vestory Being the Half Yearly Vestory held at Mr. Gosses 26th of Oct...........

		Abraham Mann	}	Chearman
	{	Wm. Olney		
	{	Thos. Twidle		
Presant	{	Joseph Eames	}	Churchwarden
	{	John Olney	}	Overseer
	{	Thos. Willis		
	{	Thos. Gurney		
	{	Thos. Eames		

John Giltro (?), James Gates, Wm. Parrott, Joseph Stanbridge, D. Ellingham

Applied to have their Taxes taken off
Not Granted[18]

Because of the anomalies of this system, the smaller farmer who could not afford to employ the pauperised labourer was forced to pay in taxes for those men to break stones in the road, whilst his own fences needed repair, or his crops needed setting in. He was forced to watch those men at the thankless, demoralising task of fragmenting stones whilst thistles and couch grass choked his fields. He was forced himself to uphold a system which by the enormity of the taxes, and the distribution of lands to the larger landholders, would crush and abase him to a labourer and then in turn to a pauper himself.

The surviving Overseers of the Poor Records[19] for Stanbridge start in 1824, and show that over forty agricultural labourers, families or widows in Stanbridge were receiving regular payments from the poor rate at that time. Amongst these were regular payments made to John Dock from the beginning of the accounts. Throughout December of 1824 he was receiving payments of 2/3d most weeks and during the first half of 1825, 2/9d per week. Later this was reduced to 1/6d, rising again in March, 1826. Similar amounts are shown for later years.

Relief to the poor did not end with supplementing their wages. Payments could be made for burials and for the marriage of a man willing to marry the mother of a bastard child. The man could even have been the father, but it was cheaper than allowing the woman and child to become a burden on the poor relief. A payment could be made also for clothing.

In that same year, John Dock was granted 5/- for an overcoat:[20] (sic)

The Twelveth Select Vestory held at the Church on Friday the 7th December............

		Thos. Woodman	}	Chearman
		Wm. Olney		
Presant	{	Thos. Twidle		
		Bar. Wilks		
		Joseph Eames	}	Churchwarden

John Dock applyed for a Great Coat. Granted him 5/-
Susan Huatt applyed for Relief. Not Granted

Unfortunately, Susan Hewitt did not have the same luck – her application

Distress of the poor. There were many applicants for parish relief.

for relief was refused, as was Susannah Gurney's application for her husband, and Widow King's for more money at the Vestry meeting two weeks later. But William Pickett who applied for relief for his sick wife was more fortunate – his was granted. In November 1828, there are payments to both John Dockrel and Thomas, both of 1/9d. Thomas may have been John Dockrel's eldest brother, or he could have been our accused, young Thomas, his son, who would have been just eight years old. But children were sent out to work at a very young age, so doubtless Thomas would have been obliged to contribute his share. Payments continued to John until December 1829, when they were made to both John and his ill daughter. These payments continued until May 1831, when perhaps his daughter's health improved. There is a record, too, of the marriage of Sarah Dockerill[21] to Thomas Ellingham in November of that year. In the January of the same year, John was also granted 3/- towards a coat. In May 1833, Ann Dockerill[22] married Jesse Ellingham, but still the payments were being made to John almost weekly through until January 1834 when young William, Thomas's brother, who would have been about 10 years old, also received 1/-. This payment was doubtless one made to boys who stay at home, because in February of that year the payment of 1/- to boys is mentioned and discontinued.

Feby. 6. 1834
At a Public Vestry held pursuant to public notice, the following
Resolutions were unanimously adopted..........

1st   That 1/6d per bushel for bean setting (?) shall be the
           price through the Parish.

2nd   That the shilling a week which has been allowed
           to those Boys who stay at home is after this week not
           to be continued.

3rd   That compensation be made, to Mr. John Olney
           according to Mr. F. Young's estimate for gravel digging,
           this account to be settled by the Stone Warden (?), and
           the ground to be levelled.
                  Signed G.Whyley Chairman

Also, it was resolved
        That after this week any occupier of land taking a man
off the Road shall pay him his full money – and that there be no
roundsmen after this week.
                  Signed G. Whyley Chairman[23]

In fact, the Poor Law as it stood was about to change.

The pressure to reform the Poor Relief Law was sufficiently strong
for the Government to appoint a Royal Commission to report on the old
laws, with the result that a New Poor Law was enacted in 1834. The
new law, as with the old, accepted that every person had the right to
claim relief, but it was now under stricter conditions. The old scheme
of outdoor relief was discontinued and all those claiming of able body
would now have to enter the workhouse. Conditions in the workhouse
were made even less tolerable than before, so that they would now be
worse than the conditions under which the lowest paid worker outside
lived, to discourage people from seeking relief. More stringent means

tests were made, with the intention of deterring all but the desperate. Old parish workhouses were abolished in favour of a new larger central union workhouse, generally situated in a market town and covering a radius of ten miles,[24] and operating under a board of guardians. The Union House to cover the Stanbridge area was built in Leighton Buzzard. The new laws were greeted with bitter opposition by the labourers, who watched the erection of these austere buildings with fear. And with good cause. The families of those seeking relief were immediately broken up and housed in different parts of the prison-like building. The men were set to work at menial tasks, like stone-breaking, oakum picking or grinding corn. They were fed bread and gruel with a small allowance of cheese or meat, and, until 1842, all meals were taken in silence. Life was almost intolerable. Opposition to the system was widespread, such that some parishes did not immediately implement the reform and abandon outdoor relief, but steadily reduced the scale of payments, ultimately to the same result.

On 11th April, 1834, another public Vestry meeting was held in Stanbridge, 'pursuant to public notice, the following resolutions were unanimously agreed to'...(sic)

That the Farmers and occupiers of Land in the hamlet do in the first instance (?) employ their regular number of men, as before agreed to.

That when they have the full number as above stated, such farmers and occupiers shall be at liberty to employ any man from the road at any price for a Month from this Date, paying him 4/- per week, and whatever he is further entitled to from the Parish according to Family the same to be paid and made up by the Overseer at the month end; but in the first instance the farmers so employing a labourer is to pay him his full money and to take in an Account at the end of the Month to the Overseer, who will then pay back the farmer the difference between the 4/- and his regular Parish pay.[25]

However, it was a bit premature to decide that the resolutions were unanimously agreed to, for in fact the farmers did not like the idea of having to pay out the full amount to their labourers and claiming it back. The resolutions were rejected and therefore not signed by the Chairman.

On 25th September, 1834, at an 'adjourned' Vestry of which due notice was given on Sunday the 14th ult:

A Church rate of 1/6d in the pound was unanimously granted for current expenses.[26]

For a couple of years following the Poor Law Reform, harvests were good, and the price of wheat fell, and opposition to the Poor Law gradually diminished. But by 1836 the good harvests came to an end and the country was plunged into a depression once more which was to last until 1842. These years of hardship were the worst in the history of the nineteenth century. Unemployment reached hitherto unknown proportions, with high food prices and inadequate poor relief. Faced with the terror, shame and degradation of the workhouse, criminal acts of social protest, petty theft, and vagrancy continued. The Settlement Act of the late eighteenth century, which was designed to prevent labourers moving to another county where they might 'settle' and thereby become eligible for poor relief, had by now broken down in most areas. In its wake, vagrancy, and those itinerant workers associated with it, brought continual problems to the area of Bedfordshire. Tramps, often men moved by Poor Law authorities, road-gangs and railway navvies were responsible for a lot of the petty thefts and poaching. Road-gangs and railways navvies were aplenty in the area, with the coming of the railway. But it was hard to distinguish between the vagrants and those hawkers and harvesters genuinely seeking employment.

It was around this time that things were put into motion by those interested parties to begin the process of enclosure of the village of Stanbridge.[27]

.........*And whereas Millard Adams Daniel Claridge and William Twidell three of the Proprietors of or persons interested in the open and common arable meadow and pasture lands or fields in the township or Hamlet of Stanbridge in the County of Bedford did by writing under their hands bearing date the twentieth day of September One thousand eight hundred and thirty six give notice in the manner prescribed by the said first mentioned Act that a Public Meeting would be held in the Church of Stanbridge aforesaid on Thursday the thirteenth day of October then next at eleven o'clock in the forenoon for the purpose of taking into consideration the expediency of inclosing the open and common arable meadow and pasture lands or fields in the said Township or Hamlet of Stanbridge and to extinguish the right of intercommonage which then existed as well over as in respect of such land. And whereas a Public Meeting of the Proprietors and persons interested in the said open and common fields and lands in the Township or Hamlet of Stanbridge aforesaid was held on the said thirteenth day of October One thousand eight hundred and thirty six in the Church of Stanbridge aforesaid pursuant to such Notice And it was then and there resolved amongst other things that in the opinion of that Meeting it was expedient to inclose the open and common arable meadow and pasture lands and fields in the said Township or Hamlet of Stanbridge and to extinguish the right of intercommonage which then existed as well over as in respect of such land and the Proprietors and persons interested as aforesaid present at such Meeting did severally consent and agree in writing to such Inclosure. And it was further resolved at such Meeting that the said Inclosure should be proceeded with in accordance with the provisions of the said first mentioned Act so soon as the consent in writing of two third parts in number and value of the Proprietors and persons interested in the said land should have been obtained. And whereas the consents in writing of two third parts in number and value (such value being ascertained as in the first mentioned Act expressed in that behalf) of the several persons seized or possessed of or entitled in possession to or interested in possession in any rights of common or other rights in the said lands intended to be inclosed for such Estates as in the first mentioned Act in that behalf expressed having being obtained and such their consents having been obtained and such their consents having been signified in the manner prescribed by the first mentioned Act the said Inclosure was proceeded with. And whereas the major part in number and value of the Proprietors of and persons interested in the said lands intended to be divided and inclosed or their known Agents who were present at a Meeting called for that purpose at the House of Thomas Goss known by the sign of the Five Bells in Stanbridge aforesaid Did on the sixteenth day of March One thousand eight hundred and thirty seven nominate and appoint in writing under their hands me the said Thomas Bloodworth (being a person not interested in the premises) to be the Commissioner for dividing allotting and inclosing all the open and common arable meadow and pasture lands and fields in the Township or Hamlet of Stanbridge aforesaid which had been agreed to be divided allotted and inclosed as aforesaid And did also appoint me the Surveyor for surveying and admeasuring such open and common arable meadow and pasture lands and fields and for the performance of all other duties appertaining to the Office of Surveyor which should be requisite to be performed in carrying the said first mentioned Act into execution And I the said Thomas Bloodworth did on the said sixteenth day of March One thousand eight hundred and thirty seven take and subscribe before Richard Thomas Gilpin Esquire one of Her Majesty's Justices of the Peace acting as and for the Division of Woburn in the Hundred of Manshead in the side County of Bedford within which Division and Hundred the said Inclosure was intended to be made ....*

(sic)

seized possessed entitled or interested as aforesaid or of the Guardians
Trustees Feoffees Husbands or Committees aforesaid of such of the
said persons who might be under disability as aforesaid (such
value to be ascertained as therein mentioned *Provided also*
that no such Inclosure should take place nor should any
Agreement for that purpose be binding until a Public Meeting
of the Proprietors and persons interested in the lands intended
to be inclosed should have been previously called for the
purpose of taking the expediency of such Inclosure into
consideration by notice under the hands of three or more of
such Proprietors or persons interested such notice to be
affixed on the principal outer door of the Church or Chapel
of the Parishes Townships or places wherein the lands intended
to be inclosed should lie or in case there should be no such
Church or Chapel then on the door of the Church or Chapel of
some adjoining Parish Township or Place and also advertized
in some Newspaper circulating in the County wherein such
lands lie at least fourteen days before the said intended
Meeting *Provided* that such Inclosure might after such Meeting be proceeded
with by and with the consent in writing of two third parts in
number and value of the Proprietors and persons interested in
the lands intended to be inclosed notwithstanding some of the
parties who might approve of and consent to such Inclosure
might not be present at such Meeting and might signify their
consent thereto after the same should have been holden *And
it was* by the said Act further *Enacted* that whenever the
persons whose consents were thereby rendered necessary to any such

A notice was affixed to the door of the church. *MA60*

Throughout these years, John Dockerill and his family were living in one of the parish workhouses in Stanbridge. Outdoor relief could still be awarded to those unable to work through illness and John must have suffered bad health for a number of years. In 1837 records show that he is receiving parish relief because of sickness and it seems that his daughter, Kingsmill, was also in poor health. On 17th January he was granted two payments of 2/- and 5/-, then another 5/- on 24th January. On 31st January he received 5/- at the Vestry and throughout most of the year he received 8/- per week. Unfortunately, here the records end.[28] It is obvious that to put food in their mouths, the Dockerills would have had to forage what they could. At the very least they would have poached. Any skills, both legal and illegal, that had been acquired by the adults, would have been passed on to the next generation. They were uneducated, but wise in the art of survival. But it was Thomas who developed the grudge against the system, it was Thomas who would steal rather than starve.

Young Thomas was now sixteen years old. He was tall for those times, making him seem older than his years, and his maturity was further heightened by the responsibility of the family which fell ever more increasingly on his shoulders. It would appear that he was a wild youth, but with his father being ill for so many years he had probably lacked parental guidance. His liaison at the tender age of sixteen with Rebecca White led to her pregnancy and their marriage, six months into her confinement, when he had just turned seventeen, but their union was saddened by the death of the baby daughter, Ann, shortly after her birth in December 1837. However, a year later Rebecca gave birth to their second child, this time a healthy boy whom they named Ephraim after their baby nephew Ephraim Emmerton who had died earlier that year at the age of two years. But sadly the joy of Ephraim's birth, too, was overshadowed by the death of Thomas's sister, Kingsmill, at the age of twenty-one.

Seemingly, Thomas's father never recovered his health, but sank further and further into decline. He died on 9th March, 1839, just over five weeks after Rebecca's mother Lucy. With him at the end was William Botsworth, his daughter Kingsmill's young husband who himself had not long been made a widower. John was buried three days later near his daughter in Stanbridge graveyard.

Later that year, on 6th June, there was a meeting of the ratepayers at the Parish church. Now that the Union Workhouse was centralised in Leighton Buzzard, the Guardians of the Poor sought to sell the workhouse cottages in Stanbridge, including the one in which John Dockerill's family lived.

Township of Hamlet of Stanbridge Leighton Buzzard Union Counties of Bedford and Buckingham. At a Meeting of the Rate Payers of the said Township or hamlet and owners of Property therein entitled to vote pursuant to the provisions of an act passed in the 4th and 5th years of the Reign of His Late Majesty King William 4th instituted(?) "An Act for the amendment and better administration of the laws relating to the Poor in England and Wales" held at the Parish Church in the said Township or hamlet on Thursday the sixth day of June 1839 Pursuant to a Notice of such meeting duly given

(Signed)   G. Whyley Chairman

It was resolved by a majority of such Rate Payers and Owners present in person or as respect owners by proxy at such meeting. That this Meeting do consent to the Guardians of the Poor of the said Union selling the premises described in the margin hereof, under the provisions of an act passed in the 5th and 6th years of the reign of his late Majesty King William 4th instituted(?) "An act to facilitate the Conveyance of Workhouses and other property of Parishes and of Incorporations or Unions of Parishes in England and Wales" in such manner, and subject to such rules, orders and regulations touching such sale, the conveyance of such property, and the application of the Produce arising therefrom, for the permanent advantage of this Township or hamlet as the Poor

Law Commissioners shall in that behalf direct.

(In Margin) All that freehold Cottage now and for many years past used as two Tenements situate standing and being in the East end of Stanbridge in the County of Bedford now in the occupation of William Eddins (?) and John Dockeriell together with the piece of Garden Ground yard and other appurtenances thereunto belonging. And also all that freehold cottage divided into and used as four tenements situate standing and being in Stanbridge aforesaid near the Church there now in the several occupations of Edward Boskett, Thomas Bodsworth, William Hewitt and Susan Hewitt with the appurtenances thereto belonging subject to a chief Rent of one shilling and eight pence per annum. And also all that piece of freehold land being near the wash brook and estimated at half an acre more or less awarded to the parish under an Act of enclosure in lieu of land in the open field called the Haywards back[29]

(Signed)	G. Whyley	}	Minister
	John Franklin	}	Churchwardens
	Thomas Eames	}	
	Thomas Eames	}	Overseers
	Thomas Mead	}	
	Thomas Thorpe		
	Rowland Gadsden		
	Thomas Willis		

By this time, the process of enclosure of the villages Stanbridge and Eggington was well under way, and the names of the committee administering the affairs of the village featured heavily in the awards.

Another person to benefit from the enclosure, also the chairman of those proprietors interested in the enclosure of Eggington, was Richard Thomas Gilpin Esq., already an extensive land owner in Hockliffe and Eggington and Chalgrave.[30]

Eggington Award

Bedfordshire } *Be it remembered that on the fifteenth day of March in the fourth year of*
to wit } *the Reign of our Sovereign Lady Victoria by the Grace of God of the United Kingdom of Great Britain and Ireland Queen Defender of the Faith and in the year of our Lord One thousand eight hundred and forty one a certain Deed Poll or Instrument in writing purporting to be an Award was left with me Fred Pearse Clerk of the Peace for the County of Bedford which said Deed Poll or Instrument is in the words following.*

We the undersigned Proprietors of and persons interested in the open and common Arable Meadow and Pasture Lands and Fields situate lying and being within the limits and boundaries of the Hamlet of Eggington in the Parish of Leighton Buzzard in the County of Bedford and the rights of Common over and in respect of the same and the known Agents of Proprietors being the major part in number and value present at a Public Meeting held at the Unicorn Inn in Leighton Buzzard aforesaid on Monday the eleventh day of September Once Thousand eight hundred and thirty seven for the purpose of nominating and appointing two persons (not interested in the premises) to be Commissioners for dividing allotting and inclosing the said open and common Arable Meadow and Pasture Lands and Fields do by virtue of an Act of Parliament made and passed in the sixth and seventh years of the Reign of His late Majesty King William the fourth instituted "An Act for facilitating the Inclosure of open and arable fields in England and Wales" hereby nominate and appoint Thomas Bloodworth of Kimbolton in the County of Huntingdon Gentleman and Daniel Lousley of Blewberry Farm in the Parish of Blewberry in the County of Berks Gentleman to be Commissioners for dividing allotting and inclosing the said open and Common Arable Meadow and Pasture lands and fields.

> *Richard Thomas Gilpin Chairman*
> *Richard Thomas Gilpin As Agent for*
> *Richard Gilpin*
> *Millard Adams*
> *Daniel Claridge*
> *John Vaux Moore*
> *William Smith Sen.*
> *Wm. Smith Jun.*
> *Wm. Smith as Agent for H.W.Smith*
> *Thomas Wynter Mead*
> *Thomas Wynter Mead as Agent for*
> *Maria Lucy Parkinson*
> *David Lee Willis Agent to Anne Russell*
> *Mary Anne C. Justice F.W. Justice*
> *Maria Whitworth Russell,*
> *Henshaw S. Russell, John Russell*
> *and Caroline Elizabeth Russell.*
> *David Lee Willis Agent to Charlotte Willis*
> *Fred. Willis.*

Franklin John	89		Jacksons Close		2	3	26
"	132		Homestead and Home Close		5	2	20
"	133		Meadow		3	3	30
"	137		Meadow Close		1	2	2
"	205		Homestead and Home Close		2	2	4
"	210		Brockers Close		3	2	25
"	213		Germans Close		4	1	6
"	217	1	East field	Freehold	53	2	18
"	94	2	Fishells	Ditto	5	3	32	230
"	202	3	On the Green	Ditto	2	0	27
"	244	4	Mead Field	Ditto	28	1	29
"	226	5	Naldwick Field	Ditto	10	.	.
"	227	6	Ditto	Ditto	2	3	.
"	228	7	Ditto	Ditto	10	2	.
"	229	8	Ditto	Ditto	20	.	.
"	230	9	Naldwick Field and Mead field	Ditto	71	.	12
"	141	10	On the Green	Ditto	1	3	18
"	138	11	Ditto	Ditto	.	.	26

John Franklin, churchwarden, featured in awards. *MA60*

Gilpin Richard Esquire	37		Hill Hicks	
"	125		Pot Ash Close	
"	129		Meadow	
"	131		Homestead and Home Close	
"	209		Brockers Close	
"	142	1	On the Green	Freehold
"	117	2	Ditto	Ditto
"	25	3	Muggenden Home Field and Long Furlong Field	Ditto
"	107	4	Mill Field	Ditto

Richard Thomas Gilpin Esq. Enclosure awards. *MA60/61*

Lieutenant Colonel Gilpin who resided at the Grange in Hockliffe was a genial squire and enthusiastic sportsman. During his life he was a Member of Parliament serving as High Sheriff of the County of Bedford and in his position of magistrate he chaired the local Petty Sessions. And his was a name that Dockerill would have cause to remember as their paths crossed in the years to come.

In 1841, the time when these enclosures came into force, Dockerill and Rebecca were shown to be living in a cottage in Stanbridge, by the Church, one of those which the Guardians of the Poor sought permission to sell in 1839. Thomas's younger brother, William, lived in the Tilsworth Road, with his younger siblings.[31]

The serious depression during the early 1840s had forced Commissioners to change their way of thinking because the scale of unemployment meant that workhouses were not large enough to take in all applicants for funds, and they had no choice but to accept that it was impossible to totally prohibit all outdoor relief. But once again they failed to tackle the problem of poverty at its root cause. Their answer was to issue a Labour Test Order in 1842 forcing men into menial labour such as breaking stones on roads in return for outdoor relief, causing more loss of self-respect and creating more disillusionment amongst the poor with the disparities of the system.

By 1845 Thomas and Rebecca had moved to Puddle Hill and their family increased with the birth of their son Joseph. But once again their joy was blighted by the loss of Thomas's mother, Kingsmill, who had been ill for some fourteen months, because on the 29th September, 1845 she haemorrhaged and died.

Life seemed to be settled now for Thomas. Or was it? Thomas had grown up, but he had much suffering to contend with at a very young age. He had lost a daughter, father, mother and sister all in those few years, and memories of his childhood of poverty were not far behind him. And were things better for the family now? With the recent enclosure of his native village, he was forced to confront the injustice of the system and evaluate the gap between the rich landowners and the poor labourers.

Plenty of food for the rich.

He could brood on the fact that his compatriots went hungry whilst the rich congratulated themselves on their land acquisitions over their laden tables. Whilst these corpulent beings with their bellies full threw their meaty bones to their dogs, the starving inmates of one workhouse, who had been set the task of grinding bones from the local butchers, fought

No food for the poor.

over the pitiful scraps of meat which still adhered to the bones, causing a riot. The bonds of poverty are hard to escape and it appears that Thomas had not lost the chip on his shoulder. He had little time for authority, had a grudge against the police and he considered that if he did not have food to provide for his family, then he would help himself to it. It was not long before this attitude manifested itself and Thomas was in trouble.

On 9th February, 1846, just five days after George's arrest, he struck police constable Attwood, resulting in an appearance at the Petty Sessions and a fine of 20/-. Then followed a very hot summer, after which they had to contend with an outbreak of typhoid in the autumn and the death of Emily, George's wife. Now there was another very harsh winter which caused much hardship and distress for labouring families. They were hungry, and were at a loss as to where to find food to put on the table. To make matters worse, early in 1847, Rebecca discovered she was pregnant once more, and things were brought to a head.

During the night of 5th March, under cover of darkness Dockerill and one Thomas Lancaster crept into a barn on Thomas Pratt's farm at Thorn. They struck a lucifer match and lit a candle which Dockerill held. After stripping the straw off a heap of oats, they filled two sacks (later described as being stolen from one Edward Barnard by Dockerill), carefully smoothing the pile and replacing the straw afterwards. Unfortunately they were not quite so careful in their escape, and they left a trail of oats leading to their cottage. Unfortunately too, for the men, there was a witness, one Silas Sheppard, who, after working all day on the farm, was asleep in the barn. After seeing the men take the sacks and making off with them, Silas raised the alarm. Farmer Pratt's son went for the police and he and police constable Sinfield together followed the trail of oats and the men's footprints which led them near to Dockerill's house and Lancaster's van, where they found the oats. William Carter, described as a farmer at Houghton, and who had also had a quantity of oats stolen, went with Sinfield and compared the foot marks. He had no doubt that they were made by Dockerill and Lancaster.

The census of 1841 shows that Thomas Pratt's farm at Thorn was the first one to be reached from the Turnpike Road, and was near to the Whites' cottage. The Pratt family also leased Carcutt farm from one Lieutenant Colonel Richard Thomas Gilpin.[32] William Carter, the other farmer mentioned, is shown as living with his mother on a farm at Chalk Hill, at one time called Greenman farm. Greenman farm was rented by the Carters from the Duke of Bedford's estate. Edward Barnard too leased Bidwell farm from the Duke of Bedford.[33] In 1850, on the Land Tax Assessments, the Lancaster family are shown as living in a cottage at Puddlehill owned by Ann Green, George White's sister.

Dockerill and Lancaster were both charged to appear at the Bedfordshire Lent Assizes.

Thomas Dockerill (27) labourer, Houghton Regis, charged with stealing, on 5th March, a quantity of oats, the property of Thomas Pratt; also of stealing, on the same day, two sacks, the property of Edward Barnard.[34]

Thomas Lancaster (30) labourer, Houghton Regis, charged with stealing, on 5th March, a quantity of oats, the property of William Carter; also of stealing, on 5th March, a quantity of oats, the property of Thomas Pratt.[35]

On Monday 15th March, Dockerill and Lancaster stood before Mr. Justice Coleridge at the Bedford Crown Court.

Dockerill's first trial

On Saturday 13th March, 1847, Mr. Justice Coleridge, one of the Judges appointed for the Lent Assizes for Bedfordshire, arrived into Bedford at 5 pm escorted by R. Newland, the High Sheriff, and other dignitaries and the ordinary staff of javelin-men when the Commission was opened at the Shire Hall.

On Sunday morning, his Lordship attended divine service at St. Paul's church with the Sheriff and the Mayor and other members of the Corporation. The Reverend J. Gaskin read the prayers, after which an appropriate and impressive sermon from Proverbs xiv, 34 was preached by the Reverend H.J. Williams of Kempston, chaplain to the Sheriff. He traced the various causes of the increase of crime and in particular the neglected state in which children were allowed to grow up by their parents. He suggested that it would only be checked by a thorough system of education, which would act as a preventative, and to which end he hailed the proposed scheme of government as a step in the right direction. Also, by greater attention to the dwellings of the poor that they might be brought up with due regard to the common decencies of life, and with self-respect. And by an improved system of correction, which, instead of discharging persons after punishment, in a more depraved state than before, would tend to restore them to society as useful and honest members of the community. He regretted that there was so great an increase in the number of juvenile offenders, and that Bedfordshire stood not only low in educational statistics, but proportionably high in regard to crime.

The following morning, Mr. Justice Coleridge took his seat at the Crown Court shortly after 10 am. After the usual preliminaries had been gone through, His Lordship swore in the Grand Jury

Lord Chief Justice Coleridge.

and read the usual proclamation against vice and immorality. He then delivered the charges.

The fact that there were more cases to deal with than normal on the calendar was accounted for in some degree by the long period that had occurred since the last sitting of the Court, as well as from the hard winter and great amount of distress that had prevailed. As many as eight cases were for taking small quantities of potatoes and wheat. There were also two cases of arson. The first was one where the prisoner yielded to temptation without knowing why, but the second was more serious as to motive. The prisoner named Goodliffe was out of work and made an unsuccessful application for relief. Thus rejected and in a temper, possibly irritated by suffering and privation, he set fire to the stack of the Guardian to whom he had applied for relief. His Lordship directed the jury to give great consideration as to the motive in all these cases.[36]

HOUGHTON REGIS

Thomas Lancaster, (30) and Thomas Dockerill (27) labourers, Houghton Regis, charged with stealing, on the 5th of March, a quantity of oats, the property of Thomas Pratt.

Mr. Birch, having stated the facts of the case called the following witnesses:

Silas Sheppard, labourer, deposed that he ? after employment to Mr. Pratt, on the 4th of March, slept in the barn during the night; was disturbed by two men coming into the barn; they struck a light with a lucifer match, and lit a candle; they stripped the straw off the heap of oats, and filled two sacks; after doing so, they made the heap even and swept round it, and then covered it up; they then took the two sacks of oats, and went away; he alarmed Mr. Pratt's people, and they got up. The taller prisoner, Dockerill, held the light.

Robert Pratt, son of prosecutor, deposed that he awoke early on the morning of the 5th of March by last witness, and told what had happened; he went with a policeman and searched the house of Lancaster; found a quantity of oats in his van, they were black and white oats mixed, corresponding with the oats in his father's barn; took the sacks off the prisoner, and gave them to the police.

Police-constable Sinfield produced the oats taken from Lancaster's van; there were footsteps of two persons leading all the way from Mr. Pratt's barn to near Dockerill's house; there were black oats strewed along the track; the footprints of both prisoners corresponded with the track.

William Carter, farmer at Houghton, went with Sinfield and compared the foot marks, which he had no doubt were made by the prisoners.

A sample of the oats was produced from the heap, as also those taken from Lancaster's van, and shown to the jury.

Mr. NAYLOR, in addressing the jury for the defence, dwelt upon the imperfect evidence given by the witness Sheppard, who admitted that he was awoke in a state of alarm, and, owing to the flickering light of a single candle, and the distance from which the men in the barn must have been from him to have been unobserved by them, was unable to speak distinctly as to their features; the more particularly when the witness's vision was so very dim that he had the courage to swear that the green smock now on the prisoner Dockerill's back was a brown one. Verdict, Guilty. Sentenced to four months' hard labour.[37]

Dockerill and Lancaster were taken to Bedford prison to serve their sentence. Prison records for this offence show that Dockerill was married, and that he was residing in Houghton Regis. The record also states that he was slender with a scar under his left eye.

He was imprisoned in the New House of Correction at Bedford Prison, and was put to work in the mill for four calendar months' hard labour. This mill was in fact a discipline mill with tread wheels on which the prisoners were required to take a set number of steps before every meal and until this was achieved there was no food for them.

But whilst Dockerill had to endure his term in prison, Rebecca had to endure four months of her pregnancy without the support of her husband, for it was the 12th July of that year before he returned to his family, now a convicted criminal.[38]

What did I learn from you father? What was the lesson you taught?
I learnt that whilst poor men hungered, rich men killed game for their sport.
That the hide and seek which I played as a child was no game,
And the man whom we hid from no friend,
That his gun was no toy,
And his net was a trap
But I laughed as I hid just the same.
For your comforting self was beside me, and excitement in me bred,
Now we'd caught a rich-man's rabbit, and our bellies would be fed.

The upper class attitude – the labourer's answer lay in prayer.

CHAPTER 6

The Rise in Crime

During the childhood years of our accused, the standard of living for the general labourer had grown steadily more into decline. For the Dockerills, it was a lifetime of poverty on parish relief, each generation inheriting the demoralising existence from their fathers before them. For the Whites, although in employment, it was a hand to mouth struggle for survival being such a large family. Whereas salaries of the upper classes had been substantially raised on the grounds that the cost of living was more expensive, the agricultural labourer was the poorer. It was a period of want and distress, a time when it was not uncommon for the labourer and his family to live mainly on bread and cheese, sometimes never tasting meat for a month and children were to be seen eating scraps from pig-troughs. The potato became a favourite because it was the suitable companion for misery and filth.[1] It was a time when a Suffolk labourer who was out of work and convicted of stealing wood, begged to be sent at once to a House of Correction where he hoped to find food and employment.[2] For it was believed that prisoners in jail were better fed and clothed than the working labourers.

In the summer of 1830, four harvest labourers were found under a hedge dead of starvation. When they were opened up by surgeons, their stomachs contained nothing but sour sorrel. Lord Winchilsea, considering this incident was worthy of mention in the House of Lords, stated that this was not an exceptional case.[3] However this social dispossession and plight of the labouring classes was met by a sanctimonious upper class whose attitude was that industriousness reaped rewards and that poverty was merely evidence of labourers' transgression. It was therefore obvious – the labourer's answer lay in prayer. Such ideas did not help those trapped in poverty. The parson with his full belly could preach all he liked about public morals, and about how to starve without complaining. In the uneducated labourer's view, his answer did not lie in prayer, but in poaching and thieving. He was driven to the wages of crime. It was either that or starve to death.

In the earlier part of the century, there had been many protests and disturbances by labourers in many parts of England. But the uprising during the winter of 1830, which started with fires and destruction of threshing machines in Kent during the summer, became much more serious. It quickly spread through Sussex, Hampshire and Wiltshire, and was led by a romantic but mythical figure named Captain Swing. Hundreds of letters with this signature, but in different handwriting were delivered to farmers and gentry under cover of darkness by rioters. Before long the rising had reached Dorset, Gloucestershire and Buckinghamshire. Here, in addition to the rising primarily occurring for a living wage, the villagers had other scores to settle, and they took advantage of the situation to seek further redress. At Walden, in addition to demanding extra wages and a reduction in tithes, they sought to change the improper distribution of parish gifts.[4] In High Wycombe there was destruction of paper-making machinery by the unemployed.

Northampton Mercury 1830 Dec. (sic)

Paper Fortress. – The paper-mills of Mr. Alderman Venables, in the vicinity of High Wycomb, owing to the alacrity and vigilance of the workmen, wholly escaped the attack of the mob, who proved so destructively mischievous to similar property in that quarter.

On Saturday night about 160 labourers proceeded to Stone, and destroyed all the machinery belonging to Mr. Kingham. They then proceeded to Mr. Farnborough's at Bishopstone, to Mr. Todd's of Sedrup farm, Hartwell, and thence to the Misses Monk's farm adjoining, to Mr. Monk's at Stone, at all whose premises they destroyed every description of machinery. In all these instances the men conducted themselves with great civility, and removed the machines from the yards to prevent injury arising to the cattle from the nails and splinters which fell from the machinery.

The Magistrates at Aylesbury were occupied the greater part of Saturday, in investigating cases of violent outrages. The first was a charge against seven men and boys, all of Waddesdon, for destroying a draining plough and a chaff-cutting machine, the property of W. Rickford, Esq, M.P. at his farm at Blackgrove. None of the labourers employed on the farm were of the number of those assembled. The next was for destroying a threshing machine at Mr. Bigg's of Cublington, by a mob led by a chimney sweeper named Jarvis; a third, for destroying a winnowing machine at Waddesdon, the property of Mr. Hirons; and a fourth, for breaking a hay machine at Eythorpe.

The Bucks Yeomanry have been marching about during the week; they secured ten prisoners at Waddesdon, and seventeen at Stone.

Marlborough, Nov. 25 – There is scarcely a night but some of the farmers around are suffering by fire. The Wiltshire Yeomanry are called out; the Staff are at the Armoury, night and day. There is a troop of dragoons stationed here till the alarm has subsided.

In Oxfordshire, after destroying threshing machines, the labourers demonstrated against a proposal for land enclosure. A large proprietor in the parish, a Mr. Newton, had made one of many unsuccessful attempts to obtain an Enclosure Act for the parish of Benson, or Besington. The labourers were expecting him to try and fix an Enclosure notice on the church door, and upwards of a thousand persons assembled in the churchyard in wait. When he did not appear, they proceeded to his house to extract from him the promise that he would not attempt the enclosure again.[5]

Now the riots reached Bedfordshire, and although there was apathy in some areas, in others there was found a breeding ground in mobs of already resentful and demoralised men.

Here, in 1829 there had been an affray that had a devastating effect on the morale of the local villagers. Early that year two brothers were apprehended by a gamekeeper whilst they were poaching in the village of Wootten, a few miles from our defendants' villages. The two men, the Lilleys, fearing capture, fired on and wounded the keeper whilst they tried to make their escape. They were apprehended, held in Bedford Gaol, tried, and hanged at the Spring Assizes. The elder of the Lilley brothers was twenty-eight years of age, married with two small children, and a pregnant wife. He had been unable to obtain work in his own parish but if he ventured further, he was sent back because of the anomalies of the poor relief. He received 7/- a week for which he was expected to work on the roads from light until dark and he had to pay three guineas a year for the hovel in which he and his family lived. The other brother was aged twenty-two and unmarried. He received 6d a day.[6] It was reported that in Bedford Gaol, at the same time as the Lilleys, were ninety-six prisoners, seventy-six of whom were able bodied, in the prime of life and generally of good character. They had been driven there by sheer want. Amongst this number were eighteen poachers awaiting trial for the capital offence of using arms in self-defence when attacked by gamekeepers. Of these eighteen men, only one was not a parish pauper on poor relief.[7]

What was considered to be the unjust hanging of the Lilley brothers appeared at first to have the required deterrent effect on the local men. But, gradually, fuelled by lack of work and food, and fuelled too by visits to the local alehouse, the poachers were to be seen around the fields again. Late at night, garden gates were to be heard squeaking in protest as first one, then another, would venture out, stealthily creeping into the hedgerows, regrouping in gangs for protection in numbers. Whereas before some men poached alone, they now adopted a gang approach for their own defence. Even after the sale of game was made legal in 1831, and men could take out licences to kill it, precious few did so.

Because now the conflict between poacher and gamekeeper had reached a new level, it had been stepped up a pace and had become a personal war. The local gamekeepers were hated men. Although usually born and bred in the villages and so were one of them, the very nature of their work ensured that they were never accepted socially. The villagers would lapse into sullen silence when they approached, their loathing apparent in their hostile gaze.[8] The men now carried weapons, ready to use against any gamekeeper who got in their way. They armed themselves with anything – guns, sticks, nets, ropes. Those that before had relied on their fists to fight themselves out of capture, enjoying every moment of it, now armed themselves with whatever they could find. The fate that befell the Lilleys was not going to happen to them. They became wilder, more aggressive, and more antagonistic towards the unfair system. The system which saw squires striding jauntily over land which had previously been theirs to roam and hunt at will, but was now out of bounds. Which saw their guns cocked ready to capture their prey for the sport rather than to satisfy their fat bellies, still replete from their last meal. To capture for their pleasure the docile pheasant whose gay feathers mocked the half-starved labourers bent over their back-breaking task of breaking stones on the road for a pittance, and hare which would have kept the villagers from starvation. Which saw their bloodthirsty hounds, intent on their own destructive course, spoil as much wheat in a morning as would have fed the whole village. Which saw the smug satisfaction in their pursuit deriding the labourers' poverty.

Now that the punishment was so abhorrent, they had more reason for violence. Now on a cold, still, moonlit night, the shouts and curses of sullen men and sickening thuds of blows from bludgeons and gunshots were commonplace, the men knowing that, if they were caught, they would suffer the punishment of transportation, or worse, the fate of the Lilley brothers.

So when the riots in 1830 spread to areas all around them it took little persuasion for these already demoralised men to join in and voice their protests. Villagers with a grudge against the system took their revenge on the hated administrators, the overseers and churchwardens, the clergy and larger farmers. The labourers demanded more wages. Some smaller farmers joined the labourers, demanding exemption from crippling taxes.

Northampton Mercury December 1830

Ampthill, Beds. – At about six o'clock of the night of 27th ult, a terrible and destructive fire broke out in the stack yard of Mr. Benson, an extensive farmer at Wotton Pillinge, a lone farm situated between this place and Bedford, by which 11 stacks, consisting of hay, clover, beans, and wheat, and other grain, together with all the outbuildings attached to the premises, have been entirely destroyed. The farm-house itself, being a little distance from the stacks, is fortunately preserved. The cattle, consisting of a number of horses and cows, and other animals, were removed in safety. The fire engine from Ampthill was soon upon the premises, but the wind blowing very brisk; notwithstanding the utmost exertion, it could render but very little service. It may not be amiss to remark that no thrashing machine was used on the farm, and that it is held under Sidney College, Cambridge. Mr. Benson is neither churchwarden nor overseer, and bears amongst the labourers a liberal character. He is unfortunately not insured, and is a widower with ten children. No doubt can exist of this calamity being the work of an incendiary, as the fire broke out in a haulm stack very recently erected. Several persons have received threatening letters with the signature "Swing".

Bedfordshire. – On Thursday last, one of the most desperate riots that have occurred of late, took place in the village of Stotfold. Late on Wednesday evening, the labourers began to assemble together, and many of the more peaceable inhabitants were forcibly dragged from their beds, and compelled to join the rabble. They then proceeded to the residences of the more respectable inhabitants, demanding an increase of wages, &c. One of these gentlemen, however, had the precaution to tell them, that if they had any reasonable complaints to make, they should be attended to at a vestry in the morning at ten o'clock. With this understanding they separated for the night but long before daylight in the morning, they collected again, and proceeded to every farm house in the village, and compelled every man and boy that was willing to work to join them, positively declaring, with the most horrid oaths and imprecations, that neither man nor horse should proceed to work that day; which threat they literally carried into effect. In this state things remained until about ten o'clock, when the vestry assembled. They then demanded, first, to be wholly exempt from the payment of taxes. This was agreed to. They next demanded the dismissal of the assistant overseer. This was also acceded to. They then required that every man should receive 2s per day for his work. This was objected to as a general principle; but as nothing short of recognising this principle would satisfy the mob, the vestry broke up after much fruitless discussion. The infuriated assembly (from 100 to 200 in number) then proceeded to acts of violence, and went through the village, demanding bread from the bakers, beer from the publicans, and money from the inhabitants generally; and such as had the hardihood to resist their demands, had a forcible entrance effected into their houses, and were eventually obliged to comply with their demands, or suffer their property to be forcibly taken away. Late in the evening they separated, hinting that, if their wishes were not granted on Saturday, they would on that evening have recourse to further violence. On the Friday they resumed their labour; but a meeting of the principal inhabitants was held in the afternoon, which was attended by J.G. Fordham, Esq. of Odsey, Herts, who has an extensive corn and seed-mill in the village, which was threatened with destruction by the rioters, and a communication of the circumstances was made to W.H. Whitbread, Esq., the magistrate, who took immediate measures for the apprehension of the ringleaders. Accordingly, on the Saturday morning a considerable number of special constables were sworn from the neighbouring villages by Mr. Whitbread and the Rev. John Hull, clerk, another county magistrate, and intimation of the affray having been communicated to the Lord Lieutenant, he despatched upwards of 100 constables to assist Mr. Whitbread, if necessary. With this combined force, after every necessary arrangement had been made, assigning to different individuals (powerfully supported) the several parts of their duty, the magistrates proceeded to Stotfold, and in little more than half an hour, ten of the ringleaders were apprehended, and forthwith committed to the county gaol, to await a further investigation into this lamentable affair.

The disturbances spread north, and an article to appear in the Times on 6th December lent its support to the 'tens of thousands of Englishmen, industrious, kind-hearted, but broken-hearted beings, exasperated into madness by insufficient food and clothing, by utter want of necessaries for themselves and the unfortunate families'.

Magistrates, under intimidation, had suggested a uniform rate of wage, but this was quashed by Lord Melbourne, the Home Secretary. His answer was not to give in to the labourers' demands but make the punishment so severe for the perpetrators with sentences of transportation and death that it would thereby suppress the rebellious. If the miserable wretches had something to complain about before, now they would really have something to complain about. From now on, labourers were constantly watched for any sign of dissent. Meetings were banned, those who had called for higher wages were thrown into prison, and gaols were overflowing.[9] Under one section of an Act of 1827, the penalty for destroying a threshing machine was transportation for seven years, and under another section, the penalty for firing ricks was death.[10] The hundreds of village labourers awaiting trial were fearful for their lives, and the temptation to give evidence and so betray their colleagues was almost insurmountable. In some cases it was that or the penalty of death.

Throughout the country prisoners were convicted and sentenced to capital punishment. Most were transported for life. But some were to be executed. In Winchester, although during the riots not one life had been taken, nor a single person wounded, there were one hundred and one capital convictions, of those ninety-five were transported for life and the remaining six were to be executed.[11] The scenes of distress about the gaol were terrible. As a result of public protest, four of the lives of these men were spared, but two were hanged.[12] Similar scenes resulted as trials took place in other counties. In Buckinghamshire there were one hundred and thirty-six prisoners for trial, only eighteen of whom were forty years or over. Forty-two of those involved in the breaking of the paper-machinery received the death sentence, but this was later commuted to life transportation for one, seven years transportation for twenty-two and various other terms for the rest. There were two exceptions; two men were sentenced to execution. Of these two men, one was thirty years old with a wife and three children. At the time of the riots he was a roundsman, and received 1/- a day from the overseers and 1/6d a week from a farmer. He said he would rather endure imprisonment and even transportation than have his wife and children cry for bread. The other man was fifty-six years old with a wife and six children. He was of impeccable character and kept a small beer shop. After petitions for the men were gathered, the sentences were commuted to transportation for life.[13] No comfort to the wife and children of the first, who would still cry for bread.

Despite the quelling of the riots acts of arson still continued and so Lord Melbourne proposed that an Act of 1826, the forbidding of spring-guns and man-traps, be repealed. Melbourne now proposed that persons could apply for a licence from two magistrates to protect their property by these means. But although the Bill was passed in the House of Lords, it would appear that nobody saw fit to put this abhorrent law into practice.

Although there was much debate in Parliament about the plight of the labouring classes, nothing constructive came of the riots, in spite of the Reform Bill of 1832. In the autumn of 1831 an Act was placed on the statute books empowering churchwardens or overseers to hire or lease, and under certain conditions to enclose, land up to a limit of fifty acres for the employment of the poor.[14] But with the cessation of the riots the Government was lulled into a sense of security. So too were the larger farmers, who 'Tranquility being now restored, are of course reducing their wages to that miserable rate that led to the recent disturbances.'[15]

Then came the New Poor Law Act in 1834. Despite great hatred of it and of the Guardians who instituted it, an uneasy peace prevailed through better times, but was interspersed with unrest during bad times. Conditions had not improved in general for the labourer. Acts of arson and petty crime were rife.

Following the establishment of the Peel's Metropolitan Police Force in London in 1829, there had begun a campaign to improve public law and order. But there was dislike and distrust of the police by all classes, and crime in country areas was still rising fast. In parts of the country where crime rate was high, gentry and farmers took matters into their own hands and formed their own protective associations, appointing their own men to guard their property. Then the County Police Act of 1839 was passed permitting counties to raise and equip paid police forces, and the first constabularies were established. Initially only about half of the counties in England and Wales took advantage of the first rural police legislation. There followed a second rural one in 1840 and in 1842 a new Parish Constables Act was passed, which was at a time of political unrest associated with the Chartist Movement. The appointed Parish Constables were part-time and poorly paid, sometimes unpaid, so the posts attracted a low calibre person who, not surprisingly, for such a pittance was not prepared to risk life or limb. In fact, at this time, it fell upon anybody to 'arrest' anyone they suspected might have committed a crime and take him to the magistrate, the magistrate then deciding what should be done with him. The most common offences they had to deal with were petty larceny, poaching, assault and drunkenness. For crimes that the magistrate considered minor, he could try them in his own home and if he considered the person innocent he took no further action. For other more major crimes he would send them to be tried by two magistrates, but no jury, in a court at the Petty Sessions. From here, if those magistrates considered that the prisoner had committed a fairly serious crime, then he could be sent to be tried at the Quarter Sessions, held four times a year with judge and jury. For other very serious offences they would be sent for trial at the Assizes, held every year with a Circuit Judge and jury. The judges travelled round several counties on a "circuit", holding the courts when they arrived in a county town. In Bedford during the 19th century, the Assizes were usually in spring and summer, the judges travelling round the counties of East Anglia and Buckinghamshire.

It could be said that a certain amount of the more serious crimes dealt with, such as sheep stealing, arson, and even murder, were personal, committed by those who wished to settle a score with an unpopular employer, or with a Poor Law official who had refused their relief or a squire who had possibly turned somebody out of their home. The burning of corn-ricks was common-place and targeted farmers could only watch as their barns went up in flames. Many farmers and landowners suffered continually from these attacks, many which could be attributed to the appallingly low wages and unemployment. A certain amount of inter-village warfare could also be blamed for some of the petty crime and lack of education. It was noted, in 1847, that Bedfordshire stood not only low in educational statistics, but proportionably high in regard to crime.[16]

Bedford Times. 22nd November 1845

FIRE – On Saturday night last, a lone barn containing a quantity of barley and oats in the occupation of Mr. Scroggs, of Houghton Regis, near Dunstable, was discovered to be on fire between eleven and twelve o'clock, and its contents together with a hovel adjoining, were entirely consumed. It is supposed to have been the vile act of an incendiary. The same night, three ploughs, the property of Mr. Cook, of Houghton Regis, were broken in such a manner as to be rendered totally useless. Two men, named David Humphrey and David Tennant, since committed to Bedford Gaol on suspicion of committing the offence, have, we understand, made confession of their guilt.

Bedford Times. 14 March 1846

ARSON – On Saturday last David Tenant and David Humphrey, labourers, Houghton Regis were brought up in custody of Mr. Tregenza, gaoler and charged with feloniously setting fire to the premises of Mr. John Cook, senior, Houghton Regis, on 12th November last. (1845) After the examination of several witnesses, the prisoners were fully committed for trial on this charge. They were already in custody on a charge of setting fire to the farm buildings of Mr. Scrogg on 9th November.

These two men from Houghton Regis, David Tennant and David Humphrey, were convicted for several acts, including setting fire to a barn and other buildings, the property of Mr. Henry Brandreth, the Squire, on 9th November. David Tennant is shown on the 1841 census as an agricultural labourer living on the farm of Mr. Fisher Scroggs at Sewell, so possibly he was one that bore a grudge against this farmer over some matter. But the 12th November 1845 happened to be the day of Dunstable fair and the defendants had spent a considerable amount of the day drinking. One witness at their trial swore that on meeting the defendants at Houghton Green during the evening, David Tennant said "We will have another blizzy at old Jack Cook's tonight." David Humphrey stated that as he had already been judged (suspected) for the fire at Squire Brandreth's, then he would go.

But, during this time, there were also the acts of very petty crimes, which carried disproportionately harsh penalties.

Bedford Times – 24th October 1846

Joseph Bowers, labourer, Dunstable, was indicted for having, on the 21st of September, at Houghton Regis, stolen a quantity of stubble, the property of Richard Howes.

Police constable Hornall said there was a quantity of stubble in heaps in a field in the occupation of Mr. Richard Howes. He saw the prisoner come out of the field with a quantity of stubble under his arm. Took the prisoner into custody; he wanted to settle the matter at his house. He said he found it in a ditch.

Richard Howes missed some stubble from three of the heaps in his field; had missed a good deal before. There is a gap in the hedge near the prisoner's residence. John H. Smith, a little boy, aged seven years, was put into the witness box, but, being unable to reply to the questions put to him as to the nature of an oath, the Court decided upon not taking his evidence.

Mr. Fitzpatrick addressed the jury for the prisoner, who called two witnesses to character.

Guilty : One week hard labour.

So fearful were the authorities of a repeat of the riots of the early 1830s that hungry villagers, banding together to discuss their plight, were liable to find themselves falling foul of an Act of 1714 and becoming what was described as a riotous assembly.

Before T.C. HIGGIN, Esq.

Robert Roe, tailor, Eaton Bray, was convicted of having, with divers others, on the 19th of May inst, riotously and tumultuously assembled at Eaton Bray. Sentenced to be imprisoned for 24 hours.

Bedford Times – 24th June 1848

Petty Session, June 19th 1848 – Present Rev. Dr. Bland, and Rev. W. M'Donall.

SHOOTING RABBITS – Thomas Young, of Peter's Green, Luton, was charged with trespassing on the land of John Smith Leigh, Esq., on the 14th instant. The defendant acknowledged that he was shooting rabbits, but said he was on the footpath, and thought he had a right to be there. The Bench, however, told him to the contrary; but as it appeared that he committed the trespass from ignorance, a small fine of 7s 6d. was inflicted, and costs 12s. 6d.

There were also cases of arguments between neighbours which were summarily dealt with by the magistrates.

Petty Sessions May 29th 1848 – Present Rev. W.B. Wroth and H. Brandreth. Esq.

Village Brawls – Soloman King, a genuine specimen of the 'profane vulgar', with a head of unusual bulk, placed on shoulders of corresponding dimensions, and roughly attired, was charged with using indecent and threatening language to Mrs. Mary Robins; both parties reside at Houghton Regis. From the statements of the parties it appeared that this case arose out of one of those neighbourly rows which so frequently occur in certain villages in Bedfordshire. The complainant, a sharp-featured person, which an ill-natured physiognomist would describe as that of a scold, had applied to defendant the obnoxious term of 'bull-headed', whilst he in return christened his fair adversary 'bottle-necked'; each of these compound adjectives being accompanied with nouns too expressive to be repeated except in the unadulterated regions of Billingsgate. The husband of complainant confirmed the evidence of his partner, whose tongue moved so quick that it seemed to be endued with the perpetual motion, and it was not until she was removed to a distance, that that little restless organ subsided into anything like a quiescent state. Both witnesses stated that they were in bodily fear. The defendant, who appeared half lushy, denied the charge and became very noisy and rude. The Bench told him he must be bound over to keep the peace towards the complainant, and pay the expenses. On hearing this, the defendant became greatly excited, stared fiercely around, and opened his capacious jaws, as if he was about to attack the first person he could lay hold of, and then swore he would go to prison sooner than pay a farthing. He continued his violent exhibitions till removed by Millard into a corner, where his ruffled passions gradually sank into repose. Subsequently, not being able to procure sufficient sureties he was committed for six months.

The problems of arson continued throughout these years. Although our men stood accused on the side of the sinners, there is also evidence that they too were on the side of the 'sinned against'. For the White family did not entirely escape from the spate of fires. Early in July 1848, John's slaughterhouse and barns at Chalk Hill caught fire, and, although it was not attributed to arsonists, it is certainly very probable that it was their work, possibly in retaliation for something else.

Bedford Times – 8th July 1848
FIRE – On Friday morning, about 2 o'clock, a fire was discovered on the premises of Mr. John White, butcher, of Chalk Hill, Houghton Regis, which burnt to the ground a barn and slaughter house. By the exertions of those who were called to the spot, the flames were prevented communicating to the house. Mr. White is the owner and occupier of the house in question.

Fires were also being reported in other parts of the area. From the same edition of the Bedford Times:

THE LATE FIRES AT DAGNELL AND STUDHAM. A reward

of £100 has been offered for the discovery of the perpetrators of those incendiary fires, an account of which appeared in these columns a few weeks ago, but no clue to the parties has yet been obtained.

It is into such an environment that our accused men were born. In so many cases where crime was caused by lack of employment and low rates of pay, the general conditions of rural workers can certainly be said to be a contributing factor to transgression. There is no doubt that these circumstances had a great deal to do with influencing villagers to break the law and that also, both settling scores with neighbouring farmers and lack of education played their part. Such was the life which our accused men inherited. This was their schoolroom, and the lessons were hard.

CHAPTER 7

Caught in the Act

As dawn broke on the morning of 24th January, 1849 in the small village communities of Houghton Regis, Stanbridge and Eggington, there was nothing out of the ordinary, nothing to indicate that the day would be any different from any other.

On the farms, the labourers were at work early despite the cold January weather. There was much to be done. It was the time of year for mending fences, tending to drainage operations, for top-dressing pastures and carrying manure to fields. There was the ploughing to do, the cattle and sheep to tend, and grain to thresh ready for sale. In the cottages, the women and children were already hard at work plaiting their straw. They were cold but still their nimble fingers picked up from where they had left off the night before. After all, they were used to being cold.

In fact it was a day just like any other, with nothing to suggest the events which would unfold later that day, events which would affect the lives of so many people in this small community. The winter was harsh and it was the time of year for coughs and colds. In her little cottage in Groom's Yard, Houghton Regis, Sarah White went about her daily routine looking after her young baby. She could hear coughing coming from next door through the insubstantial wall of the terraced cottages where her neighbour, John King, was ill in bed, his wife, Ruth, tending him with regular doses of medicine.

That same evening at about 6pm., William Scrivenor, a local fishmonger, was doing his rounds in the village of Houghton Regis selling his fish. About half an hour later, he called into the Cock Inn, an alehouse just opposite the All Saints Church, on the road leading to Bidwell. He had just one lot of fish left and was hoping to sell it there. He was observed by James Rhodes, a labourer from Houghton Regis, who was sitting in the alehouse supping his pint. A little after 6.30pm George White entered the Cock with an empty jug and asked for it to be filled with ale. The fishmonger was a relative by marriage to Sarah, George's wife, so knew him well. He approached George, asking if he would buy his last lot of fish, but George replied that he didn't want any that evening, took his jug of ale and left.

At about 10pm, Ruth King heard somebody doing up the door of the house next door. Finding that she had no lucifer matches left, she called through the wall to ask if they had any she could borrow. It was Sarah who called back that she had, and Ruth went round to the back door to get them. She was to state later that, as she arrived there, George was just going up the stairs with baby Eliza in his arms. As her husband seemed quite poorly she was up with him until 1am when she gave him a dose of medicine.

Meanwhile, at Chalk Hill (Puddle Hill), William White wandered round to his neighbour, Stephen Inns, at about 8.15pm and both were to state that they sat chatting whilst they plaited straw until about 10pm when William returned home. There he found his brother waiting and the two had supper together before Charles returned to his nearby home at about 11pm.

Shortly after 10pm., Daniel Billington, a shoemaker by trade, met two men in the Tilsworth Road coming from the direction of the main road and walking towards Stanbridge situated about a quarter of a mile away. One of the men was wearing a smock frock and a low crowned hat. Daniel said goodnight to the men and they replied the same, one calling him by his name. Although it was dark, he thought that he knew the men.

At his cottage in Stanbridge, Thomas Dockerill was expecting company. He busied himself in his downstairs room, preparing for his visitors. Just about 11pm the two men came, one after the other, but

The fishmonger on his rounds.

separately now, from the direction of Tilsworth and stopped at his yard gate. The gate creaked as the second man opened it and went in. Thomas heard the squeak of his gate and welcomed his visitors.

But he was not the only one to hear it. Unknown to the men, two others, both bitterly cold, lay in wait under the cover of darkness, listening quietly from behind a hedge just eight to ten yards away. They were police constables, James Parrott and William Clough who had been detailed to watch the activities of Thomas Dockerill and his associates. They heard the footsteps of each man stop at Dockerill's house, the first waiting there a couple of minutes for the second man to arrive and they too heard the opening of the gate as the men went in.

After about a quarter of an hour the sound of two or three men, leaving the house and proceeding quickly along the road in the direction of Eggington, reached their ears. The police constables gratefully shifted their cold bones and followed, skirting a field into the road which the men had taken.

Once more they manouevred themselves under a hedge by the roadside, this time about one hundred and forty yards from Dockerill's house and remained there quietly in the dark for nearly two hours until their patience was finally rewarded when they heard the three men returning along the road. As they got nearer, the constables could see that each man was carrying something which, from the outline, looked like a sack on his back and head, but it was too dark to recognise the identity of the men.

As they drew level, Police Constable Clough sprang out, seizing one of them who instantly dropped his sack. The other two men immediately responded to the attack by throwing down theirs, one was carrying a gun and the other sported what looked like a bludgeon. The man with the gun, who was later identified as Dockerill, shouted to the others "Go in at them". The other attempted to strike Clough with his stick, but Clough managed to shield himself with his captive whom he still had tightly held. The man then attempted to swing at constable Parrott with the stick. Dockerill raised his gun in an attempt to hit Clough with the stock, but again Clough shielded himself with his captive. Constable Parrott shouted a warning to Dockerill, that if he attempted to hit Clough, then he, Parrott, would fire his pistol at him. Dockerill made as if to level his gun at Clough, but again Parrott called out that if he offered to move or injure anyone he would shoot him and, so saying, he pointed his pistol at Dockerill. But Clough could see a new danger behind Parrott, and called out to him, "Parrott, look out you will be knocked down in a moment". Parrott turned round and saw the other man in the act of hitting him with his stick. He shot at the man, but missed him.

Now that a shot had been fired, the bloody events of this disastrous night were stepped up a pace. On hearing the shot fired by Parrott at his friend, Dockerill levelled his gun at Parrott and fired. Parrott was hit in his left shoulder and cried out "I am shot". He staggered for some distance in an attempt to get away, but fell to the ground in the road, where he was knocked about by the two men, mainly Dockerill. Before he lost consciousness, Parrott heard one of the men say "There you have done for him, he'll not get up again".

They then turned their attention to Clough, who still had hold of his captive. Clough felt a blow to his head from the bludgeon and he himself fell to the ground, letting free his captive as he fell. As he lay there, he felt two or three more blows to his head; this time he believed it was from the stock of the gun. Clough then lost consciousness, but before doing so had managed to identify Dockerill whom he had known for some six or seven years. He had also seen the face of the man carrying the bludgeon several times even though it was dark.

Whilst the constables lay there insensible, the three men made their escape, Dockerill back to his cottage, and the other two men in the opposite direction. The sacks, containing the spoils of their robbery, lay abandoned in the road. Dockerill, knowing that he could be identified, made sure that he had no evidence upon him. One of the other men took away the gun, which had been broken in the affray, and the skeleton keys with which they had entered the farmer's barn. The keys were the first to be disposed of in a pond in Stanbridge, the barrels of the gun by the side of a ditch about a mile away, and the stock hastily shoved in a hedgerow about two miles away near the footpath that led from Stanbridge to Houghton Regis. This man had narrowly escaped injury. The shot from Parrott's gun had passed through the front of his smock but missed his person, so the smock was the next thing which had to be disposed of. The third man, who had been restrained by Clough, had been hit on the head during the attack and knew that the injury could identify him if he was questioned. He returned to his home and lay low. Tonight, the darkness was their friend. As it swallowed the evidence of the gun and the keys, so it swallowed their crime. But could it make them forget? For, when it was daylight there would be no darkness to blur their guilt, no ally in the reality of dawn.

Some time later, Constable Clough regained consciousness and staggered to the house of William Gadsden nearby. As he did so he noted that the sacks were still lying in the road, but there was no sign of the men, or of Constable Parrott, who in his semi-conscious state had somehow made his way in the other direction towards Eggington.

Parrott, on regaining consciousness, found himself on the Eggington Road, near the farm of William Adams, a quarter of a mile away from the spot where he had been attacked. William Adams was a farmer of some two hundred and nineteen acres near to Eggington House, which was occupied by the Reverend Cumberley (Cumberledge), the Vicar of Tilsworth and Curate of Eggington. It was here that he knocked urgently on the door, begging to be let in. The time was now a quarter past two in the morning, but his desperate cries were finally heard by Thomas Bates, a gardener, who also lived at the house. Seeing Parrott's appalling state, Bates first had him put to bed, before listening to his unhappy tale.

He then called upon William Adams, and, together with a man named Blythe or Bligh, the three men went back to the spot described by Parrott. Here they found evidence of the affray which had earlier taken place. There was blood on the ground and the three sacks still lay in the road together with a policeman's staff. One of the sacks had William Adams' name on it and contained about four bushels of undressed barley which Adams believed to be his own. The second sack also contained undressed barley, and the third contained some loose peas and meal in a bag which also contained six dead fowl, still warm. Blythe and Bates took two of the sacks and deposited them at the premises of Mr. Mead, a miller, in Stanbridge. Bates leaned the sacks against the gate. At 3.15am. George Allen, a baker who worked for Mr. Mead, collected the third sack and put it with the others, waiting to be handed over to the police as evidence. Meanwhile Gadsden had tended to Constable Clough as best he could whilst he listened to his tale. After hearing of the assault, he called on John Franklin, the constable at Stanbridge, and, with several other men, they went to Dockerill's house. When they arrived there, at a little before 4am, Dockerill was standing in his downstairs room. He unlatched the door of the little cottage which opened into the street and went into the room before them. Losing no time, John Franklin apprehended Dockerill and charged him with the assault.

The constable then asked for permission to search the house, which Dockerill allowed him to do freely. But, in spite of searching thoroughly, he was unable to find the gun that had been used in the assault. On being questioned about its whereabouts, Dockerill stated that he did not have a gun. When asked where the gun was that he had been seen with the day before, he replied that he had given it to its owner in the afternoon. The constable asked who that owner was, but Dockerill replied "You have that to find out". Dockerill had repeatedly been seen carrying a gun.

After having dealt with the sacks, Thomas Bates went along to Dockerill's house to assist the police. It was still not yet daylight, and the men were still searching the cottage. Whilst they did so, Dockerill sat calmly eating his breakfast. After about an hour, Bates found a round frock in the corner of the room. The smock appeared to have fresh blood on it.

Superintendent William Ralph Young of the Woburn Police now arrived and Bates handed over the smock to him. In the pocket was a piece of candle and some lucifer matches. Superintendent Young searched Dockerill and found string and gun wads in his pocket. Dockerill was formally handed over into the charge of the superintendent.

Young then went to Mr. Mead's between 6 and 7am to take possession of the three sacks which had been left there. He noted that the string taken from Dockerill's pocket corresponded exactly with that tied around the bag containing the fowls. The case against Dockerill looked conclusive.

Later that morning, P.W. Wagstaffe, a surgeon at Leighton Buzzard, was called to attend to P.C. Clough at Gadsden's, where he had remained, unfit to be moved. He found him to be suffering from concussion and he remained mostly insensible for several days. He had two wounds to the right side of the head each about an inch in extent. His face and jaw were very swollen and the contusion wounds looked to the surgeon as if they could have been caused by the butt of a gun, or the tip of a shoe. He pronounced Clough to be in a very critical state, having lost a lot of blood. It was not until Friday 2nd February that Wagstaffe finally considered him out of danger, but the constable still remained quite ill for a month.

Having apprehended Dockerill, the hunt had begun for the other two men. Both Parrott and Clough, in his confused state, had given descriptions of them to the police. Clough could identify Dockerill and he had seen the face of one of the other men several times. The man was described as wearing a low cap and light smock frock, breeches with leggings and bright buttons. The third man whom Clough had captive, he described as the youngest and smallest of the three, with dark cap and smock frock. He was wearing a fustian jacket with a very large collar, quite unusual, underneath the smock, which could be seen where the smock was slit. He had no whiskers and very light hair, worn long. Parrott also told them that he thought that he might have hit one of the men.

Having noted these descriptions, the police began to look amongst the associates of Thomas Dockerill, and in particular concentrated on members of the White family, Thomas being married to Rebecca White.

On the morning immediately following the assault, another police constable, Sharp, together with Mr. Mead, the baker, went to the house of George White in Groom's Yard, Houghton Regis. George was at home with his wife, Sarah, and baby daughter, Eliza. Their neighbour, Ruth King, saw the police arrive and, curiosity getting the better of her, went next door to see what was going on and to lend support to Sarah. Police Constable Sharp examined George's head looking for any trace of a shot or a wound. He found none. Sharp said to Mead "Be you satisfied that it is not the man?" Mead replied in the affirmative and they went away. At this stage, Ruth King offered no evidence, never mentioning that she had seen him when she went round to George's house the night before.

The same morning, the police also went to the house of William White, in Chalk Hill. Again they found no evidence that William was involved.

There was, however, the evidence of the shoemaker, Daniel Billington, who by now had come forward to state that he had met two men on the Tilsworth Road that night, men he thought to be George and William White. He was certain that the man who had answered "Goodnight, Daniel" was George. He knew both the Whites, and that they had both lived in Chalk Hill at some time.

On the following Monday, 28th January, George White was arrested and charged with having taken part in the affair. Now both Dockerill and George were in custody in Bedford Gaol, where, on admission, they were subjected to normal prison procedure; placed in a reception cell and searched by the governor or warder, anything considered dangerous or sharp, or could aid an escape, was removed and any personal effects were taken and entered into a property book, the governor taking charge of any monies. They were examined by the surgeon, cleansed in a bath, either warm or cold, and if considered necessary for health or hygiene by the surgeon, their hair was cut. As prisoners on remand, they were allowed to wear their own clothes, if considered suitable.

Two days later, on Wednesday, 30th January, George was taken to Leighton Buzzard for identification by James Parrott. Although he had not previously known George, Parrott immediately identified him as one of the men, but this was mainly because he was wearing a light smock, breeches, leggings with bright buttons, and a low cap, the same as had been given in an earlier description. George was taken immediately to Woburn to attend the Petty Sessions where he appeared alongside Dockerill, who had meanwhile been taken from gaol on a special warrant whilst awaiting examination of P.C. Clough at Stanbridge. Both George and Dockerill were charged with felony and remanded to appear again on 2nd February.

But William's troubles were not over. On 1st February, the police again called at his house in Chalk Hill. They conveyed the distraught William to Stanbridge to be identified by both constables who had been assaulted. Clough was still not fully in control of his senses and afterwards could not recollect that William had been taken to him. In fact, William was one of several men taken to him for identification, but Clough, although he was aware of several men's presence, was not in a position to remember details, later recalling only Constable Sharp by name. William was told to put on his cap so that he would appear as the man did on the night of the incident. Constable Parrott hesitated in his identification, thinking that William was not so tall as the man whom Clough had held, and his clothing was different, the smock being the only similarity. In spite of the fact that he could not be certain, Parrott stated that he had a strong impression that William was the man. But it was enough to cause doubt and a respite for William. He was freed and the police concentrated their efforts on Dockerill's brother, John.

John Dockerill was arrested and taken to Woburn to appear alongside George and Thomas at the Petty sessions on 2nd February. All three were charged with felony by Superintendent Young. George and Thomas were further charged on two other counts by John Batchelor and William Adams who were the victims of the theft on the night in question. George and Thomas were remanded until 9th February. John was released.

On Friday 9th February, Dockerill (who was also given the alias of 'Dock') and George were brought before the Reverends E.O. Smith and J.V. Moore, Cols. Gilpin and C.H. Smith and W.L. Smart at the Petty Session held at Woburn by the Deputy Chief Constable, Mr. Jebbutt, and formally charged with firing a gun loaded with shots at Police Constable Parrott, with intent to resist their lawful apprehension. Dockerill's heart must have sunk when he saw Colonel Gilpin on the bench. As one of the major land owners in Eggington and Stanbridge he had probably fallen prey to Dockerill's activities at some stage in the past, as had his tenant farmers, and doubtless he had a vested interest in Dockerill's committal.

Evidence was given that Constables Clough and Parrott were

watching Dockerill's house at Stanbridge on the night of the 24th January, and that they heard two men come along the road to the house just before midnight; that soon after, three men left the house and the police constables followed them, by the sound, part of the way to Eggington, when they lay up in a hedge about one hundred and fifty yards from Dockerill's house to await their return. About two o'clock they saw three men coming back, with a sack each on their shoulders. The police constables endeavoured to apprehend them, when the men threw the sacks from their shoulders, and a conflict ensued, in which Police Constable Parrott was fired at and wounded in the shoulder, and both he and Clough afterwards brutally maltreated with bludgeons, and left in the road for dead. However, after lying insensible in the road for nearly an hour, they contrived to crawl away, and gave an alarm. It was alleged that the prisoners were two of the three men; that Dockerill fired the gun, and White knocked Clough down.

Thomas Bates was called, and on examination stated that he was aroused by Police Constable Parrott, all muddy and bleeding; he went to the spot and saw the marks of a conflict; he also saw three sacks lying in the road. He then stated that he saw a smock-frock in prisoner Dockerill's house, which he saw Superintendent Young take possession of.

Jeremiah Borham, a miller, deposed that the sacks left in the road by the men were very recently in Dockerill's possession, for he had brought them to Mr. Mead's mill at Stanbridge, with wheat in them to be ground, and he had received them back again.

Superintendent Young said he opened the sacks and found two of them contained barley, undressed, and one peas and meal and six fowls. Also attached to the neck of the bag which contained the fowls was a piece of string, and on searching Thomas Dockerill he found string which exactly corresponded – it being rather particular string. He also found in the pocket of Dockerill's smock-frock a piece of candle which had been lighted, and the remains of several lucifer matches, partly burned.

Mr Batchelor and Mr. Adams, both from Eggington, identified the barley and the fowls found in the sacks, and Daniel Billington stated that he saw George White and another man come through Tilsworth towards Stanbridge after ten o'clock that night. John Franklin gave his evidence that Dockerill had recently been in possession of a gun but, when he was asked where it was, Dockerill said "Ah, that's it"; and refused to say more, only that he had returned it to its owner on the afternoon before the night of the robbery.

Both prisoners had nothing to say, and were then fully committed for trial.[1]

Ruth King, George's neighbour, in an attempt to give him an alibi for the night in question when he was allegedly in Stanbridge, travelled to Woburn for the Petty Session. She intended to state that she had seen George at home that night when she went to borrow some lucifer matches, that he was just going upstairs with the baby, and later, around 1am, she heard him talking to the baby through the wall of the house, that wall between the two houses being so thin. She was specific about the times, as her husband was ill at the time and she was tending him. However, this plan was not to work, because, when she reached Woburn, she was not allowed in to the Petty session, and although she stated that she had come to speak for George White she was pushed away.

Meanwhile, the hunt continued for the third man, and police attention was still centred on William. The 19th February was the first day that Clough was allowed to leave the house of William Gadsden, and he was straight away driven to William's home at Chalk Hill, accompanied by Constable Sharp. Clough had no recollection of seeing William before at Stanbridge, but he immediately identified him as being one of the men who had been present on the night of the attack. William protested his innocence, saying that he had been at the house of Stephen Inns, nearby, from 8.30pm until 10pm. Both men had been occupied straw-plaiting. William's brother, Charles, confirmed this, saying that he was at William's house that night until 11pm and stayed there for supper, and that William had come in around 10pm. In spite of the alibis, Constable

Sharp arrested William, and he too was taken into custody.

William was transported to Woburn to appear at the petty session on 23rd February. On the journey, William desperately protested his innocence to the driver, Henry Isau Jubbett, saying how hard it was to suffer for another person and that he was not the third man the police had been looking for. On being questioned by Jubbett as to what he meant William cited Tom Hines, his uncle, and brother-in-law of George and Thomas Dockerill who lived next door to him at Chalk Hill as the man they ought to have. Jubbett then asked William what sort of man Tom Hines was, and William described him as a man about 5ft 10 or 11inches with black whiskers and dark hair.

Unfortunately for William, this description of Tom Hines in no way resembled that of the third man given by the constables. That man they had described as fair, like William. Thomas was dark with whiskers, and a good deal taller. Clough maintained that he knew Hines and that the man had been nothing like him. And Parrott, having now seen William in different clothes than those which he wore at Stanbridge when he was brought to him for identification, thought the clothes he now wore looked very much like those which the man whom Clough had held was wearing that night. He thought the jacket was the same one, and as for the man, if he had whiskers at all, they must have been very light ones as he had seen his face plainly. He described the collar of the jacket, his light long hair which he saw just before he was shot, and the cap of Billcock that he was wearing.

So William too was remanded for trial along with George and Dockerill, and at the Lent Assizes on 8th March was charged with the assault on the constables.

The Sheriff's procession.

CHAPTER 8

The Bedfordshire Lent Assizes 1849

The Bedfordshire Lent Assizes commenced on Thursday 8th March, 1849 with the arrival of the learned judges, Lord Chief Baron, and Mr. Baron Rolfe at Bedford from Aylesbury by special train at two o'clock. They were received at Bedford Railway Station by the worthy High Sheriff, Humphrey Brandreth Esq., the Deputy Undersheriff, C. Austin Esq., the Sheriff's Chaplain, the Reverend W.B. Wroth, and, with beautiful equipage and the usual retinue of officers and javelin men, they were escorted to the Shire Hall. The Commission was then opened, after which their Lordships were taken to their lodgings at Mr. S. Wing's, Potter Street. Shortly after three o'clock, the judges attended divine service at St. Mary's Church with several of the members of the Corporation. Prayers were read by the Reverend Charles Brereton and the sermon was preached by the Reverend Wroth, who took his text

The retinue of officers and javelin men.

from the xvith Luke, 27th and 28th verses; "Then he said, I pray thee, therefore, father, that thou wouldest send him to my father's house: For I have five brethren; that he may testify unto them, lest they also come into this place of torment." The service concluded sooner than was expected and so the Judges were detained for a considerable time in Church whilst they awaited the Sheriff's carriage to transport them to their lodgings.

At ten o'clock the following day, Mr. Baron Rolfe took his seat upon the bench at the Crown Court, and after the roll of the magistracy of the county had been called over, the gentlemen of the Grand Jury were sworn in:

GRAND JURY.
Sir C.G. Payne, Bart, Foreman

F.C.H Russell, Esq.	W.C. Cooper, Esq.
T.C. Higgins, Esq.	Chas. Moore, Esq.
S.C. Whitbread, Esq.	W.S. Addington, Esq.
J. Harvey, Esq.	G.P. Livius, Esq.
J. Gibbard, Esq.	R. Lindsell, Esq.
R.T. Gilpin, Esq.	H. Littledale, Esq.
J.P. Leigh, Esq.	F.L. Pym, Esq.
W.B. Higgins, Esq.	W.H. Colquhoun, Esq.
C.L. Higgins, Esq.	T.J. Green, Esq.
R.L. Orlebar, Esq.	H.W. Beauford, Esq.
W.A. Orlebar, Esq.	H. Elliot, Esq.

Once the proclamation against vice and immorality was read, his Lordship proceeded to address the Grand Jury, stating that there was very little in the calendar which called for any particular observations from him, and that they would find no difficulty in the duties which they were called upon to discharge. He perceived that there were nearly forty prisoners, consisting mainly of persons committed since the last Quarter Sessions. There was one case of a serious nature where a woman was charged with the murder of her child, but on looking over the depositions

The procession of the learned judges into church.

it appeared to him that they would not find sufficient evidence to warrant finding for the capital offence. If they were not satisfied the child was born alive, of course they would return a bill for concealment of birth.

He then drew the attention of the Grand Jury to the case against Dockerill, George and William White. He alluded to the terrible outrage committed by three men on two policemen. But he stated that there was some difficulty in bringing home the charge of shooting. They would perceive that, as there was only one gun, the trigger could only be pulled by one man. One member of the Grand Jury, recognizing Dockerill's name, was paying particular attention to his words, and that was Lt. Col. Richard Thomas Gilpin Esq, the committing magistrate. For it was on this Squire's 'patch' that the events of this case had taken place.

His Lordship went on to the second case in the calendar, in which a person was charged with an unnatural offence; and indicated that they would probably not find for the capital one, but merely with an attempt.

Then, after making some remarks upon a clause in a recent Act of Parliament, relative to statements of prisoners being taken at their examination before the magistrates which were to be used as evidence at their trial, without proving the signature of the committing justices, he dismissed the Grand Jury to their duties.

The men of the Grand Jury rose and retired to their chambers where they reviewed the bills laid before them and listened to witness evidence. They had the power to judge the cases on such, and to dismiss any with insufficient evidence, or prepare bills of indictment for those to be brought before the court.[1]

Squire Humphrey Brandreth sat in attendance in his role of High Sheriff, and as Mr. Prendergast and Mr Fitzpatrick got ready for their first case, the Petty Jury was sworn in:

PETTY JURY[2]
Joel (?) Burr

James Butcher

Samuel Burr

Jonathon Cranfield

John Imery

David Fuller

Samuel Hartoff (?)

William Loxley

Wm. Johnson Neal

Richard Quimbey

Daniel Ross

George Woodward

TRIAL OF THE PRISONERS

Samuel Taylor, (38), was charged with stealing, at Flitton, a bushel of potatoes from John Maddams. – Joseph Walker said he was out on the morning of the 24th, and saw two men on the premises of prosecutor; they ran away and he followed them, and found them standing by a smock-frock filled with potatoes. – The prosecutor stated that, in consequence of what the last witness had told him, he went to his potato pit, and found that it had been broken open. In another part he found a quantity of potatoes scattered about which were like those in his potato pit; as also did those which Joseph Walker found in a smock-frock. A police-constable proved that the smock-frock belonged to the prisoner. The jury found the prisoner guilty. Sentenced to three months.

Elizabeth Collinson, (40), bonnet sewer, Luton, was charged with stealing, on 29th January, at Luton, a worsted shawl, the property of John Cook. – Maria Cook, wife of the prosecutor, was staying at the "Three Brewers" public-house, in Luton, on the day in question. She gave her shawl to the landlord, and on asking him for it in the afternoon, it could not be found. – A young woman named Burrows stated the prisoner went to the "Three Brewers" on the above day, and when she went away she had a shawl hanging on her arm. Hardwick, driver of the mail cart, found the shawl on the premises. – The prisoner called a witness named Morgan, who deposed to being with the prisoner at the public house, and that she had a shawl, but did not know the one produced in court. His lordship summed up, and said it appeared a weak case. The jury acquitted the prisoner.

John Odell, (34), labourer, Clophill, was charged with having, on 3rd March, stolen a pottle of potatoes, the property of James Horn. – James Horn deposed that he went to the prisoner's house on Saturday last, with the policeman, and found a quantity of the Pheasant-eyed Champion potatoes in his possession, which he identified as his property. The policeman corroborated the above evidence, and also that the prisoner's shoe marks agreed with those found near the potato pit. – The prisoner said his wife stole the potatoes, and then told the policeman he had committed the theft. – His lordship briefly summed up, and was remarking upon the shoe-marks, when the prisoner called out that his wife put his shoes on (laughter). The jury found the prisoner guilty. A previous conviction was then proved. His lordship said the story about his wife might be true; but no doubt he was with her. He then sentenced him to four months' imprisonment with hard labour.

George Stapleton, (21), labourer, Ridgmont, was charged with stealing, on 3rd January, one pottle of peas, the property of Abraham Wing Crouch. The prisoner pleaded guilty, and was sentenced to one month imprisonment.

MANSLAUGHTER AT EATON SOCON

William Partridge, (38), labourer, Eaton Socon, Beds, was charged with the manslaughter of Wm. Skinner, of Eaton Socon. Mr. Worlledge conducted the prosecution and stated the case, which will be found in the following evidence. Mr. Tozer appeared for the prisoner.

John Mayes, agricultural labourer, said he was working in Mr. Topham's field at Staploe, on the 29th July last, with six or seven other reapers. It being the first day of the harvest they drank 8 pints of beer each. Just before they left the corn-field at night a dispute arose between the prisoner and Miles. Skinner said, 'If you are going to quarrel I'll go home,' prisoner replied, 'if you will go home, go; and tell your master what a drunken fool you are,' or words to that effect. Skinner turned round and said, 'can you make a fool of me.' Other words passed, and Skinner went up to Partridge with his fists clenched; the latter then struck Skinner on the face with the back of his sickle-blade, and they fought a round. The father of prisoner tried to part them but could not. Witness then parted them, but they fought two more rounds; in the last of which Skinner ran at Partridge with his head downwards, when the latter struck him on the back of his neck; and two blows in the ribs as he was falling. Skinner then said to the prisoner, 'You have given me my death blow.' Miles pulled out Skinner from the wheat and laid his head on a sheaf; he was afterwards carried to the barn.

Another witness was called who corroborated the foregoing facts. Mr. Evans, surgeon, of St. Neots, stated he was called in, and found the deceased suffering from palsy in the lower parts of the body; he died on the following Wednesday. Three of the vertebrae in the neck were fractured and driven upon the spinal cord, which he had no doubt was the cause of death. It must have been a very severe blow to have produced such an injury. He thought it unlikely a blow could have such an effect.

Mr. Tozer addressed the jury, and contended that although there was blame attached to the prisoner for the part he took in the transaction, he thought, under the circumstances, he could not be deemed guilty of manslaughter. They would bear in mind the prisoner did not begin the quarrel, but merely interfered between the unfortunate deceased and another man, and that he was resisting an attack made upon him.

Mr. Joseph Topham, farmer, and another respectable witness of Staploe, gave the prisoner a good character.

His lordship summed up, and concluded by saying that if the jury believed the evidence of the witnesses, there could be no doubt of the prisoner being guilty of the charge. The law in such cases was that if two men fought, and one of them should be killed from a blow by the other, the survivor was guilty of manslaughter.

The jury returned a verdict of guilty, but recommended the prisoner to mercy, on account of the mitigating circumstances of the case.

Sentenced to 14 days imprisonment.

James (or John) Edwards, (30), and **Robert Newton**, (18), sweeps, tramps, London, charged with having, on the 15th February, at Streatley, stolen twenty-three bushels of soot, the property of Thomas Smith. They were further charged with stealing thirty-seven bushels of soot, at the parish of Totternhoe, the property of Abraham Fossey. The prisoners pleaded Guilty, and were sentenced to 4 months' imprisonment, hard labour.

Jacob Smith, (41) labourer, Luton, charged with having, on the 28th December, stolen one iron mattock and two iron wedges, the property of Thos. Lawrence. The prisoner pleaded Guilty. There was another indictment against the prisoner, to which he pleaded not guilty. Thomas Thoroughgood deposed he lost his mattock on the 16th of December, and had not seen it again till that morning, when it was shown to him by police-constable Millard. A Mrs. Welch proved that the prisoner brought the implement to her house. The prisoner said he bought the mattock on Luton Market-hill. His lordship summed up the evidence, and the Jury returned a verdict of Guilty. Sentenced to six months' imprisonment.

Sarah Heeds, (19), servant, Sandy, charged with having, on the 27th of January, at Sandy, stolen two rings and other articles, the property of John Powers. The prosecutor stated he missed from £3 to £5 out of his cash box on the 20th, and sent for a policeman, who came and examined the prisoner's box, and found 10/- in silver in a paper, and 50/- in a purse, two rings, a pair of curtains, three quarters of a yard of lace, and two cuffs. The policeman was next called, and confirmed the statement of the prosecutor. Mrs. Unas Augusta Sarah Powers identified the articles. The prisoner in defence said she picked up the two rings in Mrs. Powers' sleeping room; the thimble she found in the kitchen, and the curtains and other articles she found amongst some old rags. The Jury found the prisoner Guilty, and his Lordship sentenced her to six months' imprisonment with hard labour.

William Hardwick, (20), labourer, Toddington, charged with having, on the 3rd of February, at Toddington, stolen three pecks of potatoes, the property of James Forster. James Forster, senior, missed about three pecks of potatoes from his garden on the day in question. The policeman Elliot brought a quantity of potatoes on the following day which he identified as his property. The son of the prosecutor saw some foot-marks in the garden which were proved to correspond with the shoes of the prisoner. The policeman deposed he found the potatoes in the prisoner's house; they appeared to have been just taken from the pit. The prisoner said the potatoes were his property, and called several witnesses to character. Guilty: Sentenced to two months' imprisonment.

John Seymour, (48), labourer, Shefford, was charged with stealing, on the 23rd January, at Shefford, twenty pounds of lead, the property of Widow Sarah Dace Whitehouse.

Mr. Prendergast prosecuted and Mr. Tozer defended.

Police-constable Hann went to Mr. Goodman's shop, in Shefford, on the 8th February, and found some lead, which he took to an empty house belonging to Mrs. Whitehouse. The lead fitted on the portico, from which lead had been taken. He then went to Geo. Hays, who told him he had bought some lead from the prisoner.

Thomas Barcock, of Shefford, deposed that the prisoner brought him some lead on the 27th of January. Witness told him he had a suspicion he knew the lead. He said another person brought it to him. He was with the policeman when he fitted the lead on the house, and it exactly corresponded.

Geo. Hays, of Campton, marine-store dealer, deposed to buying lead from the prisoner, which he sold to another man named Wm. Bray; the same lead was afterwards produced before the magistrates. Wm. Bray and his brother also gave evidence to having had dealings with the prisoner for lead, and said they were in the habit of buying lead or any mortal thing that came their way.

A quantity of lead was then produced in court, which the several witnesses swore as being the lead they bought from the prisoner. No evidence having been given that the house in question belonged to Mrs. Whitehouse, his lordship said the indictment could not be sustained. Mr. Chas. Stafford, agent of the prosecutor, was sent for, but he was not at home. The jury, therefore, acquitted the prisoner.

Thomas Church, (19), labourer, Leighton Buzzard, was charged with stealing, on the 3rd of January, a bushel of potatoes, the property of Widow Elizabeth Bennett Flemans. He pleaded guilty and was sentenced to three months' imprisonment.

James Dennis, (75), labourer, Leighton Buzzard, was charged with having, on the 14th of January, at Leighton Buzzard, stolen a spade and a cwt. of wood, the property of Richard Irving Byers. The prisoner also pleaded guilty, and was sentenced to one month's imprisonment.

William Ellis, (43), labourer, Luton, was charged with stealing a frying pan, the property of Charles Clarke, on the 9th of February. He pleaded guilty. One month's imprisonment.

Charles Horne, (23), labourer, Royston, Herts., charged with having, on the 13th of January, at Milton Earnest, unlawfully obtained from William Solesbury the sum of 2/6d.

There were three indictments against the prisoner, to two of which the prisoner pleaded guilty and the other not guilty.

His Lordship said he should not go into the third charge. The prisoner was then sentenced to six months' imprisonment with hard labour.

John Hack, charged on oath with having on 16th of July 1848, at the parish of Tingrith, feloniously stuck, stabbed and cut George Coleman, with intent to do him grievous bodily harm.

The prosecutor deposed that he was at Tingrith feast on the day in question, and saw the prisoner there. Between 9 and 10 in the evening he met prisoner walking along Toddington land, with his brother and two or three girls or women; a young woman named Ann Walton was with witness. He spoke to Hack and wished him good night. The prisoner used some vulgar expressions and witness asked him what he meant. He doubled his fist in his face, and witness then slapped his face; the prisoner called out to some persons to come back again, then put fists in his face; witness hit out and knocked him down. More hard words passed between them, and witness tried to strike him again, but the prisoner stooped down, struck him in the ribs but he then felt himself wounded and, putting his hand to his side, found it covered with blood. The prisoner ran away. He was taken to a cottage, and afterwards was removed home.

Ann Walton confirmed the testimony of Coleman, and another witness stated that he saw a knife in the hand of the prisoner, and that when Coleman missed his blow the prisoner struck him on the side with the knife.

William Abbott, police-constable, took the prisoner into custody, and found a knife concealed in his clothes. He expressed sorrow at what he had done, and hoped Coleman would get better.

Mr. Green, surgeon, deposed that he attended Coleman, and on examination found a wound near the left groin, about two inches deep. It was not a dangerous wound, but would have been so had it taken an upward direction.

The prisoner said the wound was made by a fall, and called several witnesses with a view to proving that the quarrel was commenced by Coleman, and that the injury occurred from an accident.

His Lordship summed up the evidence, and said the jury was not to decide as to who began the quarrel, but whether the wound was willfully given by the prisoner.

The jury consulted for a minute, and then returned a verdict of Guilty.

His Lordship, in passing sentence, strongly condemned the conduct of the prisoner, and awarded twelve months' imprisonment.

Henry Humbles, (40), labourer, Leighton Buzzard, was charged with stealing 3lbs. of sugar, 3 oz. of tea, 3lbs. of soda, 6 yds. of linen sheeting, 2 yds. of printed cotton, and other articles, the property of Leah Windser, on the 20th of January.

Mr. Dasent prosecuted and Mr. Fitzpatrick defended the prisoner.

Leah Windser deposed that she was outside the "Ewe and Lamb" public house, at Leighton Buzzard, and left her two baskets and contents there, while she went a few yards off to speak to her son. When she came back, a minute or two afterwards, the baskets, with the contents, were gone. The policeman was informed of the circumstance, and he brought them to her the same night.

Peter Dimmock saw the prisoner walking very fast towards his own house, with the two baskets. The baskets produced in court are much like those he saw in the possession of the prisoner.

Police-constable Parrott, acting on information received, went to the house of the prisoner and found the two baskets, with other articles, which were identified by the prosecutor. Another police-constable also deposed to having met the prisoner in another part of the town with a bundle; he told him of the robbery of pork and the other articles, and suspected he had got some of the goods in the bundle. Witness then tried to search the prisoner, but he resisted. He afterwards apprehended him at his house.

A statement made by the prisoner before the magistrates was then read. The prisoner said he was going along the street, and kicked against the baskets, and not seeing anybody took them away with him.

Mr. Fitzpatrick addressed the jury for the prisoner, and contended that the evidence amounted to a mere matter of suspicion. His Lordship, in summing up, said he never heard of a clearer case of robbery, according to the prisoner's own confession. If the prisoner's plea were to be accepted, a person may go into the field of another man, take his horse or anything else he found, and take them away because he saw no one near.

The jury immediately returned a verdict of Guilty, and the prisoner was sentenced to six months' imprisonment.

Edward Holmes, (78), labourer, Toddington, was charged with stealing 4lbs. of hog's fat, the property of John Crawley, on the 5th of January. The prisoner pleaded not guilty. A little girl deposed to having seen the prisoner take a quantity of fat from the prosecutor's house, and put it under his arm. Guilty. Three months' imprisonment, hard labour.

Geo. Hays was charged with receiving a quantity of lead, knowing the same to have been stolen.

John Kirkby, of Shefford, stated he missed some lead from his father's house in the parish of Campton, in Sept. 1847. Police-constable Hann cut off some lead that was remaining in the kitchen, and compared it with other lead found in possession of the prisoner, which corresponded.

Police-constable Hann went to the prisoner and asked him if he had any lead in his possession; to which he replied he had not, but, if he bought any, he would let him know. He then went to Goodman's some time after, and saw some lead which he identified as Mr. Kirkby's property. Mr. Goodman said he bought the lead from Wm. Bray, and the latter stated it was brought to him by the prisoner. He then went to the latter, and asked him where he got the lead from he sold to Bray; after some hesitation, he said John Heathfield and Geo. Clarke.

The lead was here produced in court, and exhibited to the jury.

Wm. Bray was then called, and stated he bought a quantity of lead from the prisoner, and his brother that he had sold it to Mr. Goodman.

Mr. Burcham addressed the jury, and contended that there was no satisfactory evidence to show that the prisoner had any guilty knowledge of the lead having been stolen at the time he made the purchase.

His lordship went through the evidence, and left it to the jury to decide, from the statements of the witnesses, whether the prisoner was guilty of the charge.

The jury consulted for a few minutes, and returned a verdict of guilty. Deferred for sentence until the following day, and the session for the day was brought to an end.[3]

The following day the court rose as Mr. Baron Rolfe entered, and at nine am precisely the trials of the prisoners were resumed in the Crown Court. A new jury was sworn in:

PETTY JURY
John Allen
Joshua Burr
Jonathon Cranfield
James Heuman (?)
Benjamin Jeffries
Charles ?
Joseph Harman
John Heath
Charles Allington (?)
John Whiton
Thomas Whitwell
Samuel Abraham

The reporter for the 'Bedford Times' sat poised ready to take his notes.

Thomas Pettit, (33). The first case to be heard was against one Thomas Pettit, aged 33, who was charged with committing an unnatural offence. The prisoner presented the appearance of a miserable half-witted mortal, in the garb of a farm labourer. The evidence was described in the Bedfordshire Times dated 17th March as being totally unfit for publication, as in all similar cases. A man by the name of Thomas Ellington was called to prove the charge. Mr. Prendergast addressed the jury for the defence on the absurdity of attempting to prove such an improbable case. His Lordship summed up, and the jury returned a verdict of guilty. The prisoner was sentenced to twelve months' imprisonment with hard labour.

Rachel Ann Simms, (18). Mr. Prendergast was again appearing for the defence in the next case, which was that against Rachel Ann Simms, an 18-year-old lace maker from Northill who was charged with infanticide. The young girl had been delivered of a bastard child that she attempted to conceal by throwing the infant into a little brook that ran by her father's garden. She had been charged with murder under the coroner's inquisition earlier, but the grand jury threw out this bill and found for concealment of birth. The girl at first pleaded not guilty, but, when her father appeared in the witness box to give evidence against her, she became greatly excited and subsequently withdrew her plea, and pleaded guilty. His lordship, after a suitable admonition, sentenced the girl to four months' imprisonment.

At this point one of the jury was excused and David Fuller was sworn in place.

David Wing, (29), and **Charles Smith**, (22). The next to appear in court, were David Wing and Charles Smith, a pair of labouring tramps from Bedfordshire who were charged with breaking into the house of one James Glover at Little Staughton on the morning of 21st January. Mr. Prendergast this time was appearing for the prosecution of the men who were undefended. James Glover stated that he went to bed about ten o'clock on Saturday night 20th January, leaving doors and windows fastened. He rose at 5 am the next day and found the money drawer removed from the place in the shop and taken into the storeroom, the window of which had been entirely taken out. Other articles were also removed from their usual places in the shop. The wife of the prosecutor deposed there were 14/- or 15/- worth of coppers in the drawer on the previous night. Two loaves had disappeared from a window by the storeroom. A cotton dress-piece was shown to her by the police on the Tuesday following, which she identified as her property. From the evidence of other witnesses, it appeared the prisoners were seen in Little Staughton on the evening of the robbery, and that they afterwards called at the "Bell" public-house, in St. Neots, where they wanted to hire a room for the day and night. They had with them two half-peck loaves, which they freely distributed to sundry "navvies", who happened to be drinking in the house. Their night's lodgings and beer were paid for in copper. The burglars were subsequently traced by police constables Hemp, of the Huntingdon police, and Beach, stationed at Great Barford, to St. Ives, where they were captured at the "Crown and Mitre". In the pockets of Smith were found 2/93/4d in copper coin, and in those of Wing 3/8d. The cotton dress owned by Mrs Glover was found under the person of Wing, on a seat in the tap-room, where the men were quietly boozing, when the sudden appearance of the police interfered. A foot mark by the store room window was found to correspond with the left shoe of the prisoner Smith. Other evidence was adduced to prove both the men were professional thieves and vagabonds. Mr. Baron Rolfe summed up the evidence very minutely, and the jury, almost immediately, returned a verdict of guilty against both prisoners. A previous conviction having been proved against Smith, he was sentenced to ten years' transportation, and Wing to eighteen months' imprisonment, with hard labour.

John Goodman, labourer, charged with stealing a loaf of bread on 8th February, the property of Samuel Stapleton.[4]

These cases had all been dealt with quite quickly, and the court now prepared itself for the main case of the day.

A court jury.

CHAPTER 9

The Trial

At approximately 11am. the judge, his Lordship, the Right Honourable Baron Rolfe, read out the charge against George and William White and Thomas Dockerill, "that on the 25th January, 1849, at the parish of Standbridge (sic), they did unlawfully and maliciously wound James Parrott and William Clough, with intent to prevent their lawful apprehension, and that the said Thomas Dockerill did unlawfully and maliciously shoot at and wound the aforesaid James Parrott." The prisoners all pleaded 'Not guilty'.

Mr. Prendergast and Mr. Tozer for the prosecution gathered their notes, and the jury sat ready for the first witness to be called. Mr. Burcham, for the defence, was still feeling unwell but had his colleague, Mr. Power, sat next to him whom he could call on if needed.

The audience now sat hushed as the first witness was called.

William Clough, the police constable who had been hit with the bludgeon, entered the courtroom and stepped into the witness box. After he was sworn in, he made his statement:

William Clough, *Police Officer :*

"I was watching Dockerill's house at Stanbridge at 11pm on the 24th January. I was near.

I saw a man come from direction of Tilsworth towards Dockerill's house. Tilsworth is in the same direction as Houghton. Houghton is beyond Tilsworth where I was.

The man went towards Dockerill's yard gate. I could not see him go in. I was behind a hedge, it was dark. I am sure he

His Lordship, the Right Honourable Baron Rolfe.

did not go past the house, the footsteps stopped at the house, a minute or two. Afterwards another man came from the same direction and went up to the gate. I heard the gate then sound as if opening. I was perhaps eight or ten yards off.

In about a quarter of an hour I heard sound as if two or three persons leaving the house. I could not see them, the footsteps went towards Eggington. I went round the field to get into the road to Eggington. Parrott was watching with me all the time and he went with me to the road round the field.

The footsteps were going quick.

Parrott and I waited under the hedge by the road side 140 yards from Dockerill's house.

We waited an hour and a half or two hours.

Then I saw three men coming from the direction of Eggington into Stanbridge.

When I first saw them they were 130 or 140 yards off. Each man was carrying something like a sack on his back and head.

We remained quiet till they got opposite to us.

Then I sprang out and seized one of the men.

The three prisoners were the men. I seized William White. Parrott was at my side doing what he could.

The sacks were immediately thrown off their backs into the road.

Dockerill had a gun. George White had a bludgeon or heavy stick.

Dockerill said go in at them, George White attempted to strike me with the stick.

I protected myself with William White.

George White attempted to strike Parrott with his bludgeon. Dockerill levelled his gun at me but I turned William White quickly round between me and the gun.

Then Dockerill levelled his gun at Parrott and fired.

Parrott called out 'I am shot'. I looked towards him and saw him stagger. Then George White struck me a heavy blow on the head with the bludgeon and I fell immediately.

When on the ground I felt two or three blows on my head, I believe from the stock of the gun.

I became insensible. I never left go of William White till I dropped down.

I saw George White's face several times. I am sure of his identity, also Dockerill.

I knew Dockerill before, not the Whites.

I have known Dockerill six or seven years.

George White had a smock-frock and a cap. He had not a smock-frock on when I saw him in custody, he had a cap on then, I believe the same.

He had leather leggings on.

I could see

The barristers gathered their notes.

plainly that William White was the youngest and least of the three, he had a dark cap on and a smock frock, no whiskers and very light hair.

I gave description of him before he was taken.

When I recovered I got into Stanbridge at William. Gadsden's as well as I could.

I saw the sacks in the road.

I remained at Gadsden's for a fortnight. I was attended by Wagstaffe.

I know Hines, he is not at all like William White."

Mr. Burcham, for the defence, cross-examined Clough in a severe attempt to discredit his evidence, in particular that regarding William White. But Clough was not going to give up one of the accused now that he had him in the dock, and replied that he was certain as to the identity of William:

Cross-examination.

"Stanbridge is three or four miles from Houghton.

Tilsworth is about a mile short of Stanbridge.

I first gave information about Dockerill in the morning at Gadsden's house. I, at that time, gave information of the other men.

I did not see William White till 19th February. On that day I saw him at Chalk Hill in the parish of Houghton. Sharp was with me then and the person who drove me over. I saw William White in a house there.

I never recollect seeing him before that time. I gave him into custody as soon as I saw him.

I was not in my proper senses for four or five days.

People were brought to me there.

I don't recollect that William White was brought there to me. I don't recollect that anyone was told to put his cap on.

Sharp was there, several persons on one or two of the occasions when people were brought.

I saw William White at his house, at Houghton.

I gave him into custody immediately to Sharp.

I said I was certain he was the party.

It was much lighter at 2am than it had been before.

When we sprang on the men I called out to Parrott that one of the men had a gun.

I did not see him level his pistol, but I heard two reports of fire arms.

William White was four or five minutes in my hold.

I observed the motions of the other two while I had hold of him.

I never told anybody that one of the men was wounded.

I never told Sharp so.

I never gave directions to look after a wounded man nor after any other men.

I believe one man was brought to me when I stated to be very like one of the men, but I could see it was not the person. I said so at once."

The Prosecution then re-examined during which Clough answered:

"19th February was the first day I was able to go out.

I had been taken to Woburn before in a conveyance.

I had communication with William Young three or four days after the affray as soon as I was able to be spoken with."

William Clough then left the box and Police Constable James Parrott was sworn in. He confirmed the testimony of William Clough up to the time the attack was made on them, when he proceeded to furnish additional details. In spite of being unsure enough to question that William was the right man when he was asked to identify him on 1st February, Parrott now also stood convinced that William was the guilty party:

James Parrott, *Police Officer:*

"I was with Clough watching the prisoner's house.

The two or three persons started from the front of Dockerill's house towards Eggington.

Clough and I followed, and stopped in the hedge 140 yards from Dockerill's house, on Stanbridge Hill.

After about two hours I saw three persons – all them had a sack – each had one.

There were two gates nearly opposite each other close by where we were.

When they came just opposite the gates Clough and I came on them.

Clough seized William White. I have not the least doubt of the man.

Dockerill had a gun. The other, George White, had a bludgeon. I have no doubt of his person.

As soon as Clough seized William White they all threw down their bags and Dockerill said 'now lads go to work' and directly raised his gun to hit Clough. I presented my pistol at him and said if he offered to hit him I would shoot him.

Then he passed away and was apparently going to level his gun at Clough. I told him if he offered to move or injure anyone I would shoot him. I pointed my pistol at him.

Clough called out to me 'Parrott look out you will be knocked down in a moment'.

I turned round and saw George White in the act of hitting

me with a large stick.

I shot at George White, but missed him.

Then I turned round and saw Dockerill levelling the gun at me. He fired and I was shot on my left shoulder. I staggered for some distance and was about to get away but I was followed by Dockerill and George White. I fell down on the road and then I was knocked about by Dockerill and George White, chiefly by Dockerill, on my head, arms and hands.

I could not see what happened to Clough.

The last thing I recollect was a blow on my head when one of the men said 'there you have done him he will never get up again'.

Then I became insensible.

When I recovered my senses I found myself near Adams's farm at Eggington a quarter of a mile from the spot.

I knew Dockerill before by person, not by name.

I did not know George White before, he had a low cap, a light smock-frock, breeches with leggings with bright buttons.

I saw George White afterwards, he was brought to me on the 30th at Leighton Buzzard. I knew him immediately.

I did not know William White before. I saw him on 1st February. He was shewn to me at Stanbridge. I had a strong recollection of his dress but I thought he was not so tall as the man. I had however a strong impression he was the man but I hesitated and would not be certain. The man whom Clough had hold had a smock-frock on.

When William White was brought to me at Stanbridge he had a smock-frock but his dress was otherwise different from what it had been in the night in question.

I afterwards saw him in a different dress from that in which he was first brought to me.

That was like the dress of the man whom Clough had hold of.

That man had a smock-frock on and a fustian jacket underneath which I saw where the frock was slit. The collar was very large, remarkable and unusual.

I could see him just before I was shot, he was stooping. I saw his collar, his long hair and the side of his face. I said it was light hair.

I think that is the same jacket which he now has on.

If he had whiskers they must have been very light, I could see his face plain.

He had on a cap or Billcock.

Batchelor's farm is about three-quarters of a mile off, a little further than Adams's.

I saw the sacks lying on the ground near the gates before I was insensible.

I was very ill some time, not as bad as Clough."

During the testimony of James Parrott, Mr. Burcham had been compelled to leave the court for a few minutes, being somewhat indisposed. On his return, he attempted to cross examine the witness, but again he had to stand down. In the end he transferred the defendants' case to Mr. Power, but managed to remain in court, to assist him for the remainder of the trial.

On cross-examination by Mr. Power, James Parrott replied:

"I did not see any of the prisoners till the 30th. Then I saw Dockerill and George White.

I gave description of William White, the best I could.

A man named Howdell was brought to me to look at.

He resembled Dockerill.

More people were brought – two or three more.

I did not say a man had been hit. I told the Superintendent perhaps I might have hit him.

William White was brought to me by a Police Constable on

the 1st February to be looked at, not in custody."

James Parrott was excused and Daniel Billington, the shoemaker from Tilsworth, who was walking along the Tilsworth Road on the night in question, was called. Daniel recounted the meeting, stating that he mentioned the circumstances to his brother the following day.

Daniel Billington:

"On the night of the 24th January, I was in Tilsworth Road at a little past ten.

I met two men going towards Stanbridge. I thought they were George White and William White. I said good night. They said the same. I thought it was George White who spoke – he said 'Goodnight Daniel'.

I knew them before.

George White had a smock-frock on and a low crowned hat."

Upon cross examination, by the Defence, Daniel recalled:

"This was a quarter of a mile from the beginning of Stanbridge.

The Whites used to live at Chalk Hill, two miles from Stanbridge. I don't know whether they live there now."

When he left the court, Thomas Bates was called to the stand. He described the incident, stating that he had been roused on the night in question by Parrott who had presented a sad spectacle; he had been shot and had blood streaming from his head.

Thomas Bates:

"I live at the Reverend's, Mr. Cumberley (Cumberledge) of Eggington.

At about a quarter past two Parrott came to our house.

*He seemed in a desperate state and wished me to let him in.
I gave directions to have him put to bed.*

*In consequence of what he said I went with Blythe (or Bligh)
and Adams to the spot by the two gates.*

There I found three sacks, and a policeman's staff.

*I saw marks of a struggle near the sacks, I saw blood. Blythe
took two of the sacks to Mr. Mead's yard. Mr. Young afterwards had
them. I saw him. I set the two sacks up against the gate.*

*I went to Dockerill's house the same morning before daylight,
he was at home.*

*I found a round frock in a corner of the room where they sit.
I gave it to Young. There was blood on it, apparently fresh."*

Upon cross examination he went on:

"After a while he had breakfast, he has a wife and children.

I had been in the house an hour before I found the frock.

Dockerill was in custody before I got to his house."

Several more witnesses were called to give evidence in an attempt to
prove several points in the charge against the prisoners, but which more
particularly involved Dockerill.

George Allen, *Baker:*

"I work for Mr. Mead of Stanbridge.

*At half past three, I went to the gate and there found a sack
which I brought to Mr. Mead's.*

The name was on it.

Young took it."

John Franklin, *Constable at Stanbridge:*

*"I went to Dockerill's house with Gadsden and several others
at a little before 4am on 25th – others were before me.*

When I got there Dockerill was standing in the downstairs

room. *I apprehended him.*

It was known what he was charged with. I told him I should take him first.

I looked for a gun. I searched his house closely but could find none.

I asked him for his gun. I said there is one thing more we want. That is your gun.

He said 'I have not got one'.

I said you had one yesterday where is it now?

He said 'I gave it to the owner yesterday afternoon'.

I asked him who the owner was, he said 'you have that to find out'.

I had repeatedly seen him with a gun."

Cross Examined.

"His house opens into the street.

He came to the doorway, and when I came up he went in before me.

I asked him after I had taken him whether I might search his house, he allowed me to do so freely."

Wm Ralph Young, *Superintendent of Woburn Police :*

"I went to Stanbridge to Mr Mead's on the morning of 25th January between 6 and 7am. I there took possession of three sacks which I now produce.

One contained undressed barley about four bushels.

The second contained about the same.

The third contained some loose peas and meal in a bag in which were six fowls dead but warm.

I produce the skins of the fowls and the bag in which they were.

I had been before that to Dockerill's house and I had found some string in his pocket and some gun wads. I produce them.

I produce the smock which I got from Bates.

In the pocket, I found this piece of candle and these lucifers.

Dockerill was handed over to my custody.

The string corresponds with the string of the bag in which the fowls were."

Jeremiah Borham, *Journeyman Miller to Mr. Mead of Stanbridge:*

"Dockerill has had corn ground at our mills.

I produce the sort of sack he sent to our mills.

He had only one, it corresponds with this. The same make exactly:

T Gadsden Eaton Bray No 1

It was delivered to him on the 13th January.

On 4th January he brought some barley to our mills in a sack, same marks as this."

Inwards Houghton:

"I believe it to be the same. The sack with the ground barley was delivered to him on 19th January.

I had received particular instructions to observe them."

Gaius Batchelor, *Son of John Batchelor farmer of Eggington :*

"He had some fowls.

This is the skin of one of them.

We had never sold it.

We had a large quantity of fowls, I am satisfied we have lost some.

Those six were not fat."

William Adams, *Farmer at Eggington:*

"I was called up by Parrott on the morning of 25th.

I saw the sacks that morning

I believe one to be mine, it had my name on it.

I had undressed barley in my barn similar to that in sacks. I compared it with the bulk. I am convinced it was the same.

I believe the peas were mine, they were very particular."

P. W. Wagstaffe, *Surgeon at Leighton Buzzard :*

"I was called to Clough on the morning of the 25th.

He was in bed labouring under concussion of the brain very slightly sensible.

Two wounds on the right side of the head about an inch in extent each, face and jaw much swollen.

Contused wounds.

It might have been done by the butt end of the gun.

I considered him in a very dangerous state. On Friday week 2nd February I thought him out of danger, not before.

He was not well for a month.

He had lost much blood."

Henry Isau Jubbett:

"I conveyed William White to Woburn on 23rd February to Petty Sessions.

He said it was very hard to suffer for another person, he said he was not the third person they wanted.

I asked him what he meant. He said the person we ought to have had was Tom Hines who lives next door to us at Chalk Hill.

I asked him what sort of person Tom Hines was; he described him as a man about 5ft 10 or 11ins. with black whiskers and dark hair."

Mr Power, for the prisoners, addressed the jury at great length and contended that the only evidence against the Whites was the identification by the two policemen. After commenting on the inadequacy of this he put it to the jury that they would see the necessity of pausing before they convicted upon such unsatisfactory testimony. He concluded an able address by stating that he should be able to produce evidence to show that the policemen were totally mistaken in the identification of the two Whites, who were at their own houses on the night in question.

Mr. Power then proceeded to call the first of his witnesses for George and William. Apart from two character witnesses, these were all giving evidence in an attempt to give the two men an alibi on the occasion in question. For these witnesses, the defence had looked amongst George and William's friends and relatives. The first of those to be called for

George was Ruth King, his next door neighbour.

Ruth King:

"On 24th January last, George White lived next door to me at Houghton. Next day the police came to the house.

On 24th January I heard someone do up the door of George White's house. I had no lucifers and so I hallowed have you got any lucifers? She said 'yes'.

It is a very thin wall between our houses, we can talk to each other through it.

I went straight to her back door to get the lucifers. When I got in George White was going upstairs with the baby.

My husband was very ill, I did not go to bed till past 1am. Then I went upstairs to give my husband some medicine. I heard George White talking to the baby.

Next day Sharp the policeman came and Mr Mead a baker and miller.

Sharp examined George White's head and found no trace of a wound and then he went away."

Cross Examined

"George White was taken up on the following Monday for this affair.

I went to Woburn to the Magistrates, they would not let me in. I said I came to speak for George White, they pushed me away, not the police, gentlemen standing about.

I did not tell George White I had come to speak for him.

I went into White's house while Sharp and Mead were there. I saw them examine his head. I never mentioned that White was at home the night before.

As soon as I got in they examined his head and Sharp said to Mead, 'Be you satisfied it is not the man'? Mead said 'yes'.

White is related to Dockerill's wife.

My husband was bad about three weeks."

Re Examined

"I went nine miles to Woburn to tell the same story what I have told now."

Ruth had done her best. She left the stand and the next to be called was William Scrivenor. William was a relative by marriage of George's wife, Sarah. At the time of the trial he was described as a fishmonger, but in a later post office directory of 1854, he is the publican at the 'Unicorn's Head' in Houghton Regis.

William Scrivenor, *Fishmonger at Houghton:*

"On the 24th January I went round the Town of Houghton with my goods about 6 pm and at half past I went to the Cock Public House. In a few minutes George White came in. I asked him to buy some fish, he said no he did not want any that evening.

He had a jug and had some beer put into it and took it away. I remained in the house.

I never knew anything against him.

Both he and William have borne very good characters.

They are uncle and nephew.

On the 25th I heard the police were gone to George White's house to see if he was shot or wounded."

James Rhodes, *Labourer at Houghton:*

"I was at the Cock when William Scrivenor was there.

I saw George White there.

Scrivenor asked him if he would buy the last lot of fish.

I have known him all his life, he has always been upright among his neighbours.

I never heard anything against William White."

The last to appear for George was a character witness, Thomas Randall. Thomas was fifty years old and a carrier by trade. He was also the father of Maria, who subsequently married David, George's younger brother.

Thomas Randall:

> "*I live at Houghton.*
>
> *I have known George White all his life.*
>
> *I never heard anyone say anything against him, nor against William.*"

Apart from that of Ruth, the evidence of the other men placed George in the Cock Inn on the evening in question, but not late enough. He would certainly have been able to reach Stanbridge by the time in question. However, together with Ruth's alibi, it might have been enough to cause doubt that he was the guilty party.

Mr. Power then called the first of the witnesses for William, Stephen Inns. Stephen was a twenty-seven-year-old labourer and was William's neighbour at Chalk Hill. Stephen maintained that William was with him until 10pm and that they spent the evening plaiting straw.

Stephen Inns, *Labourer at Chalk Hill five yards from where William White lives:*

> "*On the 24th January William White came to my house at half past 8pm and stopped with me till 10. I was plaiting and he was plaiting.*
>
> *Next day was the alarm. Half a dozen people or more came to William White's house. He is a married man.*
>
> *I never heard anything against him.*"

The next witness was William's younger brother, Charles. Charles was twenty years old and still living with their parents at Chalk Hill. He confirmed that he had supper at William's house that night and was there until 11pm.

Charles White, *Brother of William White:*

> "*I remember his coming home on the 24th January.*
>
> *I was in his house. I stopped there till 11 and had some*

supper.

> *Next day was the alarm."*

Samuel Burgess:

> *"I live at Dunstable, Tailor and Draper.*
> *I have known William White from his childhood.*
> *He has always been of a very good character.*
> *I don't know much of George White.*
> *Dunstable is a mile and a half from Houghton."*

Mr. Prendergast replied for the prosecution.

Mr Baron Rolfe then went through the evidence very minutely, and was particular in making a distinction between the case of Dockerill and that of George and William White. He stated that the evidence against Dockerill was very conclusive, but as regards George and William there was a great deal of conflicting testimony. His Lordship then explained the law of the case: "Where several persons concerted together in the dead of night, with arms for the purpose of resistance, should they be detected in the act, if death or any injury occurred to the parties who endeavoured to apprehend the person or prevent the robbery, all the parties engaged in such unlawful practices, and resisted with violence their lawful apprehension, all were responsible in the eye of the law."

He then pointed out the circumstances favourable to the Whites, and adverted to the evidence of the witnesses who were called to prove an alibi, and said it was entitled to every consideration. If the testimony of the witnesses for the defence was to be relied upon there was a reasonable probability that the Whites were not the men who took part with Dockerill in the outrage; but if they trusted entirely to the statements of the policemen to the identity of the men it would be impossible for them to come to any other conclusion than that all the prisoners at the bar were guilty of the crime laid to their charge.

The Jury deliberated for some time, and then pronounced a verdict of "Guilty" against all prisoners. The foreman added that they considered William White guilty to a certain degree, but not with the intention of doing bodily harm. This qualification was however withdrawn, on his lordship observing that it could not be received; the Jury must return either a verdict of acquittal, or say he was guilty of the charge.

His Lordship, in passing sentence, said the prisoners had been convicted of an atrocious crime; it was only by the providence of God that the lives of two persons were not sacrificed to their brutal outrage, and their punishment would be most severe. He could conceive nothing more dangerous to life and property than a number of persons going about armed for the purpose of plundering, and to resist to the death should they happen to be interrupted in their nefarious practice.

At this point, George and William protested their innocence.

But the jury had decided otherwise, and His Lordship, Baron Rolfe, as judge, was duty bound to carry out the law. He stated however that he would make a difference in the sentence he was about to pass; for though the case for the Whites was bad enough, it was not so bad as that of Dockerill, upon whom would be inflicted the fullest extent of punishment. He then sentenced Dockerill to be transported for life; George and William White both to transportation for fifteen years.

George and William still loudly protested their innocence, and Dockerill asked the judge to recall the sentence against William White, as he was innocent.

His Lordship said he would be sorry if he had sentenced an innocent person, but the jury had come to a contrary conclusion, and he would not alter it.[1]

William then attempted to address the court, but failing to do so, he fell down in a swoon and in that state was conveyed from the dock.

CHAPTER 10

William and
Squire Brandreth

N ow they had been convicted, the three prisoners were led off back to Bedford Gaol to begin their sentences. The first stage would be a period in solitary confinement, initially spent in Bedford Gaol, before their second stage in a public works gaol, after which their final sentence would be carried out; in the case of Dockerill, it was transportation for life, and for both George and William, transportation for fifteen years.

The distraught families of the men returned to their cottages to face the prospect of bringing up their children without the support of their husbands. Sarah returned to Houghton Regis, and Mary and her father-in-law, John, to Chalk Hill. The outcome of the trial was not what they had hoped for. They thought that the case for the defence had been strong.

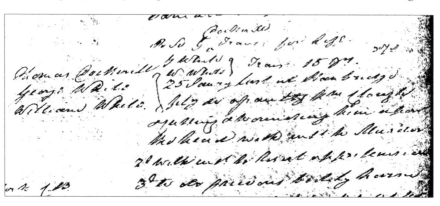

Bedford Prison record, showing Dockerill and George and William White. *ASSI 33 14/2*

The Verdict is anounced.

Rebecca alone must have been prepared for a conviction, although she doubtless had wished for a better outcome. Rebecca returned to Stanbridge to a cottage in the Slough along the main Tilsworth Road, where she now faced life on parish relief, continuing the curse of the Dockerills.[1]

But behind the scenes, the conviction had caused some disquiet, for there were those who were convinced that there had been a miscarriage of justice. Among them was the High Sheriff of Bedfordshire, Squire Humphrey Brandreth, who resided at Houghton House, on the Green at Houghton Regis.

Humphrey Brandreth had been born plain Humphrey Gibbs, but he had inherited his estate, mansion and lands from his uncle, Henry Brandreth, whose only child had pre-deceased him, on condition that he changed his name to Brandreth. Once he became the Squire, he quickly occupied himself with village matters, assuming his right to authority, unquestioned by the villagers who had grown up in the shadow of the 'House'. Whilst there were some squires who chose to mix only with the company of their equals, there were others who were committed to public service, giving generously of their time. Although patronizing they invariably might be, they played a leading and charitable role in village affairs and organizing festivities.[2] Squire Humphrey was a philanthropic gentleman who saw fit to share his good fortune on occasions with the villagers.

From Bedford Times Saturday 2nd September 1848:

HOUGHTON REGIS

RURAL TREAT. – The inhabitants of this place have, during a few months past, had many opportunities of meeting together, and enjoying themselves in mirth the most innocent, and recreation the most joyful. The generous lord of the manor, H. Brandreth Esq., seems continually anxious to contribute to the pleasure and happiness of all around him. On Wednesday last, he kindly opened his park and gardens for the pleasure of the Houghtonians and their friends. A large party was invited to play a game of cricket, which commenced at two o'clock, between eleven gentlemen chosen by Mr. E. Foster, and the same number chosen by Mr. Jos. Inwards, of this place. The batting was exceedingly good, and the bowling such as would have done credit to Lords' Club. B. Gibbs, Esq., joined in the game, and added much to its interest by his superior play. A booth and other accommodations for the company were provided for the occasion, and, the weather being fine, happiness and joy beamed from every countenance, and each one seemed to regret the approaching "shades of evening" which terminated the merry village holiday. In the evening a supper was generously given in the park, and, full justice having been done to it, the party separated, highly gratified with the entertainment. It is seldom these rural treats are given, but when they do occur they are well estimated in this neighbourhood. For this additional kindness of Mr. Brandreth the most unbounded gratitude was expressed, and, for many and many a day will the remembrance of it be warmly cherished.

From Bedford Times Saturday 23rd September 1848:

HOUGHTON REGIS v DUNSTABLE

On Thursday last, Sept. 14th, a match was played between the parish of Dunstable and the parish of Houghton Regis, which terminated (as will be seen by the score), in favour of the latter by 88 runs. H. Brandreth, Esq., kindly opened his park for the occasion, and, in accordance with all his other acts of kindness, generously regaled the cricketers with an excellent cold collation. The playing was very good, especially the batting of Swift and Abell. We expect the return match will be played in a few days.

From Bedford Times Saturday 29th July 1848:

Houghton House, the residence of Squire Humphrey Brandreth. *Z50/63/10*

HOUGHTON REGIS
A GOOD EXAMPLE TO THE GENTRY OF BEDFORDSHIRE.

– On Wednesday last, H. Brandreth, Esq., of Houghton House, gave tea to the whole of the Sunday School children belonging to the parish of Houghton Regis, under a booth erected for the purpose in the park. The liberal gentleman would have no distinction made between the Church and the Dissenters, but was determined that each should enjoy a holiday, when upwards of 600 children assembled together and partook of his hospitality, and seemed to enjoy themselves exceedingly.

POOR RATES. – A number of persons of Houghton Regis were summoned for non-payment of poor rates. Some, from extreme poverty, were recommended to the parish authorities to be excused, and others were given time for payment.

In his position of Squire of the Manor, Humphrey Brandreth managed his estate through a bailiff, and collected his rents from his many tenants. For the Squire owned much land and property around Houghton Regis, Sewell and Puddle Hill, and he now also owned the cottage and shop where John White junior, William's father, lived and ran his butchery.[3] In his position of High Sheriff, he dispensed justice at Petty Sessions, and in his role on the local board of guardians, he oversaw the execution of the Poor Law. He was a busy man. But he was a fair and just man and he was convinced of William's innocence. Doubtless, being William's father's landlord, he had been informed by John of the true circumstances of the event, or maybe he started making his own enquiries. Either way, he was certain that he would be able to convince the authorities sufficiently to obtain a free pardon for William and quickly set in motion proceedings to begin an appeal.

In the meantime, William had no choice but to suffer life inside prison. But the thought that somebody of the Squire's importance saw fit to take up his cause must have been a tremendous relief for William and given him new hope. For he had already unjustly endured nearly four weeks in prison, a week of that being with hard labour.

On 15th March, just a week after the trial and the sentencing of the three men, Squire Brandreth set off to visit Bedford Gaol in order to interview William, Thomas and George with a view to obtaining new statements from them. William's statement, given in the presence of the Squire, was brief, just declaring his innocence of all charges.

Statement of William White

William White of Houghton Regis in the County of Bedford, labourer, who was committed on the 23rd day of February last, by the Revd. E.O. ?, clerk and Henry Charles Hoare, Esq, charged on oath with having on the 25th day of January 1849, at the parish of Stanbridge unlawfully and maliciously wounded William Clough, and James Parrott, with intent to prevent the lawful apprehension of him the said William White, and who at the Lent Assizes holden

on the 9th & 10th of March instant was found guilty, and sentenced
by the Rt. Honourable Baron Rolf to be transported for the term of
Fifteen years.

faith, I am not guilty of the offence with which I have been
charged and of which I have been found guilty, and I have upon
no occasion been engaged with either Thomas Dockerill or George
White, the other two persons that have been tried and convicted for
the offence above charged against me in any unlawful acts.

and I therefore humbly pray her Majesty's most gracious
pardon and remission of the sentence passed upon me.
   William White
Witnessed

P Banfield
Gaoler

The above statement was made before me.

Humphrey Brandreth
Sheriff
Bedford March 15 1849   *(sic)*

Next it was the turn of Dockerill, who had decided to make a clean breast
of it. His statement not only exonerated William but named Thomas
Hines as the third man, confirming the plea that William had made
when he was transported to the Petty Sessions at Woburn. However,
Dockerill's statement also removed all doubt that George was indeed
guilty. Thomas gave his version of what happened that night, during and
after the assault. He confirmed that he had fired the gun that wounded
Constable Parrott, and that it was George who had struck Constable
Clough. The bullet that Parrott fired had passed through the front of
George's smock sideways, missing his person, and George subsequently
destroyed the smock. It was Thomas Hines who had been hit on the
head during the affray, and that Hines had indeed been injured. So, had

the police looked for the injury to Hines when William named him, they would have found their evidence. Dockerill went on to say that the gun he had used was broken when he hit Parrott on the arm. George took the gun and disposed of it on his way home, the barrels by the side of a ditch about a mile from the place of the affray and the stock in a hedgerow about two miles away, near the footpath that led from Stanbridge to Houghton Regis. The skeleton keys which they had, George threw into a pond at Stanbridge.

Statement of Thomas Dockerill

Thomas Dockerill who was tried upon the same ? as the above named William White and convicted of the same offence & who is now under sentence of transportation for life. faith. That William White who was convicted as being present, was not present and was in no way concerned in the Robbery or in the attack upon the police, but that the guilty person is Thomas Hinde,(Hines) who is a brother-in-law of his, he also states that Thomas Hinde (Hines) is the person that the policemen, Clough, first seized, that it was George White who also stands convicted of the above offence, & who is sentenced to fifteen years transportation, who struck the Policeman Clough, with the bludgeon and that Thomas Hinde (Hines) was struck on the head by the Policeman Clough, and which blow caused his head to bleed. He also states that the shot the Policeman Parrott fired passed through the frock of George White sideways, in the front of the frock, but never wounded him & that George White destroyed the frock. He also states that George White threw away the skeleton keys into a pond at Stanbridge, in John Ongs (Black House) Close.

He also states that he, himself, broke the gun when he hit Parrott on the arm – that George White took the gun and (hid?) it as he went home, the barrels by the side of a ditch a mile from the place, and the stock in a hedgerow about two miles from the place, near the foot path that leads from Stanbridge to Houghton Regis.

He further states that he, Thomas Dockerill, was the man who fired the gun and wounded the policeman.

The Mark of
Thomas Dockerill

Witness
P Banfield   Gaoler
The above statement was made before me

H^{phrey} Brandreth
Sheriff
Bedford March 15th 1849   *(sic)*

George White's statement was brief, merely confirming that made by Dockerill. All three statements were signed, William's with his signature, George and Dockerill's with their marks, and were witnessed by a gaoler, P. Banfield in the presence of Squire Brandreth.

Statement of George White
George White who was convicted for the above offence and who stands under sentence of transportation for Fifteen years states that the above account given by Dockerill is correct, and says that William White is not guilty.

The Mark of George White.
Witnessed
P Banfield Gaoler

The above statement was made before me

Humphrey Brandreth
Sheriff
Bedford March 15 1849   *(sic)*

Houghton House
Nr Dunstable, Beds.
March 17. 1849.

Sir,

Enclosed I have the honour to transmit to you a prayer from a prisoner of the name of William White, who is now confined in Bedford Gaol, under sentence of transportation for 15 years, for a supposed assault on two policemen, who were engaged in apprehending certain delinquents, together with the confessions of two other men, who were tried for, and convicted of, the like (?) offences.

From enquiries I have made relative to the charge against the said William White, I am induced to believe that he is not the guilty party and I am further induced to believe that if secretary, Sir George Grey, should think proper to refer the enclosed petition to the Right Honourable Baron Rolfe, the Judge who tried the convict, it will be found that he will support the present application for a ? and remission for the sentence.

I beg also to enclose a ? copy of the Calendars(?)which I think will facilitate a reference to the case I now wish to bring before the Secretary of State's notice.

I have the honour to be
Your very obedient servant
Humphrey Brandreth.
Sheriff of Beds

To Horatio Waddington Esq,
Under Secretary of State   *(sic)*

Letter from Humphrey Brandreth Esq.

Once returned to his family seat at Houghton House, Squire Brandreth lost no time in forwarding the statements to the Secretary of State, recommending consideration for a free pardon. On 17th March he wrote to Horatio Waddington in the State Office, enclosing the statements, adding his own conviction that William was innocent. He urged the Secretary of State, Sir George Grey, to forward a copy of the statement to the Judge who had tried the case, the Right Honourable Baron Rolfe, whom he believed would add his support to the case for William.

On receipt of the Squire's letter, Mr. Waddington granted him an interview to discuss the case, after which, on 21st March, Mr. Waddington wrote to Baron Rolfe enclosing a copy of the statements. On 9th April, from his address at 40 Upper Brook Street, Baron Rolfe wrote to Sir Geoffrey Bowl, enclosing a copy of the notes that he had made during the trial. He stated that although he had no doubt that Dockerill had

40 Upper Brook St

3757

9 April 1849

Sir

    I have to acknowledge the text of a letter from Mr Waddington dated the 21st ult. transmitting for my perusal an application on behalf of Wm White who was convicted before me at the last Bedford Assizes of feloniously wounding Willm Clough with intent to prevent the lawful apprehension of himself & others & with intent to do grievous bodily harm.

    I enclose you a copy of my notes of the trial by which you will see that the prisoner was indicted with 2 others Thomas Dockerill & Geo White & they were all found guilty.

    The case against Dockerill was free from all doubt - But I was by no means satisfied with the propriety of the verdict as to the two Whites, particularly as related to William.

    With respect to George, there is now no doubt.

    But as to William I strongly incline to think he was not one of the party. There was no evidence against him except the positive oaths of the 2 policemen, & they had never seen him before. One of them when first he saw Wm White after the outrage did not think he was the man.

    The Demeanour of William at the trial did not appear to me to be that of a guilty man & I thought the alibi sworn to had every appearance of being true.

    Under the circumstances I think it wd be proper to recommend a pardon.

    I have the honour to be

        Your very obedient servant

        R.M. Rolfe

P.S.

I return the papers sent to me by Mr. Waddington

Sir Geoffrey Bowl   *(sic)*

Letter from Baron Rolfe.

been guilty, he had been by no means satisfied with the verdict against George and William White, particularly William. He was inclined to think that William was not one of the men involved. He thought that there was no evidence against him other than the positive oaths of the two policemen who not only had never seen him before, but one of whom had, at one stage, thought he was not the man sought. Baron Rolfe further thought that William's demeanour was not that of a guilty man and that his alibi was probably true. Of course, with respect to George, there was no longer any doubt. Under the circumstances, he recommended a pardon for William.

William White   22
Bedford Lent Assizes
March 1849
Wounding &
15 Years Trans.
Gaol Report   Char Good
Write to Mr. Baron Rolfe

The High Sheriff of Bedford
sends the Declarations of
the persons Convicted with
the prisoner that he is not
guilty, & he states that he
has reason to believe that
if reference is made to
Mr Baron Rolfe, he will
Recommend a Pardon

Answered 27 April 1849
Free Pardon 21 April 1849

left and above William White's appeal.
HO18/261/43

right above William White's pardon. *HO13/96*

right below Squire Brandreth's letter of
thanks.

William received his free pardon on 21st April 1849, having wrongly been imprisoned for two months.[4]

Mr. Waddington wrote to Squire Brandreth on 27th April, informing him of the decision of the Home Secretary Sir George Grey that he had recommended William for a free pardon, and Her Majesty had been pleased to comply with that recommendation. The Squire was away at the time, but on his return he replied to Mr. Waddington on 9th May, thanking him for the courtesy shown at his interview on the subject and expressing his satisfaction that justice had been served. William was a free man once more.

Victoria R

William White }   Whereas Wm White was
Free Pardon }   at a Gaol Delivery holden in & for the County of
Bedford in March last, convd of Feloniously Wounding, &
sentenced to be transported 15 years for the same, We in
considn of some circs (?) humbly repd unto Us are Gy pleased to
extend Our Grace & Mercy unto him & to Grant him our Free
Pardon for the crime of which he stands convd. – Our Will ?
To Our Trusty & Well beloved   }   dated 21 April 1849
The High Sheriff of the County }   By HM Command
Of Bedford, and all others ?   }   G Grey

5102

Houghton House
May 9. 1849

Sir   On my return home I have had the pleasure to find your letter of 27th ultm informing me that Secretary Sir George Grey had been pleased to recommend William White, who was sentenced to 15 years transportation at the Bedford Lent Assizes, Her Majesty's consideration and ? gracious free pardon and that Her Majesty had been pleased to comply with that recommendation.

        I beg that you will do me the honour to express to Sir George my ? thanks for his attention to my application, and assure him that I am most thoroughly satisfied that my application was founded on justice.

        I beg to thank you for the courtesy you were so good as to shew me when I had the pleasure of an interview with you on this subject.

        I have the honour to be you most obedient humble servant,

Humphrey Brandreth
H Waddington Esquire   (sic)

Bedford Prison. *Drawn by the author from a picture by T. Fisher.*

CHAPTER 11

Life in Bedford Prison

As William rejoined his family and friends in Chalk Hill, George and Dockerill were beginning the fourth month of their incarceration. It would have been little comfort to them that the awful conditions they were experiencing were in fact some improvement on those that prisoners before them had to endure. Or indeed that the death sentence which at one time would have been compulsory for the crime they had committed was now considered by magistrates to be too harsh, for between 1801 and 1837 thirteen executions took place in Bedford Gaol. But prisons, albeit still grim, had undergone great change since the 18th century. Then, they were overcrowded, filthy hovels with the prisoners massed together, providing no privacy or protection from others. There was very little fresh water, they had to pay for their own food and many were dependent on relatives or friends to bring it to them. But for those whose relatives were not able to provide from their own grinding poverty, and for those who had no money to pay their gaoler for any, they simply had no choice but were forced to beg from people who passed by the prison. For they had to pay their gaoler for every service; even punishment, such as being shackled in irons or being whipped. Disease was rife, due to the unsanitary conditions and poor diet.

There were those reformers who considered that keeping prisoners in such conditions would not influence them to change their ways. John Howard (1726–1790) was one such person. He was the High Sheriff of Bedfordshire from 1773 until his death and he made a study throughout Europe of prison conditions. It was his opinion that prisoners should be provided with their own cell at night where they could contemplate the error of their ways in private, and that they should attend Church and be given Christian teaching. He also believed they should be given work to do and should be supplied with fresh food to eat and water to drink.

Newly built prisons were based on this theory. Gloucester prison, built to a new design in 1792, separated the prisoners into different categories. Minor offenders were put in a House of Correction, prisoners on remand and awaiting trial were housed in a gaol, and those who had committed major offences in a penitentiary where each prisoner had his own cell. They were no longer at the mercy of family, friends or gaolers for their food, but were fed a strict diet by the authorities. They were also provided with clothing, a uniform with arrows on it and were made to wash regularly. All were made to work, some on hard labour. The system was gradually adopted throughout the country, including Bedford, which was extended considerably between 1801 and 1841 to provide for longer term prisoners and the increase in the prison population.

Early in the 19th century the inmates of Bedford Gaol were allowed to work for local businesses to earn a small amount for their keep, the gaol-keeper no doubt taking his cut of the earnings. But in 1816, following the theory that prisoners should be made to work for the prison, a mill with a new tread-wheel to grind corn was built. On this torturous instrument, prisoners climbed for ten hours a day, in silence. Even during rest periods they still had to walk around in a circle, and only eating time provided brief respite. The tread-wheel earned money for the gaol and the prisoners were paid a small amount.

By this time the prison which had been intended to hold forty prisoners was now holding one hundred and one as a result of the growth in crime which followed the return of soldiers and sailors from war and now swelled the numbers of unemployed. Because of the vast overcrowding, a new House of Correction for minor offenders was added in 1820. The tread-wheel was considered by the authorities to be such a great success as a form of punishment that this was built with a discipline mill with tread-wheels. Once the prisoners had worked their allotted time on the wheel they were allowed to attend school run by a turnkey to learn to

A treadwheel – prisoners were made to climb ten hours a day.

read and write. For this service, the turnkey was paid 3/- per week.

In spite of this additional accommodation, still the problem of overcrowding occurred, with prisoners sharing cells and some sharing beds. So, although the goal and House of Correction were meant to operate on the silent system and prisoners were not allowed to communicate with each other, albeit they were allowed to work together, it was impossible to enforce the system. In spite of the fact that they were punished for it, prisoners could not be kept from talking to each other whilst taking exercise, going to chapel or signalling to each other by coughing or waving. They sang at night and shouted to each other from their cells. As a result of this the system became stricter and all new prisons were then built so that all prisoners could be separated.

Bedford Prison was a very unpleasant, cold, damp, inhospitable place. There is evidence of the grim conditions of the prisoners in reports of the prison inspectors. In the report of 1839 there is a graphic description of the prison cells, stated as being just 6ft 2ins by 3ft 9ins, with those on the lower galley just 7ft 10ins in height.[1]

Fourth Report of prison inspectors 1839 on prison accommodation at Bedford Gaol:

These cells were constructed merely as night cells and are, with the exception of two, of the following dimensions: six feet two inches long, three feet nine inches broad and in height seven feet ten inches in the lower gallery and ten feet four inches in the upper gallery. There is only one small aperture in the door for the admission of air and light, and a few small holes near the ceiling for the escape of foul air, but which are quite insufficient to maintain a proper degree of ventilation. The cells are far from being light. The prisoners, during this close confinement, have no access to a privy. When the cells were formerly occupied by day, the doors were kept open for the admittance of light and air; but as facilities were thus afforded for communication the doors were ordered to be closed.

Since 1815 prisoners no longer had to pay for their own keep, but nevertheless the authorities wanted to keep the cost of feeding them as low as possible. They wished also to ensure that inmates were not fed better inside prison than they would have been outside, in order to discourage the petty criminal from re-offending just to get fed. From 1820 published dietaries ensured a basic diet, but although regulated it was poor quality. Then, from 1843, the government brought in new minimum standards throughout the country. Prisoners serving different sentences were given different amounts of food; those with longer sentences had a better diet as their work was harder. However, authorities would still strive to keep their costs as low as possible. There is also evidence of the disease and illness that these conditions and poor diet caused from a report to the Home Secretary both in 1840 and from the visiting surgeon in 1841.

1840 Extract from a report to the Home Secretary on the health of prisoners in the new House of Correction in Bedford (Fifth Report QGR 1/1-4)

The prevalent disease is petichia, or land scurvy, a disorder which, though it is now exceedingly rare in this country, is always to be found in this prison. It is a disorder very destructive to health, and constitutions affected by it are greatly broken down, and those who are afflicted with it are generally long in recovering their strength, and in many cases never do so. We had a long and full conference on this subject with the surgeon, who expressed his opinion to the above stated effect in very decided terms - and we ascertained in reply to the questions put by us to this officer (who is a very able and experienced surgeon, and most attentive to his duties) that he attributed the bad state of health and the prevalence of petichial disease to the strict discipline of the prison, the scantiness of the diet, and the defective ventilation of the cells.

1841 Extract from Report by Charles Short - visiting surgeon for the gaol (QGR 1/7 1841)

There has been more illness in the last quarter than has usually occurred in former corresponding periods, taking into account the number of prisoners. The prison is however now in a more healthy state.........Two men came to prison with hernia. Several men have been attacked with abdominal pains and diarrhoea. Two have obstinate chronic disease of the liver, all those have terminated favourably. There have been some cases of pleuritic and pulmonary disease and catarrhal fever; the latter have left the men in a state of great debility. The petichial (land scurvy) disease has reappeared in four instances of men sentenced to long imprisonment; they are recovering. Two men had vomiting of blood and haemorrhage from the bowels; they have both recovered. There have occurred only four cases of continued fever, which terminated favourably. Sciatic rheumatism has been rather prevalent but not of long continuance. One man had a very distressing retention of urine attended with severe pain; he was relieved by repeated use of the catheter, warm baths and other means and ultimately recovered. A few cases of disorder of the stomach have occurred. One of leprosy. A man came to prison with varicose veins of the leg; he and the two with hernia (though sentenced to hard labour) were not allowed to work at the wheel. Several vagrants have been brought to the prison in a most filthy state. Some with itch in its worst form; they are well.

> **Thirteenth Report of the prison inspectors 1847-1848 (QGR 1/16 QGR 1/17)**
>
> *There is a small opening in the door for the admission of air and light, but hoppered to prevent the prisoners seeing into the yard when the door is closed, and the ventilation is effected by means of a pipe, two-and-a-half inches in diameter, which is carried through the roof into the open air. There are no means of warming the cells and the ventilation is bad. Indeed one can scarcely imagine any place intended for a lengthened confinement of prisoners in the present day more painfully cold in winter or more distressingly hot in summer than these cells on the ground floor and roofed with copper. The prisoners having nothing to wash themselves in but their soil pots, which each brings from his cell and cleans out with water and rotstone before he uses it as a basin.*

Now that they were convicted prisoners, this was the life which George and Dockerill could expect. Whilst on remand they had been allowed to wear their own clothing, if it was considered fit and proper by the authorities. If not, or if it was necessary to preserve their clothing for the trial, then they were furnished with a plain suit of clothing made of coarse plain cloth. George, at least, wore his own clothing whilst on remand because it was described by Police Constable Clough in his statement "he had a cap on then, believed to be the same (as on the night of the affray). He had leather leggings on". But now convicted, their clothing was taken into the charge of the prison governor, and they were issued with standard prison dress by the authorities, a coat, waistcoat, trousers, shirt, shoes and stockings. Once they had been examined by the surgeon they were required to take a warm, but more likely cold bath, and their hair was cut if he deemed it necessary for hygiene. In an attempt to improve hygiene standards, they were made to wash regularly. In fact they would now wash daily, shave at least once a week and their hair would be cut once a month. Convenient places for the prisoners to wash themselves were provided with sufficient allowance of water, soap, towels and combs. If the surgeon advised, they would bath at least once a month. They were provided with a hair, flock, or straw mattress, two blankets and a coverlid but, if the surgeon ordered it, might also have two sheets and a pillow. These were to be kept properly clean and the straw changed when necessary. Clean linen and towels were allocated once a week. The cost of their clothing and bedding to the Authorities was 3/- per head.[2]

George and Dockerill, being prisoners under sentence in solitary confinement, would have been made to work for the minimum of ten hours a day hard labour. The theory now introduced was that prison was meant to punish, not provide an income, and so penal labour was enforced. Both the Gaol and the prisoners lost most of their income as a result.

Bedford Prison Rules

Prisoners Sentenced to Hard Labour:

He shall be employed unless prevented by sickness at such hard labour as can be provided, and for so many hours (not exceeding ten, exclusive of the time allowed for meals), as hereinafter provided, except on Sundays, Christmas day, Good Friday, or public fast and thanksgiving days. He shall not be allowed any portion of his earnings; neither shall he receive an extra allowance in consequence of any labour performed by him.[3]

In spite of the fact that the use of treadwheels was on the decline in some gaols, it was still a favoured form of punishment in many, and a preferred form of punishment by authorities in their plans to enforce the separate system of confinement. This soul destroying occupation was loathed by prisoners, and even in the opinion of inspectors of prisons was only detrimental in all respects to the moral and physical well-being of the convicts. In 1846 one group of visiting inspectors wrote to the Home Office voicing their objections to the system and also to state their opinion against the use of dayrooms for untried prisoners, considering them rendering "frightful contamination from unrestrained association".[4]

London 31st March 1846

Sir,

We request that you will inform Secretary Sir James Graham, that we learn, with much regret, that Plans of Prisons professedly framed with a view to the carrying out of the separate system of Prison discipline have been certified by the Secretary of State in which Treadwheels have been provided as the ordinary discipline for Prisoners sentenced to hard labour.

We regard this circumstance as one of considerable importance, because we are apprehensive that the sanction given by the Secretary of State to such Plans may be the means of encouraging and perpetuating a system of Labour which has been for some time on the decline, and which we are of opinion should be discontinued. We therefore beg to lay before Sir James Graham the objections which we entertain to this species of Hard Labour.

With reference to the use of Treadwheels for the enforcement of Hard Labour, Experience has shewn that it is not conducive to reformation – that it is mere punishment without improvement – and that it hardens and irritates the Prisoner; – that so far from producing industrious habits, it creates a distaste for every kind of Labour, that it has no deterring influence, and has no effect in diminishing the number of recommitments: Great improvements have, of late, been made in the discipline of Prisons, having for their object the effectual correction, and the moral amendment, of Prisoners; and Treadwheel Labour, being considered unfavourable to these objects, has greatly declined in the estimation of enlightened Magistrates and experienced Governors of Prisons. Treadwheel Labour has also, in the opinion of high Medical Authority, been deemed prejudicial to health, and wherever that species of employment is still retained, a larger amount of diet is found indispensable to sustain the health and strength of the Prisoners.

There is another subject connected with new Plans for Prisons, to which we are anxious to call Sir James Graham's attention – viz:

the importance of discontinuing, in every case, the erection of Day-Rooms.

The adoption of Day-Rooms in the new Gaol for the County of Bucks justifies our apprehension that Sir James Graham's certificate of approval to this Plan may lead to the inference that he is not unfavourable to this objectionable arrangement, and we therefore beg to submit to him the grounds on which we are induced earnestly to recommend the discontinuance of Day-Rooms in Prisons.

So long ago as the year 1835, the Committee of the House of Lords, appointed to enquire into the State of Gaols and Houses of Correction in England and Wales, recommended "That the use of Day-Rooms, as such, should be discontinued"; assigning as the reason for such recommendation, "That every motive of humanity as regards the individual Prisoners, and of Policy as regards the good of Society in general, requires that the most efficient regulations should be established, in order to save all Prisoners, and especially the Untried, from the frightful contamination resulting from unrestrained association." We submit that if Day-Rooms are provided for the Untried, "unrestrained intercourse" and "frightful contamination" must be the inevitable result, or else intercourse between the Untried when brought together in the Day-Rooms must be prevented by the enforcement of Silence, which we believe to be illegal with reference to the Untried, and which can only be attained with any degree of effect by numerous restrictions, and frequent and severe Prison punishments.

It is important that these very objectionable parts of our old and defective systems of Prison Discipline, viz. The use of Tread Wheel Labour and of day-rooms, should not be perpetrated in Prisons expressly built, or extensively altered and amended, in order to give effect to an improved system of Prison Discipline. Our Experience had convinced us that, when once a body of Magistrates has been persuaded that either the construction of a new Prison, or extensive alterations in an existing Prison, are absolutely necessary, they may be induced by a judicious but firm and persevering course of proceeding, to render their Plans at once complete and effective: If, however, half measures are adopted, and a considerable sum is expended without securing all the essential requisites of a good Prison, great disappointment is the result, after calls for money to supply deficiencies, and render works complete, produce much irritation, and in order to avoid such after calls, modified and defective arrangements are adopted, and the enforcement of a really sound system of Prison Discipline is abandoned.

We would, therefore, earnestly submit, whenever these highly objectionable arrangements, to which we have referred, viz: Treadwheels and Day-Rooms, form part of the Plans submitted for the approval of the Secretary of State, that every effort should be made to induce the Magistrates to abandon so injudicious a mode of construction; and in the event of their not adopting such a recommendation, which we confidently anticipate would very rarely occur, that then the Secretary of State should withhold his certificate from Plans so decidedly defective and objectionable.

We would further submit that it is highly necessary that duplicate copies of all Plans of Prisons certified by the Secretary of State, should be transmitted to the Home Office, and there preserved. This would not only be most advantageous in many respects; but is in accordance with the provisions of the 4th :Geo:1V:C:64:Sec 15: which enacts that Plans of Prisons, and of all alterations in and additions to such Prisons shall be transmitted to, and carefully preserved in the Office of the Secretary of State.

We are,

Sir,

Your most obedient humble Servants

{ Wm. Crawford

{ Whitworth Russell

{ John G. Perry.

Inspectors of Prisons

M. Phillipps Esq.   (sic)

The crank – this one at Dartmoor Prison.

Another form of solitary punishment introduced into Bedford Gaol was the crank, a handle attached to a set of cogs, which had to be turned by the prisoner in his or her cell, all day, without any product of their hard work. The crank handle pushed a paddle through sand, and as an extra punishment could be screwed up to make it harder to push.

Whilst the crank was a soul destroying task having no end product, another which did have a purpose was picking oakum which entailed pulling apart tarred rope into its individual fibres, to be used for other purposes. Vast quantities were utilised by the Royal Navy for caulking ships' timbers to make them waterproof. This work made prisoners hands bleed, and was very painful. Another task was picking rags, separating different sorts of material and tearing them into strips. Prisoners were also expected to sew prison uniforms or other cloth items needed in prison and sold outside.

The execution of George and Dockerill's sentence carried a mandatory period in solitary confinement, and although the new prison, built under the separate system, was not yet completed, the prison rules (1840) stated that 'There shall be an adequate number of solitary cells for the reception of prisoners sentenced to solitary confinement; from

Oakum picking, a task which made the prisoners' hands bleed.

these cells the bedding shall be moved during the day.'[5] Therefore, any communication they had with others was restricted to visits by the chaplain and prison disciplinarians. As families were no longer required to bring in food or clothing for the prisoners, their visits were restricted to twice a year. Authorities now believed that, as well as being kept away from the bad association of other prisoners, they should also be kept away from the influence of their families. So they could not look forward to any communication from their families for at least six months, neither by visit nor by letter, as the latter, too, was restricted. They would also be aware that they would soon be sent on to another prison in the country to await transportation, and once they were removed from Bedford it would not be so easy for any member of the family to visit them.

But they could look forward to the same meals each day, never varying, being fed in accordance with dietary rules laid down by the authorities. And after they had served a certain amount of time of their sentence, the amount of food would increase accordingly. Whilst on remand, they would have been Class III prisoners and would have been fed as such. Once convicted they had to work their way through from Class I to Class IV.[6]

CLASS I.

Convicted Prisoners for any term not exceeding One Month.

	BREAKFAST.	DINNER.	SUPPER.
SUNDAY...	1 pint of Oatmeal Gruel, 8 ounces of Bread.	8 ounces of Bread and half a pound of Potatoes.	1 pint of Oatmeal Gruel, 8 ounces of Bread.
MONDAY	Ditto......................	Ditto......................	Ditto......................
TUESDAY...	Ditto......................	Ditto......................	Ditto......................
WEDNESDAY	Ditto......................	Ditto......................	Ditto......................
THURSDAY...	Ditto......................	Ditto......................	Ditto......................
FRIDAY......	Ditto......................	Ditto......................	Ditto......................
SATURDAY...	Ditto......................	Ditto......................	Ditto......................

CLASS II.

Convicted Prisoners for any term exceeding One Month, but not exceeding Three Months.

	BREAKFAST.	DINNER.	SUPPER.
SUNDAY...	1 pint of Oatmeal Gruel, 8 ounces of Bread.	8 ounces of Bread and 1lb of Potatoes.	1 pint of Oatmeal Gruel, 8 ounces of Bread.
MONDAY	Ditto......................	3 ounces of Cooked Meat, (without bone), 8 ounces of Potatoes, 8 ounces of Bread.	Ditto......................
TUESDAY...	Ditto......................	Ditto......................	Ditto......................
WEDNESDAY	Ditto......................	8 ounces of Bread and 1lb of Potatoes.	Ditto......................
THURSDAY...	Ditto......................	3 ounces of Cooked Meat, (without bone), 8 ounces of Potatoes, 8 ounces of Bread.	Ditto......................
FRIDAY......	Ditto......................	Ditto......................	Ditto......................
SATURDAY...	Ditto......................	8 ounces of Bread and 1lb of Potatoes.	Ditto......................

CLASS III.

Convicted Prisoners for any term exceeding Three Months and not exceeding Six Months. Prisoners committed for Trial and for Re-examination-First Class misdemeanants-And destitute Debtors.

	BREAKFAST.	DINNER.	SUPPER.
SUNDAY...	1 pint of Oatmeal Gruel, 8 ounces of Bread.	8 ounces of Bread and 1lb of Potatoes.	1 pint of Oatmeal Gruel, 8 ounces of Bread.
MONDAY	Ditto.....................	4 ounces of Cooked Meat, (without bone), 8 ounces of Potatoes, 8 ounces of Bread.	Ditto.....................
TUESDAY...	Ditto.....................	3 ounces of Cooked Meat, (without bone), 8 ounces of Bread, 1lb of Potatoes.	Ditto.....................
WEDNESDAY	Ditto.....................	4 ounces of Cooked Meat, (without bone), 8 ounces of Potatoes, 8 ounces of Bread.	Ditto.....................
THURSDAY...	Ditto.....................	8 ounces of Bread and 1lb of Potatoes.	Ditto.....................
FRIDAY......	Ditto.....................	4 ounces of Cooked Meat, (without bone), 8 ounces of Potatoes, 8 ounces of Bread.	Ditto.....................
SATURDAY...	Ditto.....................	3 ounces of Cooked Meat, (without bone), 8 ounces of Potatoes, 8 ounces of Bread.	Ditto.....................

Females to have 2 ounces of Bread less at each meal.

Note. – 1. The Gruel when made in Quantities exceeding 50 pints, to contain 1½ ounce of Oatmeal per pint, and 2 ounces per pint, when in less quantities. The Gruel to be seasoned with Salt and to be delivered hot.

Note. – 2. All the Rations to be delivered at three different periods of the day in the quantities specified.

Note. – 3. Convicted Prisoners sentenced to longer terms of imprisonment than one Month, are not to be placed at once on the Classes of diet provided for such longer terms, but are to be transferred from one class to another as their respective terms of imprisonment advance.

CLASS IV.

Convicted Prisoners for any term exceeding Six Months

	BREAKFAST.	DINNER.	SUPPER.
SUNDAY...	1 pint of Oatmeal Gruel, 8 ounces of Bread.	3 ounces of Cooked Meat, (without bone), 8 ounces of Bread, 1lb of Potatoes.	1 pint of Oatmeal Gruel, 8 ounces of Bread.
MONDAY	Ditto.....................	4 ounces of Cooked Meat, (without bone), 8 ounces of Bread, 1lb of Potatoes.	Ditto.....................
TUESDAY...	Ditto.....................	3 ounces of Cooked Meat, (without bone), 8 ounces of Bread, 1lb of Potatoes.	Ditto.....................
WEDNESDAY	Ditto.....................	4 ounces of Cooked Meat, (without bone), 8 ounces of Bread, 1lb of Potatoes.	Ditto.....................
THURSDAY...	Ditto.....................	3 ounces of Cooked Meat, (without bone), 8 ounces of Bread, 1lb of Potatoes.	Ditto.....................
FRIDAY......	Ditto.....................	4 ounces of Cooked Meat, (without bone), 8 ounces of Bread, 1lb of Potatoes.	Ditto.....................
SATURDAY...	Ditto.....................	4 ounces of Cooked Meat, (without bone), 8 ounces of Bread, 1lb of Potatoes.	Ditto.....................

In spite of the fact that these dietary conditions were laid down to be followed by all prisons, Bedford prison authorities continued to look for ways of reducing theirs costs. In 1851, some two years after George and Dockerill had 'moved on', the Bedford magistrates asked the Home Secretary to allow them to give a lower quality diet to the prisoners in Bedford Gaol in an attempt to save money. They maintained that prisoners preferred the diet in the gaol to that in the Union Workhouse and even suggested that some prisoners were committing petty offences to get the 'better food' in the gaol. A Captain Williams was sent by the

Home Secretary to compare the diet in the two institutions. As a result of his report the diet as recommended by the Home Secretary was maintained.

QGV2/6 1851 Report of Captain Williams:

Tables No. 1 and 2 of the prison dietaries, which extend to twenty-one days imprisonment, are infinitely below that of the union, although the latter is so framed as not to offer any inducement to the able-bodied to remain there when work is to be got. In the Bedford Union the able-bodied men work at a crank labour machine which is applied to the grinding of corn. It has been frequently stated that the paupers prefer Bedford jail to the Union, but all my inquiries tend to prove the very reverse of this assertion. I examined separately every prisoner in the gaol and house of correction, to the number of sixteen, who had been in the Union workhouses, and with one solitary exception they all expressed their decided preference of the workhouse to the prison.

The magistrates in thus pressing for diminution of the food allowed to prisoners appear to consider the diet as the sole penal element in the separate system, and that its success or failure is wholly dependent thereon, but the very reverse is the case. The efficacy of the discipline mainly depends upon the complete isolation of the prisoners, the compulsory hard labour in solitude, the only interruption being the time given for devotion and moral and religious instructions, the visits of the medical and discipline officers. Experience has proved that under such depressing circumstances the quantity and quality of the prisoners' food should be larger and even more nutritious than when in association. I beg not to be understood as advocating the issue of more food for prisoners than is absolutely necessary for their maintenance in health while in jail, and their physical fitness for labour on their discharge.

The grievous results arising from the withholding of a sufficient supply of food from prisoners are still deeply impressed upon my memory, by the many instances witnessed in my earlier labours as Inspector of Prisons but perhaps no more striking case is afforded than in the Bedfordshire prisons when formerly scurvy, typhus, ague and the whole train of low diseases, which invariably follow depression of the mind and body, prevailed for a series of years, and did not wholly disappear until the occupation of the new building.[7]

In an attempt to make them repent their sins, visits from the chaplain were encouraged. Prisoners also attended services in the chapel where they sat apart from each other, facing the preacher. George and Dockerill, along with all prison inmates, were now getting compulsory instruction in reading and writing with great emphasis placed on the scriptures, the latter in an attempt to make the felons recant their evil ways. Bibles and other books of a moral and religious character were provided and they had daily prayers and sermon on Sundays. On 3rd April 1849, the Chaplain of Bedford Prison gave his report on to the Justices of the Peace who were assembled at the General Quarter Session. He expressed himself pleased with the conduct of the prisoners, which at the time included all three of our convicted men, Dockerill, George and William. The Chaplain also seemed delighted by the fact that his instruction in spiritual teachings did not appear to be in vain, citing the fact that prisoners sometimes returned books to him observing parallels between passages in the book and their own lives, thereby confirming that he or she had indeed studied their Scriptures and contemplated their meaning. Occasionally a prisoner would beg to be given a Bible on discharge from prison, so that he might study further on his return home. A less virtuous person than the Chaplain might have questioned the sudden conversion of his student from rogue to honourable citizen, and wondered if possibly the Bible might have been destined to be sold on, or to provide a little warmth on their meagre fires.[8]

Bedfordshire   *Report of the Chaplain of the Prisons*

in the said County, to Her Majesty's
Justices of the Peace. Assembled at their
General Quarter Sessions holden at
Bedford on 3rd of April 1849

My Lords and Gentlemen

I have the honour of submitting to you my Report for the last three months.

The Prisoners, committed during the last Quarter, have varied but little, as respects both mind & morals, from those that had preceded them. It is unnecessary therefore to detail their characteristics on the present occasion.

With the conduct of the Prisoners, as far as I have been conversant with them, I am glad to say I have had much reason to be pleased. No men could behave better than they did during the time of private instruction in my own room; & in the public services very seldom indeed was there cause of complaint.

The progress made by several in reading, writing, and scriptural knowledge, has been very considerable. And I am humbly of opinion there is reason for believing that in some instances the instruction has not been in vain. Very often, on the returning of a book, are observations made as to the application of certain passages to the history and condition of the reader, & the earnest hope expressed parental care that the truths thus made known to them might be attended with a blessing from on high. Occasionally, too, a Prisoner, when about to be discharged, begs to have a Bible to take home with him, adding that it is his intention to give practical heed to it in future. I have always a supply of Bibles in readiness to meet such gratifying requests as these. Many of these unhappy creatures might have been very different both in principle and practice, had they had in the days of their youth any thing like the admonition with which so many of their more privileged fellow creatures have been blessed. The early history of many a Prisoner is such as, if known, as it ought to be, would awaken the deepest & most compassionate interest in the hearts of those who can feel for the neglected & oppressed. I am humbly of opinion that under the Divine Blessing, much benefit may be expected to accrue to these poor creatures from the new system of Discipline, now so soon to come into operation.

I have only to add that the Schoolmaster having resigned, another had been appointed by the visiting Justices on the recommendation of the Chairman of the visiting Justices and myself. This person, William Mellows, I have been acquainted with for the last sixteen years; & Mr. (?), I have reason to think, has been acquainted with him for four & twenty. He is a man of great steadiness of character, & strictness of principle, & is said to possess an aptitude for teaching. There is ground to hope that the training he will have previous to the opening of the new Prison, will render him an efficient & valuable officer in that Institution.

I have the honour to be
My Lords and gentlemen
Your Most Obt. Servant
Geo. Maclear

(sic)

In his second report (overleaf) the Chaplain seems quite surprised by the lack of religious knowledge of his inmates, and in particular pays emphasis to the plight of a young lad of twelve years old who had been imprisoned for stealing gooseberries. He draws attention to the fact that this poor unfortunate, whose father had been sentenced to transportation before he was born, had been employed to watch sheep on the Sabbath, when he should have been learning his scriptures. He considered that had he been allowed the opportunity of doing so then he might have become 'a blessing to his fellow creatures and heir of immortal glory'. It did not seem to occur to him that the boy might have stolen the gooseberries because he was hungry.

Expansion of the gaol had become essential to house the increasing number of prisoners. Despite opposition, particularly from ratepayers who resented the cost, it was decided to proceed with the project. At the beginning of June, 1849, the justices wrote to the Home Secretary to request authorization for the removal of those convicts under sentence of transportation to Millbank penitentiary. But, because of problems housing them at Millbank, there was some delay and they were finally removed on 8th August, 1849.[11] The remaining prisoners were moved to the new house of correction. Possession of the empty gaol was handed over to the builder and on 6th October, 1849, the Home Office was informed that the new prison was completed. The new gaol was built to the same pattern as Pentonville, whereby each prisoner had their own cell in which they worked all day in solitary confinement, and each cell was equipped with its own water closet. Prisoners were allowed to leave their cell for exercise but they were kept separate by each being made to hold a knot in a rope, held taut between prisoners, each knot being fifteen feet apart. Now one hundred and fifty prisoners could be accommodated in separate cells, whereas previously, only fifty could be accommodated in separate sleeping cells, and one hundred and fifty in cells sleeping more than one prisoner.

Bedfordshire

Report of the Chaplain of the Prisons
In & for the said County, to her
Majesty's Justices of the Peace
Assembled at their General
Quarter Sessions holden at
Bedford on the 16th of October
1849

My Lords and Gentlemen,

In the Report which I have now the honour of submitting to you, I confine not my attention, as heretofore, to the Prisoners committed during the quarter immediately preceding, but extend it to the whole collective number, committed during the last twelve months. And in doing so, instead of any detailed description, I beg leave to lay before you three Tables, which will present a concise and comprehensive view of the Prisoners, in those aspects which appear to me of most importance. In regard to the two first Tables, it is not necessary for me to say any thing. They speak for themselves. But in relation to the third a few remarks may be advisable to prevent mistake. When, therefore, it is there marked that such a number could read, though very imperfectly, let it not be supposed that those poor creatures could read with any degree of intelligence. Far from it. They could not collect the meaning of the simplest verse in the Bible. When, too, a certain number, though comparatively very small, are represented as being able to read tolerably well, let it not be supposed that this small number had turned this faculty to any beneficial account, by rendering the medium of possessing their minds with the truths of Holy Writ (?). Any thing but that. With very, very few exceptions, they were as ignorant in this respect as those who were unacquainted even with the Alphabet. Indeed of the 688 Prisoners who were committed during the last year, only five or six possessed any knowledge of the leading facts of Scripture, & the great Truths of the Gospel. Of this melancholy state of things, my Character Book presents the most convincing & affecting evidence. Permit, my Lords and Gentlemen, to lay before you an extract of two from my private Character Book, in proof of these positions. "?.?" "age 15. read pretty well. Said, The Holy Ghost was the "Soul". "J. W.(?) age 32. School five years. "Baptised and Confirmed. Not been to any place of worship for seven years" "Ignorant of veriest elements of Scripture. Read Tom Pagres' "Age of Reason & Rights of Man. Habitual drunkard." "? ?" age 22. Fearfully ignorant. School, never. Repeat neither "Lords Prayer, Creed, nor Commandments. When asked to say The Lord's Prayer, he said, "Matthew, Mark, Luke & John, bless the bed that I lie on". Such is the condition of the vast majority of our Criminal population, on their first reception into Prison. And surely every effort ought to be made to remedy this lamentable state of things. I cannot resist the impulse to trouble you with one other extract, & especially because there is much reason to fear it is but one of very, very many such instances of Sore(?) Moral Wrong. "W.(?) F. age 12. In Prison for Stealing Gooseberries". "lamentably ignorant. Father transported. Says he went a little to a Sunday School, but not for the last twelve months." During last year, he has been employed by – to keep sheep on the roadside, on the Sunday."

Mark here, my Lords and Gentlemen, the Sore moral injustice inflicted upon this poor boy. Morally an orphan from his cradle, (for his father was transported shortly before he was born), the individual for whom he toiled, during six days of the week, not only exposed him to the temptations of the roadside, at those hours, when most people were attending Divine Worship, but cruelly robbed him of the only opportunity his poverty had left him, of learning to read those Scriptures, by imbibing whose spirit, he might have become a blessing to his fellow creatures, & an heir of immortal glory. These are deeds of cruel injustice, that surely every Christian man ought to discountenance, & as far as possible, prevent. In vain will you endeavour to repress crime & remove the evils that disturb society, by any form of Prison Discipline, however improved, except a simultaneous, vigorous, & well sustained effort be made, in dependence on the Divine Blessing, to impart to the poor of the land, as sound, scriptural, Christian education.

It is with the greatest pleasure, I am able to Report favourably, of the general conduct of the Prisoners, during the last year. When under instruction, both public & private, their demeanour was generally marked by decorum & attention. And many have expressed themselves as very thankful, for the expositions given them, both in class and in the Chapel. This instruction, there is reason to hope, has not been altogether in vain. I believe some have been, thereby, awakened to a sense of the importance of spiritual & eternal things. Of the Transports who were removed in July, two or three seemed to feel deeply, what an "evil & bitter thing it is, to live without God in the world", & professed if to be their fixed purpose to make the Scriptures their daily study, during the remainder of their days. Seven of those men took with them large Bibles, with Marginal References, which were procured for them with money, which they begged their friends to collect for them.

The Schoolmaster still continues to afford me the utmost satisfaction. He is a very valuable Officer, & possesses many attributes peculiarly important in his vocation, especially a remarkable aptitude for communicating information to poor people. He seems to aim, in all he does, to please Him who "tries the heart".

Now has come to its close, the old system, so to speak, of Prison Discipline in your County, to be replaced by another, which possesses, at least, one invaluable provision, that of complete separation. May your fondest and most sanguine expectations be thereby realized! And in order of this, may every officer imbibe the spirit of his office, & identify himself with its object. And above all, may the Divine Blessing largely attend it. But may I be permitted, humbly, & respectfully, to remind you, that the root of our Social evils, lies deeper than in any defects of Prison Discipline ?

I have the honour to be,
My Lords and Gentlemen,
Your faithful Servant,

Geo. Maclear

The Magistrates,
Bedfordshire.

(sic)

The number of Prisoners at present confined within the walls is as follows:-viz:-

Males 76

Female 5   -   81

They are thus divided:-

	Males	Females
For Trial	*21*	*1*
Convicted	*44*	
Want of sureties ..	*4*	*1*
Re Examination	*2*	
Bastardy		
Assaults	*1*	
Debtors	*2*	
Vagrancy	*2*	*3*
	76	*5*

The conduct of the whole has, during the brief period I have had charge of them, been submissive and orderly. They were not, at the time of my entrance to the Establishment subject of any work in their cells, the only labour imposed being the Treadwheel, and the Pumps; but as the former, from an inadequate force of Prisoners, had not for some time past been regularly worked; I felt it incumbent on me to provide suitable labour for them in their Cells, in compliance with the Prison regulations.

They were then employed on Oakum Picking, which is performed under task; and I have already perceived its value on the Prisoners, particularly that class who come under the Vagrant laws; or from Union Workhouses. It has not only been pronounced a healthful employment; but was considered a most degrading, salutary, and preventive punishment; and moreover possesses an advantage over other kinds of Prison Labor, from its not requiring so much of the Man's mental attention, as to deprive him of the means of moral instructions. Indeed I am disposed to consider it an incentive, than otherwise, to improvement of the mind. Thus by force of habit, induced by compulsion, the prisoners may be turned from idleness.........

Because of the influx of prisoners from the common gaol, the house of correction was greatly overcrowded so, without waiting for any approval from the Home Office, the justices moved the prisoners to the new building once it was completed. But in December, Captain Williams reported that during his inspection the cells were not sufficiently dry to justify being given a certificate. Despite Captain Williams' opinion, on 5th March, 1850, Whitehall sent to the justices a set of rules and regulations for their new establishment, signalling their approval.

Our two prisoners were to spend a total of five months in Bedford Gaol after their conviction. There is no record of any visits from their families whilst they were there, but they would not have been eligible as they had not served the qualifying time.

On the 7th August they were interviewed by the visiting magistrate, who, having been convinced of their contrition, wrote to the Home Secretary to recommend clemency. But that day was the last that they were to spend in Bedford Gaol, for before the reply came back from the Home Office, they were removed and transferred to their next place of internment. When the answer did arrive, it was not good news. Their application was refused.

224/13

Thomas Dockerill   29
George White   24
Bedford Lent Ass
March 1849

Shooting ?

Dockerill   –   Trans For Life
White   –   ditto   15 years

Gaol Rept. –   Dockerill Convicted before
                White – Char. Good

Nil. H.W.

One of the Visg. Mag. Redeemed the prisoners to favourable consideration on account of their contrition and good conduct in prison.

Ans. 16th August. 1849

Received. H.O. Aug.8 1849.

8514

Bedford County Gaol

7th August 1849

Sir,

On the removal of the Prisoners who have been sentenced to Transportation I beg to forward for your information the enclosed Memorial in favour of Jesse Fisher convicted of Horse Stealing.

I would at the same time venture to recommend for your consideration the case of George White as well as that of Thomas Dockerill, both convicted of feloniously and maliciously wounding with intent to resist their lawful apprehension – I am bound to say that these Prisoners appear to be deeply affected by the thought of their offence and the situation in which it has placed them; and their good conduct during the long period they have been in confinement has evinced, as far as one can judge, the sincerity of the repentance.

I have the Honour to be Sir

Your Obedient Servant

George P. Liv?

Visiting Magistrate[12]

CHAPTER 12

Millbank, Cholera and Shorncliffe

I
t was the normal procedure for prisoners under sentence of transportation to spend the first part of their sentence in the prison where they had been confined prior to their conviction, until the Secretary of State ordered their removal. Now that the authorities required the gaol at Bedford to be emptied so they could begin their alterations, they sought permission to remove them to Millbank Prison to begin the next stage of their sentence. Originally dated 15th June, 1849, this was finally given on 1st August, and carried out on 8th August, when along with thirteen other felons George and Dockerill were transferred to Millbank.[1]

> *H.S. Bedford* } *To Remove Wm Fenson, Jesse Fisher, Richd Hall, Wm Kifford, William King, George Brain, Jas Richardson, Chas O.Cortin(?), Reuben Dean, Wm Woodward, Wm Warner, Chas Smith, Geo White, Thos Dockerill, Wm Sinfield*

On their journey, they had the company of a fellow villager from Houghton Regis, one William Sinfield who had been convicted at Bedford Sessions on 3rd April, 1849 and sentenced to ten years for receiving stolen goods. William was twenty-nine years old, married with three children, and had a previous conviction for which he had received a sentence of seven years transportation.[2] Along with the men went their "caption papers" stating the date of their conviction, the offence, and the length of sentence.

The first sight of the grim exterior of Millbank Prison must have caused the prisoners' hearts to sink. Formerly named the Penitentiary, Millbank was a gloomy forbidding place built on the bank of the river Thames where the Tate Gallery now stands, the ground on which it stood raised just a little above the river. The prison building was based on the work of Jeremy Bentham who had in 1791 produced his ideas for prison management, a round prison with cells on the circumference facing a core at the centre where guards would sit and view all cells, thereby creating the appearance of constant surveillance. Bentham had been unable to secure funding for the prison, and the government took over the contract, completing it in 1821. This modified version was shaped like a six pointed star, the external walls built like a fortress enclosing more than sixteen acres of low, marshy land, seven of which was covered by the prison building itself. Despite enormous sums of money being spent to improve the drainage and improving the soil, and although it was kept scrupulously clean and well ventilated, the prison was still very damp and very unhealthy, due both to its locality and poor diet. It was the largest prison in England, with three miles of labyrinthine passages and winding staircases. One warder after years of service still marked the walls with chalk so that he did not lose his way.[3] The forbidding building could confine one thousand, two hundred prisoners in separate cells where the inmates, both male and female, sat despondently all day with nothing else to look forward to except the endless toil of making shoes and stitching mailbags. Every convict under sentence of transportation was sent there to serve that part of his sentence in solitary confinement before being transported. Here they remained for at least three months, at the end of which time the inspectors reported to the Home Secretary and recommended the place of transportation.[4] Their conduct was also carefully noted, with the most deserving receiving good-conduct badges to wear after they have been in prison a certain length of time. Although the majority of prisoners were in separate cells, there were some who

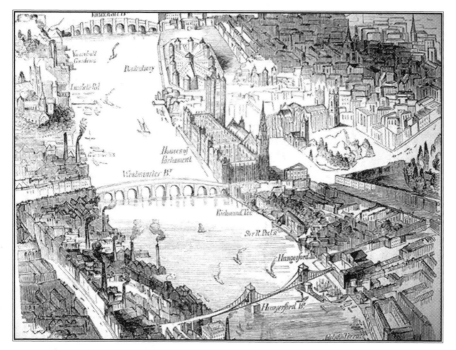

Millbank Prison on the bank of the Thames near the Houses of Parliament.

were allowed to work together under strict superintendence of the warders, in places such as the kitchen and bakehouse. The policy of reform by rigid rules, hard work, but mostly by religious influence was strictly enforced, so every prisoner was given religious instruction and attended chapel regularly.

Each of the six pentagons converged on the centre and had three floors with four wards on each floor. The first pentagon contained the reception ward where all prisoners were incarcerated in separate confinement. The second pentagon housed prisoners occupied in various trades, but still in separate cells. The third housed the female prisoners, mostly in solitary cells. In pentagon four was the infirmary, and both separate and communal accommodation. Pentagon five, in addition to the separate confinement cells, contained a general ward, consisting of four cells knocked into one, and every effort would be made to gain admission to

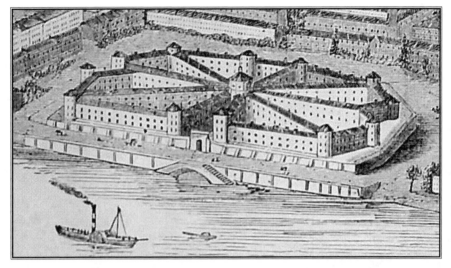

The imposing Millbank Prison. Prisoners were sent here to serve part of their sentence in solitary confinement before being transported.

this cell by those old lags eagerly seeking the company and conversation of their fellow inmates.

On their arrival, George, prisoner number 17732, and Dockerill, number 17733,[5] followed the same procedure observed by every prisoner. They were bathed, examined naked by the surgeon and placed in the reception ward before being allocated their cell for separate confinement for six months. George was taken to Pentagon 1, Ward 4, Cell 24. Dockerill to Pentagon 6, Ward 4, Cell 9. Their general description was entered into the surgeon's book together with any marks they might have on their body. Their hair was cut and the rules of the prison were read to them, the latter being repeated each week. The cells in this reception wing were situated down a long high passage and were about twelve feet long by seven feet wide. Each cell had a double door, the inner one being of wood and the outer of iron cross bars. The inner door was left open from 9am to 5pm so that the prisoner had some semblance of communication with the outside world, but any misdemeanour and this privilege was removed and the door bolted. Each cell had a hammock and a signal wand, which the prisoner could push through an aperture and so communicate his needs to the warder. There was also a ventilating aperture for the release of foul air. The cells in the second pentagon, instead of the hammock had an iron frame rested on two stone supports, or a board.

But now, after their admission to Millbank, George and Dockerill's fortunes were to take a separate path. For during 1849, the country was in the grip of an epidemic of Asiatic Cholera. Throughout the year, one by one, counties and institutions had succumbed to this dreadful disease. The town of Cardiff published its report of cholera cases and put up posters offering a reward to any persons giving information leading to conviction of those landing Irish passengers illegally.[6]

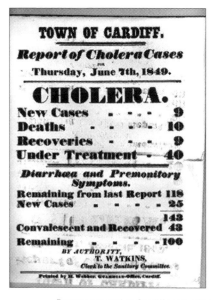 

Posters erected at Cardiff in an effort to combat the cholera outbreak.

The plight of the Irish, trying to escape starvation in their land, was a big problem to the authorities on the coast, as is seen by an extract from a letter at this time, the poor creatures heightening the concern of the cholera outbreak:

.........Cardiff is full of Irish lodging houses and every tide adds to the number of these poor wretched creatures who throng here. They are brought over in the Coal Vessels as live ballast to save port dues, and other similar interruptions to this odious domestic slave trade. The shippers make no provision for them and the roadside are covered by parties who are said to sleep under hedges and in ditches. Deaths from cold and want in the open fields and roadsides are frequent. This is the emergency which has to be met, and I promised the Committee of the Guardians to state the matter to the General Board of Health in order to have from it some decision as to the amount of accommodation which should be provided in the refuge. The number of beds judging from experience elsewhere need not exceed 100, but if the demands of these poor needy creatures were to increase.......[7]

Gaols sought to remove their inmates by transferring them to another prison, but as most other prisons in the country were affected, some applied for permission to release their prisoners early:[8]

The Visiting Magistrates of Hertford Gaol have the Honour to transmit to Sir George Grey a list of Persons, whose sentences will expire within the present or next month, and whose cases they submit for the consideration of Sir George Grey. – They feel it their Duty, however, to call his attention to the fact, that there are circumstances connected with the breaking out of Cholera within the Gaol, which, in the opinion of Dr. Davies, Surgeon to the Gaol, lead to the inference that it may be contagious, and they cannot but be alive to the danger of spreading the contagion, if there is contagion, through the different districts of the County, to which the Prisoners belong. –

They must, therefore, humbly submit the decision of this important subject to Sir George Grey, and if he shall, under the circumstances, not deem it impediment to remit the sentences of the Prisoners, the Visiting Magistrates most earnestly request that he will have the goodness to suggest some other move of relieving the overcrowded state of the Gaol, which is without doubt very much to be desired.

Another difficulty has occurred to the Visiting Magistrates, upon which they very much desire to have the direction of Sir George Grey –

The weekly commitments average about twenty – of which five are for trial. If the Disease should continue to rage, it would be manifestly improper to expose fresh Persons to the Danger – There is no other legal Place of Confinement within the County, over which the Visiting Magistrates have undisputed Authority, and it is doubtful whether they could under the 52 Clause of 4 Geo 4 @ : 64 – appoint any other place of Confinement, but those at present in existence – They wish, therefore, to be advised, whether they might remand such cases to the custody of the Police, until more satisfactory arrangements can be carried into effect – It will be recollected that the commitments for trial are made not to the Gaoler, but the Officer of the High Sheriff, who is responsible for their safe custody.

The Visiting Magistrates beg to remind Sir George Grey of the Interview which

Mr. Franks, one of their Body, had with him yesterday as the reason for this communication and to refer Sir George Grey to the Report of Capt Williams, the Inspector of Prisons, who will wait upon Sir George Grey with this minute.
Signed. ? Salisbury, William Franks, Charles ?, Thomas Mills

As a result of this appeal, the Secretary of State lost no time in granting a free pardon to some forty-three prisoners, releasing them from prison on 9th January, the same day that he received the plea. In June came another appeal from Gloucester gaol, where they reported several cases of cholera, that twenty-two male and four female convicts be removed to Millbank prison. But when the response came from the Home Office, it was not what they wanted to hear, for Millbank was full. There were already one thousand, two hundred and fifty male convicts in the prison and there were orders to receive one hundred and thirty more. And it was for the same reason that there was the delay in accepting prisoners from Bedford.

But, in spite of the fact that these gaols were turning to Millbank to offload their convicts, Millbank was not immune to the disease. For its part, London was playing host to a health hazard of tremendous proportions, the River Thames. This seemingly innocent scenic beauty was in actual fact an open drain of filth and debris. Into its sludgy depths was indiscriminately poured the excrement of society; household rubbish, sewage, refuse from knackers' yards and slaughter houses with a total disregard for hygiene, born out of ignorance. Into it, too, were discourteously tossed bodies of rotting flesh which only shortly before had been wept over in some overflowing graveyard, only to be dug up again by unscrupulous gravediggers once their grieving relatives had aborted their posts. Thereby their vacated resting place made way for another dearly departed who would eventually suffer a similar posthumous demise.

The health problem in this murky killer might be defused when diluted after a lot of rain, and the stench diminished briefly, but as fast as it cleared, it was filled up again. Thick black sludge oozed round the outfalls, and viscous scum covered the exposed banks at low tide.

This contaminated slime was the Londoners' drinking water. Naturally, the water used in the prison was also obtained from this ever flowing tap, and although it was filtered through sand and charcoal, and looked clear enough, it was in fact most unsanitary and contaminated, and led to periodic outbreaks of cholera.[9]

Cholera Cases London	Deaths	Under treatment	Recovery
16th July 1849	58	48	4
18th July 1849	72	52	24
19th July 1849	45	41	13
20th July 1849	45	43	2
21st July 1849	55	57	7
16th August 1849	112	120	11
21st August 1849	136	65	10
23rd August 1849	108	79	14
19th September 1849	48	35	7
21st September 1849	40	42	10

During that year of 1849, when George and Dockerill were transferred to Millbank, there were forty-eight deaths from cholera amongst the inmates, amounting to 4.3% of the average number of prisoners, a much higher rate than at other prisons where water was obtained from a different source.[10]

The advance of the symptoms of cholera was a terrible sight to behold, the unfortunate victims suffering firstly with diarrhoea and violent retching which increased in its intensity, with thirst and dehydration. Their skin took on a bluish-grey hue and was accompanied by severe pains in the limbs and stomach, by which time the progression was usually fatal. The bodies of those forty-eight prisoners who succumbed to the disease were buried in the small prison churchyard, but there were so many corpses that the authorities thought even the graveyard unhealthy. So after this, bodies of prisoners were buried at the Victoria Cemetery, Mile End. In the bleak prison graveyard of Millbank, there were no head stones for those poor wretches so stricken, no evidence of the grief and desolation of their mourners, no records which might have served as a memorial to disquiet the prison authorities, only the earthy mounds covered by an abundance of marigolds.

As a result of the cholera outbreak, permission was now sought to remove prisoners from Millbank, and on 16th July a warrant was issued appointing the barracks at Shorncliffe to be a place of confinement of male offenders under sentence of transportation, a military camp built in 1808 which stood high on a hill overlooking the village of Elham, near Folkestone in Kent.[11]

Warrant appointing the Barrack at Shorncliffe in the County of Kent a place for the confinement of Male Offenders under Sentence of Transportation	*Victoria R*
	     Whereas by an Act passed in the fifth Year of the Reign of His late Majesty George the 4th Intituled 'An Act for the Transportation of Offenders from Great Britain", It is among other things enacted that it shall be lawful for Us from time to time by Warrant under Our Royal Sign Manual to appoint places of confinement within England and Wales, either at Land or on board Vessels to be provided by Us, in the River Thames or some other River, or within the limits of some Port or Harbour of England & Wales for the confinement of Male Offenders under Sentence of transportation.
	     Now We do by Virtue of the said Act hereby appoint the Barrack at Shorncliffe in the County of Kent, to be a place for the confinement of Male Offenders under Sentence of Transportation, under and according to the Provisions of the before Mentioned Act - Given at Our Court at St. James the Sixteenth day of July 1849 in the thirteenth Year of Our Reign.
	                     By H.M. Command
	                               G. Grey

A further warrant was issued on 17th July to the Governor of Millbank Prison authorizing the removal of three hundred and thirty-nine convicts to Shorncliffe.[12]

The Governor of Millbank Prison	*Sir* *Whitehall, 17 July 1849*
	     I do hereby Authorize and require you to cause the Male Convicts named in the Margin and on the other side hereof, now under sentence of Transportation in the Millbank Prison to be removed therefrom to the Barrack at Shorncliff in the County of Kent, which has been appointed by H.M to be a place for the confinement of Male Offenders under sentence of transportation pursuant to the Act of the 5 Geo 4 Cap 84
	                         (?) G. Grey

Still the threat of cholera persisted, and more warrants were issued, one on 15th August for the removal of another twenty-eight men to Shorncliffe by G. Grey, and one by Palmerston for the removal of one hundred and sixty-six convicts. George was one of those selected to be evacuated there.

The transfer of these prisoners caused much concern among the local residents of Folkestone and Sandgate who were worried about the spread of the disease, and the presence of the convicts so near, but assurances were made that only the healthiest would be sent.

July 1849 Maidstone & South Eastern Gazette.
500 Prisoners sent to Shorncliffe Camp

CONVICTS – Much anxiety has been felt during the past week by the inhabitants of Folkestone and Sandgate, at the report that 500 convicts from Millbank Penitentiary were to be located at Shorncliffe barracks on account of the increase in cholera at that prison. Upon enquiry, we find that there are no grounds whatsoever for alarm, as only the most healthy of the convicts will be brought here. About 100 arrived by special train on Saturday morning last at Coolinge Bridge near Folkestone, and were marched off to the barracks which had been prepared for their reception, under the superintendence of Capt. GROVE, the governor of the Millbank Penitentiary. The barracks are situated on an eminence, and entirely isolated. A more healthy spot could not be selected.

In spite of these assurances, there is evidence that cholera was indeed found amongst those transferred. Prison records show that a young lad of seventeen years old, John Howells, serving his first sentence for breaking and entering a shop, died of cholera at Shorncliffe Barracks on 11th September, 1849. Convicts were still being transferred to Shorncliffe into 1850, forty on 7th January and one hundred on 24th January. A further fifty-six were sent on 22nd February.[13]

Shorncliffe Barracks, appointed a temporary place of confinement for prisoners.

Meanwhile, Dockerill, who was not fortunate enough to be one of those evacuated, was to serve almost a year in Millbank. From the reception wing he was taken to his first cell, for he was to move four times during his incarceration there.[14] The cell was 8ft square, and was all made of stone, the walls, ceiling and floor. In the outside facing wall there was a heavily barred window, into which light mocked its inhabitant. Dockerill now wore the Millbank uniform, a grey jacket, brown trousers with a thin red strip in the fabric, a blue cravat also with narrow brick coloured thread and a grey cap.

Prisoners were made to produce various commercial items; this meant to serve as a punishment whilst developing an appreciation of labour. Most of the work carried out in Millbank was tailoring; they made clothing for most of the public works prisons, Portland, Pentonville, Dartmoor, Portsmouth, for the Hulks, and for the Navy. Some were employed shoemaking, but generally only if that was their trade. Others picked coir, but mostly this was by those with no trade, or if they were suicidal, so that they had no tools with which they could harm themselves. But there were also wards where blacksmiths, carpenters, masons etc. were employed.

On 2nd April, 1850, Dockerill's wife, Rebecca, was allowed to pay him a visit in the prison.15 It would appear that she made the visit alone, as hers is the only name in records. This was probably the first time that poor Rebecca had made such a journey to London, maybe by stagecoach, but possibly by train and the last part by river, which would have given her a first memorable view of the forbidding building of yellow-brown brickwork against a softer backdrop of Vauxhall Bridge, its open iron work embellishing its arches. It was certainly a different world than she was used to, that of her narrow village life. Maybe she wondered at the houses of the upper class as she tramped over the cobbles of the London streets, where inside the portly figures sat devouring their multi-coursed, multi-choice meals and quaffing their ale, oblivious to this poor woman, heart gladdened at the prospect of seeing her husband, but anxious too at her daunting task.

As she approached the prison, signs of the moat which once surrounded it would still have been visible, the earth with which it had now been filled yielding a crop of rank grass adding a gloomy atmosphere to this already forbidding vista. The entrance from the street was an austere and imposing vision of architectural offence. Firstly, a dark solid archway and from this, the expectation of forthcoming hopeless depression was heightened by the mighty portcullis spear-pointed, ready to sever the unfortunate convict from the outside world. Inside the archway, the great iron gate shadowed the pacing armed warder.

Though probably apprehensive of this censuring exterior, Rebecca would have been spurred on by the thought of seeing her husband after so long. Once her summons was answered by the gatekeeper by the outer door, she was ushered into the small triangular hall. If her nervousness allowed her to take the time to look around she would have seen stairs leading to the gatekeeper's rooms, and a table in front, on which stood letter boxes like the poor boxes in churches, one each for male and female officers, one for Clerk of the Works, and one for prisoners. From the hall she had to cross the gravelled outer yard of the prison, between the first and sixth pentagons, to the barred inner gate where the gatekeeper entered her name into a record book. Once these formalities were completed, Rebecca was allowed to see her husband. This was probably the first time she had seen him since he stood in the dock next to her brother and nephew. Perhaps in her joy at being re-united with him she could ignore his white prison-ravaged face. For there is no doubt that Rebecca loved her errant husband.

Millbank Prison records showing George White and Thomas Dockerill. *PCOM 230/113004*

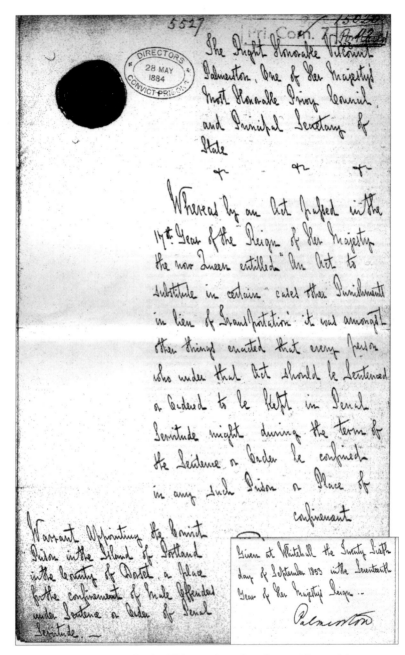

Warrant appointing Portland Prison a place of confinement for convicts.

CHAPTER 13

Portland Gaol

On 5th July, 1850, a warrant was issued instructing the Governor of Millbank prison to remove twenty-eight convicts to Portland Gaol.[1] Portland was a penal service institution on the south coast housing some one thousand, five hundred convicts from all parts

Warrant for removal of prisoners, including Thomas Dockerill, from Millbank to Portland Prison. *TNA HO15/1* of Britain who were generally serving the second stage of their sentence on public works, having spent the first stage at a prison specially modelled for solitary confinement where it was hoped this period of isolation had enabled them to truly repent of their crimes without the bad influence of others. On 9th July, Dockerill bid a thankful farewell to the sinister Millbank when he and twenty-seven of his fellow inmates were transferred to Portland,[2] where he became prisoner no. 1569.[3]

A month later on Saturday 10th August, 1850, the prisoners were employed in their usual capacity in the quarries outside the prison. The weather, which had started off dreary, got progressively worse and as the evening was so wet they were called in from their labour early, at 5pm. During that day twenty-one new prisoners had arrived from Pentonville, but the Governor was somewhat vexed as these were not all he was expecting. Eventually during that evening, through the driving rain, the next consignment climbed slowly up the hill, the sound of their chains reaching their fellow sinners as the great gates were thrown open to devour this sodden assemblage of new arrivals. Of the seventy-three of this latest assortment of criminal disrepute, sixty-three were from Millbank, and ten were from Shorncliffe. It was 9pm before they were finally distributed through the halls and the Governor felt himself much inconvenienced by their late arrival. One of the prisoners taking in his new surroundings, after spending a year in Shorncliffe Camp, was no.1710, George White.[4] George and Dockerill were once more re-united in their common incarceration. Now, for them both, their period of solitary confinement was over, and the second phase, that of public works, had begun.

Portland Island on which the gaol was built was not an island at all but a peninsula and gained the term from the fact that travel to the island was by ferry from Weymouth across the stretch of water known as Portland Roads. The neck of land which joined Portland to the mainland was but a mound of treacherous shingle.

The gaol itself was built on top of a precipitous escarpment of stone, and even in the summer months this austere building was often eerily

View of Chesil Beach from the convict quarries.

engulfed in low cloud and sea mist. But on a clear day, almost as if a deriding contrast to the forbidding view of stone walls which the prisoners inside endured, once outside there was a splendid vista of the Channel and over to Cherbourg. Weymouth and its promenades were on one side, and below, gently riding the waves, lay the majestic sailing ships at anchor in the bay. Occasionally one would sail in, its magnificence a mockery to the inmates of the prison, soon to be subjected to the grim conditions that her welcoming hulk would provide for her human cargo. For this was a convict transport ship, ready to take on board the unhappy inmates who would shortly say goodbye to England for the last time, a miserable group of rogues who would be shackled and then shuffle unwillingly to their fate. Thereby, they were easily dismissed by the authorities whose indifference was tempered only by relief, the poor wretches thus relegated to the ranks of the forgotten by all except their grieving families.

Upon their reception in Portland, Dockerill and George followed the same procedure undergone at previous prisons. Each was given a full medical inspection, and then made to bathe. Next was a change of clothes – an outfit consisting of fustian, over which a blue smock frock with white stripes was thrown. Those convicts who had misbehaved or tried to escape were made to wear a more distinctive dress, a coat of more striking character instead of the smock frock.[5] They were then instructed in the rules and regulations of the prison and examined in their educational abilities, so that they might be given their correct classification. There were four of these, each class earning payment according to his ability. This payment was kept for the convict and paid to him partly when he reached his destination of transportation, and partly when he received his conditional pardon.

From Jebb, 45 Parliament St. to H. Waddington. 13/06/1849
PRO HO45/2954

Rules for Portland Prison

No Prisoner during the period of his Confinement or Employment on Public works has any claim to wages or Remuneration of any kind, but as a reward for Industry and good conduct, certain ? gratuity will be credited to deserving men of such an amount and under such Regulations, as may from time to time be established. –
The amount of the Gratuity will depend on the Class in which a Prisoner may be placed, but as far as possible opportunities will be afforded for gaining an additional amount for extra exertion or work.-
The Gratuity according to classes will for the ? be as follows

1st Class per week	9d
2nd Class per week	6d
3rd Class per week	4d

The cases of Prisoners in the Infirmary or otherwise incapacitated by accident from going to work to be specially considered.
Prisoners misconducting themselves or under punishment forfeit all advantages. –
A Prisoner by Extra Exertion will be eligible to be recommended ? Gratuity from 3d to 6d per week in addition or for any less ? according to circumstances. –
The amount placed to a Prisoners Credit will be transmitted to the Governor of the Colony to which the Prisoner may be removed and the payment will be afterwards advanced to the Prisoner under certain restrictions or be otherwise ? to his benefit as may be considered desirable.

Following this they received an appropriate address from the chaplain and were allowed to write a letter to their relations.[6] After these preliminaries, they were taken to their allocated cell which contained a hammock and all that was required for personal cleanliness. Each cell

DESCRIPTION OF GOOD CONDUCT BADGES WORN BY THE PRISONERS.

EXPLANATION

This Badge indicates that the Wearer has been sentenced to 10 Years Tranportation. Has been 8 Months in Prison and that his conduct has been "Good" 6 of them.

EXPLANATION

This Badge indicates that the Wearer has been sentenced to 12 Years Transportation. Has been 8 Months in Prison and "Very Good" all the time.

EXPLANATION

This Badge indicates that the Wearer has been sentenced to Transportation for 15 Years. Has been 2 Months in the Prison and "Good" all the time.

NOTE A Prisoner is not entitled to the V.G. or "Very Good" until he has been 3 Months in Prison.

EXPLANATION

This Badge indicates that the Wearer has been sentenced to Life. Has been 24 Months in the Prison and "Very Good" the whole time.

NOTE The Badge is worn on the Left Arm, is made of Black Leather with an edge of Red Cloth, the upper Figure is of Red Cloth and the moveable slip of White Moleskin stamped with Black Letters.

Size of the Badges 5" x 3" Circles 1" in diameter

Good conduct badges at Portland Prison.

opened on to a corridor in a sleeping block which was light and well ventilated. The sleeping blocks were three or four storeys high and could contain from one to five hundred men.[7]

The prisoners' day began at a quarter-past five when they were roused by the prison-bell. An hour was allowed for washing, dressing and breakfast which consisted of 12oz. of bread and one pint of tea or cocoa. Breakfast over, they attended morning service in the chapel, a fine building that could hold fifteen hundred men. After their daily spiritual guidance, the men collected in the yard in gangs of fifteen

Convicts at work in the quarries on Portland.

to thirty men to be searched by their appointed officer to see that
they had nothing hidden. He also examined their number to see that
it was in order. Each gang would then march through the gate, the
officer calling out the number of the gang, and the number of men it
contained to the chief officer, who entered it in his book.[8] Under the
charge of their respective officers, each gang was then marched off to
work. Being young and able-bodied, George and Dockerill would either
have been employed in quarrying stones for the breakwater below, or

above and right Convicts at work in the quarries on Portland.

in constructing the enormous barricades and fortifications which the Government had ordered as a defence for that part of the world. There were two types of quarries on Portland, the Government ones and the private ones. The former, in which the convicts were employed, were 300ft above sea-level on the east side of the island. The convicts had to work hard, for the contractor depended on them for the supply of stone that was sent down the tramway to the breakwater,[9] but most of the men at Portland had been accustomed to hard labour all their lives.

The convicts remained at their various tasks until eleven, when they returned for dinner which consisted of 1 pint of soup, 5½ oz. of meat, 1lb. of potatoes, and 6oz. of bread or pudding. At half-past twelve they were again paraded, and dismissed to labour until six. Supper, consisting of 9oz. of bread and 1 pint of gruel or tea, was distributed to each cell at half-past six, and at seven evening service was held once more in the chapel. The prisoners then returned to their cells where they were allowed a book from the library. In winter-time their labour finished at half-past four, prayers were read at five, and supper was served at six, after which the prisoners returned to their cells.[10] Lights were extinguished at eight and silence reigned, broken only by the footsteps of the night guards.

Prison diet was strictly controlled, although it is shown from the Governor's Journals that some effort was occasionally made to humanise the circumstances. On 9th August, 1850 he wrote that the Medical Officers had recommended a prisoner named William Browning, reg. No. 1489, should have extra diet in consequence of his large frame. The Governor referred the question to the Directors, considering that the rules gave the Medical Officers the power of altering, but not increasing, the diet of a prisoner who was not under medical treatment. He also considered that giving way on such grounds to the craving of the prisoner's appetite was likely to produce many similar applications and cause discontent among other prisoners.[11] Interestingly it would appear that the Medical

Officers were allowed to decrease but not increase prisoners' diet. There is no mention of the outcome of William Browning's application, but it would seem apparent from the Governor's comments that it was not successful.

Prisoners who were less able-bodied were employed in mending clothes, or making shoes, in baking, or brewing, carpentry or making tools. Some were also needed in the school-room, or other offices necessary in such an enormous establishment.[12]

On Sundays, they would attend chapel and walk in the open air, and each prisoner was allowed half a day's schooling per week. But never far away was the threatening presence of a sentry standing near with loaded gun ready to shoot an absconder if necessary.

There is no doubt that Dockerill would have welcomed George's arrival at Portland and that they were both glad to be in each other's familiar company once more, even though this was restricted to their workplace. Whilst there, they would have been able to talk together, as it was impossible for the authorities to prevent it. It had been some eighteen months since their trial, and a year since their common removal from Bedford to Millbank prison. But their undoubted pleasure would have been diffused by the knowledge that their transfer to Portland meant that their transportation would soon take place, and therefore their reunion would be short lived. For although they might have hoped that they would be transported together, it was unlikely that this would happen. But until that day came, George and Dockerill could enjoy this brief respite, coming as a welcome relief after the separate incarceration already suffered. For George, too, it was a chance to catch up on news from home, Dockerill having received a visit from Rebecca, George's sister, not long before whilst he was in Millbank. As for the future, all they had to look forward to now was the final stage of penal servitude in the colony to which they were transported.

It is certain that both men wrote, or had somebody write, to their families to let them know that they had been removed to Portland, and would therefore shortly be transported. There is later evidence that

Dockerill did write and receive letters from Rebecca when he was allowed to do so. George must have known when his departure was imminent, for he received a visit from his brother, John, on 14th December of that year, 1850. This was not an easy journey for John to undertake, so he must have had a special reason to do so, which must have been to say goodbye forever to his young brother. After a somewhat gruelling journey to Weymouth, the passage in one of the numerous steamers which plied between Weymouth and Portland

The track up the cliff to the prison.

normally took half an hour. The principal entrance to the gaol was reached after a climb of another half an hour up the steep hill and once at the top, the bell rung to signify his arrival and his letter of introduction handed though a window. His name was then entered into a book by a janitor, who sat in a wooden cage. Only after all these formalities were undertaken was he was allowed to see his brother.

Both brothers must have known that this was to be the last time they would see each other, and that in fact it would be the last time that George would see any member of his family. John made the journey alone, for there is no record of any other visitor accompanying him. It is almost certain that John gave George a sum of money to take with him as the brothers said their final farewells. It is recorded that George had with him the amount of £3 1s 2d on his arrival in his new land, with only £1 of this coming from prison earnings, the rest being personal money.[13] Compared with that of other convicts, it was a large amount. There were probably other goods from the rest of his family, but unfortunately there was nothing else recorded.

It can only be surmised as to what emotional conversation took place

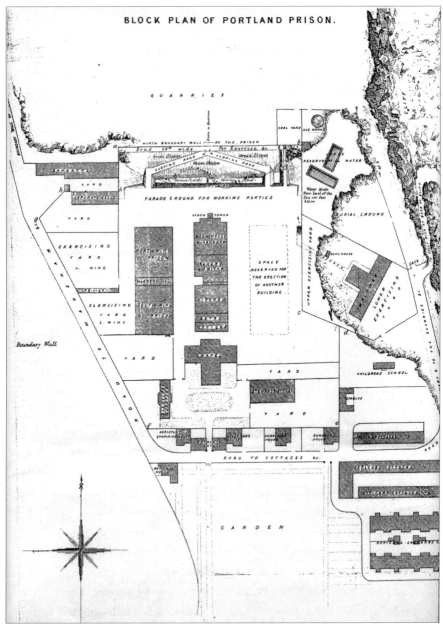

Proposed plan of Portland Prison showing the cliff path taken by John from Folly Pier at base of cliff.

No.	Name
1539	William Thompson
1541	John Cooke
1545	John Stayner
1546	Matthew Smith
1547	George Draws
1548	William Calahou
1549	Charles Barriton
1550	Bullough Bullough
1555	William Bailey
1560	Benjamin Foggatt
1563	James Harris
1564	Henry Priest
1565	Thomas Brown
1604	John Peace
1605	Robert Fergus
1606	Robert Dixon
1607	William Smith
1608	Charles Brooks
1662	John Wood
1678	James Hamilton
1687	William Clark
1688	Daniel McDonald
1690	John Melhuish
1691	John Reeks
1692	Phillip Dixon
1693	Richard Barry
1695	Job Weston
1696	George Clamp
1698	Alexander Fegan
1700	Alexander Anderson
1703	Joseph Brindley
1710	George White
1711	George Mann
1712	Henry Playfer
1713	George Westwood
1714	Thomas Ryder

True Copy of List signed by the Convicts

Cash list of prisoners at Portland transported on the Mermaid convict ship. The list shows that George White had the sum of £3. 1s. 2d. *ACC 128/26*

The breakwater at Portland, for which the prisoners quarried stone.

between the two brothers as they met again for the final time. George would have been eager for all the news of his family, and his baby daughter, Eliza, who by now was over two years old.

But John did not have good news for George from home. For George's wife, Sarah, was four months into her pregnancy by Thomas Inns, the man with whom she was now living. Even if she had wished, she certainly could not have made the journey to say her goodbyes to her husband, but poor Sarah must have already closed her heart to him when he was convicted, for she would have had little choice than to find somebody to support her and her baby, Eliza, who was only four months old when her father was taken.

In any event, George had nothing to prevent him from making a completely fresh start in his new country.

CHAPTER 14

Western Australia and the Transport System

T he 1700s heralded an era of exploration and great discovery for Great Britain and other European nations with whom great rivalry existed in the building up of trading empires. For trade could make the difference between a rich nation and a poor one, and Great Britain could boast some of the most prosperous merchants in Europe. Expeditions sailed the seas searching for new lands with which to trade, or better still, conquer, and once they had taken possession of these, they sought to colonize them. It was during this time that Great Britain saw the reformation of the penal system and the answer to the problem of both overcrowded gaols and a labour shortage in the new colonies. It was the dawning of the transportation system to Australia.

For the working class people, life in general was the worst it had been since the Middle Ages with thousands unemployed and starving. To feed their large families, they poached and many turned to crime. They had little choice. The increase in crime was enormous, and the upper classes, concerned about this lawlessness, looked for ways to protect themselves. The Government, which naturally consisted of these upper classes, drew up new laws. Up to this time there was no mercy shown – there was no difference made between a man convicted of murder and one convicted of stealing a morsel of food to feed his family. Both were sentenced to die and were hung. But people began to protest about so many executions, so instead those convicted were sent to prisons which were vastly overcrowded and conditions appalling, cells were unbearably cramped, filthy and stinking. Prisoners were hungry and ragged, vermin flourished, and disease was rife.

Great Britain needed more men in the navy and the army and to work in the dockyards, so a number of convicts were pardoned on condition that they enlisted. But transportation too was popularly used by the courts as a form of punishment. At one time they were sent to America, and by 1775 there were thirteen British colonies there, but upon the declaration of independence in 1776 America refused to take more convicts and other destinations were sought.

Old ships were already being used to store coal and gunpowder, and, assuming that the need was only temporary, it was decided that they could also be made into prisons, and the convicts they contained put to work on hard labour. Parliament agreed to this, and in 1776 authorized the use of hulks for the period of two years. They were to last for eighty-

Prisoners on board a hulk.

The Warrior, a prison hulk moored at Woolwich.

two.[1] The masts were cut off, and the hulks were anchored along the banks of the Thames at Woolwich, and in harbours such as Portsmouth. Conditions in prisons might have been bad, but the hulks were worse. On these, they were terrible, badly ventilated, cold, damp and even more crowded. At one stage over two thirds of all prisoners were incarcerated on the hulks. During outbreaks of disease such as cholera, large numbers of prisoners died because of the insanitary conditions and the use of water for all purposes from the polluted Thames. During the day, prisoners were ferried out to work on hard labour along the river and back at night, when they were chained to their bunks to prevent them from escaping ashore. But still the jails overflowed.

There had been favourable reports of housing a colony at Botany Bay in Australia – from there escape would be difficult, but at this time the

Commons Committee were favouring incarceration in penitentiaries in England with prisoners kept in solitary confinement on hard labour. But as crime increased, conditions in British jails worsened and grew more cramped, and the government decided to begin transportation again. After considering various sites for their convicts, Gambia, South Africa, Madagascar, Algiers and the West Indies, they decided on New South Wales, and the first fleet of convicts was sent there in 1787. Once there, the prisoners were assigned to 'masters' who were, in effect, in control of their life. Other penal settlements followed and they became the destinations for the most hardened criminals. But not always. Amongst those transported were four hundred and sixty-four agricultural labourers, not hardened criminals, but ordinary men sent to Australia after riots in the winter of 1830/1. The majority of these men were married, and they were older than those normally sent. Only a little less than a quarter of them had been convicted before, and that was generally for minor offences such as poaching. Most of these unfortunates were sent to Van Diemen's Land.

Meanwhile in England, the whole system of transportation was being questioned. During the Napoleonic wars, despite bad harvests and distress, crime did not seem to be such an urgent problem as it had been or as it was subsequently to become. Convict labour was greatly required in the dockyards, and prisoners could be handpicked for selection in the Army and Navy. But a rise in crime at the end of the French Wars caused a further shortage of prison accommodation; there were so many prisoners with such long sentences that the jails were overflowing. To solve the problem of overcrowding the courts began to sentence more prisoners to transportation. Despite much debate on reformation of the prison system in the early 1800s, this was still the favoured method of dealing with the criminal classes as it was cheaper than building new gaols. And if it did not deter crime, at least it got rid of its perpetrators.[2] In 1823 an act allowed the use of convict labour in any colony of the King's determination, so up to four hundred were sent to Bermuda on hard labour in the dockyard with a further two hundred in 1827.[3]

From Illustrated London News

The principal islands of the Bermudas consisted of Long Island (chief town Hamilton, the seat of Government), St. George's, and Ireland Island; the latter was a mass of fortifications, principally erected by convict labour under the supervision of the Royal Sappers and Miners. Ireland Island contained a spacious dockyard and arsenal, and a large "camber", capable of containing the largest ships of the line. In this camber convict hulks were moored, the Dromedary, Thames, Coromandel and Tenedos.

The convicts commenced work on the breakwater and fortifications in 1824, quarrying and cutting stone. At their completion it was understood that the convicts were to be withdrawn, it not being intended to make Bermuda a penal settlement, but by 1848 the number of convicts confined at the Bermudas averaged about one thousand, six hundred. All were employed on Public Works except those incapacitated by illness, or the few who were best behaved and qualified who were employed on board their respective hulks as clerks, cooks, servants, carpenters, shoemakers etc. For this labour every man was paid by the Board of Ordnance three pence per diem ; one penny of which he was at liberty to expend in the purchase of the cheap luxuries of the colony, and the remaining two-thirds of his earnings were reserved by the overseers, to be given to him on his liberation.

Bermuda's climate was very healthy, but occasionally an outbreak of yellow fever occurred; during 1843, a great number of soldiers, convicts and civilians died from the disease.

The dress of the convicts consisted of a frock and trousers of white duck, (with the name and number of the prisoner conspicuously marked thereon), straw hat, shoes, cotton shirt, and drawers; the latter articles being necessary to absorb the excessive perspiration engendered by exposure to the rays of a tropical sun.

Rules for the guidance and observance of the convicts were, until the year 1844, very lax; but owing to a mutinous outbreak on board the

THE CONVICT DRESS AT BERMUDA.

The convict dress on Bermuda.

Thames hulk, and the subsequent escape of twelve prisoners to the United States of America, the regulations became more stringent and the punishment then inflicted on the convicts for crimes committed on board the hulks, or on the public works, varied with the nature of the offence; stoppage of pay, solitary confinement, being placed in heavy irons, and flogging, being the usual inflictions.

No overseer was permitted to inflict more than five dozen lashes at one time without an order from the Governor of Bermuda (Captain C. Elliot, R.N.), who was ex officio the superintendent of convicts.[4]

In 1837 the young Queen Victoria came to the throne and with her a new reign of hope began. New ways of dealing with criminals were considered. Already the number of crimes punishable by hanging had been reduced, and penalties for more petty crimes were lessened. Conditions in prisons had improved in that criminals were divided into groups in prison, those awaiting trial, the hardened criminals, and those in prison for the first time. Now people began to criticise the system of transportation. Different people had different ideas, the cost of building new prisons to house those with shorter sentences against the cost of sending them to Australia.

The anti-transportation league found a champion in Sir William Molesworth, a member of the House of Commons, who persuaded his colleagues to form a Select Committee to examine the facts of transportation and to determine what was to be done. The Committee concluded that transportation did not work very well, and that it did not deter people from committing crime. They recommended that transportation in its present form, that is the assignment of convicts to masters, should be abolished, and replaced by gang labour on public works. They were firstly to be isolated in places where there were no free settlers, by so doing the settlers would be protected from the convicts.

But even then, the assignments system had it supporters, it being economically viable, cheap and easy to conduct even taking into account that paid overseers were difficult to obtain.[5]

Bearing in mind that four thousand convicts who were sentenced to

Sir William Molesworth.

Lord John Russell.

transportation every year had to be disposed of somewhere, Lord John Russell, the Home Secretary, made his proposals. They were that transportation would continue for long term convicts who would be sent to Van Diemen's Land. An experimental penitentiary to house a thousand men would be built in England, an experimental project would be carried out on Norfolk Island, more men would be sent to Bermuda, and more would be kept on the hulks in England.[6] In fact the hulks were being used more and more as holding prisons for men waiting to be transported. It was also decided that every male convict would work out the initial term of his sentence on hard labour in public works such as road building.

Then in 1839 Parliament decided to stop transportation to New South Wales, but not to Van Diemen's Land. By this time, New South Wales had become somewhat successful and well developed and it was considered a desirable place for free settlers. Not only did those settlers object to the immoral influence of the convicts, but it was considered that it was no longer a punishment for the criminals to be sent there. So more and more were sent to Van Diemen's Land. The last convict ship to sail for New South Wales for the present time arrived in Sydney on 18th November, 1840.

By the time the third Earl Grey took over as Secretary of State, other outlets were being sought in which to deposit convicts to relieve the financial burden on Van Diemen's Land. The Ionian Islands, Table Bay, New Brunswick and Nova Scotia were approached, but each refused, citing excuses such as "costing too much", by authorities in Corfu, to being "distasteful to every class in the community", by those in Nova Scotia.[7] Earlier in his career, Grey had expressed his misgivings about the costs of building new prisons in England, so he was opposed to long imprisonment in England and in favour of an 'exile' system. The prison authorities heartily concurred. They wanted to get rid of as many convicts as possible. Grey considered that if they were distributed throughout the colonies, the benefits of their labour force to the communities would outweigh the social disadvantages. As a sweetener to those colonies he proposed that an equal number of free emigrants would be sent, along with the wives and families of those convicts who were well-behaved. He favoured the Australian Colonies in that they had the advantage of distance; it would be difficult from there to return to England.

So the system of transportation would now be classified into three categories. 'Separate confinement' in prison for the first part, followed by a term of penal labour, and then 'assisted exile' to the colonies. The

Her Majesty's Cabinet Ministers, Earl Grey and Sir George Grey.

suggestion was that only those deserving convicts would be sent as a reward for their good behaviour, not as part of their punishment but as a security against them falling into crime again. Once in their place of exile they would receive a conditional pardon and would have payment for their passage deducted from their earnings.[8] So now the convicts were to pay for their transportation. On 5th March, 1847, Grey addressed the House of Lords with his proposals.

Later in 1847, under this new system, volunteers were sought for exile from amongst those on board the hulks who had served a period of time on public works, with a view to granting them their ticket of leave on arrival in Australia. Not surprisingly there was no shortage of convicts volunteering, considering that the conditions they could expect in their new land were infinitely preferable to those endured on board the hulks. They could look forward to their freedom in exile, on condition that they did not return to England. So Grey seemed to have found the solution to ridding himself permanently of the convicts, and never mind what happened at the end of the voyage, just as long as it was not on his doorstep. With Grey's assurances that his 'reformed' ticket of leave convicts would be of great advantage to the colonies, New South Wales agreed to take more consignments of convicts who had 'undergone some portion of their punishment'. They were also assured that their families would be sent out 'whenever their conduct should be such as to entitle them to the indulgence', and that an equal number of free emigrants would be sent at the cost of the British Treasury, 'still further to guard against the social evils which have heretofore resulted from....transportation'.[9] With the supply of labour still short in New South Wales, the scheme looked attractive, but was agreed to only on the understanding that the equal number of free emigrants and the men's wives and families were sent with them.[10] Grey however had second thoughts, and without a thought that this might be considered a breach of faith, he sent a letter in September 1847 informing them that he would send out convicts without migrants whilst waiting for further advice from them.

Report from Bedford Times 25th December 1847.

FREE CONVICTS FOR NEW SOUTH WALES

The Elphinstone, hired barque, dropped down the river yesterday to moorings opposite the Royal Arsenal to receive on board convicts from the Warrior and Justitia convict hulks at Woolwich, who have voluntarily preferred proceeding to New South Wales, where they will, on landing, obtain free tickets, with the opportunity of following any plan they may choose to adopt in that country for an honest subsistence, on condition that they do not return to this country again. The convicts under sentences here for long periods appear very glad to accept the stipulated conditions, and numbers have volunteered, and are now having each two suits of plain clothes made for them without any of the convict badges attached, and these clothes will be given to them on their embarkation. Two other vessels have been hired to convey convicts to the same destination, and are at present taking stores at Deptford. A new series of regulations is to be adopted relative to the convicts who will remain in this country, and the alteration will take place at the commencement of the new year. The free-ticket system must be a source of prospective hope to many of that unfortunate class, and it is far preferable for them to commence a new life in a distant land than be discharged here as one was last week, who, having no friends and being reluctant to return to his native place, is still about Woolwich nearly penniless, having soon expended the savings made while he was a convict – Times'

However, despite Grey's decision to abolish transportation by calling it exile, he did not delude the authorities in Australia for long, before New South Wales woke up to the fact that convicts, whatever they might be called, were still arriving. Grey's system and broken promises aroused ill feeling and mistrust in the colonies, but not before five ships with one thousand, four hundred and five convicts had arrived.[11]

By this time it was free assisted migrants who were seeking work

Meeting at Cape Town to oppose the introduction of convicts into the colony.

in New South Wales, and they had no desire to have to compete with the convict classes. Few of the convicts had a skilled trade, so many employers were inclined to favour more immigrants than convicts to relieve the shortage of skilled workers. On 11th June, 1849 a mass gathered at Circular Quay in Sydney in the pouring rain to demonstrate against the 'beautiful waters of their harbour' being polluted with 'a ship freighted not with the comforts of life, nor the commodities of commerce but with the moral degradation of a community – the picked and selected criminals of Great Britain'.[12]

Grey looked in vain for other places to send his 'exiles'. Ceylon, Mauritius and New Zealand all refused – the latter reasoning that the men would have an 'irresistible temptation' to get into the interior and cohabit with the women of their native population.[13] In 1846 the Admiralty had agreed to an extra three hundred convicts being sent to work in the dockyards in Bermuda, and Grey was assured that there was work for two thousand men for twelve years, but this proved unpopular because the men on Bermuda, as did those on Gibraltar, looked forward to being discharged at home as a reward for good behaviour and not sent on to Australia.[14] The outcome of all his enquiries was that nowhere was willing to take them unless Britain would pay for them, which Britain refused to do, and unless they could look forward to the convicts being returned to England once their period of public works was ended. This was unacceptable too; Grey and the Prison Inspectors wanted the men released in the colonies at the end of their term, and there was no way that they wanted them back in England. This rejection by the colonies meant that nearly all prisoners were still being sent to Van Diemen's Land. Grey began to rethink his policies, wondering if under the right conditions the old scheme of transportation, which he had so heartily rejected, was possibly the better and instructed that prisoners be released to 'approved' employers, but in country districts.[15] But there were more protests and the system was near to collapse. Neither New South Wales nor Van Diemen's Land wanted any more criminals, and Grey was unable to attract the free migrants he required to pacify the colonists or to counteract the convict influence.[16] Until 1851 Victoria was still part of New South Wales, and was receiving its quota of prisoners until 1849 when the people there refused to let a convict ship land. The protests in New South Wales continued, calling for the resignation of Earl Grey.

'With respect to the anti-transportation movement, we learn that a monster league meeting had been held at Sydney, at which was carried a petition to her Majesty for the removal of Earl Grey from her council. This firm and unequivocal exhibition of the colonists' feelings must speak volumes. Referring to the document, the Sydney Press says: "One thing at least cannot be said by his minions as an objection to it, that it was Dr. Lang and his agitation that did it;" the truth being, as the colonists aver, Earl Grey and Sir Charles Fitzroy have done it, and the are denounced as the real enemies of her Majesty's Australian colonies. It is not expected that the petition will reach her Majesty; and the Press says: "We doubt whether the petition will reach her Majesty. The unworthy etiquette of Downing-street forbids it – unless a deputation were sent to present it. But it does not much matter. Let it be published to the world. The right, the dignified, the honourable way to the throne, if it cannot be direct, is through the press." [17]

However, salvation came in the form of a request from the Western Australian Government.

By 1830 there was a small group of settlers established at Fremantle just down river from Perth. What began with such high hopes for this small band, though assured of many of the essentials for survival, good soil, healthy climate and fresh water, it soon became apparent that they lacked another necessity and that was labour. [18] In spite of the settlers' efforts, they were too isolated and conditions were too harsh for them to prosper. By 1850 there were still only four small settlements in Western Australia, Perth, Fremantle, Albany and Bunbury. From the beginning these settlers had determined that the Swan River Colony would remain a "free labour colony". But gradually this attitude began to change. More skilled labour was leaving than arriving, and more was needed if it was to grow. Trade between the settlements was difficult as there was no infrastructure in place. But the old attitude continued until 1848 when the colony was in such a bad economic state that something had to be done – it was time for the colonists to swallow their pride. When Governor Fitzgerald arrived in February 1849, they held a public meeting in Perth. It was agreed that, should the British Government wish to establish another penal settlement, then the settlers of Western Australia would be glad for their colony to be considered and that this request should be sent to Earl Grey. [19] This was just what Earl Grey and the prison inspectors wanted to hear – the British Government would be only too happy to agree to the transportation of convicts to the Swan River Colony. Consequently, it was declared by an order-in-Council as a penal colony on May 1st, 1849. As a general rule, the convicts sent there would be selected on account of their good behaviour, who, having served a time on penal works, were entitled to receive their tickets of leave. Initially a limited number would be employed on public works to assist the colony. The assignment system would not be applied in

Western Australia. In addition to the convict labour force, it was agreed to send with them military pensioners and their families to ensure the security of the colony and enough free women to equalize the sexes.[20]

As with Van Diemen's Land, retired soldiers were recruited to accompany convicts on the voyages to Western Australia and in most cases they were accompanied by their families. On 28th July, 1849, the War Office issued regulations pertaining to the conditions that some might be provided with free passages. Convict guards on the voyages, up until then furnished by Regiments of the Line, would in future consist of pensioners wishing to settle in Australia. They were to be engaged to serve for a period of six months or until the termination of the voyage, at the rate of 1/3d. per day for a private, 1/6d. for a corporal, and 1/10d. for a sergeant with an advance of four months pay before sailing, but in lieu of that pay, no enrolment money would be issued to them. Each pensioner would be equipped with one frock coat, one shell jacket, one pair of trousers and a cap to be worn when on duty. On the termination of six months, or arrival in Australia, his military engagement would cease but he would be liable to attend exercise in any company formed locally for twelve days in each year. For this he would receive pay accordingly:

	In aid of Civil Power	On days of Exercise
Sergeants	3s. 6d	3s. 0d. per diem
Corporals	3s. 0d.	2s. 3d. per diem
Privates	2s. 6d.	2s. 0d. per diem

In consideration of the expense incurred by the government in sending out the Pensioner and his family to the colony he would not receive the annual enrolment money of £1 per year, but he was bound to keep up the usual stock of necessaries, consisting of one pair of boots, two shirts, two pairs of socks and one stock. On termination of his engagement he was required to register his abode in the books of the person who paid his pension, obtaining permission if intending to change residence.[21]

Although they were not retained as permanent convict guards after their arrival in Fremantle, and generally sought work among the free settlers of the colony, they were always on hand to help in case of an outbreak among the prisoners. They were encouraged to stay in the colony by a gratuity of £10 and an offer of an allotment of ten acres of land with the use of convict labour to help clear it. This land they could lease for seven years after which they would own the freehold.

This was doubtless an attractive offer to a retired soldier who had served in a harsh British Army, generally recruited from rural labourers and often under dubious circumstances. Many found themselves living in filthy overcrowded barracks in charge of convicts in military prisons. Their daily rations were unsubstantial, consisting of a pound of bread and coffee for breakfast and three quarters of a pound of boiled meat for lunch. They earned a basic wage of a shilling a day but from this was deducted their living expenses, including food.[22] Many absconded and found themselves in prison, alongside those whom they had recently overseen. There were those who believed that the life of the convict was better than their own and that transportation was preferable to army life, so they committed acts of insubordination against their superior officers in order to be transported.

Military Prison
Gibraltar, January 17 1856

Sir,

Availing myself of the kind permission of his Excellency the Lieut. General Commanding – I have the honor to submit for his consideration the following suggestions relative to the disposal of transported soldiers, in the hope if they appear to merit it that His Excellency will be pleased to support and recommend them for adoption to the Secretary of State for War.

During eight years' experience as Governor of Military Prison at this Station, numerous instances have come under my observation of premeditated acts of insubordination having been committed by ill disposed soldiers, with the object of seeking transportation to free themselves from the Service and its discipline, which together with the total indifference manifested by a certain class of Soldiers to the terrors of Transportation, has impressed me with the conviction, that, if all soldiers were sentenced to undergo this punishment in a Military Prison (or a portion of the punishment) where the discipline partaking of a Military character is consequently more distasteful to a Military Offender than that which is enforced in the existing Convict Prisons, the crime of insubordination would be considerably diminished and it would tend to support materially the discipline of the Army.

Prisoners have been committed to my charge who have declared in my presence that "they would get transported", some of whom effected that object on their discharge from Prison, it is a common assertion amongst ill disposed soldiers, that the position and advantages of the Convict is preferable to that of the Soldier, the first fact in support of this assertion invariably being that "the convict has every night in bed" and the next that "convicts being civilians are not subjected in their discipline to any kind of Military tyranny"; it would appear therefore that among a certain class of Soldiers (to be found in every Regiment) transportation does not deter them from crime but induces its commission.

The Military Prisons at Home and in the Colonies might be made available for transported Soldiers by each (or some of them) having additional wards be constructed expressly for such soldiers or a trial on probation might be made in one of them, say for instance, that at Gibraltar, where all Soldiers sentenced to Transportation at that, and all the Mediterranean Stations might be sent. The discipline of the Military Prison being severe, much shorter terms of transportation might be awarded than heretofore, and in some particular cases, where there was reason to believe that a reformation had been effected some men might be permitted to rejoin the Service.

The principal outlay that the adoption of the above system would entail, would be rendering the Military Prisons practicable for the purpose, but after this, the cost of each prisoner would not exceed that incurred at the convict Prisons, if after probation the system be found successful, then the expediency of establishing penal settlements for Military Offenders might be taken into consideration.

I have the etc.

(signed) Fredk. Brome

Governor Mil. Prison

Gibraltar

The Ass. Military Secretary,
Gibraltar[23]   *(sic)*

Although their life in the British Army was hard, it was orderly and there was basic sustenance. But once discharged they discovered that conditions outside the army for the civilian worker also were wretched. Bearing that in mind, the offer of a free passage to a new land, a grant of land, and the princely sum of £10 would have seemed very tempting to those who had nothing, never mind the long hazardous sea crossing and an unimaginable existence in a strange land. But it was a different matter to attract free and single women.

The first consignment for Western Australia consisted of seventy-five convicts, one hundred and sixty-three pensioner guards and their families. They arrived in Fremantle on board the Scindian on 1st June 1850, the twenty-first birthday of the colony, after eighty-nine days at sea. The convicts on this first ship were all men of good conduct, near to receiving their ticket-of-leave so deemed unlikely to make any attempt to escape. This was just as well because the Scindian arrived prior to the ship which carried the official notification of their arrival. Hence the colony was totally unprepared and the ship had to stay anchored at sea in Gages Road for two months because there was nowhere to house them. Whilst the convicts remained on board, Captain Henderson, the

Controller General in charge of the convicts who had travelled out with them, sought premises which could be used for their accommodation. He found a woolshed and other outbuildings, consisting of a stone store, two large wooden stores and cottages, which he rented from Captain Daniel Scott, the former harbourmaster of Fremantle. These buildings were situated where the Esplanade Hotel in Fremantle now stands, which at that time was on the water's edge, facing the beach and with swampy land behind.

Excerpt from **The Independent Journal** Friday 7th June 1850

Arrival of the "Scindian" with Convicts

The arrival of the Scindian with the first batch of convicts and the staff of officers for the formation of the Penal Establishment, took place on Saturday last, the 22nd anniversary of the foundation of the colony – a curious coincidence and a very fit day for the commencement of the new order of things. She has had a quick passage of 88 days from Portsmouth, which she left on 4th March..........

......On Tuesday His Excellency proceeded to Fremantle, for the purpose of arranging, in concert with Capt. Henderson, for locating the prisoners, and an agreement was made with Capt. Scott to take his premises upon lease for five year, at a rental of £250 per annum, to expend £1,000 in improvements for which interest at the rate of 4 per cent, is to be allowed out of the rent.

We understand that, after the erection of their own buildings, the first public work proceeded with will, in all probability, be the erection of a Pier to run out from Arthur's Head, for the protection of Gage's Road.

We also hear that the Scindian has on board 400 tons of Government stores, including tools, iron-work, and everything the establishment is likely to require for the erection of gaols, carrying on works, etc.......

Firstly the buildings had to be repaired, for the woolshed had no floor and only part of a roof, and the other buildings were in an even worse condition, their derelict state reflecting the decline in the economy of the colony and the necessity for convict labour. Captain Henderson lost no time. He landed a working party of pensioner guards to prepare a part of the building, which would hold about twenty-five prisoners. These prisoners were chosen not only for strength and health, but for their good conduct. Some had two stripes on their jacket sleeve and 'VG' indicating them to be of the best class, and the remainder had one stripe and 'G' for good.[24] This brawny gang worked on the repairs of the other parts of the building and by the end of June they had done sufficient for it to house all of the seventy-five convicts who had arrived on the Scindian. But even after this, the premises were not very secure; there was no fence or wall around the buildings which meant that the convicts were able to roam about pretty much as they pleased. It was even reported in the local paper that four convicts wandered into a hotel for a drink. It was not until the end of 1852 that they were more securely housed.

Despite the fact that they had been unprepared for the convicts, the colonists were, in the majority, delighted by their arrival, seeing their contribution of labour as the answer to the depressed economic situation they were in. A public meeting was convened on Wednesday 10th July 1850 to consider the propriety of a Memorial to Earl Grey.[25]

PUBLIC MEETING

Perth, Western Australia,
June 7, 1850.

SIR, – We, the undersigned, do hereby call upon you to convene a PUBLIC MEETING at the Court House, Perth, on Wednesday, the 10th July next (if convenient to yourself), to consider the propriety of a Memorial to the Right Hon. EARL GREY, thanking His Lordship for his prompt attention to the wishes of the Settlers, in sending out the first draft of Convicts by the *Scindian*, lately arrived, and further to urge his Lordship to continue the emigration of that class of persons to an unlimited number, accompanied by a supply of free labour, and the establishment and protection rendered necessary by such a system.

We are, Sir,

Your obedient servants,

L. SAMSON	L.S. LEAKE
J.W. TURNER	F. CROFT
C. DEANE	R. HABGOOD
J.G.C. CARR	H.L. COLE
H.H. HALL	S. DUFFIELD
H. DEVENISH	E. STIRLING
G. SHENTON	R. JONES
G. GLYDE	T. HELMS

To G.F. STONE, Esq., Sheriff, &c., &c.

In furtherance of the above requisition I herby appoint Wednesday, the 10th day of July next, at 2 o'clock in the afternoon, at the Court House, at Perth, at which time and place, the Public Meeting will be held.

GEO. FRED. STONE,

Sheriff.

June 9, 1850

In the course of the Public Meeting, reference was made to a letter of intent of the Home Government, which had been addressed by Captain Henderson to His Excellency the Governor[26]:

H.M Government having been led to believe that this colony was languishing for want of supply of cheap and abundant labour, and for which there existed a considerable demand, and that the colonists were willing and anxious to receive as labourers men selected from the prisons in England, in consideration of the expenditure consequent upon a convict establishment being formed here; had, therefore, resolved upon sending in the first instance a limited number of men to the colony. The men are selected for their good conduct and willing industry, and the time they will have to serve on the public works will average from one to three years. The number proposed to be sent to the colony the first year is 150, and the further supply will depend upon the demand which may exist for their labour. Captain Henderson supposes that the absorption of 500 men during the next three or four years, is quite as much as can be anticipated, although it is possible that with the increased encouragement afforded to agriculture, stockbreeding &c., and the inducements to carry on other pursuits which the certainty of cheap labour would give, a larger supply might be required. The number of convicts to be introduced it appears will be influenced in a great degree by the demands made by settlers upon the Local Government for supplies of labour. Speaking of the men by the *Scindian*, Capt. Henderson has so high an opinion of them, that he would not hesitate a moment to receive any one of them into his own service.

Earl Grey, by way of Captain Henderson, had dangled his carrot, and the settlers, fighting for the survival of their colony, grabbed at it willingly. A resolution was put forward that *"whilst they thus most thankfully receive the boon conferred on the colony, by this measure of Her Majesty's Government, and do not in any manner wish to impose on it any conditions, feel it, nevertheless, necessary to express their opinion that the objects for which the colonists prayed for the introduction of convicts, would not be fully attained if their numbers were limited to a small extent, and any doubt existed of the permanency of the system of transporting convicts hither. And therefore this Meeting desire to make it known this their opinion to Earl Grey, with their earnest request that all the establishments may be formed upon a scale calculated to receive large bodies of prisoners, and that Her Majesty's Government will continue, by degrees, to send out, on the system explained in Mr. Hawes's letter of the 24th Dec., 1849, to the Manager of the Colonial Assurance Company, such numbers as may be commensurate with the works which are necessary for the improvement of the colony, and to develop and render available its resources and capabilities.*"[27] Mr. Helms, in seconding the resolution, expressed his firm conviction that it would likely be a serious evil if labour was sent to be employed with the capital they possessed at the time. Everything necessary to the colony's progress was wanting – roads and bridges scarcely in existence. But if the Home Government could be induced to form a permanent large establishment, then they would be able to open out the resources of the colony. He believed the colony would be the cheapest penitentiary in the world. But by the letter from Captain Henderson he feared the views of the Home Government were too confined and the numbers to be sent too small to be of any service.

The memorial to Earl Grey was subsequently drawn up and unanimously signed by the settlers in the various districts.

WESTERN AUSTRALIA,
JUNE 12th , 1850

To

> *The Right Hon. Earl Grey, Her Majesty's Principal*
> *Secretary of State for the Colonies.*

The Memorial of the undersigned Landowners, Stockholders, and Landholders in the Districts of York, Northam, and Toodyay. Humbly sheweth:

That your Memorialists deeply sensible of the great boon conferred on them in the hour of their distress, and when nearly at their last extremity, by your lordship kindly acceding to their request, in making this colony a penal settlement, and forwarding the first convict ship, 'Scindian', just arrived – beg to return your lordship their most grateful thanks, and to assure your lordship, that they consider the introduction of convicts on *a large scale*, the only means of placing the colony in a prosperous condition; as it will enable your Memorialists to render available its many *valuable natural productions*, which hitherto, from the very great scarcity and high price of labor, and the want of good roads, have never been turned to advantage. Your Memorialists therefore, urgently request that your lordship will be pleased to continue their introduction here as speedily as circumstances will permit, *accompanied* with a proportion of *free labor*, and *sufficient protection* in the shape of troops and pensioners.........

Before Earl Grey had received the memorial, the second consignment of convicts was on its way.

The Hashemy, with one hundred convicts and one hundred and thirty-one passengers, arrived at Fremantle on 25th October 1850. These hundred convicts were all from Portland Gaol, and details of their forthcoming transportation were recorded in the Governor's Journals.[28]

15th July 1850 Monday
The Surgeon Superintendent of the Ship 'Hashemy' (which vessel arrived yesterday in Portland Roads) inspected the convicts (100) selected for transfer to the public works in Western Australia and rejected none – no instructions have yet been received as to the day of embarking these men – they have been selected as generally useful hands, whose minimum period on public works would expire in this country within the period from March 1851 to December 1852 and had chiefly received sentences of 14 or 15 years.
17th July   Received instructions to embark convicts on Hashemy.

But now Earl Grey had carte blanche to rid himself of his problem – he had found a colony that was actually requesting him to send convicts in large quotas. It must have been beyond his wildest dreams. He lost no time in fulfilling their request. The third ship set sail from Portsmouth on 9th January, 1851. This ship was the *Mermaid*, and her consignment consisted of two hundred and eight convicts and ninety-one passengers, the latter all pensioner guards and their families.

Meanwhile new prisons were being built in England. Condemning reports had been made about the appalling conditions on the hulks, and opposition to the system of transportation was growing. In 1850 Grey reported to Parliament that there were still two thousand men in the hulks in Great Britain and Ireland. There was room for only twelve thousand, nine hundred men in total in all the prisons in the United Kingdom, Bermuda and Gibraltar, including the hulks. Five thousand men a year were sentenced to transportation each year, so prison accommodation would have to be nearly doubled to house all transported prisoners at home.[29] The following year the new prison at Dartmoor opened, and together with other new prison buildings it made it possible to house sixteen thousand convicts. It was found that imprisonment in England was costing less than had been expected and that transportation had become the more expensive punishment.[30] It cost £100 per man to transport a man for the whole of his sentence whilst the net cost of imprisonment at home was £15 per year per man.

Gradually transportation ceased. On 27th November, 1852, the last convict ship bound for Hobart sailed. During 1853, sentences of seven years transportation were replaced by four years' penal service, and proportionally up to fourteen years. The longer terms remained. Gradually over this decade, the hulks were less and less used, and by 1857 most had been burnt. By 1861 a new prison at Chatham replaced the hulks there, and in 1862 those at Bermuda were scrapped.[31] It was seen by the War Office and the Admiralty that there was an advantage to employing cheap convict labour, so the need to transport the convicts had lessened. It was no longer expedient for Great Britain to have the expense of transporting cheap convict labour to Western Australian when it could be used at home. It was announced that after 1867 transportation would cease and on 12th October, 1867, the last convict ship sailed for Fremantle.

However it was not without a price. The scrapping of the hulks, together with the end of transportation, caused many problems within the prison system. In Bedfordshire, for instance, it was thought by the authorities that transportation and prison hulks would always be there to take surplus prisoners, and, therefore, with that in mind, they had built the gaol too small for the increasing number of local criminals.

"Mermaid"
209 Male Convicts for
Western Australia
30th Decr 1850

Name	Where convicted	When	Term of ye
George White	Bedford Assizes	5 March 1849	Fifteen
William Newnham	Dr	16 July 1849	Ten
William Bailey	Bucks Assizes	12 July 1849	Fourteen
John Raven	Cambridge (Cambridge Quarter Sessions	19 October 1848	Seven
Henry Mauser	(Isle of Ely Quarter Sessions)	3 January 1849	Fifteen

Excerpt from the Mermaid convict list, showing George White bound for Western Australia.

CHAPTER 15

The Voyage of the Mermaid

What have I learnt from you Daddy
though too young to remember your face?
For I was only a babe in my mother's arms
when they took you away in disgrace.
But my eyes are like yours
My hair too is brown
And your pain is the pain that I feel.
The sound of your chains ever haunts me
I learnt catching sparrows is real.

Whilst George was contemplating the final break from his family, England and all that was familiar to him, the 473-ton barque, Mermaid, was lying in dock at Woolwich awaiting her first contingent of human freight. The Mermaid was a fine-looking vessel built in Calcutta in 1817, of teak and sheathed with yellow metal. She had undergone extensive repairs in the last few years, including new topsides, and was equipped ready to carry the third of the thirty-seven shipments of male convicts destined for Western Australia.

On board were the crew, thirty-two able bodied seamen, their Captain, J.P. Anderson, and the Surgeon Superintendent for the voyage, Alexander Kilroy. The consignment consisted of two hundred and eight convicts and ninety-one passengers, the latter all pensioner guards and their families.[1] These were made up of twenty-nine pensioner guards, twenty-three wives, twenty sons and nineteen daughters, all of whom had elected to become settlers on arrival in Australia, a commitment they undertook, in effect, in return for their free passage, a ten-acre grant of land, and assistance in building a dwelling.

Since the beginning of the transportation of convicts, authorities had learnt many lessons. Conditions on earlier voyages were terrible, the men confined behind bars below decks on the prison deck, sometimes waist deep in water, and in many cases they were restrained in chains, half-naked for the entire voyage. Cruel masters, harsh discipline, dysentery, scurvy and typhoid resulted in a huge loss of life. When the miserable wretches died, their comrades allowed them to lie there until the stench of their rotting flesh became intolerable for even them to bear, because, until the death was reported, they could claim their rations to be shared between the starving men.[2]

But by the time George sailed, conditions had improved somewhat. The surgeon, Alex Kilroy, had the sole responsibility for the welfare of the convicts, and they had a Religious Instructor to educate the convicts and attend to their spiritual desires. Charterers were also paid a bonus to land the prisoners safely and in good health at the end of the voyage. It was in the Government's interest to keep the prisoners in good health as their labour was desperately needed in Western Australia. In fact, existence on board a convict ship could often now be deemed an improvement for the prisoners after being confined in one of the prisons or hulks.

In 1846, The Times published an article on the conditions on board convict ships:

"1846. Idealistic account of Conditions on Convict Transports taken from The Times. England. August 23rd. "Convict Ships. In the report of the Inspectors of Millbank Prison, issued within the last few days, a statement is given of the improvements effected in convict ships. Until a somewhat recent period, four or sometimes five prisoners slept together during the long voyage to Australia in

The Mermaid. *Author's adaptation of sketch by John Acton Wroth.*
Courtesy Battye Library Accession 2816A/3

one sleeping berth. The prison deck being entirely dark, neither employment nor instruction could be carried on. According to the approved method of fitting up seats for the convicts on prison deck in masses of eight, and at night each convict has a separate sleeping berth. Illuminators are introduced on each side of the deck extending the whole length of the ship, and the convicts are thus enabled to read, write and work. A religious instructor accompanies every party of male convicts. A useful collection of books and arithmetic has been provided in order that school instruction may be carried on during the voyage."

It was agreed that all those convicts sent to Western Australia were to be able-bodied and in good health, though some might have bent the truth a little in order to escape their harsh prison life.[3] Medical examinations tended to be slack as some English authorities also whitewashed the true facts in order to get rid of certain convicts.

On some voyages, embarkation began on the Thames, before the convict transporter sailed around the coast to the south shore to take on board more contingents. On other voyages, convicts were transported by road or rail from the inland prisons or from the Hulks and put aboard the Transport Ship in batches as they arrived at Portsmouth. As they were transported through the town on wagons, sometimes thirty in number, the shop windows and doors were all closed, and troops lined the streets. At Point Beach, as soon as they embarked on the boats which were ready to row them to Spithead to the Ship, they gave three tremendous cheers.[4]

On 20th December, 1850, at Woolwich, the Mermaid was ready for her voyage. First to embark were fifty-one prisoners, twenty-four from Pentonville wearing black caps and twenty-seven from the Hulk, Justitia, in striped caps, and some of the pensioner guards. Meanwhile on the dock at Gravesend, the remainder of the guard, their wives, two of whom were heavily pregnant, and their children, waited impatiently with their baggage for the appearance of the ship. One of the wives, Mrs. Maher, watched anxiously over her children, Susan, aged four and Dennis, aged two, both of whom had developed a cough and seemed unwell. On the 21st December the Mermaid sailed slowly into sight and the families, some excited at the thought of their new lives and others reluctant, scrambled to embark and claim their berths. With her new cargo she set sail for Portsmouth arriving at Spithead on 25th December. This was the end of the voyage for one of the convicts, who was returned to Pentonville on 26th for misconduct.

The sick children had become increasingly worse over the few days of sailing and chose the afternoon of their arrival at Spithead to break out in an eruption of spots. That evening Mrs. Maher decided to seek the advice of the Surgeon Superintendent, Alex Kilroy, who diagnosed measles. After treating them as best he could, the following morning, he wrote to the Director General informing him of the outbreak of the disease. On the 27th December, Alex Kilroy received an order from the Admiral Superintendent of Portsmouth Dockyard to remove all sick children and send them to Haslar Hospital. The two young Maher children together with their parents were taken on board the Firequeen Steamer and transported to Portsmouth. Once they had disembarked, their bedding and berths were fumigated with Chloride of Zinc.[5]

For a few days whilst the Mermaid was gently rolling towards Spithead, George, along with the rest of the convicts in Portland whose time had come to bid their reluctant farewells to England, enjoyed a brief period of respite. Those selected were those men of long sentences who in ordinary course would be entitled to their ticket-of-leave at different periods up to 1854.[6] For this reason Dockerill had, this time, escaped selection as, being under a life sentence, he was not entitled to his ticket-of-leave during this period. The men chosen had to undergo medical examinations and attend an address by the Director of Prisons on the benefits they would receive at the end of their transportation in a colony where there was plenty of work and good rates of pay. They attended a special service in chapel and were issued with new clothes, two shirts, two flannel shirts, two pairs of cotton drawers, two pairs of worsted stockings, four checked handkerchiefs, two worsted caps, one pair of shoes, a jacket, waistcoat and trousers with a smock frock, a pair of braces, two combs, a brush and linen towels.[7] They were now ready for their fate.

Meanwhile the Mermaid had received instructions to proceed directly towards Cowes, for it had been decided by the Admiralty that to sail the Mermaid into Portland to embark the convicts might endanger her, they were therefore to be transferred to Cowes by steamer.[8]

Whitehall 16 Dec 1850

Lt Col Jebb

Sir

I am directed by Secretary Sir Geo Grey to acquaint(?) you that it appears by a communication which has been received from the Lords Commissioners of the Admiralty that it being considered that the Convict Ship "Mermaid" might be endangered by embarking Convicts at Portland, directing (?) leave being given by their Lordships for H.M. Steam Vessel "Echo" to proceed to Portland to convey the Prisoners from thence to Cowes there to be embarked on board the "Mermaid" and also that similar orders will be given in the case of the "Lady Kenneway" Convict Ship when she is ready to receive Convicts.

I am ?

H. Waddington

It was on Friday 27th December, during the evening, that the Government steamer Echo arrived in Portland Roads, where the master reported himself in readiness to take on board the convicts, thence to be embarked on the Mermaid. The steamer lay in wait for her consignment, just a small speck within the imposing cliff, the first view the convicts had as they shuffled outside the walls of Portland Prison at early dawn on 28th December and stared through the gloom down the hill. Then the depressing sound of the convicts' chains was to be heard as they marched down, one hundred and sixteen of them, ten to a chain. Some who left no families behind would have had firmer steps, already eagerly anticipating a new life, but others would drag on their shackles, wretched to leave their loved ones. In the sea mist, the sound of the chains again as, at 8.30am, the convicts boarded the Echo to take them to the Mermaid. The little steamer, full of England's outcasts, then pitched and rolled on the waves all day until she reached her objective, where she regurgitated her human cargo on to the deck of the Mermaid.

Once on board, their chains were unlocked, and the men stood, some mute and motionless, staring blankly around at their new surroundings, bewildered and unsure of procedure, others moaning in protest, until their numbers were called and they were pushed roughly towards the hatch and below into the darkness beyond. At the same time, forty-three young juvenile offenders, mostly in their late teens, were embarked from Parkhurst Prison on the Isle of Wight. This pathetic band of comparative innocents, distinguishable by their red worsted caps, shuffled on board and stood, hapless protégés, next to their elder examples, wondering

Letter from Horatio Waddington stating that the Mermaid may be endangered if she embarks convicts at Portland.

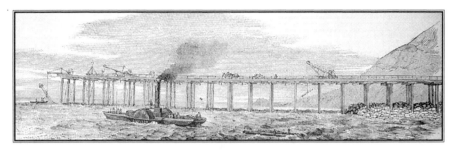

A steamer passes alongside Portland breakwater.

how life could have dealt them such injustice. For the assurances of the authorities that only convicts of a lesser sentence would be sent to Western Australia was short-lived, and by the time the Mermaid sailed, just a few short months after the first consignment, she contained more hardened criminals, eleven of whom had been convicted to transportation for life, with three of those for murder. But, to prove the anomalies of the system, and the harsh degree of punishment for military offenders, one of those men sentenced to transportation for life was for the offence of striking a superior officer. With this consignment too was a man sentenced to fifteen years for writing a threatening letter, and one to the same for returning from previous transportation. There were five arsonists, generally for firing a haystack, highway robbers, receivers, burglars and a rapist. And mixed with this motley gang were the young Parkhurst boys, most with seven-year sentences for theft. One was for stealing a handkerchief, one for stealing shoes and one clothes. Another unfortunate was the recipient of a seventeen-year sentence for stealing boots, and one lad received fourteen years for stealing a shirt. But for all of these, however long or short their sentence, they might as well have had a life sentence when put in the context of being removed from their families, for it was doubtful that more than a handful ever saw them again. The miserable group of youngsters clung to their parcel of clothing, probably containing more than they had ever owned in freedom.

All the convicts were formally handed over to the master of the ship at the beginning of the voyage to be transferred to the Governor of the

Colony at the end of the transportation. When the last of the convicts had been sent below, the barred doors of the hatchway were locked, and the convicts mingled with each other jostling to claim their sleeping space, some might excitedly recognize an old acquaintance from a previous prison. But for all on board there would have been a tremendous feeling of apprehension. Many would not even have seen the sea before, others only if they had served some of their sentence at a prison such as Portland. It was a vast unknown, and particularly at the time of year that the Mermaid sailed, the sea could be cruel. Their environment was alien to them and noises of anchor and rigging could have been frightening, especially to the young lads.

The Mermaid had been ably fitted for the transportation of convicts. They were confined between decks from the main hatchway to the fore part of the ship. The space mid-ship between the fore and main masts was occupied by two hatchways leading to the convict quarters. Boatswains were appointed to ensure that no more than one person went into either of the two water closets at any one time and to ensure that nothing was

DRESSES OF THE OFFICERS AND PRISONERS.

Parkhurst lads with an officer.

thrown in that might choke the pipes. There were four metal ventilators, two long ones in the hatchways and two short ones cut through the deck, one on each side with two wind-sails which were canvas funnels or tubes, used to ventilate ships' holds. There were also eight port holes measuring three inches by two inches, with glass in them to provide light, which could be opened for additional ventilation. Ten upper-lights made the port part of the quarters quite light and cheery, but the other end, in the bows and before the fore hatchway, remained dark and gloomy.

Looking upwards through the bars could be seen the sky by day and the stars at night, this simple pleasure a welcome sight after their incarceration in cells for so many years. On deck, they were to breathe in the sweet cold smell of liberty, as a contrast to the foul stench of human incarceration surrounding them once below. Because there, in the darkness, the first few days were terrible for the men, unused to such close confinement of so many in such cramped conditions, with seasickness and its accompanying odour, depression at being parted from their families, and the merciless pounding of the waves on the sides of the ship.

Just one of the convicts below sat as detached as possible from his unavoidable shipmates. He was John Acton Wroth, a young man just turned twenty years of age who had embarked on the Mermaid amongst the Parkhurst Prison lads. Wroth had been convicted in August 1848 at Ipswich Assizes. He came from a reasonably well-to-do background, his father being a respectable brewer, and was educated, having attended school for nine years before being apprenticed to a printer. As such, he considered himself superior to his fellow shipmates, and kept himself aloof from them during the whole voyage, thinking them coarse and vulgar. But it is fortunate that he kept a diary of the voyage, and thus placed on record the conditions which the men experienced on board the ship.

In the convict quarters, each side of the deck was fitted with two rows of bunks, one above the other, where each convict was allocated his own sleeping space, separated from his neighbour by a ten inch high board. Four berths of the lower tier and four of the upper tier constituted a mess, and these eight berths were so constructed that, during the day, they formed a table with a seat on each side of the table which seated four men. Those prisoners occupying the mid-ship places slept in hammocks, which were slung up each night over the tables.[9] The younger lads from Parkhurst occupied these hammocks whilst the men occupied the bunks. George therefore would have been in a bunk which measured 5ft 6in by 14in and was furnished with a mattress, pillow and two blankets. The lads in the hammocks had two blankets only.

Now the preliminaries were completed, the sentries were posted and articles specified in the inventory committed to the charge of Sergeant McGall. Sails were unfurled, the anchor weighed and the Mermaid was ready for her voyage. On the upper deck in the passengers' quarters, the wives and children of the pensioner guards watched the disappearing shore apprehensively, knowing that this would be their last sight of the coastline of Hampshire. But some of the wives remained in their quarters watching anxiously over their children for any signs of illness which might hamper their proceeding with the voyage. As the sea roughened, the Mermaid returned to Spithead to monitor the situation, but signs of the measles outbreak, which had manifested itself at Woolwich, appeared to be abating.[10] However, on the 6th January, their worst fears were confirmed. More children of the pensioner guards had fallen ill and developed signs of measles. Three children of the Fahey family, Mary, aged seven, Anne, aged five, and Kate, aged three, all had spots appear in the morning and in the afternoon were sent to Haslar hospital by Admiralty order. The same fate befell James Rooney, aged five, and Anne Rooney, aged three. These children and their parents were disembarked on 7th January.[11] Fate had ruled that for these three families, the Mahers, the Faheys and the Rooneys, the eagerly anticipated life in a new land was to be denied them.

That same day, the ship was visited by one of the directors of the convict prison, anxious to wash his hands of the responsibility of the convicts and see them hastily dispatched. He recommended that the

Mermaid should set sail forthwith and that no more passengers should be disembarked. But the weather had worsened and the ship prepared for a storm, an anchor dropped from the starboard bow, and all cable eased out.

The following day, as soon as a reinforcement of guard had arrived to replace those sent ashore, the crew once more prepared for departure. On 9th January, at 1pm she once again sailed from Spithead, but the weather was still rough and by 8pm half of the convicts were sick and vomiting. Conditions were terrible as the storm continued, with most seasick and seven more cases of measles diagnosed between leaving Spithead and the 12th January. Six of these were within the families of the pensioner guards, but now it appeared it might have spread to the convicts as one of them contracted the disease. However, all the cases except one seemed slight.

The hospital on the ship was small taking into consideration the demand that was made on it, just 15ft by 10ft 8in, and averaged just under 6ft high. There were three iron bedsteads which were placed on bunks. Light was provided from part of the main hatchway (portside) and one skylight, with further ventilation admitted in fine weather. Hospital patients were treated with a diet of sago, arrowroot, preserved meat and vegetables with tea.

For several days the ship heaved, as she tacked along the English Channel, her human cargo tossed mercilessly in their bunks and hammocks, until finally, on 13th, the heavy weather forced her to put into Torbay for shelter. The following night general alarm broke out as the ship drew a great portion of her cable as she weathered the storm.

Some prisoners took the opportunity to apply their dubious talents whilst their shipmates were otherwise occupied, resulting in several being brought before the Surgeon Superintendent on a charge of stealing with one being 'boxed'. Incarceration in the 'box', a confined space in the bows in which a man could neither lie down nor stand, was the usual punishment meted out for offences, even minor ones such as insolence, disobedience and smoking.

The Mermaid remained weather-bound in Torbay until 18th January, when she attempted to set sail once more. But still the malevolent sea pitched the ship savagely and the vomiting returned amongst the men. The following day she was obliged to seek sanctuary again, this time at Falmouth. As the sea calmed the seasickness subsided, but still the cases of measles continued with two children of the guards and three convicts falling ill. However, the surgeon reported that, in general, the convicts were in a healthy state when they embarked and most remained so despite the poor conditions, apart from a great many cases of diarrhoea which were cured with a dose of chalk mixture.

The Mermaid remained at Falmouth for a further two weeks to ride out the storm. Whilst there, it was noted that a foreign vessel also took shelter in the harbour, but a schooner was not so lucky, going down with all hands lost but one.[12]

For the whole of the month of January the ship had been able to make little or no progress in sailing, and the time seemed tedious and long. The men, when not sick, were hungry, dissatisfied and contentious.[13] A few were boxed, for disobedience of orders and smoking, and a watch went missing. But the prison was kept clean with the air well-circulated and the Surgeon Superintendent, along with the sergeant was attentive to those placed under his care. A visiting captain expressed his approval at the state of the decks. Supplies of fresh provisions were taken on board on the 27th and 28th January, and on 1st February, with a fair breeze behind her, the Mermaid weighed anchor and set sail once again bound for Western Australia. Six days into the voyage there was just one more case of measles reported before it abated, although the surgeon was of the opinion that many more mild cases went unreported. Chloride of Zinc was freely used to purify during the prevalence of the disease.

So the convicts began their journey with no knowledge of what fate awaited them at the end of their voyage on the other side of the world.

George found himself in the company of William Golding, a butcher from Chesterton, who was convicted at the Cambridge Quarter Sessions on 5th July, 1849 for sheep stealing and sentenced to ten years' transportation. William was just about the same height as George, at 5ft 7½ins, and a year younger with light brown hair and grey eyes, long face and fresh complexion. William had distinguishing marks WGAGEG on his right arm, a permanent reminder of his young wife, Amy, and baby daughter Emily whom he had been forced to leave behind. The two men had a common interest in that their babies were just about the same age, Emily being born just a few months before Eliza. The friendship forged early in the voyage between the two men was to last throughout the first few years of their transportation.

The convicts were divided into messes of eight men, one of each elected to serve out provisions, and wash the utensils after each meal. Each mess was supplied with cooking and eating utensils consisting of eight tin pint mugs, eight spoons, one wooden eight pint tub called a kid, one six pint tin can, one meat dish and one circular wooden bowl. A knife and fork was issued to each convict every dinner time and collected after the meal had been finished. At night, light was provided by two oil lamps in the hatchways. Cooks were required to be ready for duty at 5am and the prisoners out of bed by 6am, with their bed rolled up ready to be taken on deck at 6.15am, after which they had to make up the mess tables. Bread was served between 6am and 7am. From 6.45am they were allowed on deck, three messes at a time. A typical breakfast of one pint of gruel, half a pint of cocoa, and six ounces of biscuit was served at 7.45am, after which the mess-men went on deck to clean the utensils. Dinner, comprising of pea soup, eight ounces of salt meat and six ounces of biscuit was served at noon. On Sundays and Thursdays they were also served with half a pound of "duff", a pudding made of flour, suet and currants. Supper at 5.30pm consisted of four ounces of biscuit and half a pint of tea or chocolate. A pint of vinegar and half an ounce of mustard were issued to the messes three times a week, with glass bottles to preserve it until the next issue.

The three cooking galleys were situated in the fore part of the ship, one on the starboard side for the use of the prisoners in which there were two coppers, one large, one small and two ovens. The cook in this galley was assisted by two prisoners. On the larboard (port) side there were another two galleys, one for soldiers and one for the ship. Two cooks served in the soldiers' galley, assisted by a prisoner, a Portland man, whilst that of the ship had one cook assisted by a Parkhurst lad. The cook's assistants were selected from the better-behaved prisoners as were those for other shipboard duties, some being given the jobs of hospital orderlies and some boatswains. The latter were required to keep order amongst their fellow prisoners, especially below decks at night, making sure that none of the prisoners left their beds. They worked in shifts of two hours and for these duties they received small privileges. Strict rules were to be observed and these were posted up by the Surgeon. Prisoners were called up for washing prior to the issue of breakfast biscuit. Soap was only allowed twice a week for shaving, and shaving utensils were issued only to those who had reached 'maturity'. Salt-water baths were provided in warm and sultry weather, early in the morning, about 4am. Monday was washday, and on that day each mess was provided with eight scrubbing brushes. During the first week of the voyage routine was established and seasickness began to abate. Fair progress was being made although it was hampered by the breaking of a boom. Salt rations were commenced on the 4th February, along with an allowance of one gill of Cape wine which was served on deck. But by the 6th February the wind had changed once more, little progress was being made and diarrhoea broke out amongst the men. Odd occurrences of disobedience and insolence resulted in punishment. Each Sunday prayers were read on deck by the Surgeon Superintendent. On the 10th the ship sailed past the Canaries and Madeira at 9.15am, about 14 miles distant.

On 12th February, John Wroth was recommended to the Surgeon Superintendent by Sergeant McGall for the position of school assistant, an appointment which suited him very well, as it commanded him extra privileges, an extra gill of wine on wine days and a half a pint of lime juice added to his ration. He also had access to books, of which he noted there were '147 library books, 112 schoolbooks, comprising of lesson books for classes, arithmetic etc, and miscellanies 135'. Library books were issued five to a mess, a welcome relief for those who were literate[14] to alleviate the boredom of the voyage. Although there were some convicts willing to attend school and grasp the opportunity to attain knowledge, others would do all they could to avoid it, and only compulsion made them attend. The classes were conducted by four schoolmasters, or assistants, under the superintendence of Sergeant McGall, who expressed great interest in his task, wishing to promote knowledge to those who were willing among the less literate.

By mid February most of the passengers had become accustomed to the movement of the ship, and a routine for work was established amongst the convicts. Skeins of wool and bolts of cloth and canvas were removed from the stores and on 14th February the men were put to work. Some were employed in making up clothing, duck canvas trousers, and grey suits. These were superintended by a prisoner from Woolwich. Others were put to the task of knitting stockings, mostly the Parkhurst boys, and superintended by a prisoner from Portland. There were four shoemakers constantly employed in repairing shoes. Others were on general cleaning of the mess and utensils.

Sightings of other vessels, and wildlife such as dolphins, whale and sharks, occasionally relieved the boredom, but apathy was setting in, some convicts became insolent, three daubed others with pitch, and all were 'boxed' for it. One guard received the same for abusing his wife. The surgeon thought it fit to introduce diversions.[15] On 22nd February, two fiddlers were given their violins from the sergeant, and evening entertainment began. Wroth reported that after tea, at 4pm, beds were taken in from their airing down to their respective berths, decks were swept and scrubbed, after which the men found themselves a convenient place on deck to sit if they wished to be present. The fiddler would then appear from between decks and seat himself amidst the chattering throng and immediately strike up a tune for singing or dancing, to the enjoyment of all in attendance, who would clap and hoot their appreciation. The ladies on board also honoured them with their

Diversions were introduced on board ship to combat boredom.

presence. This recreation served to relieve the boredom of the men until 6pm when they reluctantly obeyed the order to return below.

On 2nd March, the Mermaid crossed the equator and, after a violent thunder storm, was now making good progress southwards. On 7th the messes received only half their allowance of biscuit and one stock of biscuit was rejected by the men as being bad and thrown overboard.[16] Anne Miller, the wife of one of the guards, was delivered of a child during the first week of March, but the baby was still-born. This week, divine service was read by the Captain in his clear audible voice, doubtless with prayers for the unfortunate infant and its mother. A week after the birth Anne was still ill, complaining of intense pain and swelling in the left leg and thigh, together with headache and thirst, and it was not until 9th April, after having her leg bandaged from toe to hip, that Anne was discharged from the sick list.

The weather was now becoming much hotter, some days sultry and oppressive with little headway made, others more temperate and agreeable when the ship was able to make good progress, sailing gently towards the Cape. The shoes of each prisoner were inspected to see if repairs were needed. All on board eagerly anticipated putting in to Cape Town for supplies, but after inspection of the water casks and supplies it was decided that there was sufficient on board, so there would be no need to replenish the stock. In the distance a great number of Cape birds could be seen, and in the dazzling water a shark was spotted, one of a number to be seen over the next few days, and although great efforts were made to catch it, the shark won the day.

Another of the wives, Mrs. Griffin, was more fortunate than Anne Miller. She was delivered of a healthy daughter at 11.30am on 19th March, the infant being christened Maryanne by the captain at a service in the cabin four days later.

But discontent had set in amongst the men once more. They were disappointed they were not to put in at Cape Town, and arguments broke out about the portions of meat. By now, night time in the convicts' quarters was becoming exceedingly oppressive, being tainted with the perspiration and foul breath of the men. John Acton Wroth found the state of them distasteful, as they lay about almost naked. He resolved to have nothing to do with his fellow convicts, considering them ignorant of the meaning of respect, remarking that they were constantly chattering and singing until the bell struck 8pm when the boatswains interposed with an order for bed, which they obeyed reluctantly. He considered that they were 'destitute of moral rectitude and etiquette with their obscene language, avarice and envy; that it was not surprising they had been exiled and it was a good thing for society that they were. Every encouragement was given by both the Surgeon Superintendent and the Sergeant to those who evinced any desire to conduct themselves with propriety'.[17]

To alleviate the boredom and dejection, the fiddlers were joined by two other men, one with 'bones' and one a tambourine, and they were permitted to stay on deck until a quarter to eight to entertain the emigrants.[18]

By 18th March there was an improvement in dietary conditions, the state of the provisions being considered moderate and satisfactory. The sergeant was now filtering the water, which was a great improvement both in taste and appearance. The arguments about the portions of meat, which included pork and salt beef, had been resolved by cutting it into twenty-six pieces (the number of the messes). This was carried out by the boatswain, after which an appointed man would turn his back on the meat whilst another asked him which piece was to be allocated to which mess.[19] Thus all grounds for disturbance were removed.

In spite of the seeming improvement in the water, there were still many cases of diarrhoea and dysentery reported amongst both convicts and passengers. The surgeon reported that the health of the pensioner guards and their families was not generally as good as that of the convicts, although their berths were more roomy and better ventilated. There still prevailed feelings of nausea, and now many suffered inflamed and pustulous legs and rashes caused by the heat of the sun.

On 31st March, the Mermaid rounded the Cape buffeted by near gale force winds from the south. The sea was rough but with no heavy swell, the weather a great deal colder. To the disappointment of all, the Mermaid sailed on past Cape Town, now being driven east by a strong cold westerly wind, the swell now increasing. An albatross measuring 9ft 2ins across its wing tips was caught with a hook and cork.

Sadly one little boy aged two years, James McCormick, the son of a pensioner guard, died on 5th April after thirty-three days of illness, which was diagnosed as tabes, a wasting disease, and diarrhoea. According to the surgeon, the child was embarked in an unhealthy state, malnourished, suffering from bad or insufficient food.[20] He was buried at sea at noon, with the Captain and Surgeon Superintendent present.

The allocation of wine was at times suspended, no doubt to make rations last, but lime juice continued. Punishments were still being handed out, although in general they were quite lenient in most cases. A man was put in the box on 11th April for fighting, and put in irons after being taken out the following day at 2pm. A sheep was killed on 12th, and efforts were made to catch porpoises. For another week the ship continued to make good progress; it was noted on Thursday 17th, the day before Good Friday, that the sea had changed colour to a peculiar green.

Although there was no apparent sign of disease, the health of one of the convicts from the hulk, Samuel Heathfield aged fifty-three years, had gradually fallen into decline as he reached the tropics. From the beginning of March he was given extra food, but by the third week his appetite had begun to fail. Even though he was carefully monitored and treated by the Surgeon, had fresh meat daily from the cuddy, by the 12th April he was reported to be sinking fast, and by 16th April was no longer able to eat. He was greatly emaciated, being little more than flesh and bone. He died on the 18th April at 6.15pm. The Captain was with him a few hours before his death, conversing with him upon his approaching dissolution, endeavouring to direct his mind to the merits of his Saviour.[21] Frequently on the day of his death he was to be heard imploring the Lord to have mercy upon him and to take him to himself. He was committed to the deep on Saturday, 19th April, Easter weekend at 10am, his body being wrapped in linen, then sewn in canvas with 24lb of iron wrapped at his feet. He was then placed on the hatch which rested on the bulwark and covered with the Union Jack. The prisoners all attended the funeral service, which was read by the Captain. During a raging tempest following the conveyance of Samuel Heathfield to the water, John Acton Wroth wrote an elegy to commemorate his passing (opposite).

The tempest that night was violent. Vivid and frequent lightening and frighteningly loud thunder struck the men with awe, but the following day the wind subsided and the ship became becalmed, the weather wet and miserable.

It had been anticipated that they were only about ten days sailing to their destination, but little progress was now being made, there was a strong headwind, and it became apparent that it would take longer. On 24th April the guns were removed from the quarter deck down to the

Despised by all those from whom love was due
Bereft of all those whose love he well knew
Friendless and alone from his country he's sent
To toil in some distant land till his life he had spent
The stroke too severe – his nature gave way
He sank under the weight from premature decay
His spirit has fled from all troubles and pain
To his Maker returned - in sweet peace to reign
No useless coffin did his body enclose
Or funeral knell bespoke his death's last repose
Closely shrouded in his hammock he was borne
    towards his grave
Covered oe'r with the colour: he was launched in the
    wave
The waters closed oe'r him: he sank in the deep
Without a tear being shed: or one seen to weep.

April 21st 1851
John Acton Wroth

stores. By this time, the tailors had completed two hundred suits of grey material and three hundred and fifty pairs of duck trousers, and the boys had knitted seventy-seven worsted stockings, all to the satisfaction of the director. With the work complete, all began to anticipate the end of their voyage, now eagerly looking forward to their arrival which surely could not be much longer.

After a few days of making better headway the popular opinion was that they were near land, supposedly the island of St. Pauls, but the men were disappointed thinking they were nearer Australia. Flour ration was stopped, but two dolphins were caught and eaten, the flesh tasty. On 1st May, Australia was computed to be some one thousand, eight hundred miles distant. Several vessels were spotted near the island, and as two studding-sails were carried away and pieces of wreck floated past the ship amongst the seaweed, it was a disturbing reminder of how cruel the sea could be.

CHAPTER 16

Gibraltar

Once again George and Dockerill's paths had taken a different course. As George became just one of the statistics of convict transportation when he was taken on board the barque Mermaid bound for Western Australia, his partner in crime continued to serve his time in Portland Prison, but it would not be for long, as Dockerill's departure too was imminent.

In February 1851, H.M. hired convict ship Cornwall, under her master, Captain Maundrell, and Surgeon Superintendent D. Geddes M.D., which was anchored in the Thames at Woolwich, made ready to receive her consignment of convicts. Her first destination was the island of Gibraltar where three hundred (two hundred and ninety-eight?) convicts were to be disembarked before taking on board their replacements, those unfortunates destined for Van Diemen's Land.

On 4th and 5th February, the unhappy process began when a total of one hundred and eighty-three prisoners from different gaols were embarked, together with two non-commissioned officers and fifteen privates (pensioners). On the 8th she slipped anchor and slowly moved down the Thames to Gravesend where the remainder of the guard, thirteen men, and twenty-four women and forty-five children were received on board.[1] Then on the 10th she set sail once more, this time heading for Portsmouth, arriving at Spithead on 14th February. Here she remained, at anchor once more, her bowels not yet replete with her human cargo.

Meanwhile, Lt. Col Jebb, Governor of Prisons, had written to the Home Office regarding the inadequacies of the steam vessel used to transfer the prisoners from Portland to convict vessels at Spithead, and on 20th February Mr. Waddington sent his reply. It would appear that the Admiralty had objections to using their Man of War vessels for the likes of convicts.

Whitehall 20th February 1851

Lt. Col Jebb

Sir,

      Referring to your letter of the 11th inst. representing the insufficiency of the Steam Vessel employed in removing Convicts from Portland to Spithead. I am directed by Sec. Sir Geo Grey to acquaint you that it appears by a communication which has been received from Capt. Hamilton on this subject that the Board of Admiralty have instructed Admiral Sir. ? Capel at Portsmouth to send the Echo to perform this service during fine weather, another Sprightly or some other Man of War when there are fresh breezes, but that their Lordships are of opinion that it is very objectionable to employ Men of War in the conveyance of Convicts.

I am, ? H. Waddington

In spite of conflict of interests which was taking place between authorities, on the morning of Sunday 16th February during Divine Service a uniformed visitor presented himself to the Governor of Portland Prison. The caller was the Commander of the Sprightly, Government steamer, there to formally notify the Governor of the arrival of that vessel in Portland Roads. He was charged with the task of transporting the assignment of convicts to Spithead, to be embarked on the Cornwall, where she lay in preparation for sailing, bound for Gibraltar. The Commander required the removal of the prisoners to take place early the following morning to enable him to reach the ship at Spithead before dark.[2] However, the Governor thought differently. He did not intend that the order and quiet of the Sabbath should be disturbed by the preparation of those convicts selected for departure, and he informed the Commander that the men would not be ready until the Tuesday morning, 18th February. On the Monday evening, the Commander of the Sprightly sent a message to say that he had been ordered off and that the convicts would be transferred on the Government steamer Echo in her stead.[3] Possibly the authorities had seen fit to appease the Admiralty and their distaste in using their Man of War vessel for transporting convicts and had ordered the transfer of steamers.

The following day the Governor chose not to attend Morning Service, but to oversee the embarkation of the prisoners, possibly glad of this diversion, because it seems that the Governor would often find an excuse not to attend morning and evening services.

At 8am those convicts selected to be employed on public works in Gibraltar, being mostly men of long sentence, were finally embarked on the Echo. Among them was convict no. 1569 Thomas Dockerill, for it was now Dockerill's turn to bid farewell to his mother country. Although Gibraltar was not the other side of the world like Australia, this would have made little difference to him. He would still have believed that he would never see England or his family again, for Gibraltar was just another stage of public works servitude before the final transportation to the antipodes. And this was exactly what was happening with this consignment, the three hundred embarking in England bound for Gibraltar, replacing the same number to be removed from there and transported to Australia. Finally, after loading the remainder of the convicts on to her open upper deck, the steamer Echo set off bound for Spithead. She took until 6pm to transport her cold and miserable cargo.[4]

Meanwhile, whilst she was awaiting the eighty one prisoners from Portland, the Cornwall had taken on board the rest of her consignment, one corporal, his wife and three children, and thirty-four prisoners from the hulks. But it was not until 24th February that the Cornwall was finally ready for her journey, and by this time bouts of sickness amongst the prisoners had begun to manifest. Most were ill with diarrhoea, but amongst those men from Portland many complained of catarrh for some days.[5] The Surgeon Superintendent attributed the latter to the fact that they had been exposed on the deck of the steamer Echo for such a long time.[6]

There appear to have been no other health problems amongst the prisoners, or the guard and their families during this part of the voyage, a fact attributed by the surgeon to the measures taken:

> The prison and sleeping berths were cleaned daily by dry scraping and sweeping and on no occasion was water used in cleaning the prison from the time that the convicts embarked until they finally left the ship.
>
> Chloride of Zinc was several times daily sprinkled about the water closets and prison as well as in different other parts of the ship and was evidently the means of contributing much to the comfort of all on board and of preserving the health of a population, amounting nearly to 500 individuals, crowded together within so small a space as they were necessarily confined to.
>
> The prisoners were admitted upon the upper deck on all occasions, during the day, when the weather was favourable for their being there.[7]

On 3rd March, as they neared Gibraltar, Dockerill and two other men reported sick with what appears to be 'illeus'(?), a blockage of the bowel. But in all of the cases of illness, none were considered of a serious nature and all were declared in a state of good health when the ship arrived in Gibraltar the following day. On 5th March all the convicts were disembarked, those who had reported sick being discharged fit for duty. On the 8th March, three hundred wretched convicts who had been in penal service on the island were embarked on the Cornwall in their stead, and on 15th she set sail once more bound for Van Diemen's Land, leaving Dockerill to become convict no. 1557[8], together with two hundred and ninety-seven fellow rejects, on Gibraltar. The main town

Copy of Sick List of H. M. hired Convict Ship "Cornwall" during a voyage from England to Gibraltar in February & March 1851

Date	Name	Age	Quality	Disease	When put on Sick List, how disposed of
1851 Feb. 25	Chas. Taylor	24	Prisoner	Catarrhus	March 2 Duty
28	J. Salley	24	Do.	Diarrhœa	March 1 Duty
March 1	Wm. Muniford	38	Do.	Diarrhœa	March 4 Duty
" "	Rd. Brown	20	Do.	Diarrhœa	March 6 Duty
2	Thos. West	28	Do.	Diarrhœa	March 4 Duty
"	Alfd. Rush	27	Do.	Catarrhus	March 5 Duty
"	Geo. Marshall	44	Do.	Catarrhus	March 5 Duty
3	J. Henry	43	Do.	Herpes	March 5 Duty
"	Hend. Keeling	25	Do.	Ulcus	March 5 Duty
"	Th. Dockerell	48	Do.	Ulcus	March 5 Duty
"	John Farmer	42	Do.	Herpes	March 5 Duty
"	Robt. Wilson	41	Do.	Ulcus	March 5 Duty

D Eddes M.D
Surgeon R.N.

Excerpt from the sick list of the Cornwall, showing Thomas Dockerill. *ADM 101/17/10*

View of Gibraltar, showing inspection of troops.

on Gibraltar housed a mixed population, including a garrison of British soldiers and was the entrepôt for much of the trade between Spain and Morocco. The fortifications with their terraces and covered galleries, wide enough for carriages, were cut out of the solid limestone and marble of the Rock and ran for a length of two or three miles and had formidable batteries in every direction. There was the King's Bastion, the Albert Bastion, the Victoria, the Orange, and several others, with very powerful guns, making it one of the strongest fortresses in the world.

The penal establishment here was founded in 1842, and by 1845 there were some five hundred prisoners held there. During the month of March 1847 a hulk arrived, which could house an extra three hundred men.[9] At this time, Gibraltar, along with Bermuda, was regarded by Earl Grey, the Secretary of State, to be only the second or penal stage in the punishment system, whereby the convicts were to spend one to three years on public works as their 'reformatory period', and then be sent on to Australia as exiles. But the Governor of Gibraltar, Sir Robert

Wilson, had a different view. He considered his penal establishment to be very successful, but this success was built on the understanding by the convicts that, from here, as a reward for good conduct, they might be sent home rather than on to Australia. This was a great stimulus for hard work and good behaviour. So although the Governor reported to Grey that he could take more convicts, Grey was not so co-operative. He was unwilling to go to the expense of sending them there if, after a period of time, they were to be returned to England.[10] That was not what he wanted at all, for, having got rid of them, he would far rather they did not return home.

The accommodation for prisoners at the Military Prison on Gibraltar was a very makeshift affair. According to the Superintendent there were only fifteen 'very faulty' cells. Consequently the convicts were housed in open wooden barracks where they were considered to be at the prey of one or two 'disaffected men' who could influence the minds of the rest of the prisoners.

Dockerill was one of those convicts set to work constructing the moat around the Battery Wall, which meant working in water up to his middle. Under these conditions, the clothes the men wore became very heavy and rubbed the skin from parts of their legs making them very sore. Once the day's work was finished, there was no opportunity for a change of clothing, so they would have to remain in wet clothes and footwear.

Dockerill on Gibraltar, *PCOM 2 137/113004*

From Harry Blair to Jebb   British Library of Political and Economic Science JEBB 3/14
Memo

Gibraltar Prison
4th March 1856

The Prisoners under Sentence of Penal Servitude have proved themselves, in the Prisons in England, more unruly; and less amenable to Discipline, than those sentenced to Transportation.–

At Portland, where they have conducted themselves very badly every facility exists in the Construction of the Prison itself (being divided into Separate Cells) for effectually restraining these men.

But besides this, by the Rules established at Home, Prisoners who seriously misconduct themselves, are removed from Prison, and sent back to Solitary confinement at Millbank or Pentonville –

At Gibraltar, no such means exist.

It is prohibited to remove Prisoners, and send them back to England.

There are 15 Cells, and these of a very faulty description; and the whole body of Prisoners, instead of being confined in separate Cells as at Portland and Portsmouth, are located in open, wooden Barrack Rooms, where the amount of mischief which once disaffected men, possessing influence over the minds of their fellow Prisoners, may produce, is, almost incalculable. –

To men sentenced to Penal Servitude, there is no hope held out! – nor can any effort, however prolonged, no attempt at reformation however sincere, no amount of industry or hard work, however perseveringly pursued, possibly shorten by one day, the Prisoners Sentence; nor can any amount of misconduct, nor any degree of sullenness nor idleness be the means of prolonging the period of detention beyond the hour previously fixed by Law!

And what may be the result of such a system ?

I can expect nothing, but to see human nature hardened or broken hearted.

Despondency will lead to recklessness and despair, and hardening of man's heart to mutiny and every evil work.

Harry Blair
D. Supt. ?

Prison records for the Quarter ending 30th June, 1853, show that Dockerill was incarcerated on the Hulk, Owen Glendower, with an abscess. His conduct was 'very good' for that period, with eight of his preceding musters 'good'.[11] Other prison records of Gibraltar state that he was healthy and that his behaviour was very good.[12]

The men were made to work very hard on Gibraltar and a great deal of emphasis was placed on religious instruction. Discipline was harsh but with it there came encouragement and praise. It would appear that Dockerill worked hard to gain a good report from the authorities, doubtless spurred on by the thoughts of his possible return to England, for the longer he remained on Gibraltar and was not sent on to Western Australia, the nearer he got to his 'ticket-of-leave'. For the last two years, as a reward for his industry and good conduct, he was appointed a warder. This meant that for two nights each week he had two hours night watch to keep, in addition to working all day, gaining no additional benefit or privilege for doing so.[13] But he did not think a lot of the harsh sun and conditions there, for he was to complain about it in later letters.[14]

Dockerill was to spend a total of four years and eight months on Gibraltar, which was a long time to spend under the penal stage of his conviction. It would appear that he always felt that, at any time, it would be his turn to be transported to Western Australia, for he mentions in later letters that it was intended he be sent there.[15]

But here fate took a hand when he burst a blood vessel which resulted in him being invalided back to England along with twenty other sick and injured convicts on board the HMS Rhadamanthus.[16]

The voyage of the Rhadamanthus
From the Ship's Log[17]

At 1pm on Sunday 14th of October 1855 the HMS Rhadamanthus sighted the Rock of Gibraltar on the starboard bow, and at 8pm she passed Europa Point and fired a rocket, before entering Gibraltar Bay where she anchored near the HMS Prometheus and the transport ship Queen of the South.

On 15th the crew were employed cleaning, whitewashing and restoring the main hull, whilst the stokers cleaned the engine room and swept the flues. The engineers made good the defects which had appeared in the boilers, the starboard boiler having developed a leak in the furnace. At 2pm the HM Ship Saw Pariel arrived and at 4pm the Rhadamanthus was taken in tow and moored in the new mole.

On Tuesday 16th, the stokers continued to clean the engines and engine room, and the engineers worked on the defective boilers, packing the cylinder glands and examined the bottom side of port side valve. 210 tons of coal and 24 tons of fresh water were loaded on board. At 11 am members of the crew were sent to get an anchor and cable (into a lump?) (for heaving a ship?) on shore near Europa Point. The crew returned on board at ?

At 5am on 17th the fires were lit, at 7am steam up. At 8.30 working engine occasionally and at 10.15 the ship proceeded to Cabriata Point to the assistance of an American ship on shore with the Prometheus and Bustler (?) tug in company. It was impossible to render any assistance to the ship, being bilged and up to her lower deck with water. So, at 1.30 the Rhadamanthus anchored once more in Gibraltar Bay. Wm. Kinkaly (?) employed in Engine room from deck.

On 18th the fires were again lit at 7.30 am and steam up at 9am. 69 convicts received on board for passage to England in charge of Wm. Thos. Smith, chief warder. 10am weighed and proceeded. 10.15 working engines occasionally. Kinkaly and Daniel Coleman employed in Engine room from deck. 3.30pm. Abreast of Tarifa lighthouse.

19th October. Burnt a blue light and stopped engines to a vessel crossing the Bow on starboard tack. Proceeded immediately. 10am. ? with the English Steamer Melita. Steering to the ?

20th October. Watch (?) employed clearing decks of coals. The following stokers being taken ill viz. Chas Ansley, Michael Quinn, Henry Edson (?), James Billingham – Placed six prisoners on Full Allowance to take their place in Engine Room.

21st October. Noon Cape Roca. Proceeding expansively on the 3rd grade. The following prisoners employed in the Engine Room as Stokers. Joseph Mason – 1795, Richard Dearden – 2822, ? Rind – 2025, John Rivet – 2151, John Priest – 2001, John Hines – 2146.

22nd October. Set jibs and ? top sail. Watch employed cleaning ship. Prisoners employed in engine room as above.

23rd October. Prisoners employed in engine room as above. Placed three prisoners on full allowance to make necessary repairs to ship. Several sails in sight steering to the ?

24th October. A heavy swell from the ? Prisoners employed in the engine room as above. Several sails in sight. Boilers leaking in the furnaces.

25th October. A heavy swell from the ? Made all possible sail. ? with the English Ship Carland (?) steering to the south. Boilers leaking. Prisoners employed as above.

26th October. 10 am. Abreast of Falmouth. 1pm. Abreast of Plymouth. 9.30pm. Abreast of Portland.

27th October. Saturday. 8.15. Eased and stopped engines. 8.20am. Anchored at Spithead and banked fires. 9am. Fired a gun to enforce(?) signal. 11am. Customs House Boats come alongside. 3pm. Received Wm Jones Pilot. ? Steam up and proceeded. 3.30. Weighed and proceeded into Portsmouth Harbour, made ? to a mooring bay. 4.40pm eased and stopped engines. Working engines occasionally. 6pm Convicts to the Stirling Castle.

With the convicts went the sum of £273. 7. 9. which was private cash due to sixty-nine of them and which was to be handed over to Major John Shaw, governor of the "Stirling Castle" hospital ship at Gosport.[18] At 6pm on Saturday 27th October, the invalid convicts were disembarked from the Rhadamanthus and Dockerill set foot on English soil once more.

CONVICT SERVICE

Deputy Commissary General G.H. Dinwiddie in Account Current with the Right Honorable the Lords Commissioners of Her Majesty's Treasury, to 31 October 1855.

Date 1855	No of Vr.	Dr. To Receipts	£	s.	d.
		By Check No.522 on the Comm. Chest	770.	17.	3.
		" 537 "	71.	12.	8.
		" 547 "	19.	8.	3.
		" 548 "	4.	4.	5.
		" 550 "	31.	1.	7.
		" 554 "	22.	10.	2.
		" 555 "	5.	4.	2.
		By Bill No 1241 on HM Treasury	394.	12.	5.
		" 1250 "	22.	19.	8.
		" 1249 "	17.	9.	4.
		By Check No 557 on the Comm. Chest	80.	3.	10.
		" 558 "	1.	11.	8
	26	H Blair Esq. Overseer Convict Establ amt of Received & Private Cash due 69 Convicts embarked? HMS Transport "Rhadamanthus" for the purpose of being transferred to Major John Shaw Gov. of the "Stirling Castle" C.H. at Gosport and for which a remittance certificate has been granted	273.	7.	9
	30	Chas Hutchinson Esq. of Cv Naval Depart. Convict Labor & gratuities	100.	16.	7.
		£	1815.	19.	9.

Date 1855	No of Vr.	Cr. By Payments	£	s.	d.
Oct 3	29	H Blair Esq. Overseer Convict Est Pay of Officers ? of Establ for Sept.	692.	15.	1.
"	30	" Prison Contingencies Q to 30th Sept. 1855	1.	7.	7.
"	31	" Hospital " "		10.	-
"	32	" Reserves months pay due 4 guards	1.	-	-
"	33	" Convicts weekly pay	75.	4.	7.
11	51	" Gratuities to Subordinate Officers of Est.	71.	12.	8.
13	64	" Thos H Roberts Medicines suppd Convict Hosp. in Sept.	19.	8.	3.
"	66	John Sheriff Milk & Eggs supp. "	4.	4.	5.
16	70	C Pons & Co shower bath & etc " Estab. "	31.	1.	7.
"	71	John Bertrloso lumber and paper " "	5.	4.	2.
"	72	James Dadero Vegetables Convict Estab & Hosp	22.	10.	2.
18	76	A Mateos Fresh meat supp " in Aug & Sept	394.	12.	5.
"	81	Anthony C Recano Water " "	22.	19.	8.
"	83	Fredr. Bafadone Oil " "	17.	9.	4.
"	85	" Groceries " "	22.	6.	7.
"	86	" Soap Oatmeal etc "	57.	17.	3.
"	87	Jacuito Marcella Paint etc "	1.	11.	8.
23	99	H Blair Esq. Overseer Convict Est. Reserves & Private Cash due 69 Convicts transferred to "Stirling Castle" C H at Gosport	273.	7.	9.
31		Amount paid into Comm. Chest	100.	16.	7.
		Credited	1815.	19.	9.

Shilling day at the Great Exhibition.

CHAPTER 17

Arrival in
Western Australia

When they took you away we went hungry
Then another moved into your bed
For poverty was our prison sentence
And compromise, freedom instead.
But this daddy is full of compassion
For those that your crime left for dead.
He is there to dry tears and to comfort
And to make sure the sparrows are fed.

In England, the summer of 1851 began chilly and wet, but on 1st May, after a little rain, the sun shone brilliantly on the great glass edifice of the Crystal Palace in London for the grand opening of The Great Exhibition. At the same time, as he begun his fifth month at sea, George might have taken a moment to remember his first young bride, Emily Cherry, on what would have been the sixth anniversary of their marriage.

Meanwhile, the Mermaid was sailing closer to Australia. By 5th May they were making rapid progress sailing at around eleven knots. The ages of the men were noted, all books collected and school finished on 8th May when the sergeant was confined to the hospital. The following day one boy was punished with the box for evincing lewd propensities with an attempt at sodomy. Fresh birds were sighted on 12th and when the cables were brought up and bended to the anchors, the portholes cleaned and painted, the men knew that the voyage was near its end. On 13th, as cleaning of the painted ports was in progress, land was sighted.[1] There was great excitement aboard the Mermaid. First the hovering of strange birds had told them that their voyage was nearing its end, then land was sighted and the mood of the convicts had lifted. Even before this new horizon appeared, the men on board could smell it. After so long at sea, land makes a sailor aware of its presence by its bouquet. They could smell the pungent eucalyptus, the acrid bushfire smoke, the aromatic scent of flowers. They could feel the presence of land, the excitement of this strange new world.

Back in Houghton Regis, on 10th May, Sarah, George's second wife, had given birth to a daughter, the first by Thomas Inns. Little Eliza, now nearly three years old, had a baby sister, named Mary Jane. On 15th May, as Sarah and Thomas prepared for the baptism of their baby, on the other side of the world her husband was nearing his destination. At 1.30pm on 15th, the Mermaid passed Rottnest Island, one and a half miles away, and after sailing for another three hours stood by to take a pilot on board. The pilot's two oarsmen were Aborigines, a fact which caused great interest amongst those on board. The Mermaid finally sailed into Gage's Roads, between Rottnest Island and the mouth of the Swan River at 5.30pm and lowered the anchor. The following day brought two officials aboard a water police boat to speak to the Captain and Surgeon Superintendent, and to interview those men chosen for duties aboard, the boatswains, school attendants and two hospital orderlies, speaking favourably of their efforts. A supply of fresh mutton was received on board, and the men prepared for disembarkation, impatient for their first taste of their new land. All tins, mess utensils and bedding up to number 13 mess were collected. The next day four hundred and fifty-two lb loaves of soft bread were received sent by prisoners ashore, to be enjoyed with pumpkin soup. Then the men began to disembark, the first being two lots in sailing boats. With these, the surgeon deemed it wise to send two sick passengers to the military hospital at Perth without delay. Fred Stone, a pensioner guard, aged thirty-six, had been ill on board since 27th February complaining of a violent pain in his right side and loins. Since then he had been regularly attended by the surgeon who had diagnosed hepatitis. He had apparently had a similar attack some years before. The other was also a pensioner guard. Arthur Eggar, aged thirty-five, first complained of diarrhoea at Spithead on 2nd January and, although he recovered briefly in February sufficiently to return to duty, he had fallen ill again and had continued to have treatment for the rest of the voyage. He had been invalided from the artillery with the same complaint which he had suffered for more than two years, and the surgeon considered that he had not been fit for embarkation.[2]

The following day the sea became agitated, with winds high and strong. All the cable was eased out and an anchor dropped. Unfortunately for those remaining on board, the severe weather hampered the process of disembarkation and the Mermaid was forced to stay at anchor to ride it out. The disappointed men were forced to carry on the day to day monotonous routine they had so long endured. That day, prayers were read by a schoolmaster. On 19th May, mess utensils and bedding were issued once more. It was evident that there would be nobody going ashore that day. The next day continued squally and the men sat about dejectedly, mostly occupied catching a great many fish.

Excerpt from THE INDEPENDENT NEWS May 1851 CO 22/4

Shipping Intelligence
ARRIVED – On the 15th instant, the ship Mermaid, Anderson from London & Portsmouth, with 200 convicts, 29 pensioners, and 30 women and children. Surgeon Superintendent, Dr. Kilroy, R.N.

The Mermaid rode out the heavy gale of Monday night and Tuesday in Gage's Roads, without dragging her anchors in the slightest degree; her draught of water prevented her entering Owen's anchorage until lightened. The landing of the convicts and pensioners was completed on Wednesday.

On 21st May, the stormy weather abated, and the men could see their future. Their distant view was of a land thickly wooded with beautiful foliage, but in all directions what caught their eye was the shoreline of dazzlingly white sand. It was expected they would begin to go ashore at any time. Firstly the Captain and the Surgeon Superintendent, and then gradually the men began to disembark in small parties, the process not finally complete until nearly a week after the Mermaid had arrived.

George was taken ashore, as convict number 320, to begin his new life along with his fellow convicts, firstly to a reception ward to be cleansed. The convicts' papers were brought up to date with their personal details, their offences, sentences, date and place of conviction, trades, personal description, and a conduct report by surgeon-superintendent. George's Character Book states that his character was "good".[3] Now ashore, the convicts had the clothes they were wearing replaced by the government convict attire consisting of a jacket made of Drogheda Linen, which was a type of canvas material, with broad black arrows stamped all over; a pair of trousers, waistcoat and either a felt or straw hat. Items such as knives, watches or scissors, which had been placed in the hands of the steward on board, were now handed over in the governor's office.

One might wonder just how prepared the men were to embrace their new land and what impression they got from their first sightings. To exchange the cool green English countryside, with verdant rolling hills, oak trees and fields, for this strangely inhospitable place; the harsh sunlight, the unfamiliar smells, eucalyptus trees, exotic birds and strange animals, the flights of screeching cockatoos replacing the gentler sounds of English songbirds, and the sight of natives in their state of nudity. It was a curious new world they were introduced to as they were marched in their batches to their makeshift prison, somewhat bewildered by their surroundings but out of necessity ready to make what they could of their new lives.

Foreseeing the arrival of so many more convicts, it was decided that a more permanent prison should be built to replace the makeshift housing provided by Captain Scott's warehouse. The site chosen was on a rise

View of Fremantle in 1856.

overlooking the town and it became one of the first jobs for the convicts to build a jail in which to house themselves, from limestone quarried locally. The men on the Hashemy, the second ship to arrive at Fremantle, who were also supposedly men of lesser sentence, were already at work in clearing the ground and marking out the site for the prison.

Meanwhile, the relatively unrestrained lifestyle of the convicts in the warehouse overlooking the sea at Fremantle came as a welcome relief after their arduous crossing from England and their years of imprisonment.

From the start, this penal settlement established in the Swan River Colony was run much more humanely than those at Botany Bay and Port Arthur. The superintendent in charge of the convicts, Captain Henderson, did not believe in flogging, or making the men work in chains. The convicts had hot water to wash in and in summer they were taken swimming a couple of times a week, but in return they also had to work long hours in the open, under the blazing hot sun, conditions which they were unused to. Some of the more trustworthy men were released on restricted tickets-of-leave and sent out in parties for work on roads and other public buildings.

Excerpt from **The Independent Journal Friday 5th July 1850**

THE CONVICT ESTABLISHMENT AT FREMANTLE. – A few days since we visited this establishment, which we were courteously conducted over by the officers in charge. We went impressed with the idea usually entertained, of gangs of convicts working under restraint, that they would exhibit a sullen, sulky appearance, only kept to their tasks by fear of punishment, and every precaution by means of guards and sentries taken to prevent escape. What we saw was exactly the reverse; not a guard was to be seen, save a gate-keeper, not a discontented or a sullen countenance was to be observed in the whole body. On the contrary, good humour, alacrity, and contentment was the characteristic of all, and no person unacquainted with the fact that it was a body of convicts, could possibly have expected these fine, healthy looking men to be such, in fact we were not only surprised at what we saw, but also extremely gratified. It would appear that the authorities could not have found premises better suited for the establishment than those of Captain Scott, and they are now being fitted up with all possible dispatch; the long shed before used as a wool store, is being enclosed, and when completed will furnish sleeping accommodation for 175 men; other parts of the premises are used for offices and depot for implements, clothing, and stores of all imaginable kinds, for carrying on works of every description. The lease of these premises only extends to three years, and not five, as we before stated, a reduction of the term having been since made. It is in contemplation to erect buildings for a permanent establishment, the site of which is not yet determined upon, but it is likely that the low hills situated at the back of the present establishment, will be selected.

When the men from the Mermaid finally came ashore they too were taken to the makeshift warehouse prison, placed in wards, still in messes, and allocated hammocks. John Acton Wroth was placed in B. ward, No. 1 Division, No. 2 Mess, No. 12 Hammock with messmates J. Pearce,

G. Whittaker, T. Neale, J. Baskerfield and W. Revel. He described the accommodation as good with sufficient food and tobacco. The convicts attended chapel and school a half day a week.

Now that the Mermaid had discharged her human cargo, she remained at anchor in Gage's Roads, her empty bowels awaiting her next consignment, this time a shipment of horses bound for Madras. Meanwhile her two hundred and eight enforced immigrants had to be put to work. Their services were advertised in the local paper informing settlers when their ticket-of-leave expired, their trades and profession. At the same time a notice appeared in the same paper to potential employers of the ticket-of-leave men.

NOTICE

Comptroller General's Office,

Fremantle, July 23rd 1851

The Comptroller-General begs to call the attention of employers of Ticket-of-leave Holders, to the following Regulation respecting them; and wishes to impress upon the former, the necessity of making the required amount of stoppages from the men in their employ, - at the rate of 8s 6d. per month, - to be enabled to make the regulated half yearly payment of £2 10s. on account of each man, - without delay or inconvenience:-

1 - "Every Ticket-of-leave Holder is required to pay into the hands of the Comptroller-General of Convicts a sum of money on account of his passage to the Colony."

2 - "For the payment of this sum, every employer of a Ticket-of-leave Holder is required to pay to the Comptroller-General of Convicts a sum of £5 per annum."

3 - "All payments to the half-yearly, or at the expiration of any engagement for a shorter period."

4 - "A reduction of 2s. in the pound will be allowed, if the yearly payment is made 3 months before the end of the year."

5 - "All employers of Ticket-of-leave men are liable for this payment, which can be recovered in like manner as any other debt."

6 - "The total amount required to be paid by each man will be notified to his Employer."

E.Y.W. HENDERSON.   *Comptroller-General*

Others were placed on public works around Fremantle, some joining their compatriots of the Hashemy building the prison. The construction of Fremantle Prison was begun at the end of October 1850 and not totally completed until ten years later in 1860. It remained Western Australia's main penitentiary until it was decommissioned after it closed as a prison on 31st October, 1991. Fremantle Prison remains the only surviving intact convict-built prison in the world; a tribute to those convicts who built it. Convict labour was also responsible for the erection of many fine public buildings including Perth Town Hall, where windows in the shape of the broad arrow can be seen on either side of the clock face, and Government House.

At the same time, a road had to be built to haul the stone to the site, and houses had to be built to house the guards and their families who had arrived with the convicts, for accommodation in Fremantle was scarce, and some pensioners were being accommodated in a rented building at the whaling jetty.

In 1850 the Government decided to assist the growth of the area known as Freshwater Bay by allocating land on the foreshore and Lake Claremont to nineteen pensioner guards and their families. Freshwater Bay was a small settlement half way between Fremantle and Perth first established in 1830 by John Butler, a settler from Liverpool, who, realising the potential qualities of the area, built an inn on the road connecting the two major communities. This inn was well situated to serve those travellers between Fremantle and Perth for, as an alternative to the passage boats that regularly plied between the two places, the journey could be made on horseback, crossing by a horse-ferry at Preston Point, about a mile and a half from Fremantle. The journey would continue along a loose sandy track, passing through the open forest via Freshwater Bay. Although improvements to the road between Fremantle and Perth had been started in July 1851 by a small party of convicts, they were withdrawn in September of that year. Little was done to it for a number of years because the river was used so much for the traffic and therefore it was not considered to be of any urgency. So

Government House, Perth.

the track remained often obstructed by fallen trees, making it difficult to travel.

The pensioners were provided with two lots of land – nine and a half acres inland at the swamp north of the bay and half an acre on the foreshore, the swamp locations being chosen for their agricultural potential and the foreshore for dwellings. But life was hard for these pensioners, for although they had been led to believe in England that cottages would be built for them, in reality convict labour was given priority to other projects. Initially, their shelter was probably primitive huts thatched with blackboy rushes. Their blocks of land for cultivation, although the soil showed great potential, were in some places heavily timbered and hard to clear. Food prices were high, seriously eroding their pensions and, as the £10 cash grant intended for tools and seeds had to be spent on provisions, most were forced to find work to supplement their income, reducing the time they had available to clear their land for cultivation. Some sought positions with the convict establishment in Fremantle and some wives earned a little from washing for settlers there but, because of the distance involved, generally had to stay overnight.

However, when they could make time to take in their surroundings, they could take delight in what they saw. The area was beautiful, the landscape surrounding the clear waters of the Swan River. There was a plentiful supply of fresh spring water, and an abundant supply of fish – kingfish, schnapper and skipjack – and waterfowl, the swamp full of wild duck.

By December 1851, the year of their arrival, both George and William Golding, his acquaintance from the Mermaid, were working in Freshwater Bay as sawyers.[4] William obtained his ticket-of-leave on 17th February, 1852, nine months after his arrival in the colony. Initially, to be eligible for a full ticket, a convict must have served half of his sentence, but this rule was gradually relaxed if the convict proved to be trustworthy. By this time, many convicts had qualified, which meant that they were free to hire themselves out to those colonists anxious for their services, and to earn wages. William was employed by John Weedon at Freshwater Bay, and now William had obtained his ticket-of-leave he was allowed to employ other convicts. He employed George, to work with him. Their work would have been very hard. All along from Bunbury to Lancelin and inland to the Darling Range there was once tuart forest. The area immediately around Freshwater Bay abounded in mahogany and redgums and was covered with banksia and scrub. Tuart was a very hard wood tree and once dry was so hard that a nail could not be hammered into it, so the wood had to be drilled to drive in a nail.

The two men would have spent all day in a sawyer's pit, a hole dug into the ground approximately 6 to 7ft deep and 6ft wide, or even more depending on how thick were the trees to be sawn, by about 10ft long. Support timber was laid end to end on top of the pit and the unsawn log rolled lengthways onto the support logs. There the two men would cut the log into boards for use in building, one of them standing on the log and one of them down in the hole. Saws used were very large, around eight feet in length, called cross cut saws. To make the cut the man at the top pulled the saw up about a 6ft stroke, then the man underneath pulled it back down the same length stroke. Nowadays this method has been replaced with circular saws powered by electricity. But for the two convicts the conditions would have been terrible, especially for the man at the bottom of the pit with a day's sawdust in his clothes in the heat of a West Australian summer's day. The itch from both sawdust and mosquitos would have driven them mad. Supposedly, some men worked in the nude to combat the problem.

Initially, the two men were probably very dependent on each other for friendship in this isolated place. For, once their working day was over, the two men, exhausted by their exertions, could sit in companionable silence smoking their pipes or exchanging a yarn over their pot of tea, with the satisfaction of a hard day's work completed. They could look forward to the same tomorrow. For their life here in the bush would have been very far removed from their life in England. Here they would have at best a primitive hut in which they lived in this small community at Freshwater Bay, for the convict depot which came later was not yet built. They would combat bush flies and mosquitos, heat and dust. But they had new experiences of beautiful birds and animals like never before seen, wild flowers and a view of the Swan River, as it snaked its way in one direction towards Perth and in the other to Fremantle. In fact, now that George was able to take stock of his new home and work opportunities, life could not have looked so bad from the graceful banks of this magnificent river.

On 1st December, 1852, George also obtained his ticket-of-leave[5] although he still continued to work at Freshwater Bay with William Golding, who in turn was employed by John Weedon. Once this was approved, he was interviewed by the chaplain at Fremantle, and issued with a pair of trousers, two pairs of socks, boots, vest, cap, two handkerchiefs, a blue flannel shirt and two cotton shirts by the Accountant of Stores. Reconvicted men, colonial and local prisoners

Scale of Clothing

— to be issued to Prisoners on discharge —

Probation Prisoners

Boots _____ pr 1
Cap _____ no 1
Handkerchief _____ . 2
Shirts Flannel Blue _ . 1
_ Do Cotton _____ . 2
Socks _____ pr 2
Trowsers _____ . 1
Vest _____ no 1

Reconvicted, Colonial, and Local Prisoners

Boots _____ pr 1
Cap _____ no 1
Handkerchief _____ . 1
Shirts Flannel Blue . 1
_ Do Cotton _____ . 1
Socks _____ pr 1
Trowsers _____ . 1

True Copy

H Murray
5. 7. 73

(Sgd.) D. Francisco
Accountant of Stores

Clothing allowance for ticket-of-leave men.

had their clothing allowance reduced by one handkerchief, a pair of socks and one shirt. There was also a list kept of men who had 'made away with' the clothing supplied to them on their discharge and to whom no more clothing was to be issued in the future.

Regulations for Holders of Ticket-of-Leave:
(See appendix for full list)

(1)   The ticket holder was required to report to the Resident Magistrate within 7 days of arrival in the district. He had to report also within the first two weeks of January and June each year.

(2)   Any changes of employment or residence had to be reported within 7 days.

(3)   They were only allowed to stay in a town on a special pass.

(4)   They were not permitted on ships without authority.

(5)   They were not allowed to have a licence to keep a public house.

(6)   They could not carry firearms without permission.

(7)   They were required to pay the sum of £15 for their passage to the colony.

During 1853 a convict depot was established at Freshwater Bay for the purpose of making the Fremantle to Perth road. It consisted of three houses for officers, a cookhouse with ovens and a building to house eighty prisoners, sleeping in hammocks. The buildings were portable and made of jarrah wood and were located at the alignment of the new road. A well was dug to supply fresh water.[6] The prisoners here were engaged mainly in labouring associated with building the road, quarrying, woodcutting, lime burning and sawyer work, as well as cook, boatman and cleaner. The road gangs generally camped in the bush at night in comparative liberty. But the labour was very hard, especially in the warm weather, and water was scarce, even though wells had been constructed at intervals along the routes. Often the men had to walk long distances to and from where they were working. Limestone for firming the roads was quarried with gunpowder covering the men with white powder. It was extremely hard on their clothing and any replacements had to be paid for out of their wages, as did such extras as sugar and their one permitted solace, tobacco. But they were paid a wage higher than at the depots and they received adequate rations, although keeping them supplied with meat, generally kangaroo, was a problem. The work was physically exhausting and discontent did breed amongst some road parties on the longer routes, leading to trouble flaring up, but it was eventually recognised that this was mainly due to spending too long a period isolated in the bush, and as a result it was recommended that no man should be forced to spend longer than four months there. But other than these incidents, there was generally little trouble from the men, and some it suited, these having no desire to leave the road gangs after the four month period. The main discipline for these work parties was the knowledge that any misconduct would revoke their probationary ticket-of-leave and delay their conditional pardon.

Rations for the convicts followed a scale recommended by a board of medical officers to the Governor. From 1st June 1855, this consisted of:

Breakfast
10oz. bread, 1 pint of tea, made with 1/5oz. of tea and 3/4oz. of sugar; 1oz. treacle if obtainable.

Dinner
14oz. meat, 4oz. bread, 12oz. potatoes.

Supper
8oz. bread, 1 pint tea (as above), 1oz. treacle if obtainable
Soup to be allowed on Tuesdays and Fridays; 1oz. rice, barley or oatmeal to thicken.
On soup days, if possible, cabbage, turnips or pumpkins in lieu of potatoes.

EQUIVALENTS OF VEGETABLES

12oz. potatoes { 24 oz. pumpkins
{ 14 oz. turnips
{ 19 oz. cabbages

Captain John Bruce, the staff officer of the Enrolled Pensioner Force, worked hard for the welfare of the military pensioners and tried to assist those settlers at Freshwater Bay in many ways. But he soon began to recognise that they lacked the intelligence and thriftiness that their situation required. In contrast, amongst the ticket-of-leave wood contractors there were many individuals of superior business habits and good sense. Consequently, whilst the pensioners struggled to bring their land under control, the ticket-of-leave men began to take advantage of their situation. For the woodcutters who were prospering at Freshwater Bay held the government contract and although Captain Bruce tried to set up the pensioners with the means to contract their own supplies, he was frustrated in his attempt as they lacked the intelligence to accomplish success with the enterprise. To supplement their income, the pensioners were forced to work for the ticket-of-leave men, and to further frustrate their advancement they often took their wages in provisions instead of regular cash.[7]

It had become obvious in those early days that the lack of unmarried females in the colony was a big problem. According to the chaplain at Fremantle gaol in 1854 "many (convicts) are tempted to seek a substitute for home and its happiness on the bench of the alehouse". He "deplored that ticket-of-leave men had to struggle against a serious evil – the want of wives".[8] In an effort to redress the balance between male and female, ticket-of-leave men were encouraged to bring out their wives and children upon payment of half of their fare. In later years, the families were brought out on application for a free passage. But not many took advantage of this offer; the spouse in Britain was often reluctant to make the journey and settle in an unknown new land. After being separated from their husbands for so long, most had made new lives for themselves and had settled with another partner. Indeed, this was so in George's case, Sarah having by this time started a family with Thomas Inns. And indeed, the convicts themselves, those that were given the opportunity, had done the same.

From Government Gazette:[9]
Colonial Secretary's Office, Perth,
November 8, 1852.
His Excellency the Governor directs the following Despatch,
relative to Female Immigration to Western Australia, to be
published for general information.
By His Excellency's command,
W.A. Sanford
Colonial Secretary.

Downing Street, June 22, 1852

SIR, – I have the honor to inform you that, adverting to the
demand which is reported to exist for Female Servants in Western
Australia, and to the great importance of endeavouring to prevent
too large a disproportion between the sexes, I have instructed the
Emigration Commissioners to collect a party of female emigrants
for the colony.

For the same reason, I have also inquired into the results
hitherto of the recommendation received from Western Australia
and other places of Convicts described as eligible to be joined
by their families. I learn that several cannot be found, owing to
change of residence, and to the difficulty of tracing persons in
their condition of life, and that others refuse to avail themselves
of the offer; so that by no means all are prevented from emigration
merely from the difficulty of complying with the rule that half
the expense of passage is to be paid by them or on their behalf.
It appears, however, on an analysis of the returns, that in cases
where an entirely free passage has been offered, one third of the
number have declined or been unable to proceed, but that when
only half the cost of passage is provided, two thirds have declined
or been unable to proceed. Unwilling therefore to oppose any
obstacle in Western Australia to so desirable an object as the
speedy conveyance of their families to convicts who have earned

their tickets of leave or appear deserving of the indulgence, I have now instructed the Emigration Commissioners to offer an entirely free passage to those convicts' families who have already been recommended by you, as well as to the others of whom recommendations may hereafter arrive from you, hoping that the men may be trusted to repay out of the accruing earnings of their labour in the colony the half of the passage which is properly chargeable to them. I have directed the Emigration Commissioners duly to inform the Colonial Secretary in each ship carrying convicts' families, of the cases respectively in which half or all of the cost of passage has be en defrayed by the public; and when the whole has been paid here, you will bear in mind that the sum chargeable to the convict will not be the moiety of the actual cost, but the moiety of one uniform assumed price of £15 per adult, and half for children under 14 years of age.

I have, &c.,
JOHN S PAKINGTON.

To Governor FitzGerald, &c., &c., &c.

The daughters of free immigrants generally looked for a husband amongst those men of their own social standing and of the free class, rather than amongst the convicts, when they came to consider marriage. But something had to be done to equal out the imbalance between the sexes.

The Acting Comptroller General, Captain Wray, was opposed to the transportation of female convicts and recommended pressing for more female immigrants.[10] The Government looked for a supply of these in the union workhouses, and amongst the poor unmarried Irish girls, many of them Irish needlewomen and those who were victims of the terrible potato famine. It was considered that these would have no prejudice against marrying those of the convict class and so, between the years of 1850 and 1855, over four hundred of these unfortunates were sent out.

William Golding was one of the few convicts to find a bride amongst

Needlewomen embark on board ship, sent to increase the female population in Australia.

the free settlers. Despite having his wife Amy and child in England, William sought permission to marry. On 7th March, 1860, he wed Mary Jane McMullen, the daughter of Thomas McMullen, an enrolled pensioner guard who sailed out with the first consignment of convicts on the Scindian. Thomas was discharged from the Royal Artillery on a pension of 1/- per day suffering from rheumatism which he contracted whilst serving in Canada in the winter of 1838 on the march from St. John's New Brunswick to Quebec during the rebellion. Thomas was one of the few pensioners who remained on his allocated grant of land at Freshwater Bay after the expiration of the seven-year period which was required to qualify for application of ownership, and in 1859 he purchased two other locations of nine and half acres each.[11]

The sawyers stationed at Freshwater Bay were employed to saw timber for the depot at Mount Eliza, Perth. For this they were paid quite a high wage compared with others. In 1857 the amount was 6/- per day compared with 2/-. paid to labourers, quarrymen, constables boatmen etc. However, records for William Golding show that his rate of wages was 10/- per 100 (ft. superficial). This included the felling of trees, and sawing the timber into beams, joists, rafters, lintels boards, battens and other scantling. The nature of the timber, mahogany, tuart etc caused a much greater quantity of sawing to produce the like quantity of good stuff. This rate of pay suggests that Golding and George had a contract to produce the timber, rather than being paid a daily rate.

Advert from the Independent Journal

TO SAWYERS.
PILES & SCANTLINGS.
Colonial Secretary's Office, Perth,
May 17, 1851

Tenders *(in duplicate)* will be received at this Office up to 12 o'clock, on TUESDAY, the 27th Instant, for furnishing the undermentioned PILES & SCANTLINGS, deliverable at the Whaling Jetty at Fremantle, viz:-

    10 Main Piles, 12x9 and 20 feet long
    8 Spur Piles, 9x9 and 12 feet long. To be squared
    and perfectly straight, and one end pointed
    180 Sheet Planking, 9x3½, 12 feet long sawn, and
    one end pointed
    20 Pieces of Scantling, 6 inches deep, cut bevel, 3
    inches top and 4½ bottom, and 16 feet long
    26 Pieces of 8x4, 9 feet long
    16 Pieces 8x4, 10 feet long

The whole of the above to be of the best description of Mahogany, straight grained, and subject to the examination of the Superintendent of Public Works.

One-third of the above quantity (in equal proportions) is to be delivered within 14 days from the date of contract, and the remainder within one month from the same period.

Further particulars can be obtained at the Resident's Office, Fremantle, and of the Superintendent of Public Works, Perth.

By His Excellency's command,
T.N. YULE
Acting Colonial Secretary

Once he had obtained his ticket-of-leave George too was allowed to employ other convicts. The first man whose name appears linked with George is Frederick Williams (249). His records show that he was working with George White serving for J. Weedon from December 10th,1852. The first man named that he actually employed was William Capp (1310) from 12th July until 27th September, 1854. These two men would have shared a common bond because William was convicted at Bedford, the same place as George himself. William was born in 1823, married with three children, and his trade was shown as shoemaker, labourer. He was convicted on 1st July, 1851, for robbery with violence and was given a sentence of ten years' transportation. His description in records showed him as aged twenty-nine years, 5ft 5in tall, dark hair, grey eyes, long face, and dark complexion, stout scar on upper lip and J Clare on right arm. William arrived in Fremantle on 4th August, 1852, on board the convict ship, William Jardine.[12]

The second, James White (3827), he employed from 18th October 1856. Records show James was born in 1835, was single, shoemaker, Protestant, literate, aged twenty-one years, 5ft 4in tall, light hair, grey eyes, round head, fair complexion, middling stout, and pockmarked. He was convicted at Bath in 1853 for stealing gas fittings and received ten years. He arrived in Fremantle on 29th March, 1856, on board the William Hammond.[13]

Then from 8th May, 1858, there was a fellow inmate from the Mermaid. John Pearce (302) was convicted at York Assizes on 11th July, 1849 for firing a stack of barley and sentenced to 15 years. He is described as a miner, single, aged twenty-eight years, 5ft 10in tall, light brown hair, grey eyes, long face, fresh complexion and anchor on right arm.[14] John Pearce was also one of those who shared a mess with John Acton Wroth on arrival in Fremantle.

During his time at Freshwater Bay, George met Maria Gardiner. Nothing is known about Maria and no record has been found of her arrival in the colony. Two families by the name Gardiner did arrive in the Colony on board the Trusty in 1842, and there was certainly at least one named Maria amongst the children, but it proved not to be this person. Maybe there was a child of the other family with the same name, but this has not been ascertained. But it is also possible that she was one of the impoverished needlewomen mentioned.

There being nothing to keep him from settling down with her, George lived with Maria until her death, although there is no record that George and Maria ever actually married. They could have applied to do so, even though he was still officially married to Sarah, and it remains a mystery as to why they chose not to wed. But nevertheless Maria assumed George's name and they went on to have six children, the first four being born in Perth.

George and Maria became parents to their first-born child on 14th December, 1853, a son, George Junior, a little over six weeks before George's wife, Sarah, gave birth to her second daughter, Harriet, by Thomas Inns at his old home in Groom's Yard, Houghton Regis. Sarah and Thomas had three daughters in total, Mary Jane born in 1851, Harriet born in 1854, and Emmie, born in 1860, all half-sisters to Eliza, George's daughter, but as Sarah and Thomas did not marry until 1875, all three of Thomas's children took George's surname.

Throughout prison records, the degree of George's ability to read or write differed. From the earliest records it was stated that he could do neither, and then later that he was able to read. On some it is stated that he could write. On both his marriage certificates he has signed with a cross, so it is possible that he learnt his somewhat inadequate skills whilst serving in prison. On his daughter Maria's birth certificate in 1858, he has signed his name as informant, although on another he has marked with a cross. Further records whilst in Western Australia show that his accounts were 'indifferent'. There is a part which details 'information respecting Prisoner obtained from himself or others as to his Religious and Moral Character', but this is unfortunately left blank. Therefore, there is no record of him attending Divine Service, or receiving sacrament. His habits, intellect, state of mind, and secular knowledge, too, is blank, as is the alleged cause of his crime, and remarks on his conduct and progressive improvement. However, the record does state that he had books delivered to him from time to time in the form of Saturday magazines and 'Robinson Crusoe'.[15] So it would appear, at this time, he was able to read but of course it is possible that these were borrowed for the benefit of Maria.

George continued to work for William Golding at Freshwater Bay until June 1857 when he began working for himself. Prison records are not clear as to whether he was still a sawyer, but on all his children's birth certificates George's occupation is shown as a wheelwright. Records also show that at some time whilst he was working at Freshwater Bay George re-offended but no record of the charge has been found.[16] This would suggest it was something minor and most of the cases of re-offence for ticket-of-leave men were for being 'drunk and disorderly'.

Gradually, once the convicts began to settle, the local economy started to improve. They provided Fremantle with a demand for food, materials and services, as well as providing them with roads, housing and a cheap workforce. As the colony began to prosper, the British Government gave more money for the organisation and control of the convicts. The town of Fremantle contained about one thousand, eight hundred inhabitants; it had four churches – Episcopalian, Dissenting, and Roman Catholic; two good school-houses; and many of the streets were macadamised. The convict prison on the rising ground at the back of the town was now nearly complete for the reception of one thousand prisoners and requisite staff. From Arthur's Head, on which the lighthouse stood, it was proposed to carry out a breakwater, to form a secure harbour at all seasons of the year – the anchorage about a mile off shore being considered unsafe in winter, at which season ships had to resort to Owens anchorage, three miles south of Fremantle, or to Garden Island, where there was an excellent harbour, secure at all seasons, but which was nine miles from the town of Fremantle. Twelve miles up the River Swan, the capital city of the colony, Perth, boasted about two thousand inhabitants. It was beautifully situated on the banks of the river, and contained several churches, a large hospital, schoolhouses and many agreeable private residences. The soil in the neighbourhood of Perth varied a great deal, but much was of an excellent quality producing exceedingly good fruit, vegetables and flowers. The vine, olive and castor-oil tree all thrived, a single bunch of grapes weighed in at 26lb, and the olive tree bearing fruit in three years instead of seven as in the Mediterranean. The upper valleys of the Swan and its tributaries were studded with thriving farms and settlements. Western Australia had already received in five years as many convicts as had New South Wales in thirteen, and at one-third the cost, and to its credit there had grown there an excellent system of convict discipline, benefiting both convict and settler. Revenue increased from £9,569 in 1849 to £34,451 in 1855 and the population more than doubled.[17] This comparatively little known colony which a few years earlier saw its bubble about to burst had been transformed by the advent of convict labour, and the colonists appeared desirous for it to continue.

From the Illustrated London News 14th February 1857 p 147:

The colonists, we are assured, really desire the services of convicts of the mother country, as we gather from the following statement, numerously signed by gentlemen connected with the colony of Western Australia, which has been read and presented by a deputation to Mr. Labouchere:

To the Right Hon. Henry Labouchere, Her Majesty's Secretary of State for the Colonies, &c.

Sir, – We, the undersigned, having an interest in and knowledge of the resources of Western Australia, feel it a duty we owe both to that colony (whose real capabilities do not appear to be understood) and this country to put before the Government a few plain facts to prove that it is peculiarly adapted for a penal settlement:

1.   Because the expense of planting a convict establishment (which is always very great) has been already incurred,

substantial prisons and depots have been built, and the necessary offices prepared to receive a large number of convicts.

2. The free settlers (unlike those of other parts of Australia) are willing to continue to receive convicts, to employ them, and to pay them great wages; they merely require some modification of the present system. The convicts can be beneficially employed in the advancement of the colony, such as making roads, bridges, and tramways into the timber forests and to the copper and lead mines.

3. Convict labour has been the means of producing the necessaries of life, which formerly were very scarce and dear, in abundant supply, and on reasonable terms. The convict establishment has also created a market for food, which is amply supplied by the settlers, and at cheap rates. Flour, as an instance, was formerly from £35 to £40 per ton, now (in October last) a contract was taken at £20 per ton, delivered at the depot, and the contractor is prepared next year to supply it at £16 per ton.

4. Western Australia also possesses a fine climate, and is unconnected with other parts of Australia (at present) except by sea, and is as much an island as if surrounded by it. Convicts can only escape by sea, and the natives would very soon bring them back if they attempted the bush; indeed, the convicts well know it.

5. Rottnest Island, about fourteen miles from Fremantle, is well adapted for the refractory convicts; and there is ample room for a large number, and employment for years to come in erecting forts and other necessary public works – raising salt, cultivating the land, gardens, &c.

6.   That a large establishment may now be carried on at a
very reasonable rate, as the heavy outlay in the colony
has been increased principally for buildings, plant, &c.

We have the honour to remain, &c.,

(Here follow the signatures of the deputation.)

One of the old settlers who had dreaded the importation of convict labour aired his view:

We trust that the Government do not intend to discontinue the introduction of convicts, seeing the amount of benefit that has resulted to the colony from its having been made a penal settlement under the highly-improved system at present in operation, and how little trouble and uneasiness the ticket-of-leave population gives under the existing regulations; for not only are by far the majority of the ticket-holders reformed and better men as now treated, but we receive, free of charge to the colony, an importation of free labour of both sexes to an equal amount. Good and certain markets are formed for everything the settlers are able to produce or rear; and property of every description has acquired a value which it could not previously pretend to.[18]

The attitude of the free settlers appeared encouraging. After their term of punishment had expired, the convicts had a fair chance of regaining their forfeited position and becoming useful members of the community once more, which in England was scarcely possible, The Under-Secretary of State for the Colonies, Mr. Fortesque, later stated that he believed that Western Australia possessed the very best system of dealing with convicts that had ever yet been devised. The credit was attributed to Earl Grey, and this exercise in the removal of his unwanted prisoners was deemed a success.

Efforts were also being made by the convicts themselves to integrate themselves into the community of free settlers:

Lectures on various subjects have been delivered by the more enlightened portion of the convicts to their humbler companions in misfortune; while a manuscript weekly publication, called the Family Herald, conducted by the convicts, is stated to be got up creditably, and to strengthen the hope that there are many among them who, under the able management now exercised, may be restored to society, and do it good service.[19]

It was made clear to convicts, that before they could obtain a conditional pardon, they must repay their passage money.[20] George's sentence being for fifteen years, he had to pay £15 at the rate of £5 per year in quarterly instalments to the Commissariat storekeeper of the area. His application for conditional pardon, based on the fact that he was eligible due to the length of servitude, was made on 2nd September, 1859, [21] and on 3rd September, this was granted.[22] The application lists him as a re-offending ticket-of-leave man.

But now that this had been obtained, he was free to settle wherever he chose within the Colony. During all this time that George was around the Perth area, there is no record that he was ever in touch with any

above Conditional pardon application for George White.
right George White's conditional pardon is granted.

Colonial Secretary's Office, Perth,
3rd September, 1859.

CONDITIONAL PARDONS have been this day signed for :—

Reg. No	Name.
92	Matthew Horsfield
302	John Pearce
320	George White
333	Thomas Ashbee
340	Edward Wilding
1465	Edward Macklin
2664	John Bridger
2956	Thomas Wilding
2963	William Ramsey
3023	George Waters
3235	Thomas Grant
3461	Thomas Gallacher
3839	George Lloyd
4452	John Marshall
4690	William Jones
4703	Charles Lancaster.

By His Excellency's command,

FRED. P. BARLEE,

Colonial Secretary.

member of his family back in England. But in the Government Gazette under the 'List of Unclaimed Letters' lying at the General Post Office, Perth on 14th April, 1859, there is a letter for 'George White'.[23] We shall never know whether this was for our George, but it would be nice to think it was.

CHAPTER 18

Dockerill Appeals[1]

For once it would seem that fortune had smiled on Dockerill, for it had sent him back to England, and he was under the impression, or he had been led to believe, that, due to his injury, he would obtain his ticket-of-leave once he arrived. But here he ran out of luck once more. Instead of obtaining his release, Dockerill was taken on board the invalid hulk Stirling Castle, a hospital ship lying off the south coast near Gosport.

Shortly after the arrival of the Rhadamanthus, Sir Joshua Jebb, the Chairman of New Prison Service, visited the returned convicts at Gosport and ordered the Governor to send all of their names to the Home Office. As a result of this, shortly after, a reply was received granting all those men who had been invalided from Gibraltar a mitigation of six months on their sentence. However welcome this might have been, it was not the freedom that Dockerill had expected. Instead of this, he found himself still a prisoner on board the hulk.

After five months of frustration on board the hospital ship, Dockerill decided to petition the Home Office to try and gain his release, citing his ill-health due to the conditions that he had to endure in Gibraltar as a mitigation factor, and describing himself as 'your almost worn-out petitioner'.

This petition was received by the Home Office on 24th March, 1856:

PETITION (Copied as written)

Name, Age,   }   1422   Thos Dockerill,   Age 29
Register No., and }   "Stirling Castle" Hulk Gosport
Where confined   }

Convicted		Crime	Sentence	Remarks
When	Where	Intent		Millbank, good
8 March	Bedford	to do bodily	Life	Portland, good
1849	Assizes	harm		Gibraltar, V.Good
				S.Castle, good

To the Rt Honble Sir Geo Grey
Secretary of State for the Home Department

   The petition of Thos Dockerell humbly sheweth that he was tried at Bedford on the 8th March 1849 and sentenced to transportation for life.

   Your petitioner with submission wishes to state that after trial he remained at Bedford 5 months he was then removed to Millbank where he remained 11 months, afterwards to Portland where he served 8 months thence to Gibraltar where he served 4 years and 8 months and finally to Gosport where he has been 5 months making in all 7 years and 1 month.

   Your petitioner in addressing this his humble memorial, begs to call your particular attention to the following facts.

   That your petitioner having been confined in five different prisons for the long term of seven years and upwards and upon no occasion ever swerved from the discipline laid down for the regulation of prisoners he is proud to boast of a character exemplary.

   That during the long time your petitioner was at Gibraltar, he was the whole time working in water, in constructing a moat round the Battery wall, while so employed he unfortunately broke a blood vessel, for which he was in Hospital three weeks, and on other occasions he was through Rheumaticks in Hospital during the seven years and upwards about three months.

   That had your petitioners health allowed him to remain but a few months longer he would have been recommended for his liberty in the usual way when he had completed eight years; But unfortunately it being the will of the Almighty to cause him to be removed, he is given to understand that he must complete ten years, before the Governor can recommend him.

   Finally it is the facts stated in the 3rd section your petitioner wishes with humility to offer a remark, which he trust you will not deem imprudent. You will see that for the space of four years and five months deducting the time in Hospital he was exposed to two distructive eliments to the human frame (viz) Heat caused by the sun in a foreign clime, and water that continually inundated his work; such hardships has been the means of so undermining his constitution, that for the preservation of his declining health, it was deemed by the medical officers necessary to remove him to his native land.

Your petitioner trusts that in consequence of his having spent the flower of his time in a foreign clime and in bondage for a crime for which he is penitent, indeed the fact of his bearing an exemplary character goes to substantiate that assertion; together with his being a married man with a family of three children; You will not allow such characters to go unrewarded, nor allow extra punishment to be levied upon your petitioner in consequence of his physical powers failing while in the service of the Crown.

Trusting this will meet with the success he anticipates (viz) a commutation of some portion of his sentence; You by so doing will confer upon your almost worn-out petitioner a lasting favour, for which he will ever pray etc, etc, etc,

Signed
Thomas Dockerell

The above Petitioner ? ? was received from Gibraltar 27th October 1855. the medical report being Hemoptysis and Phthisis. His present health is very delicate.

John W. Bowles
Surgeon S.

March 19th 1856   *(sic)*

But Dockerill was to be disappointed. His application for remission was rejected by the Home Office on 7th April.

In view of his ill health and, according to Dockerill, his good behaviour, Rebecca was allowed to visit him whilst he was on board the Stirling Castle. Poor Rebecca was doubtless very excited that her husband was now back in England after an absence of nearly five years, and would have gladly undertaken the trip, however arduous the journey. But her joy in seeing him again was marred by the bad news that Dockerill had for her. Instead of being able to tell her that he was to be released as he had hoped, it was probable he might have to complete ten years in prison before being freed. If he had not been injured and had remained in Gibraltar for about another sixteen months, he would then have completed eight years. After serving this amount of time, it was the custom at Gibraltar to be eligible for a ticket-of-leave. All was not going according to plan for Dockerill.

But, still imprisoned on the hulk, he had plenty of time to think about his next move. He decided to appeal once more, but this time he would get Rebecca to petition for him, asking her to enlist the support of Squire Brandreth who would have more influence with the authorities. The Squire had been instrumental in William's pardon and Dockerill was counting on him to assist in his release as well. So, on 3rd July, 1856, after he had been on the Stirling Castle for about eight months, he wrote to Rebecca enclosing the draft of a petition he had drawn up on her behalf for her to get as he put it 'nicely copied' and take to Squire Brandreth.

Letter from Dockerill to Rebecca with petition (Copied as written).

"Stirling Castle" Hulk
Gosport
3 July 1856

1422 Thos Dockerill

To the right Honorable Sir George Grey,
Her Majestys Principal Secretary of State,
for the Home Department.

The humble Petition of Rebecca Dockerill of Stanbridge near Leighton Buzzard in the County of Bedfordshire.

Sheweth That your Petitioners Husband Thomas Dockerill, was tried at an Assize Holden at Bedford in March 1849 and Sentenced to Transportation for Life.

Your Petitioner in consequence of her Husband being invalided from Gibralter; to the Stirling Castle" Hulk, Gosport, is induced to approach the Honble Secry of State, by means of this humble memorial, her prayer may meet with mane(?) consideration upon the following grounds

That her Husband 5 months after the trial, was removed to "Millbank Prison", for the space of 11 months and from thence to Portland; where he remained 8 months; and from thence to Gibralter, where he laboured hard, for 4 years and 8 months; and was then invalided to the "Stirling Castle" Hulk, Gosport, and was given to understand, by the Authorities at Gibralter; upon leaving; that he would soon gain his liberty in the shape of a Ticket of Leave.

He has now been on Board the above Ship at Gosport about 8 months, making in all 7 years & 4 months since receiving his fearfull long Sentence.

Your Petitioner has in consequence of her Husbands good character, been allowed to visit him at Gosport, where she was to her great surprize, informed by him, that in consequence of his health failing, after being exposed for the long period of 4 years & 8 months, to the scorching sun of a foreign climate; he is fearfull from all he can learn at present, he will have to complete 10 years before he will be eligible for a Ticket of leave. And on the Contrary, had his health continued good, for the space of about 16 months longer, he would (according to custom at Gibralter) have been recommended for his License; as he would then have completed 8 years from the time of receiving his Sentence.

Your Petitioner sincerely prays, that the slight affliction which it pleased an all merciful God to lay upon Husband, will not prove to be, the means of detaining him, beyond the time, he would have been, had his health continued good and remained at Gibralter.

Your Petitioner has a family of Three children and have experienced a Task, to provide them with the commonest nice life; having had no one to render any assistance entirely depended upon her own industry, (with the ? God) for their support and have at present a home as ?ble as can be expected, under all these distressing circumstances, where she hopes shortly to enjoy the few comforts this world will afford, with a fond though unfortunate Husband.

Your Petitioner most earnestly and solemnly pray that the Honble Secry will take into his Merciful consideration; the Statements made in this Petition, (which, coupled with his length of imprisonment and general good character) will make intercession with the Queen, for such a portion of the Royal Clemency as Her Most Gracious Majesty is at all times pleased to bestow upon those; who sincerely repent of their former misconduct, and justly deserve the same; and for a humble Petitioner will as in duty bound ever pray (etc)

(Dear Wife) This is sent for you to get nicely copied, and signed by a few respectable persons around you, & forward the same to the Right Honble Sir Geo Grey. Secry of State. for his inspection and consideration; being your petition on my behalf; I wish you to see Brandriff Esqr, who thoroughly understands my case, and always promised he would endeavour to do something for me, when I had completed as he thought time enough, which I think I must have done. If he would be kind ????????? to enclose in the Petition, no doubt it would have a good effect, and at the same time obtain a letter from some of my old Employers, stating they are willing to give me employment upon my release, which is a great satisfaction to the Government Authorities, and enclose the same in your Petition. I hope you will without fail attend to this as early as possible and I have great hopes it will be the means of shortening my punishment. Have nothing more to say, but must beg of you to give my kind respects to all friends; and yourself & children to accept the warmest love of an affectionate, Father & Husband.

Thos Dockerill

(sic)

But not quite two weeks later, before his plans could be put into motion, Dockerill's health was considered improved sufficiently for him to be removed from the invalid hulk. This time he was bound for Dartmoor Prison. On his reception he was allowed to write again to Rebecca to inform her of his whereabouts. Again he stressed the importance of the petition.

Convict Establishment
Dartmoor

Convicts are permitted to write one Letter on reception and another at the end of three months. They may also receive one Letter (pre-paid) every three months during their stay. Matters of Private importance to a convict may be communicated at any time by Letter (pre-paid) to the Governor or Chaplain, who will inform the Convict thereof if expedient.

In case of misconduct the privilege of receiving or writing a Letter may be forfeited for the time.

All Letters of an improper or idle tendency either to or from Convicts, or containing slang or other objectionable expressions, will be suppressed. The permission to write and receive Letters is given to the convicts for the purpose of enabling them to keep up a connection with their respectable Friends, and not that they may hear the news of the day.

All Letters are read by the Governor or Chaplain, and must be legibly written and not crossed.

Neither clothes, money, nor any other articles are allowed to be received at the Prison for the use of Convicts, except through the Governor. Persons attempting otherwise to introduce any article to or for a Convict are liable to Fine or Imprisonment, and the Convict concerned is liable to be severely punished.

N.B. – The Convict's writing to be confined to these two pages; - In writing to the Convict direct to No. 3565 Thos. Dockerill   2132

July 16th 1856   14 / 7 1856

Dear Wife I know take the plesure of wrighting to you hoping to find you and all my Falimy in good helth as I am in the best of helth at present thanks god for it Dear Wife I have to inform you that I am removed from portsmouth to Dartmoor in Devonshire therefore Dear Wife I hope you will be Sucksesful in your pertition to howds my behalf as I hope you will under Stand it and if you do not propely under it I hope you will get sum one to inform you how to goe on and interseed into my case therefore I hope you will not leave a stone unturnd as I hope you Will beshure to go to Squire Brandriff and tell im from me that I hope he Will be so Kind as to do sumthing for me as he nows my consarn and I return my Sincer thanks to him for it as I have now been A long time confind therefore I hope and trust you will do All you can for me and wen you have got it of to London rite Back to me and Let me now all perticulars therefore Dear Wiff I conclude with Kind Love to you and all my Dear Children I and to all my relations frends so no more at present from your affectinate Husband Thomas Dock

(sic)

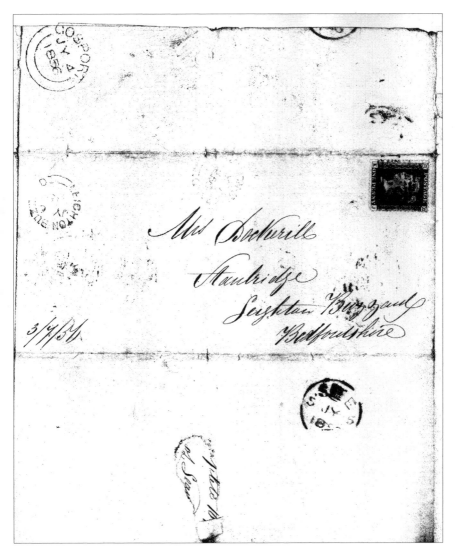

above Envelope addressed to Rebecca Dockerill.
left Letter from Dockerill to Rebecca from Dartmoor (Copied as written).

Rebecca, however, could not quite have understood, because she did not get the petition 'nicely copied', as Dockerill had requested, but took it to the Squire in its original form. She did however get the signatures of some of his supporters, expressing a willingness to employ him.

Petition from persons willing to employ Dockerill

Standbridge (sic)

Gustavus Jones	*Overseer*
George Claridge	*Miller*
Thomas Eames	*Farmer*
Josiah Wilks	*Farmer*
John Gurney	*Farmer*
William Cooper	*Gamekeeper*
John Ellingham	*Schoolmaster*
Joseph Eames	*Cattle Dealer*
John Clarke	*Builder & Farmer*

Will be glad to employ Thomas Dockerill

But, unfortunately for the couple, the Squire could not be relied on to the extent that Dockerill had hoped. He was unable to remember all the details of the incident because it had happened some years before, so he decided to write to the Police Office at Bedford for confirmation of the facts. The Police Office replied to the Squire on 11th August, giving Dockerill a bad character reference and outlining details from the Incident Book showing his previous conviction. On 17th August Squire Brandreth wrote to the Secretary of State, enclosing Rebecca's petition, and stated his impartiality. However, he also slipped in the comment that Dockerill was an exceedingly bad fellow.

Letter from Police Office at Bedford.

Bedford Augt 11th/ 56

My Dear Sir /

You are quite right. Thos Dockerill was a "most determined bad character", he shot at one Constable and all but killed another with the butt end of the gun after he had discharged it, who has ????

Charges against Thomas Dockerill from Police Book.

March Assizes 1847   Charged with one other, on three separate charges of Felony, Convicted and sentenced to 4 months, Hard Labour.

Lent Assizes 1849   Charged with two others, with maliciously wounding a Police Office, with intent to prevent his apprehension. Also with maliciously Shooting at, and wounding, James Parrott, a P.C. Also with stealing six Fowls. Also with stealing 4 Bushels of Barley. Convicted, and sentenced to Transportation for Life.

Bedford Rural Police Office)
August 11th 1856   )

Letter from Squire Brandreth.

Houghton House
Nr. Dunstable

August 17. 1856

Sir

I have the honour to send for your consideration some documents relative to the convict Thomas Dockerill – in the nominal form of a petition from his wife and friends – who was convicted in 1849.

The wife has not signed the Petition but, as it appears to have been drawn up by some of the officials connected with the Convict Establishment, I thought it had better come before you in its genuine state.

Not remembering the exact circumstances ? connected with the man's conviction I wrote to the Chief Constable and enclosed I send his reply and also a memorandum relative to charges against the man.

The man was convicted when I was Sheriff and the man White who is alluded to in the Chief Constable's letter was also convicted. The present Lord Chancellor was the Judge, and from conversation I had with his Lordship after the trial I was induced to address you to intercede for White's pardon, and which you kindly did and he received Her Majesty's pardon accordingly.

With regard to the present application I would wish to say that I simply forward Mrs Dockerill's application without offering any opinion of my own in the matter. All I know about him is that he was a bad fellow.

If I remember aright I sent a statement signed by him, after conviction, in which he not only exonerated White from any participation in the transaction, but admitted his own guilt.

Last Tuesday week I addressed a communication to you relative to the ? of the Governor of the Wandsworth House of Correction in respect of the discharge of a prisoner of the name of Evans (?), and against whom a charge had been made of running away from his wife and family, and for whose apprehension a warrant was in the hands of the Superintendent of Police of this District.

May I ask if the letter and copies of documents have been received.
I have the honour to be
Sir
Your most obedient Servant.
Hfrey. Brandreth.

The Right Honourable
Sir George Grey, ?, M.P.

(sic)

Dockerill's petition was rejected on the 2nd September, 1856. The reason was that he was "Too desperate a character to be released as yet". He had no choice, therefore but to accept his lot in Dartmoor.

Rejection of Appeal by Home Office

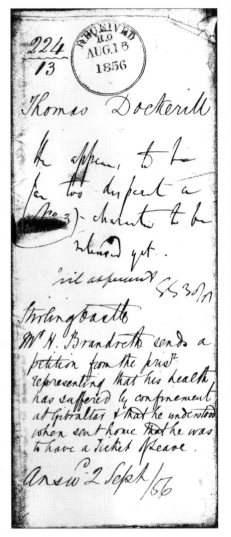

224/13

RECEIVED
HO
AUG 16 1856

Thomas Dockerill

No 3

*He appears to be far too desperate
a character to be returned yet.*

Nil at present
GS(?)

Stirling Castle

*Mr. H. Brandreth sends a petition
from the prisr representing
that his health has suffered by
confinement at Gibraltar & that
he understood when sent home
that he was to have a Ticket of
Leave.*

Answd 2 Sept / 56

Dockerill – far too desperate a character to be returned yet.

Dartmoor Prison.

CHAPTER 19

Dartmoor

Following the departure of French and American prisoners in the early nineteenth century, the original prisoner of war prison at Princetown in Devon was closed and had fallen into disrepair. But when available prisons had become so overcrowded and there were problems with the transportation of convicts, after several feasibility studies it was finally agreed in 1850 to re-open Dartmoor Prison. By September of that year, part of the prison had been made ready to house warders and military guards and on 1st November these arrived, followed by a small consignment of convicts. The latter were detailed to repair and fit the remainder of the war prisons and by December sufficient work had been done for the permanent occupation of convicts. Amongst the first to arrive were twenty-six convicts from Bedford Gaol. Dartmoor Prison was expected to be able to hold one thousand, three hundred convicts.

From Plymouth, Devonport & Stonehouse Herald, 2nd November 1850.

The prisons at Dartmoor are being put into repair for the reception of convicts, and it is said that when the whole arrangements are carried out several thousand prisoners will be sent to the spot.

The authorities, having experienced great difficulty in coming to a conclusion on secondary modes of punishment, have now determined to try the efficacy of imprisonment and hard labour on the bleak hills of the Forest of Dartmoor.

On Friday 1 November the first batch of prisoners was brought down by the mail train, and left at the late Laira Station, where an escort of the 4th Regiment under the command of Ensign Hall was in readiness to receive them, and from that place were conveyed in wagons via the Dartmoor Railway to the prisons at Dartmoor.

The convicts will, we learn, at first be occupied in repairing and fitting up the remainder of the war prisons, When the work is fully accomplished and the full number sent down the prisoners will be employed under the strictest surveillance in cultivating parts of the moor.

By the time that Dockerill was incarcerated there, the new convict prison had been converted and provided eight buildings and included a clock tower, a Church of England chapel, carpenter's shop and stores. Initially, two of the buildings were fitted out with hammocks for over seven hundred invalid prisoners, hung on hooks 2ft 4ins apart, with the average distance between the hammocks of 10ins. These were later converted to corrugated iron cells, as were installed in two other buildings, the cells in these built in tiers, back to back in the centre of the building for security, and they had no windows, the only ventilation coming from a gap underneath the doors.[1]

Conditions in the prison were appalling, icy cold winds, heavy snow, rain and blizzards for the majority of the time, with no heating in the cells. But the military guard were little better off, with unheated barracks, and having to stand on duty for hours in freezing, wet weather. The difference being that the convicts were not only also subjected to the terrible conditions and physically exhausting work but also to harsh punishments.

In spite of the atrocious weather the prisoners managed to reclaim much of the land around the prison, clearing and cultivating it, so that by the time Dockerill arrived a prison farm had become well established. The outdoor farm jobs were much preferred to others, such as quarrying and clearing land, and oakum picking. Quarrying was

Searching prisoners at Dartmoor Prison.

a particularly gruelling task, causing loss of life and injury to those unfortunate convicts detailed to remove misfired charges of powder which resulted in a number of explosions amongst the enormous granite rocks. They were also required to break the granite into small pieces with a sledgehammer for use on the roads. Oakum picking was another odious task barely more acceptable than quarrying, for the tarred rope made their hands very sore. The results of their labours were sold to the Devonport Dockyard for caulking ships.

At the end of March 1856, the year in which Dockerill was transferred to Dartmoor, the Governor, Mr. Morrish, was able to report to Colonel Jebb that the farm was standing in credit to the sum of £785. 12. 01. exclusive of gratuities of £313. 15. 04. which had been paid to officers

Prisoners at work in the smithy.

above, right and below Prison life, making shoes and tailoring.

in accordance with the Colonel's instructions. Frequent fog during the first two months of the year meant that it had been necessary to employ the prisoners within the walls.[2]

Copy of Letter from Mr. W. Morrish, Prison Governor, to Colonel Jebb

Dartmoor Prison
30th April 56

Sir,

I have the honour to transmit herein for your information a Dr. and Cr. Statement of the Farm for the year ended 31st March 1856, and in continuation of an account rendered to you on 15th Dec last, by which you will find that the sum of £785. 12. 01. stands to the credit of this department exclusive of £313. 15. 04. paid during the year as gratuities to officers in accordance with your instructions of the 31st May 55 and making a total of £1099. 07. 05 in favor of the Farm.

I have deferred sending to you my usual quarterly report of the Farm at this period of the year with a view of being able to include in it the cropping of the season and I now beg to lay before you the operational & occurrences for the months of Jan., Feb, March & April.

Altho' the past winter has in many respects been very favourable for the general work of the Farm, yet the two first months of the year were marked by frequent fogs rendering it necessary to employ the

*Prisoners within the walls – the works that have progressed since my annual report
are as follows: viz –*

1½ acre of 14 field drained, levelled, and top dressed with lime and earth.

4 acres of 25 field drained – & 15 acres of the same cleared of stones.

345 yards of Stone wall built and sodded enclosing fields 24 & 25

464 yards of ditch cut to divert the hill water from fields 23 & 24

358 yards of road repaired

74 yards of old fences repaired

*Fields 5,8,9,11,12,13 & Rundleston (?) containing 57 acres have been top dressed
with gas(?) Lime Soil, & Turf Screening.*

*Fields 6,7,22,23,24 & the garden ground within the walls making a total of 58 acres
have been dug over and prepared for the following crops, viz –*

No. 6 & inside garden ground to mixed vegetables.

Nos 7 & part of 24 to potatoes, making a total of 14 acres under this root. –

*No 23 & the remaining part of 24 to B(?) and grass seeds – a small strip in this field
has been sown with spring wheat.*

No 22 – oats & grass seeds – this crop is above ground and looking tolerably well.

Nos 5,8,9, 10,11,12,13 & Rundlestone(?) will be mown for hay –

Fields 1,2 & 3 to pasture.

    *Turf cutting commenced on the 21st last & 225 Tons have been cut up
to the present time.*

    *The Sales and supplies to the Steward for these months amount to
£283. 06. 0.*

    *The live stock at present consists of 5 horses, 23 cows, 2 Bulls, 7 3-
year-olds, 15 2-year-olds, 15 yearlings, 8 calves, making a total of 70 head of cattle
and 96 Pigs if all sizes.*

I have the honor to be, Sir

Your most obt Servt

W. Morrish.

Farm jobs at Dartmoor were highly sought after.

Dockerill, prisoner no. 3565, could count himself most fortunate because for the whole of the time he was to spend in Dartmoor he was put to work in the piggery. But consequently, he was required to start work an hour before the other prisoners, and as he was later to point out, the pigs required exactly the same attendance on a Sunday as any other. So, in spite of the fact that the farm jobs were highly sought after by the convicts, Dockerill did not seem to appreciate his fortune, but instead considered that he worked longer hours than other men and received no extra reward for it.

But nevertheless, Dockerill settled down to life in Dartmoor tending his pigs and it was nearly two years after the failure of his last petition before he thought to try his luck once more to gain his freedom.[3] He had bided his time, worked hard, and thought out his strategy. Ten years was the normal term of imprisonment for those under sentence of transportation for life, and March 1858 saw the tenth anniversary of his incarceration. This time he wrote directly to Squire Brandreth pointing out his attributes and sincerely repenting of his crime; he also deemed it prudent to show humility and gratitude to the Squire. At the same time he instructed Rebecca to get up another petition and take it to the Squire.

Letter from Dockerill to Squire Brandreth.

Special
3565 Thomas Dockerill

10th March 1858

Dartmoor Convict Establishment
Sir,

From your many and great kindnesses to my family, and also from your interesting yourself on my behalf I am embolden to trouble you with this statement and I do so with shame, and deep humiliation but I trust Sir as I have now commenced the tenth year of my imprisonment, and as my conduct has been such to merit the approbation of the authorities not only in this Establishment but at all others at which my unfortunate condition has placed me I humbly trust you will pardon this intrusion. Your great goodness to my family calls for my deepest and most sincere gratitude and never can I sufficiently thank you. I will briefly recapitulate my case but as in all its prominent features it is well known to you I need not trouble you with details.

You I believe will give me credit that not for a moment did I contemplate shooting the officer, it was on the impulse of the moment I fired the gun for after the policeman fired his pistol and his assistant crying out to fire both barrels I did not know how many pistols they had unfortunately myself fired as I thought in such a moment of peril in self defence. We were masters of the officers and could have killed them had such been the intention. I intend Sir sending to my wife to get up a petition for me for you may kindly remember that two years next August a petition was sent to the Home Secretary Sir George Grey and his answer was that he could not interfere just then. As ten years is the usual term for transportation for life unless the crime be very aggravated or the conduct of the prisoner whilst in confinement is bad and as six months is generally given for long service at Gibralter and there Sir through my exertions I broke a blood vessel and was invalided to England – I hope all this will be taken into consideration. May I humbly and most repectfully ask if you Sir will be so kind not only to sign the petition but also as you previously did forward a statement from yourself to the Home Office. – I am I trust a changed man in every respect, my heart yearns to be with my affectionate true wife, and children – Ten years Sir is a long, long, separation, and deeply do I deplore my former conduct – Misfortune and years of imprisonment are stern but most effective teachers, and never shall I forget the lesson they teach. – My wife will call on you, and if not on my account for I dare not hope from my sad career sympathy from the good, and just, yet on her behalf, and on that of my family for I am the only one who has ever disgraced them that you will try to restore a husband to the wife, and father to his children, and do believe me never shall you have occasion to regret exerting yourself on my behalf for I will strain every nerve to shew my gratitude to you my love to them.

Most earnestly, and respectfully hoping you will pardon the liberty I have taken, for I long hesitated before I could think of so doing, and trusting you will take my case into your kind consideration.

I have the honour to remain
Sir
Your most obedient humble servant
Thomas Dockerill

Dartmoor Convict Establishmen
March 10th 58   *(sic)*

This time Rebecca managed to do as she was bid, taking the petition, along with the signatures of those men willing to support her husband, to the Squire. Rebecca was obviously very well respected in the neighbourhood. She had worked hard to raise her children without the support of her husband all the time that he had been in prison, and mentions of her efforts are to be seen throughout the documents. So possibly these supporters were doing it for Rebecca rather than Dockerill. But interestingly one signature in his support was that of Thomas Eames, the overseer of the parish, one of those who had issued parish relief to Dockerill's father some years before.

Rebecca had done well. She had managed to find seven men who were willing to put pen to paper to support her husband. Among them was John Ellingham, schoolmaster, but it is not surprising that they had his support considering the fact that two of Thomas's sisters, Sarah and Ann, were married into the Ellingham family. On 28th April, the Squire forwarded the letter from Dockerill along with the petition to the Home Office, but again he expressed himself as being impartial in the affair.

Houghton House
Nr Dunstable
April 29 1858

Sir

    I have the honour to forward to you herewith a letter from Thomas Dockerill, to myself, who is now a Convict at Dartmoor.

    I also enclose a memorial signed by his wife and others on his behalf.

    Some time ago I forwarded a similar memorial and the reply was then to the effect that no sufficient reason presented itself as a claim for the mitigation of sentence.

    The Convict was convicted in 1849 during the year I was sheriff – two others were convicted at the same time – but on a representation being made by myself, backed by the opinion of the Jury – Lord Cranworth – one man named White received a True (?) pardon.

    I forwarded to the Home Office a statement made by the Prisoners after conviction and which I have no doubt will be found in the Home Office and which statement will explain more fully than I can remember the circumstances attending the charge and conviction.

    I wish to express no opinion in this matter myself.

I have the honour to be
Sir
Your most obedient Servant
H. Brandreth

Petition of Rebecca Dockerill (sic).

To the Right Honorable The Secretary of State for the Home Department

The humble Petition of Rebecca Dockerill sheweth that, her husband was convicted of Felony in the year 1849 and sentenced to Twenty years Transportation.

That he has now served full half his time and she has every reason to believe that he has conducted himself to the satisfaction of the Officers set over him and that he truly repents of his crime and has become an altered man.

She therefore humbly prays that under these circumstances and in consideration of his family his sentence may be commuted by a ticket of leave.

Rebekah Dockerill

We the undersigned Know Mrs. Dockerill well and believe her to be a Steady honest and industrious Woman and We therefore join in the Pray of the Petitioner.

Name	What calling	Where live
Gustavus Gadsden Jones	Farmer	Stanbridge, Beds
Thomas Eames Overseer	Farmer	Stanbridge
John Abraham	Farmer	Stanbridge
Josiah Wilks	Plait Dealer	Standbridge
John Clarke	Farmer and Builder	Standbridge
John Gurney	Farmer	Standbridge
Joseph Eames	Inn Keeper	Stanbridge
John Ellingham	Schoolmaster	Standbridge

above Rebecca's signature and farmers willing to employ Dockerill.
left Letter from Squire Brandreth to Home Office.

Again Dockerill was to be disappointed, for his appeal was rejected on 5th May.

But later that same year, his hopes were raised once more. On 30th September, 1858, Dartmoor Prison was favoured by a visit from Colonel Joshua Jebb, Chairman of the New Prison Service. Colonel Jebb was the official who had visited the convicts upon their return from Gibraltar, and had seemed somewhat sympathetic to their situation, allowing them a six month mitigation on their sentence. Dockerill's spirits were lifted upon being granted an interview with him, for he was encouraged to try again for his release. Colonel Jebb obviously instilled into Dockerill the importance of showing that he would be able to gain honest employment if he was released. It would appear, also, that a suggestion was made that it might go in his favour if he persuaded the authorities that he was intending to emigrate to another country. Whatever did transpire, Dockerill was convinced enough that Colonel Jebb would see his way to helping him to obtain his release, to try again. On 6th December, Dockerill wrote to Rebecca, urging her to once more plead his case with the Squire, who in turn should contact Colonel Jebb.

It must have been a great shock for poor Rebecca to find she was now required to decide to emigrate, and that she must persuade the Squire that this was the intention. In truth, whether it ever was is doubtful, but whether Rebecca was aware of this is unclear. However, once more, Rebecca, rallied by his letter, did as she was bid.

It would appear that Dockerill might now have found the magic formula for his release in Colonel Jebb. On 28th January, 1859, Dockerill was called up by the Governor of Dartmoor, Mr. Morrish, to be recommended to the Secretary of State for his liberty.

In turn, Mr. Waddington in the Home Office must have also communicated this fact to the Squire, because it is mentioned in a later letter from him.

But now things were to take another twist. Possibly Rebecca spread

opposite Letter from Dockerill to Rebecca.

N.B. The Convict's writing to be confined to these two pages, In writing to the Convict, direct to No. 3565
Thos Dockerill

Monday 6th December 1858

My dearest Wife, Since I last wrote to you I have seen Col. Jebb he was down here the last day of September. I told him the whole circumstances as regarded myself how that I met with the misfortune whilst at Gibralter of breaking a blood vessel and of my having been Invalided here on that account. I told him also that I had done Ten Years in March next. He asked me various questions. The chief one was whether if I had my liberty I could gain employment and get an honest living for myself and family. He told me that if he found my statement was a straight forward one he would see what could be done for me. I answered all the questions he put to me and I told him I had a fair chance of getting a good living when at liberty, but that I intended to take my Wife and family to Canada feeling satisfied that I could succeed much better there than any where else. Now my dear Wife I have not mentioned this to you before but I do hope that you will now think seriously of it and make up your mind to go. You are well aware that when I get my liberty I shall not be a free man and the least thing against me would send me back. I shall be certain to have some enemies at home who will try to do me an injury and if I am away I shall feel free and can be much more happy and contented than if I was in this Country. –In that Country there will be every chance for me and my family. The Children will have the best opportunity of making way in the world and you and I may have the happiness of seeing them all well settled. If you will only say that you will go I shall be satisfied and I know you will not have cause to regret it. Having made up your mind to go, you must then call on Squire Brandreth and shew him this letter, and ask him if he will write to Col. Jebb to ask him to look into my case and having done so then ask him to put you in the way of writing to the Col. In order that your letter and his may go at once. I hope you will use your best endeavours with the Squire and tell him what my intentions are, and I am certain he will be of the same opinion. – My mind is made up and I do hope you will consent to go, depend My dear Wife it will be much better for all of us especially for our dear Children. You will please tell Squire Brandreth that I am the only Man left of those who came home with me, all who had good characters have gone to their liberty except myself and they had Six months taken off their time. I want you to ask Col. Jebb in your Letter whether there is any chance of my having anything done for me. I wish you to be very particular on this head as it all rests with him and if it does not do some thing for me I may have more time to do. – I have no doubt he will inform the Squire what he would not say to you. You will tell him that my conduct since I have been in prison as been good – I have not had any reports against me since my conviction which I have no doubt will be in my favour. – You will have to state in your Letter the name of the party who has promised to employ me. You will also have to place your own case before him and ask him to take it into his serious consideration and how you have brought up your family since I have been away. I do not think that I have anything more to say now. I shall not expect to hear from you until you have made up your mind and have got all the information you can. I am happy to say I am quite well and hope you and all the family are the same, and with sincerest Love.

    I remain,

                    Your Affectionate Husband,
                           Thomas Dockerill

P.s. you will understand that when I get my liberty I shall be under a Ticket of Leave and the least thing will forfeit that, this is the reason I am so anxious to leave England.

                    (sic)

Dartmoor CONVICT Prison

1. Number. *3565*   2. Prisoner's Name and Age. *Thomas Dockerill Age 29*

3. When and Where Convicted.   *8 March 1849   Bedford Assizes.*
   Stating whether at Sessions or Assizes.

4. Offence. *Maliciously wounding with intent to resist his lawful apprehension to do grievous bodily harm.*

5. Sentence.   *Transportation for life.*

6. Gaol report.   *Once Stealing Barley.*

7. Conduct in Prison. *Exemplary.*

8. Trade.   *Labourer.*

9. Family or Friends' Names and Residences.   *Stanbridge. Bedfordshire.*

10. What are his prospects, if liberated?   } *A qualified promise of employment has been received from Mr. John Clarke,*

11. Will any person employ him?   } *of Stanbridge.*
    If so state their Name and Address.   } *The prisoner states he intends to proceed with his family to America*

12. Has Application been made to such   } *when liberated – and I think he would*
    Person, and by whom?   } *then be able to obtain employment.*

13. Has any, and what, Reply been received?   }

14. If the Reply be satisfactory, has reference   }
    been made To the Minister of the Parish or   }
    District, to verify same?   }

15. Chaplain's Remarks as to fore-going   *Has not a duly certified offer of employment.*
    Application and Reference.

Wm. Holderness
Chaplain

W. Morrish

the word around the village of Stanbridge that her husband might be considered for release, or perhaps it was her activity once more in collecting the names for her petition, because something sparked a reaction within the community of farmers whom Dockerill had terrorised. The Minister of the Parish, on behalf of the farmers, and of the police, wrote to the Governor of Dartmoor Prison, expressing the ill feeling there was towards Dockerill in the area, and the opposition there was to his returning there.

On learning of this, Dockerill lost no time in writing to Rebecca once more to stress the importance of their acceptance of a life abroad, but that she must not be pressured into signing any paper or enter any agreement that would commit their emigration without first consulting him. He was obviously worried that Rebecca might be called on by the parishioners who might bring pressure to bear upon her, and was very angry that his latest attempt for release showed every sign of being thwarted by those he had victimised. He cited them as 'throwing obstacles in the way of his release and preaching repentance but not practising forgiveness, and not showing the least particle of Christian charity, so much heard of but little seen'. One might wonder why he should be so offended that these people, whom he had obviously terrorised for years, should not wish for his return.

But also looking after the material side of things, he wished to know what assistance the community would be willing to offer should they decide to emigrate, as he considered it would be hard and unjust for them to offer none.

Rebecca lost no further time in obtaining the signatures, once more, of those willing to employ and support Dockerill. She was obviously more desirous of showing that he could be employed locally rather than emigrate abroad.

It would appear from the letter that Dockerill's son, Ephraim, who was now twenty-one years old, was intending to visit his father in Dartmoor at this time, but he discourages Ephraim from doing so, saying that it would not be worth the expense because he would only be allowed to see him

Letter from Dockerill to Rebecca.

2 / 2 1859

My dear Wife

You will be grieved, and surprised to hear the governor has received a letter from I believe the minister of your parish, stating that the farmers, and police do not think it would be prudent on the part of the Authorities to give me my liberty in England, but that it would be better to send me abroad, provided you, and my family will go with me as emigrants to one of the colonies – Now should the gentlemen of the parish call on you, and ask whether you would be willing to be sent out, you must be very particular in ascertainty what part of the world they wish me to go? What they will give you to assist us in getting out but be sure and enter into no agreement, not sign any paper 'till you have made me fully acquainted with their plans, for surely after throwing obstacles in the way of my release, after having undergone ten long years of severe suffering, and borne during that period an unimpeachable character, they cannot think of expatriating you and my children without providing you the means of so doing it would be ? harsh and unjust. – My wish, and desire is to go nowhere unless it be America to the British Colony of Upper Canada where if it meet your wishes I have no objection to go but do not agree to anything, or go anywhere unless you fully approve of it only let me know the whole of your mind for it is a most important subject and requires consideration, it certainly is my wish to go for after what has happened I should be liable to be suspected for every crime committed in the neighbourhood, for ministers and neighbours though they preach repentance, do not practice forgiveness – I was called up by the governor on 28th of last month to be recommended to the Secretary of State for my liberty, for it wholly depends on him, and as there is no positive promise to liberate a man under transportation for life for with the objection of the clergyman, police, and others of your parish I may be kept an indefinite period, for there are some who are detained upwards of twelve years in fact there is no knowing when I should obtain my freedom. Should any call on you, tell them I have conscientiously done my duty as a prisoner, have bitterly repented of my former mis-spent life the sincerity of which I have evinced by actions, rather than words and certainly was in hope after all these years of ? suffering and separation from my family, and those near, and most dear to me I might ? and it is most ungenerous, and arbitrary of those who are throwing obstacles in the road of a father's returning to his children, and a husband to his wife, neither do I think they shew the least particle of Christian charity of which so much is heard, and little seen. Mr Clarke has evinced perfect willingness to find me employment, and you will thank him for me most sincerely. If Mr Brandreth has not received an answer from the Home Office will you shew him this letter and ask if he knows what they are going to do with me and you will give my most sincere, and unfeigned thanks to him for his goodness I am afraid I shall never be able to shew him how deeply grateful I feel towards him but God will reward him to His care of my worse than fatherless children. I hope My dear boy will not think of coming here. I could only see him for twenty minutes and it would never be worth the expence, and trouble for so short a visit, may god bless him for so dutiful a desire. To you dear wife I am under a weighty obligation indeed which I hope to repay with years of devotion and gratitude to you and whether in the back woods of America, or in my native country you shall ever find me ever mindful of your love, constancy, and attention to myself and your children Heaven knows I can never repay you. Give my most affectionate love to Ephraim, his brother and sister the dearest wish of my heart *is to see you all it is my only hope in this world to find you all well and end my days with you. Will you tell me what trade to have put Mary to, and also what you are going to make of Joseph whatever it may be may God prosper them – You will not I hope dear wife make any trouble of this, for it may be very much for our good. I should have to undergo many trials, and temptations in my native place, and I am positive I could do well in America so make up your mind and let me know but first see the Squire and ask his advice for he knows better than we do what is for the best, and write to me as soon as you can, and I also when I hear anything further will let you know – and now dear Wife may God bless, and keep you and my dear children under His Heavenly protection and all will be well here, and hereafter.*

I remain my dear wife

Your most affectionate husband

Thomas Dockerill

(sic)

for twenty minutes. The Governor of the prison had also written a note on the 'Rules of sending and receiving letters' page which accompanied all letters: 'Prisoners cannot be visited by their friends without a written order from the Governor. No visits are allowed on Fridays. W.M.'

This would have been the first time that Ephraim had visited his father, or indeed seen him since he was eleven years old, and in actual fact he probably wished to visit to tell him of his forthcoming marriage the following April. But transport to the prison was just about non-existent and coupled with both his father's and the Governor's comments, Dockerill's letter had the desired effect and Ephraim did not go.

Once again, on 14th February, having gained the signatures on her petition, Rebecca braved the weather and made her way from Stanbridge to Houghton House for an audience with Squire Brandreth to beg his help once more. This time she was accompanied by John Clarke, the farmer/builder who had given a definite offer of employment.

The Squire duly sent off the letters to Horatio Waddington in the offices of the Secretary of State, at the same time expressing his concern that Dockerill was having his hopes raised and subsequently dashed by the authorities, and that it could not have a good effect on his wife and children.

Petition of farmers offering employment to Dockerill.

10th Feb 1859

Sir,

We the undersigned most earnestly beg that you will mitigate the sentence of Thomas Dockerill who was transported about ten years ago for stealing corn and release him on a ticket of Leave, we are quite willing to give him employment for the benefit of his wife and family who are highly respected.

John Gurney.	Farmer	
Josiah Wilks	Farmer	Free Holder
Samuel Tims	Plait Dealer	Free Holder
Gustavas Jones	Farmer	
John Abraham	Farmer	
Wm Ed Costin	Freeholder	
John Clarke	Farmer	

Houghton House
Feb 14. 1859

Sir,

Rebecca Dockerill and Mr. Clarke waited on me this morning and required me to forward the enclosed Petition to the Secretary of State for the Home Department in favour of Thomas Dockerill Convict no. 3565. in the Dartmoor Convict Establishment.

The Petition is got up I believe in consequence of the enclosed letter of the 1st of Dec. last and the other letter enclosed of the 2nd of this month from the convict to his wife.

In forwarding the Petition I beg to be understood as expressing no opinion or wish in the matter.

I had considered the matter as finally settled by the last letter I had the honour to receive from you on the subject.

Will you permit me to suggest that should the Secretary of State still be of opinion that it would not be desirable to release the convict then that the officials therein abstain from writing letters of the kind enclosed for him – It would appear to me that they only bring him up with hopes not to be realized and tend to destroy such reformation as may have been effected in him, and must be a constant source of anxiety to his unfortunate wife and children.

Besides which I am given to understand that there is a counter Petition got up and in consequence an unfriendly feeling is generating in the Parish.

I have the honour to be

Sir

Your most obedient Servant

H^{phrey} Brandreth

H. Waddington Esq.

> 224/13
>
> HOME OFFICE
> CRIMINAL
> FEB 14 1859
>
> ### *Thomas Dockerill*
>
> No 7
>
> Dartmoor 3565
>
> *Mr Brandreth sends two letters written by the convict*
> *and a paper signed by several persons recommending*
> *a mitigation of his sentence and promising to employ him.*

Dockerill's records show that he was indeed being considered for release that month, a qualified promise of employment having been received from John Clarke.

Dartmoor CONVICT Prison

1. Number. **3565**   2. Prisoner's Name and Age. *Thomas Dockerill 29*
3. When and Where Convicted. *8 March 1849 – Bedford Assizes.*
   Stating whether at Sessions or Assizes.
4. Offence. *Maliciously wounding with intent to resist his lawful apprehension.*
5. Sentence. *Trans. for life.*
6. Gaol report. *Once felony. Stg. Barley.*
7. Conduct in Prison. *Exemplary.*
8. Trade. *Labourer.*
9. Family or Friends' Names and Residences. *Stanbridge. Bedfordshire.*
10. What are his prospects, if liberated? } *Recommended for License*
11. Will any person employ him? } *for March 1859. A qualified*
    If so state their Name and Address. } *promise of employment has*
12. Has Application been made to such } *been received for this man*
    Person, and by whom? } *who states that he intends to*
16. Has any, and what, Reply been received? } *go to America when liberated*
17. If the Reply be satisfactory, has reference }
    been made to the Minister of the Parish or }
    District, to verify same? }
18. Chaplain's Remarks as to fore-going *Wishes to emigrate. Wm.Holderness*
    Application and Reference. *Chaplain*
    W. Morrish

But in his letter the Squire had also mentioned that there was a counter-petition in the process of being drawn up and sure enough the Home Office received the petition from the farmers opposed to Dockerill's release, in March 1859. They expressed their concern about the wisdom of allowing Dockerill to return to Stanbridge where his family still lived, and where he had been offered employment. They described him as a man of desperately bad character who had expressed his intentions of murdering those who had concerned themselves in his conviction.

One would imagine that the vestry meetings in Stanbridge would have been very interesting at this time. Because on the one hand the rate-payers attending included the likes of Thomas Gadsden who was against Dockerill's release and on the other there was Thomas and Joseph Eames who supported him. John Franklin, farmer, was also the acting constable in Stanbridge during the time of the incident and was the one to search Dockerill's house for the weapon. It is impossible to imagine that Dockerill's name did not crop up midst the parish affairs, and probably caused a fair amount of argument. But it would appear also that there was another who was assisting the farmers in their petition for the name of Colonel Gilpin features prominently on the document.

224/13

HOME OFFICE
CRIMINAL
MAR 18 1859
Thomas Dockerill

No 8

Ticket of leave in March 1861

Pres Colonel Gilpin MP

The applicants represent that the convict is a man of desperate character & that they are apprehensive for their lives if he is set at liberty. They beg that he may not be discharged on License.

(sic)

To the Right Honorable Spencer H Walpole
one of Her Majesty's principal Secretaries of State.

The humble Petition of the Undersigned being inhabitants of the township of Stanbridge in the County of Bedford.
Sheweth

That Thomas Dockerill was convicted at the Lent Assizes holdern at Bedford in the year 1849 of assaulting with intent to murder Police Constables Clough and Parrott and sentenced to transportation for life.

That it was shewn in evidence upon the trial of the Prisoner that he was seen by the two Police Officers with other persons immediately after having committed a burglary and to avoid apprehension he shot Parrott in the shoulder and then clubbed his gun and with the stock of it beat Clough over the head leaving him for dead and injured him so much that his life was despaired of for a week.

That Thomas Dockerill at the time of the commission of the offence resided at Stanbridge and was known as a man of bad and desperate character and about the period of his conviction expressed his determination to murder those persons who took an active part in the prosecution against him if he could ever get the ... opportunity to meet with them.

That in the event of the sentence upon Thomas Dockerill being commuted and his liberty allowed him it is reasonable to suppose that he will return to Stanbridge where his wife and her family reside as well as those persons who interested themselves in the prosecution against him.

That your Petitioners believe that if Thomas Dockerill is permitted to return to Stanbridge their lives and properties will be greatly jeopardised.

Your Petitioners therefore humbly pray that a ticket of leave may not be granted to the said Thomas Dockerill nor the sentence passed upon him commuted in any way.

And your Petitioners will ever pray.

Thomas Gadsden	Farmer
John Franklin	Farmer
John Olney	Farmer
Andrew Franklin	Farmer
C. Buckmaster	Farmer
Henry Woodman	Farmer

Unfortunately for Dockerill, the opposing farmers were successful in their petition. Not only was he refused his ticket-of-leave, he was recommended to be detained for a further two years.

But, despite this latest setback, Dockerill did not give up that easily. On 4th November, 1859, after licking his wounds for another eight months, he again wrote to Squire, appealing to him to speak on his behalf, as he was due once more to be recommended by the Governor of Dartmoor for licence. This time he cited the Squire as the only friend that he had in the world who would speak for him. He obviously had every faith that the Squire was on his side, and doubtless would have been devastated to know of the Squire's true opinion of him. For it is obvious that Thomas Dockerill was not well thought of by Squire Brandreth, although he did regard Rebecca with some admiration for bringing up her family on her

---

N.B. The Convict's writing to be confined to these two pages, In writing to the Convict, direct to No. 3565

Thomas Dockerill
4/11/1859

Sir,

  I once more trust to your known condescension, and kindness in pardoning the very great liberty I am taking, but as you have so generously interested yourself in behalf of myself, and family I do hope you will not consider me intrusive, for I have not a friend in the world save you to speak a word for me. In a short time I shall again be recommended to the Secretary of State by the Governor for my liberation, having been a prisoner eleven years, during which time I have borne an undeniable character for industry, and general good conduct but unless someone of standing, and influence will speak for me I am afraid even eleven years trial, and suffering, with sincere, and hearty repentance, which has been evinced by my actions, will avail me nothing, as the neighbours consider that long period insufficient punishment, and they not only wish to expatriate me, but also my innocent, and excellent wife, and industrious children. I will respectfully ask the inhabitants of Stockbridge (Stanbridge) if eleven years be not sufficient to test the genuineness of my reformation, under the stringent regulations of Convict discipline, where all faults, and breaches of decorum are reported, and recorded. I have gone on in one unvarying manner for giving not only satisfaction to myself but to my officers, and the Authorities, to whom I can appeal with

---

own without the support of her husband.

There is also on record another association that the Squire had with the White family; James White, Rebecca and George's brother, was employed by the Brandreth Estate to deepen and improve the watercourse or sewer between Houghton Regis and Leagrave in October 1851.

So in actual fact, when the Squire forwarded Dockerill's letter, he suggested that no further grounds had appeared to mitigate the sentence, and that the Officers of the Convict Establishment might be advised not to hold out Dockerill's hope for remission. He also saw fit to add that Dockerill, in a letter to his wife, had attributed the motive of the parishioners in appealing for his continued incarceration as 'revenge'.

---

confidence. My return home would also be under very great advantages I should have a home to go to, a wife any man might be proud to receive me, and children commencing life under more favourable auspices than I had any right to expect, and bad indeed must be my heart to say nothing of the miseries, and privations I have undergone, were I to do anything either to blight their prospects, or blast their characters. In the honesty, and respectability of my family would be the safeguard of my future conduct. I do think with all due deference to the prejudices of society I might now be permitted to revisit after so long, and painful separation my wife, and children, and spend our remaining years in peace, and quietude. I could materially aid them in their comforts, and sustenance, and it would be my pride, and earnest desire to prove how much I appreciate the noble exertions of my wife to bring up her children as she has done, and shew to the world that a returned convict may become an honest, and useful member of society. May I respectfully hope Sir you will once more condescend to interest yourself in my behalf, and I am certain, from your own generous disposition you would reap that inward satisfaction a noble action always gives of knowing you had restored a long absent husband, and father to his wife, and children and do believe me never should you have reason thro' any act of mine to regret having assisted the erring, and fallen to whom friends are so rare.

Earnestly, and gratefully thanking you for all your kindness.

I have the honour to remain Sir

Your most obliged, humble servant

Thomas Dockerill

(sic)

Houghton House
Nr Dunstable

Nov 27 1859

Sir

Having received the enclosed letter from the Convict Thomas Dockerill I venture to forward it to the Home Office in order that you may consider how far it is advisable for the officers of the Convict Establishment to hold that immediate prospect of remission of sentence when, as I have understood from the Home Office, no sufficient grounds have appeared to mitigate the sentence under which the convict is confined.

I have the honour to be
Sir
Your most obedient
Humble Servant

H^{ry} Brandreth

The Right Honorable
The Secretary of State

P.T. Over

I may add that in a letter which he addressed to his wife, about the same time as I received the one enclosed, he expressed himself un? at the hope held out to him not being realized and attributed the motive of his detention to "Revenge".

(sic)

So, once again fate, in the form of the Home Office, was against him. When the recommendation for licence was sent by Dartmoor Prison on 31st January, 1860, the Home Office rejected it on 6th February.

224/13

HOME OFFICE
CRIMINAL
FEB 6 1860

Dartmoor Prison

31 January 1860

PARTICULARS rendered of 3565

Convict *Thos Dockerill*

Recommended for Licence

Not at Present.

H.W.No 9

No 31.

PETITION.

Name, Age, }
Register No., and }
Where confined. }

Thomas Dockerill

Age on Conviction 29

Register 3565
Dartmoor Prison

Convicted		Crime	Sentence	Remarks
When	Where			As to Character
		Felony & maliciously		Once Felony
8 March '49	Bedford Assizes	wounding with intent to resist his lawful apprehension & grievous bodily harm	Life	Bedford – Very Good
				Millbank – Good
				Portland – Good
				S.Castle – Good
				Has been at
				Gibraltar /-
				Dartmoor –
				Exemplary

Was recommended for Licence
in March of 1859 & 1860

CHAPTER 20

Dockerill Appeals Again[1]

W hether or not Dockerill was beginning to realise that he could not entirely count on the Squire to exert the necessary efforts on his behalf, in any event he came to the decision to dispense with his unreliable services. On 18th October, 1860 he decided to try another appeal, but this time chose to petition direct to the Home Office.

He was obviously very grieved with his lot. He had now been in prison over eleven years, twelve years come January, and he considered that he had made efforts over and above his required workload whilst in the various prisons. So, in his petition, he brought this to the attention of the authorities; his extra duties as warder whilst in Gibraltar, and his extra workload in the piggeries at Dartmoor, and he compared his length of sentence with that of his fellow internees at Gibraltar. Dockerill had had enough of prison life and he wanted to return home to his family in Bedfordshire.

(Copied as written)

To, The Right Honourable The Secretary of State For the Home Department	
Prays for a consideration of his case	The petition of Register 3565
Pleas	Thomas Dockerill a prisoner
Extra services rendered, on public works at Gibraltar and Dartmoor. Promise made by Sir J Jebb Injury on public works. Good conduct.	confined in Dartmoor Prison Humbly sheweth

contonued overleaf

Your petitioner respectfully submits this memorial for your consideration, appealing more to your sense of justice than to any feeling of commiseration.

Your petitioner has been a prisoner nearly twelve years, and were he to put in the extra days, and hours, he has worked he might safely say thirteen years, during which lengthened period your petitioner has conducted himself in such a manner, as to gain the approbation of the authorities, under whom his miserable destiny has placed him; and he humbly, but honestly thinks, if any prisoner's conduct deserved consideration his does.-
He was in Gibraltar upwards of four years, the last two of which he was appointed a warder on account of his persevering industry, and general good conduct. Two nights in each week he had two hours night watch to keep; after working the whole day, often to his middle in water. His watch at night made no difference to his work, not in any way did he derive the least privilege for the loss of his nights rest. He has been now at Dartmoor four years, the whole of which time he has been employed in the piggery, consequently, he goes to his work an hour before the other men, and the pigs want exactly the same attendance on Sunday, as any other day. This extra work brings no extra privileges, no extra gratuity.

Your petitioner would next respectfully call your attention to the act under which he was convicted, and which the Judge when he passed sentence considered would be carried out in the usual manner, for the laws of England never in what are called the dark ages contemplated hopeless, and perpetual imprisonment, if the punishment then was sharp, it was short, they punished the body, not the mind. In the old rules the sentence of life was considered 24 years, and by giving your petitioner the same privilege as a twenty or twenty two years transported man, he would have obtained his liberty two years since or very nearly.

Your petitioner, with upwards of twenty other invalids came to England from Gibraltar Oct 1855. Shortly after the ship arrived Sir Joshua Jebb came down, and saw the men, giving the governor orders to send up the whole of their names, and shortly after an answer was returned granting to the whole six months mitigation on their probation, but in the interim your petitioner was removed to Dartmoor though another prisoner who came with your petitioner on making application to the Home Office had his six months granted. Now several amongst them had not been in Gibraltar more than seven or 8 months, whilst your petitioner who had been there going on five years was the only one who received no remission. There were two others with life sentences who came home with him, one who had completed about five years of his sentence died some time after, the other who had done rather more than seven years was set at liberty. Your petitioner saw Sir Joshua Jebb about two years since, and he promised to look into your petitioners case, and do something for him, but your petitioner has never heard again from him.

Your petitioner seriously injured himself whilst employed on the public works at Gibraltar, otherwise he would have gone to Australia but having ruptured a blood vessel he was sent to England as he was told for his liberty.

Your petitioner has been told both by the authorities at Gibraltar, as well as by the rules, and regulations that ten years with his conduct would be the very outside of his imprisonment, and so it would; but for regulations of which the Judge who tried him could know nothing as they were not in existence. He is being kept in a state of suspence far harder to bear than any corporal punishment. He has a most industrious, and respectable wife, hard working, honest children, and a comfortable home to which he could go. His wife, and children most anxiously waiting to receive him. His punishment is indeed most fearful, and what makes it more bitter is the fact that any other class of prisoner, no matter whether returned on ticket, or has after been convicted, receive an answer from the Home Office when they petition but now to a man with a life sentence no matter how good his conduct has been, or how sincere his repentance to his petition no answer whatever is vouchsafed that it is which makes it so heartbreaking.

Your petitioner most earnestly, and humbly, prays you will take his case into your kind consideration, and if you cannot set him at liberty, at least for humanity's sake he earnestly prays to be informed if there be any hope of his liberty. And your petitioner as in duty bound will ever pray.

Thomas Dockerill

(sic)

Thomas Dockerill   29

No. 10

Dartmoor.

The Convict represents his good conduct during the whole term of his long imprisonment, & prays to be restored to his wife and children.

Medical report annexed.

I hereby certify that the Petitioner Thomas Dockerill is in good health and bears no trace of the injury alluded to in the body of his Petition.

??

Medical Officer

Dartmoor Prison
Oct 18th 1860

Dartmoor CONVICT Prison

1. Number. *3565* 2. Prisoner's Name and Age. *Thomas Dockerill 39*

3. When and Where Convicted. *8 March 1849 – Bedford Assizes*
   Stating whether at Sessions or Assizes.

4. Offence. *Maliciously Wounding with intent to resist his*
   Lawful apprehension , & to do grievous bodily harm.

5. Sentence. *Life Tr:*

6. Gaol Report. *Once con: of Felony:-*

7. Conduct in Prison. *Exemplary*

8. Trade. *Labourer*

16. Family or Friends' Names and   *Stanbridge Bedfordshire*
    Residences

17. What are his prospects, if liberated?   } *A qualified promise of employment*
    }
18. Will any person employ him?   } *has been received for this man*
    If so state their Name and Address.   }
    } *who states that he intends to go*
19. Has Application been made to   }
    such Person, and by whom?   } *to America when liberated –*
    }
20. Has any, and what, reply been   } *Brought forward for release in*
    received?   }
    } *March 1861 in accordance with*
21. If the Reply be satisfactory,   }
    has reference been made to the   } *H. O. letter dated 23 Oct. 1860*
    Minister of the Parish or Dis-   }
    trict, to verify same?   }

22. Chaplain's Remarks as to fore-   *Has a qualified offer of employment, states that*
    going Application and Reference.   *he wishes to emigrate*

    Wm. Holderness
    Chaplain

W. Morrish
Governor

Apparently this time his plea worked. But probably he was just due for release anyway, as earlier petitions show that he was due to receive his ticket-of-leave in March 1861. His licence was issued on 28th February, 1861.

But still there was a sting in the tail for Dockerill, for it was not quite the release he had hoped for. He was excluded from returning to the County of Bedfordshire. Dockerill had won his release, but the opposing farmers had won their moral victory.

HOME OFFICE
CRIMINAL
FEB 6 1861

Dartmoor Prison

31 January 1861

PARTICULARS rendered of
Convict 3565 **Thos Dockerill**
Recommended for Licence

Licence excluding from Co Bedford 28 Feb 1861

No 12
Discharge
H.W.

On 2nd March, 1861, he thankfully bid farewell to Dartmoor prison, and made his way back towards Dunstable. For some unknown reason he went via Leicestershire, the 1861 census shows him to be residing at Ashby-de-la-Zouch, but soon after, he travelled to the borders of Hertfordshire. This was as near to Bedfordshire as he dared to go, for any non-compliance or misdemeanour would have seen him straight back in prison, and he certainly had no wish to return there. He moved into a public house on the outskirts of Dunstable, but just outside the border. Rebecca, meanwhile, had moved out of Stanbridge in preparation for his release, and moved to the main High Street of Dunstable. So they were still not together permanently, but at least she and the family could visit him regularly at his lodgings.

But no sooner had Dockerill moved into Hertfordshire, than he started planning his next move, for he was still not satisfied. In spite of the fact that he knew there was a lot of opposition to his returning there, nevertheless he still wanted to get back into Bedfordshire. So he began to formulate his next plan. He sent the long-suffering Rebecca to see the Vicar at Houghton Regis, to enlist his help in pleading his case, ascribing importance to the separation from his wife. The Reverend Smyth who was also a Justice of the Peace for Bedfordshire was a relative newcomer to the area, having moved into Houghton Regis after the crime that Dockerill and his gang committed. Therefore he did not know the facts of the case, and he was not conversant with the character of Dockerill. But he did know Rebecca, and that she was a hard working woman who deserved a break. After listening to her plea, he willingly offered

---

Houghton Regis Vicarage. Dunstable. Beds
March 12 1861

Sir,

The wife of the discharged prisoner referred to in the enclosed letter is very anxious that the restriction on her husband's pardon should be removed – it allows him to be at large anywhere except in the county of Bedfordshire.
She lives in a part of Houghton closely adjoining Dunstable where she is established in the staple trade of the County, Straw bonnets.
Dunstable is commonly stated to be in Bedfordshire, but a small part of it is in Hertfordshire, and the practical result is that he lodges at a public house in that part and is separated from his home.
Obviously no good but some harm must proceed from such an arrangement.
I offer no opinion as to the man's pardon because the offence occurred before I came into the parish and I know nothing of it or the character of the man.
His wife is a hard working woman and this of course unsettles her and her family.
I submit respectfully to your consideration whether it is worth while to maintain the restriction under the circumstances I have stated & beg to call your attention to the further particulars referred to in the subjoined letter.

I have the honour to be, Sir,
Your obt Servant
Hugh B Smyth
Justice of the Peace for Bedfordshire

---

his support for Dockerill's case, deciding to try and help by writing to the authorities. He duly penned his letter to the Governor of Dartmoor Prison on 12th March.

The Governor lost no time in replying to the letter. In it he informed the Vicar that, although Dockerill had an offer of employment, there had been considerable ill-feeling towards him in his own neighbourhood, so it was considered that he would have little chance of succeeding there. He also informed him that Dockerill had expressed his intention of emigrating to America, and therefore the exclusion clause had been implemented. However, the Governor also mentioned that he had worked hard whilst in Dartmoor Prison, and that he saw no objection to him returning to Bedfordshire if it was thought that he had a fair chance

---

Dartmoor Prison
15 March 1861

No 13

Revd Sir,
I beg to acknowledge the receipt of your letter of the 12th March respecting Thos. Dockerill a discharged Prisoner, and in reply would state that on application being made some time ago as to his prospects of obtaining employment it appeared that, although a person was willing to find him work, there was a strong feeling against him in the neighbourhood that there would be but little chance of his succeeding there.

Under the circumstances and as he had expressed a wish to go to America he was restricted from the County of Bedford. – If however the prohibition materially interferes with his chances of doing well, the Secretary of State is the proper person to whom a representation of the case should be made, with a view to obtaining its removal.-
Dockerill conducted himself well and was very useful as a Labourer here, and I have every reason to believe he intends to do well; and if, as he stated to me, his wife has a home for him, and he can gain regular employment in the County, it would appear to be a case for the favourable consideration of the Secretary of State, especially as the restriction is practically of no effect. –
I am, Rev Sir,
Your obed. Servant
W. Morrish

The Revd H. Smyth
Vicarage
Houghton Regis
Dunstable

---

of succeeding there. He told the Reverend to write to the Secretary of State with the request.

The Reverend agreed, and on 21st March he wrote to the Secretary of State with his request.

224/13

HOME OFFICE
CRIMINAL
MAR 22 1861

Thomas Dockerill

No 13

Q. Ask the Chief Constable if there is any objection.

The Revd H. Smyth JP says that it would be a great boon to this man & his family if the restriction on his Licence excluding him from Bedfordshire were removed. Its only effect is to prevent him living at home with his wife, who is a repectable woman.

Answ. 11/4/61

On 28th March the Home Office, having received the application from the Reverend Smyth, wrote to the Chief Constable at Bedford to obtain his opinion on the exclusion ban being lifted.[2]

---

28 March 1861

The Chief Constable of the County of Bedford
*   I am directed by Secretary Sir George Lewis to transmit to you the enclosed letter applying for the removal of the restriction on the Licence of Thomas Dockerill which excludes him from Bedfordshire and I am to request that you will inform him whether you think there is any objection to his application being complied with.*

H Waddington

The Chief Constable in turn made his own enquiries to see whether the feeling against Dockerill had abated amongst the farmers and on 2nd April he replied to the Home Office to the contrary. The feeling against Dockerill was as strong as ever, that he had terrorised the neighbourhood before he was imprisoned, and he did not recommend a lifting of the exclusion.

Bedford April 2nd 1861

Sir
I have delayed replying to your letter of the 28th ultimo to enable me to make enquiry as to whether, if the removal of the restriction on the License of Thos. Dockerill which excludes him from Bedfordshire, would be beneficial to him.

I beg now to state for the information of Secretary Sir George Lewis, that there is a very strong feeling amongst the Farmers against the return of Dockerill to his former neighbourhood. – I feel satisfied he would not obtain employment. He was the terror of the place before he was sent away, and I do not believe the feeling in the neighbourhood is in the slightest degree abated.

I am
Sir,
Your most Obedt. Servant
E.M. Boutsber ?
Chief Constable

H. Waddington Esq.

The petition made by the Reverend Smyth, and the subsequent enquiries made by the Chief Constable, again raised the issue of Dockerill locally. It was decided that the Reverend should be made conversant with the facts of the case and the man who considered himself responsible for imparting this knowledge was none other than the committing Magistrate at the trial, Colonel Richard Thomas Gilpin. Once again Colonel Gilpin had entered into the scenario. Not only did he acquaint the Reverend with the details of the event, but he also informed him of 'certain circumstances' about it which made Dockerill a very difficult man to deal with. Just what were these 'certain circumstances' was not mentioned, but it could have been the assault itself, or the threats that Dockerill had supposedly made which had been alluded to in other correspondence. Either way, Colonel Gilpin had the interest of the opposition firmly at heart and he certainly convinced Reverend Smyth, who was obviously devastated that he had been persuaded to give his support to such a man as Dockerill. He lost no time in writing once more to the Secretary of State, not only withdrawing his application, but also suggesting the exclusion should have included the neighbouring counties to Bedfordshire.

He also stated that the gang of which Dockerill was once a member now existed only in tradition.

ToThe Right Hon
The Secretary of the state for the Home Department

Houghton Regis Vicarag
Dunstable. Be
April 9. 186

Sir,

With reference to the case of a man named Dockerill who has been recently released on a pardon which permits him to be at large "except in the County of Bedford" and for whose wife I applied for the removal of this limitation – I beg to say that Col. Gilpin M.P. the Committing Magistrate in the case (which occurred many years ago) has mentioned to me certain circumstances connected with it, which show me that there is great difficulty in dealing with the man. I have mentioned that the offence occurred many years ago long before I came into the County – it appears that it was accompanied with circumstances of aggravation which occasioned a strong feeling against Dockerill in the locality where th offence was committed, which feeling still continues to exist in many quarters.

I think that the mistake was originally in the wording of the pardon, & that "the adjoining Counties" should have been added to the County of Bedford which would have kept him out of the neighbourhood altogether. As it is he lives in a public house in the town of Dunstable but not in the County and I fear that such a mode of life can end in no good either to him or the neighbourhood.

At the same time I do not wish to press the application against the opinion of those who know more of the case that I do. All I can certify is that the wife is maintaining herself respectably and that the gang of which Dockerill was a member now exists only in tradition, with which I as comparatively a newcomer have only a very imperfect knowledge.

I may perhaps request an answer which I may place in the hands of the applicants.
I have the honour to be

Yours faithfully
Hugh Smyth
Justice of the Peace
for County of Bedford

Meanwhile, crossing in the mail with the Reverend Smyth's letter, was the reply to his earlier petition to the Home Office.[3]

11 April 1861

The Rev. H. Smyth
Houghton Regis Vicarage,
Dunstable, Beds.

I am directed by Sec. Sir George Lewis to acknowledge the receipt of your letter of the 21st ult applying for a removal of the restriction on the Licence of Thomas Dockerill which excludes him from the County of Bedford, and I am to inform you that after due consideration of the circumstances Sir George Lewis does not think it desirable that the restriction should be removed.

H. Waddington

224/13

HOME OFFICE
CRIMINAL
APR 3 1861

Thomas Dockerill

No 14
He can easily take his wife elsewhere

The Chief Constable of Bedfordshire reports that there is a strong feeling against the return of the convict to his former neighbourhood, & that he is unlikely to get work there.
I ? having made enquiry I do not think it desirable that the restriction should be removed

---

Dockerill's petition to move back to Bedfordshire was rejected. He and Rebecca moved to the village of Northchurch, near Berkhamsted in Hertfordshire, together with their daughter Mary, who was now fourteen years old. The two boys, Ephraim and Joseph, remained in Bedfordshire.

But Dockerill was not happy, or possibly Rebecca missed her family and wanted to return to her home village. Either way, they were still not settled. Dockerill decided that he would have another attempt to have the restriction removed. In June 1862 he wrote once more to the Secretary of State, saying that he was having trouble obtaining work, and asking once more for the exclusion to be lifted.

Petition from Dockerill – copied as written.

? your petitioner is a man of grate trouble and I humbly Beg that you will once more murcefuly take my case into consideration for I might have been A happy man with my wife and all my family had I been permitted to return to them at Dunstable were they was liveing when I was let at liberty for my wife had A nice home for me to come to if I might returnde to injoy it for there was Plenty of work for me and my children but I see nothing but comeing to poverty for I have tride all I can to get a liveing withoute being A trouble to hany one I have my wife and one childe with me and the two boys I was Ablidge to leve them at Dunstable were they can have pleny of worke I my self have never had but three weeks worke never since last harvest what little money I had if have been liveing upon it hopeing to get work but I cannot for the farmers will not imploy all there own labourers in there own parishes and much less A Stanger my petitioning to yer honour is not because I whant to return to where I was convicted from or were I was brought up for I beleve there is but little work for me there but but if I might returne to Dunstable there I can have plenty of work Bless the Lord I have A good wife or I think She never could have put up with the seperation from hir children as she has Bless the Lord we have christen children and that makes us so much the more whant to be with them I know fulwell that I have broke the laws of man and god yet I know and feel that there is forgiveness with god if not with man but I whant to whiteness mans forgiveness as well as gods for I can say with A free heart that I for give every A man yes every man liveing and as I forgive every man I hope every man will forgive me for I never mean levening off praying for forgiveness this side the grave Bless the Lord if I fine not forgiveness with man I know I shall finde it with the Bless the Lord for this hope in the but if I starve I feel al this time that there is no more fealing with me for I see no pleasure in a wicked Life I have had the (leters)? but have never had the (sureaty)? As yet and I beleve I never shall either but I humely beg this simple prayer will find favour in ? singth I will humbily pray for as long as I live on the Hearth may it be so and god grant if and my soul shall rejoice in god my Savour Amen
Your petitioner is Thomas Dockerill who was liberated March the 2. 1861 and is now liveing at Northchurch Near great Burkhamsted herts
(sic)

The Home Office refused. There is no record that Dockerill made any more appeals, and he and Rebecca remained living in Northchurch until his death.

224/13   Home Office 7 Jun 1862

Thomas Dockerill

Ask the Chief Constable

*To enquire if there is
(No 16) any objection
to the granting of
this Petition
- H.W.*

Discharged Convict

*The convict prays to be
allowed to return to
Dunstable where he
could obtain work.*

*X The question was asked in 1861
In reply (No. 14)
It cannot be allowed at present.
H.W.*

The Murchison River, site of the Geraldine Mine.

CHAPTER 21

Northampton (Gwalla)

T he colonists of Western Australia were always hungry for new areas to settle. On 16th October, 1848, whilst on an expedition to find new farming pastures towards the northern part of the colony, James Walcott, a member of Augustus Gregory's surveying team, discovered lead, or galena, in the bed of the Murchison River. Once back in Perth, the men reported their find to the new Governor, Charles Fitzgerald, who was so impressed that he decided he should inspect the site personally. He and his party set sail from Fremantle on 1st December, 1848, sailing into Champion Bay three days later, before heading overland to the Murchison River, where they arrived on 7th December. They could see the lead vein, more exposed than when Walcott had discovered it, running for a distance of about three hundred metres.

The Governor envisaged great possibilities for the area, both pastoral and mineral, despite the fact that he had an altercation with the Aborigines and received a spear wound in his leg. As a result of the findings, he announced that the government was prepared to sell the rites to the lead mine.[1] The Geraldine Mining Company was founded in 1849, and the mine named the Geraldine.

From the Independent Journal December 1850:

Champion Bay and the Geraldine Mine.

The following is an extract from the report of Capt. James. It is gratifying to find that the proprietors' high opinion of the value of this mine, is confirmed by that of a practical authority such as

Mr. James:

To the Directors of the Geraldine Mining Company.

GENTLEMEN, – I have with pleasure to inform you our party are fully engaged at work, and that all reports, as represented, are highly creditable in every shape and form. * * I have not been enabled to examine the bed of the river minutely up to this date, but all that is visible is truly astonishing, At the S.S.W end there is a fine lode, averaging about 2 feet 4 inches wide; I foot 6 inches of this lode is a solid mass of galena and 10 inches of clay, zinc, and the sulphures of iron, on which I have directed the men to sink a shaft, to take this lode about 4 fathoms deep, and continue on its course for ten fathoms, if possible. The lode at the N.E. end is about 6 feet wide. The rock to sink through is of a very hard description, but in 3 months the 20 fathoms may be completed. We are not enabled to sink at present more than one shaft, which is quite sufficient to raise a large quantity of lead. I am glad to find within 3, 8, and 12 miles, and also around the mines, there is a sufficient quantity of wood to last for years. I have seen limestone about 8 miles from the mines, all on a very good road, and in the vicinity of the mines clay suitable for making common bricks. The supply of fresh water is abundant. From the direction the lode takes, I feel positive of being enabled to trace it into high ground, which will be of considerable advantage in the height of the winter.

However, there was to prove a major drawback. Due to a lack of knowledge of the local area, it was sunk at the very spot where the lead was found in the bed of the river. Unfortunately, this was prone to heavy flooding in the summer months, when monsoon rains fell into the catchment area of the Murchison district some few hundred kilometres away and rushed through the gorges and into the sea at Kalbarri. It meant that at certain times of the year the mine was inoperable due to flooding.

But at the same time, other possibilities for the area were being explored. William Burges and his party arrived in the area in November 1850 after travelling overland from the York district with stock of two hundred head of cattle and two thousand three hundred sheep. Apart from losing a few animals to unknown poisons, they arrived safe and well at the Bowes River, in fact their condition had improved on the journey. The area in which he stationed his livestock he found to be very good grazing country, suitable for cattle sheep and horses, insomuch as the grass was as green in the dry season as it would be in York in August. William Burges subsequently took up the lease of 132,000 acres of land of which 12,000 were freehold, and built a handsome residence on the banks of the Bowes River.[2]

The first shipment of lead had already been shipped out of Port Gregory, a small harbour formed by a long coral reef like an artificial breakwater, previously explored as a possible site for a harbour to service the Geraldine Mine, north of the Murchison River. Early in the 1850s a small jetty was erected and the priority now was not only to build a road to the Geraldine Mine but also to build other roads and buildings. By 1851 twenty-two ticket-of-leave men were working at the mine and with Government Surveyors in the district. But labour shortage in the area was critical. On the recommendation of Lord Grey, Secretary of State for the Colonies, the decision was taken to establish a Convict Hiring Depot, at Lynton, about seven miles from Port Gregory. On 22nd May, 1853, a party of sixty convicts and Pensioner Guards who had recently arrived at Fremantle on the 'Pyrenees', was transported to Port Gregory on the Leander. After landing in small boats they trekked inland to the chosen site and established a small settlement. The convict hiring depot was built using local limestone, and an elegant two-storey house for Captain Sandford, the supervisor of the depot. In 1852, the post of medical superintendent at Lynton was taken up by a convict named Joseph Lucas Horrocks, who had been convicted of forgery in England and subsequently transported to Fremantle. Despite having no medical training, his basic skills being acquired only whilst serving in the Royal Navy as a sick-berth attendant, Horrocks was given this post as there was no other qualified man available.

The lead from the Geraldine Mine was now being exported in considerable quantities to Singapore via Port Gregory and realised an excellent profit, but by 1857 the site of the depot at Lynton had proved unsuitable and was closed.

Joseph Horrocks moved to Wanerenooka and opened a store, but continued to tend the sick, making no charge except for medicines. In 1859 he acquired one hundred acres of land, and with financial assistance he opened a copper mine which he named Gwalla.[3] Horrocks was a man of vision. After having a road surveyed through the valley, he built a number of stone-walled cottages alongside and leased them to his married miners at low rental. Encouraged by Horrocks, his tenants grew their own vegetables, and the wives tended gardens which were well stocked with flowers. Horrocks was also responsible for the building of Gwalla Church, declaring it would be used by all denominations.[4] Hearing about his enterprise, many men flocked to the area in search of employment and the small community began to flourish.

Once George had obtained his conditional pardon in 1859, he was free to move at will within Western Australia and began to consider other areas. After hearing of the opportunities in the Northern Districts, he decided to move there. By now he and Maria were the parents of three children, George born in 1853, Mary Anne born in 1855 and Maria born in 1858, but Maria was pregnant once more, so no move could be considered at this stage and they remained in Perth until after the baby's birth. Their third daughter, Martha was born on 14th October, 1860. But the Northern Districts beckoned and, as soon as they were able, they began their move.

There is no record of how the family travelled up to the Mines area. Generally they would have used the boat service to Champion Bay, and then made their way on foot but it is possible they travelled all the way by land. This would have taken them some considerable days and would have been extremely hard with four children, and one of those a young baby.

At the time of his move the area had two towns known as The Mines (Wanerenooka) and Gwalla. The two towns were about two kilometres apart, and in September and October of 1862 the new Governor of the Colony, Governor Hampton, and other officials made a tour of the area. The party was welcomed by the delighted residents. At the entrance to the Gwalla estate a triumphal arch of flowers of every hue mixed with evergreens had been erected with the motto "Welcome to our Governor". As he neared this, His Excellency was received by those assembled with loud and hearty cheers and a modest gun salute. The mine, the site of the place of worship and the miners' houses were inspected and having been shown over the mines the official party and leading settlers sat down to dine with Mr. Horrocks.[5]

In 1863 Horrocks applied to the government for an acre of land to be set aside for a schoolhouse, and on 19th February, 1864, the township of Northampton was proclaimed, formerly the district of Gwalla and Wanerenooka and being built between these two towns on the banks of the Nookanena Brook.

George applied for one of the first town lots to be sold. It must have seemed ironical to him that he was now living in a place called Northampton, when he had lived not so far from Northampton in England. The land he purchased on 23rd September, 1865, at a cost of £ 5. 0s. 0d. was a town block, lot No. 130, fronting the Hampton road, and described as being bounded on the West side by 3 chains 60 links of Hampton Rd, on the North by 2½ chains of John St, on the South by Northampton town lot 131 measuring 2½ chains – and on the East side by a bank of the Nookanena Brook. But it would appear that his purchase did not go entirely smoothly, as he did not receive the title deeds for the land, and on 17th January, 1866, he wrote to the Surveyor General at Perth to request that they be sent to him. These were subsequently issued on the 27th April.[6]

Gwalla 17 January 1866

Sir, I have the honour to request that you will at your earliest convenience cause to be forwarded to me, the title deed of town lot No 130 Northampton purchased by me on the 23 Sep last & for which I have a receipt for the payment there of.

Sir

Your obedient servant

George White
Wheelwright

To the Honourable
    The Surveyor General
        Perth

In consideration of Five Pounds Sterling paid to the satisfaction of Our Governor of Our Colony of Western Australia Give and Grant unto George White of Gwalla in our said Colony Wheelwright All that piece and parcel of land situate and being in the Town of Northampton in our said Colony containing three Roods and twenty four Perches more or less and marked and distinguished in the Maps and Books of the Survey Office of Our said Colony as "Northampton Town Allotment No 130 and Bounded on the West by three Chains Sixty Links of Hampton Road on the North By two and a half chains of John Street and the South By Northampton Town Lot 131 measuring two and a half chains and on the East by left bank of Nokanama Brook".
Signed John Stephen Hampton Esquire

<u>Northampton Shire Records</u>
George White Lot No 130 purchased 18 April 1866
Receipt No 22506
For fee simple of his Northampton lot No 130

On this land now stands Chiverton House, a museum dedicated to the pioneers of the district. The original small cottage adjoining the museum still stands, and a plaque on the wall attributes the building (by/for) George. The cottage, however, was obviously not built in time for the birth of his sixth child, a daughter named Georgina, as she was born at Mugairay (Mugawah?) on 26th October, 1866. As on the other birth certificates, George's profession is shown as a wheelwright but it is not clear whether he ever operated as a wheelwright from Lot 130,

The original cottage on Lot 130 attributed to George White.
Drawn by the author from a photograph.

although there are wheelwright's tools and wheels still in the Chiverton House museum yard.

During this time, George again employed three ex-convicts. The first, Joseph Hindmarsh (5502), was employed from 21st February, 1866. Hindmarsh was born in 1827, single, semi-literate, Protestant, 5ft 3ins tall, light brown hair, grey eyes, oval head, swarthy complexion, and thin. He had distinguishing marks, Hannah Ellen Mary Joseph M P E J M B J P B P (indistinct P) H (reversed J) anchor on his left arm and B X H on his right. He was convicted at Newcastle on Tyne in 1857 for larceny and had a previous conviction of four years. He arrived at Fremantle on 19th August, 1859 on board the Sultana, obtained his ticket-of-leave 3rd February, 1860, and his conditional pardon 2nd February, 1861.

The second, Thomas Kerr, he employed from 9th May, 1866. Kerr was born in 1840, was single, a printer, and a Protestant. He was 5ft 7ins, had dark brown hair and dark hazel eyes, a long face and sallow complexion. He was of slight build, had a small cut on his forehead and was convicted in Glasgow in 1861, receiving a sentence of eight years.

He arrived at Fremantle on 13th December, 1861 on the York.

It is possible that he employed these men in the wheelwright business, but it is more likely to build the cottage on Lot 130.

The third man, Edward Bransby, worked as a cook from 1867. Bransby was born in 1835, was unmarried and a horsehair weaver, convicted at Spalding for pickpocketing and sentenced to ten years. He arrived at Fremantle on board the Merchantman (Journey 2) on 12th September, 1864, obtained his ticket-of-leave on 14th October, 1866, and his certificate of freedom on 7th January, 1873. Bransby left the colony on 15th May 1873, bound for Singapore.

On 16th October, 1871, George sold his block of land to John Hosken for the sum of £25.7 John was the youngest son of Martin Hosken, who built the Miners Arms Hotel at the northern end of the town.

A Memorial to be registered of an Indenture of conveyance made the 16th day of October 1871 in pursuance of an act to facilitate the conveyance of real property Between George White of Gwalla in the Champion Bay District in the colony of Western Australia Wheelwright of the one party and John Hosken the younger of ....in the said District named of the other part.

Whereby in consideration of (£25) twenty-five pounds paid of the said John Hosken to the said George White (receipt acknowledged) the said George White did grant unto the said John Hosken his heirs and assigns All that piece or parcel of Land situate and being in the Town of Northampton in the said Colony containing 3 roods and 24 perches more or less marked and distinguished in the maps and Books of the Survey office of the said Colony as "Northampton Town allotment No 130" Bounded as described in the said Books - Together with the appertainances thereto. Which said Indenture as to the execution thereof by the said George White is witnessed by "Samuel Smith".........

And is hereby required to the registered by Edward Wilson Landor(?) of Perth ? as witness his hand the twenty first day of November 1871.

Just where George and his family lived from this date until the purchase of his next lot of land is not certain, and possibly they still lived at Lot 130, renting it from John Hosken. But it would appear that he moved around the area working where needed, as the next record we have of him is in the carpenter's shop at the Geraldine Mine. There is evidence that both George and his son were working at the mine in 1873 or 1875, probably camping there whilst Maria and the other children stayed in the Gwalla district, which was some distance away.

A newspaper article from 1923 recalls a tragic event which happened during the 1860s (1865) when a small boy of six years old was abducted from land some four miles from Northampton whilst he was bringing in the cows. It was subsequently found that he had been cannibalised. When the perpetrator of the crime was discovered in 1873 (or 1875), George, then described as 'old George White', and George Junior were involved in his capture which took place in the Carpenter's shop at the Geraldine Mine. This article also mentions Captain Samuel Mitchell, the manager of the mine, who arrived in the area from Cornwall in 1867 to take charge of the mine.

Excerpt from Geraldton Gazette Wednesday 22nd August 1923

REMINISCENCES
_____

A   NORTHAMPTON
TRAGEDY   OF   THE
SIXTIES
(By "Patriarch")

It was in the sixties, shortly after the Yanganooka mine, four miles from Northampton, was first opened under the management of Captain Laurie. The late Mr. and Mrs. Edward Dunn, the parents of a well-known resident of Geraldton, were living on the property. "Ned" Dunn was a miner and worked on the Yanganooka mine. He also kept a small herd of cows and supplied the miners with butter and milk.

The Dunns' first born was a boy named Francis. He was only six years old at the time of which I write. But he was remarkably intelligent and useful for his age. He used to bring in the cows every evening from the pasture on which they grazed during the day. Late one afternoon he was sent out on his usual mission. The herd was not far off, for the bells could be heard distinctly in the direction of a valley known as "Charcoal Gully", and situated about a half a mile from the mine.

As evening approached, and the sun began to dip, the child's parents became anxious, for he had not returned. They could still hear the bells, though they were coming no nearer. The mother became distressed. She felt something must have happened, and Dunn immediately went out to "Charcoal Gully" to see what was wrong. He found the cows there, but saw no sign of his son.

On both sides of the gully there were a lot of natives camped; the Wanerenooka blacks on one hill, and the Colalli tribe on the other. Dunn shouted to the Wanerenooka natives, and asked them if they had seen the boy. The leaders came down to him and one of them said "No, nothing come on this way".

Dunn then took the cattle home, thinking that perhaps the boy saw the natives, got frightened, and ran back. But when he arrived at the house he was much alarmed to find that the child was not there. Word was at once sent round to every man off shift, and all speedily mustered and went in search, but no trace of the missing boy could be found. The Wanerenooka police were communicated with. Early next morning a constable and black-tracker were quickly on the scene. The search was resumed and continued for a week, but without result. It seemed as though the earth had opened and swallowed the child.

*   *   *

Years rolled by, and the event had been almost forgotten. In the early part of 1873 (or 75), a young blackfellow named Tommy Glass was arrested at the Geraldine mine for sheep stealing. Tommy was lodged in the local lock-up, which was then at Gwalla, the southern side of Northampton. During the first night he was in custody, a Northampton native named Toby, who had been taken in charge for drunkenness, was placed in the same cell.

At daybreak, when Toby woke out of his stupor, he found he had a mate, and he wanted to know what Tommy was in for. "I don't know," was Tommy's reply, "Might be killem that boy?" Toby asked. "What boy?" Tommy answered, "That boy Jimmy killem long time Yanganooka."

And then he went on to unfold his horrifying story. "I boy self that time. Jimmy see-em boy come, and he tellem blackfeller, 'I killem that boy; we eatem.' Some fellows wanten to stop him, and other fellow say 'let him.' Wommany all been away. Jimmy call em boy, and boy come in close mia; Jimmy hit em on head with dowark; boy tumble down; and Jimmy more hit em and kill em. Other fellows help Jimmy carry em away and take em Yuba Flat Rocks. Jimmy get em sharp stone and break em out one hand - Colalli blackfellow can't eat em that one hand. Other fellows make em fire, then cook em and all nalgo (eat). Jimmy make em mine little bit eat em. All finish, then make em big one fire want em burn up bone; then nil blackfellow walk Mideroo well. Jimmy throw em down well that one hand - that hand now in well. Me frightened, they hang em me up. What you think?"

Toby informed the police in the morning of the conversation in the cell, and Tommy repeated to them all he had said to Toby. Prompt action followed. The police went to Willow Gully and interviewed Mr. John Williams, about pulling the water out of the Mideroo well, which was on his property. Mr. Williams made all the necessary arrangements. He sent one of his station hands - a man named Frank Barker - up with the police, and they cleaned out the well. At the bottom, sure enough, and wonderfully preserved, were the bones of the right hand, which had been lying there all those years.

The police took out a warrant for the apprehension of Jimmy for the murder of Francis Dunn, and they went up to Geraldine - in which district the native was located - to arrest him. There appeared little hope of getting Jimmy without much trouble and risk. To a large extent he shunned white folk, and kept back in the bush with other savages like himself. He had, however, a singular confidence in Mr. Samuel Mitchell, who was then manager of the Geraldine mine, and who always treated the blacks with great kindness. The police knew this, placed the position before Mr. Mitchell, and asked his help.

"As it is a murder case," Mr. Mitchell replied, "I will assist you. I never gave anyone away in my life, but I'll fix Jimmy for you. I'll send out for him to come in and cut some she-oak for pick handles. He has often done so for me before. You go away, and come back at midnight; put your horses in the stable, and go down to the carpenter's shop. A place in which to conceal yourselves will be prepared for you there, and make your arrangements with the carpenter for catching him."

Mr. Mitchell sent a native out to Jimmy, asking him to come in as he wanted him. Jimmy, who would do anything for Mr. Mitchell, quickly responded to his request. Mr. Mitchell gave him instructions in regard to cutting the she-oak; provided him with rations and tobacco, and told him to take one of the axes about the place to the carpenter's shop next morning to be ground. Old Mr. **George White** was in charge of the shop, and he had on other occasions ground an axe for Jimmy.

The plan of action had been well pre-arranged. Next morning, at the appointed hour, Jimmy put in an appearance with the axe, and the grinding commenced, the native turning the stone while **White** held the implement at the proper angle. After the expiration of a reasonable period, old **Mr. White** held up the axe and examined the edge to see if one side had been sufficiently ground. That was the signal! **White junior**, slammed the door of the shop. Simultaneously Corporal Houlahan, Constable John Carroll and another constable sprang from their hiding places and flung themselves on Jimmy. He fought for his life like a human tiger, but it was five to one, and he was over-powered, handcuffed and chained.

The police took him up to the stable, where their horses were. Mr.Mitchell went to see the captive. In relating the incident afterwards, Mr. Mitchell said "I will never forget the look Jimmy gave me, and his words often come back to my mind: 'What for, master, you all time big feller babbin (friend) - what for you doem wrong way?'"

Jimmy was tried, convicted of murder, and sentenced to death. Tommy, who had been detained, was the principal witness for the Crown at the trial, which took place in the Supreme Court, Perth. He was also forced to attend the execution, the object being that, when he went back to his tribe, he would give them a horrifying account of the hanging.

Tommy, having witnessed the execution, was returned to Geraldton, given enough rations by the police there to take him to Geraldine, and set at liberty, the sheep stealing charge having been withdrawn.

The second day from Geraldton saw him once more among his tribe.

What Tommy told them can only be divined, but the story he related to the whites with awe-inspiring solemnity, was a graphic and ghoulish description of what occurred before and after the execution, and of the appearance of the body, and of the hideous deformities of the victim after the last penalty had been paid.

Tommy died about eight years ago at Yallalong in the employ of Mr. John Mitchell.

Toby, who was regarded by the white people as the principal in bringing Jimmy to the hangman's noose, was convicted in 1881 of stealing a bottle of brandy, and sentenced to three months at Rottnest. At the expiration of his time, he was engaged by the police as native assistant, and sent to Albany. He was an intelligent native, but an inveterate drunkard. He got intoxicated one day, and was creating a disturbance at one of the hotels. A constable, just returning from bush duty, appeared on the scene, and tried to arrest him. Toby resisted, hopped into the John, and was getting the best of it when the policeman pulled out his revolver, and struck the native over the head with it, laying him out senseless. He never recovered consciousness, and, in the course of a few days, had passed into the land of shadows.

Toby deserved a better fate. Until the few remaining representatives of the older generation have gone to their long rest, his name will be associated with the great mining revival which was experienced in Northampton in the middle seventies. It was he who discovered two of our rich lead lines, the Wheal Ellen and the Wheal May, and almost in the same way.

Somewhere about '74, Toby was working for the old Miners' Arms Hotel for the late Mr. John Hosken, father of Mr. Sidney Hosken, of Northampton. A horse got out of the stable on a Saturday night, and Toby was sent out early on Sunday morning to look for it. He tracked it down to Forenor Springs, and, while following its footprints, found a piece of lead which had been dislodged by one of the animal's hoofs. The rest is a matter of well-known history.

As regards the Wheal May, he was employed by the late Mr. Joe Brooks, and, in company with the late Mr. Henry Chisholm, who died some months ago, he was sent out after some cart horses, which had strayed away. While tracking them, Toby came across a piece of carbonate of lead, which one of the horses had trodden upon, and broken. Toby gave it to Chisholm; who showed it to Brooks, and, in a short time, the locality - which was the spot where the Wheal May now rests serenely - was a busy hive of profitable mining industry.

Yanganooka, the scene of the tragedy of the sixties, is no longer a mining camp. Today, from the hill where Francis Dunn was murdered, one can see farmhouses dotted here and there on landscape and fields, green or fallowed, as far as the eye can reach. In the sixties, wild bush, the haunts of savages and cannibals; in 1923, a prosperous agricultural district, whose inhabitants are availing themselves of all the appliances and aids modern science has supplied to expand and strengthen the industry to which they are devoting their lives.

Such is the advancement of civilisation.

In 1872, tenders were advertised in the Government Gazette for an engineering survey of a proposed railway line from Geraldton to Northampton, a distance of about thirty-two miles, and the lowest, that of Mr. James Major, at £35 per mile was accepted. With the forthcoming arrival of the railway, those concerned in business matters in Northampton saw possibilities of developing trade in the lower end of the town, and there began a shuffling of property.

On 18th December, 1875, John Hosken sold his land, Lot 130, to Samuel Mitchell and Charles Crowther for he had decided to build a hostelry on a site nearby. In turn, as mining was experiencing a decline, Captain Mitchell was looking to extend his business interests. In partnership with George Crowther, he imported household goods and mining equipment, extended the property on Lot 130, opened a store and built stables.

On 14th August, 1876 Samuel Mitchell and Charles Crowther, sold part Lot 70, situated in Gwalla Street to George.

A Memorial to be registered of and Indenture of Conveyance made the 14th day of August one thousand eight hundred and seventy six (in pursuance of an Act to facilitate the conveyance of Real property) Between Charles Crowther of Geraldton in the Colony of Western Australia Merchant and Samuel Mitchell of Northampton in the said colony Mining engineer of the one part and George White the elder of Northampton aforesaid Yeoman of the other part Whereby in consideration of Ten pounds sterling there paid by the said - George White to the said Charles Crowther and Samuel Mitchell (the receipt....Acknowledged) They the said Charles Crowther and Samuel Mitchell did and each of them did grant unto the said - George White his heirs and assigns for ever all that piece or parcel of Land situate in the Town of Northampton aforesaid being the South West portion of "Northampton Town Lot No 70" and bounded on the South by three chains ten and a half links of Gwalla Street On the West by two chains sixteen links of the East boundary of Town Lot 71 On the North by three chains ten and a half links of the South boundary of Town Lot 69 and on the East by a line of two chains sixteen links in length parallel to the West boundary above - described and dividing the parcel of land intended to the hereby granted from the portion of the said Town Lot 70 And the said Indenture as to the execution - thereof by the said Charles Crowther is witnessed by Stephen Henry Parker of Perth in the said Colony Solicitor and as to the execution thereof by the said Samuel Mitchell is witnessed by E W Stephens of Northampton in the said colony and is required to be registered by the said Stephen Henry Parker.

Department of Land Information, Western Australia Book V11 387 Memorial 2283 Enrolment 2596

THE RAILWAY HOTEL
NORTHAMPTON
Will be opened about 1st November, 1876, by
JOHN HOSKEN,
(LATE MINERS' ARMS)

This large and commodious Hotel has just been built, and in point of accommodation and all the appliances of a first-class modern Hotel, will be found to be second to none in Western Australia. It is pleasantly situated, within five minutes' walk of the Railway Terminus. It contains a large Commercial Room, four Parlors, and twelve bedrooms, all furnished in the best possible style.

————

Visitors.

Families visiting Northampton can be accommodated with suites of rooms, and may be confident that the best attention will be paid to their comfort. Hot and Cold Baths always procurable at the shortest notice. The stock of

WINES, SPIRITS, ALES &c.,

is unsurpassed. None but the best brands supplied.

Saddle Horses and Traps always on Hire.
Bagatelle !

Extensive and well-ventilated Stables, and a thoroughly trustworthy Ostler.

The proprietor ventures to refer to the support so kindly accorded to him whilst conducting the Miners' Arms Hotel, and trusts to obtain a continuance of that patronage which it will ever be his endeavour to deserve.

Northampton, Oct. 2, 1876

A view of Northampton showing Chiverton House, considerably enlarged on the right.

On 11th October of the same year, John Hosken advertised the opening of his hostelry in the Inquirer and Commercial News. Over the years, the Railway Hotel was the scene of many public events and concerts.

George and his son, George Junior, went on to run their wheelwright's business, probably from the property in Gwalla Street. George's charming little cottage built on this land still stands.

The original cottage on Lot 130 was renovated in 1908 and opened as the Western Australian Bank, the first bank in Northampton. Samuel Mitchell died in 1912, but the property remained in the Mitchell family until after Samuel's son, Lees Franklyn, had died. It was then sold to Thomas Williams and later to the last known occupier, Sydney Francis, who lived there and conducted a saddlery business from the premises. After being condemned twice by the council, they later purchased and refurbished it, opening it as a folk museum which it remains to this day.

The cottage on part lot 70. George White lived here until his death, leaving the property to his daughter Georgina.

CHAPTER 22

The Later Years

What legacy left you, great grandpa,
As I hid from the children at school,
From their taunts about being a convict kid,
I learnt hurting sparrows is cruel.
But what would you care that your curse lingers on
Now your debt to society's paid
And there are only a handful of sparrows to visit your far
lonely grave.

WILLIAM WHITE – pardoned

Following his release from prison in August of that year, William's wife, Mary, gave birth to their first child, a boy whom they named Joseph.

One of Mary's family also fell foul of the law; her younger brother, Samuel Tavener, was in constant trouble. He had a total of sixteen convictions at Bedford, the first in 1855 for stealing fowls when he was just fifteen years old. He had six further convictions for theft, one for stealing iron, two for barley, one for a rat trap, one for manure bags and one for cabbages. Interspersed with these were two convictions for being drunk and riotous, two for wilful damage, one for assault and one for 'suspicious person'. He was further convicted twice under the game laws. His final conviction on 15th October, 1867, was again for theft, this time for stealing a wheelbarrow to the value of 1/- at Houghton Regis for which he received a sentence of seven years. He was one of the first prisoners to be photographed at Bedford.

William and Mary went on to have a total of eleven children, three of

401

them dying at an early age. From Chalk Hill, the family moved first to Houghton Regis and then to Dunstable, the censuses showing several different addresses. Two of their children moved to Yorkshire in their adult years. William continued in his trade as an agricultural labourer until his health failed. When he became so bad that he was paralysed, he and Mary were forced to move to Yorkshire to the home of their son, William, a blacksmith.

There was no evidence that he was ever part of Dockerill's "gang". However at the Petty Session in Luton on the 5th February, 1855, before L. Ames, the Rev. F.W. Adey and Humphrey Brandreth Esquire, one William White of Houghton Regis was charged with "Illegal Sporting". It was alleged that he killed a partridge at Houghton Regis on 23rd January. He was found guilty and fined £2 including costs, or one month's imprisonment. The fine was paid.

One might wonder if Squire Brandreth recognised the accused ?

THOMAS HINES – The other accused

There is no evidence that Thomas Hines was ever charged for his part in the crime. He and Lucy and their children remained living at Chalk Hill until her early death in February 1852. Thomas then appears to have moved on but died in the Union Workhouse at Woburn. Two of their daughters, Elizabeth and Hannah, are still recorded as living in Chalk Hill on the 1881 census. At that time Hannah had two children, Matilda and George.

JOHN WHITE – The butcher – William's father and George's brother

John and Sally continued to live and run the butchery and slaughterhouse in Chalk Hill. John died in August 1865, and Sally on 30th April, 1874, and are buried in the same grave, marked by a large headstone in Houghton Regis churchyard. The business continued to be run by John's two sons, John and Lewis, along with Joseph and Elizabeth Mooring's sons. The Harrods Directory of 1876 shows Ephraim Mooring as a butcher in Edward Street, Dunstable. It also shows Lewis White as a butcher resident in Church Street. The younger John's son, Arthur, married his cousin, Lizzie Gregory, the daughter of Hannah White and William Gregory. They continued in the family trade, opening a butcher's shop in High Street North, Dunstable.

SARAH COOK – George's wife

Sarah eventually married Thomas Inns on 2nd April, 1875, twenty-five years after George's transportation. They already had three daughters.

ELIZA, George's daughter, married William Henry Mead, a bricklayer, on 26th September, 1867. They had seven children. Three of their sons, Leonard, Jesse and Harry, served in the First World War. Jesse was gassed, but died of tetanus in 1916. Leonard went missing in May 1917. Harry was gassed three times in the war but survived and went on to work at Waterlows Printers. Harry married Susan Morgan from Totternhoe, and their daughter, Kate Mead, often recalled how she was taunted at school for being a 'convict kid'.

THOMAS DOCKERILL – Transportation for life

It would appear that Dockerill did not return to his life of crime. He and Rebecca remained living in Northchurch High Street where the 1881 census shows their trade as grocers.

Their daughter, Mary, married Richard Sear, a Master Tailor. On the 1881 census Richard Sear is shown to employ three boys; one of these was Albert White, the deaf and dumb son of Charles White, William's brother, who gave William an alibi at his trial. Another of those employed was Charles Dockerill, the son of Thomas Dockerill's brother, William.

Dockerill and Rebecca's son, Joseph, eventually moved to Berkhamsted where he married in 1869. On the 1881 census he is living near his sister Mary, and is a plait dealer, but the 1891 census shows that Joseph and his family had moved back to Luton.

Ephraim Dockerill stayed in Bedfordshire, firstly Dunstable, and then

Leonard Mead, missing in action, May 1917.

below and left Three of George's grandsons, Eliza's sons, who served in the war.

Harry Mead, survived the war.

Jesse Mead, gassed and died of tetanus in 1916.

Luton where, on the 1891 census, he is shown to be a straw hat manufacturer.

Thomas's troubled life was over on 7th December, 1886. He was sixty-six years old, and died from valvular disease of the heart – the mitral valve. He had also suffered from dropsy for four weeks. Rebecca, his daughter Mary, and his son-in-law, Richard, were with him at his death.

Following Thomas's demise, Rebecca's years of exile from Bedfordshire could come to an end. She moved to Luton and lived with her son, Joseph, and his family, where she died sixteen months after her husband, on 24th April, 1888. The cause of her death was chronic bronchitis, dilation of the heart, and dropsy, the condition inherited from her mother, Lucy. She was seventy years old. Her sons were both with her at her death.

GEORGE WHITE – Transportation for fifteen years

George and his son George Junior ran a wheelwright's business, which is shown in directories between 1881 and 1899.

George Junior married a very young emigrant named Mary Moyle. They had ten children, tragically seven of them dying as infants. Their son, George Stephen, was killed in the 1st World War, whilst serving as Private 156 with 44th Battalion Australian Infantry. He died in the 3rd Battle of Ypres on 5th July, 1917, aged twenty-seven years, shortly after his British half-cousin, Leonard Mead, went missing in the war. There is a memorial tree dedicated to George Stephen in the Avenue of

The memorial to George Stephen White in Kings Park, Perth.

George Stephen White, killed in the Battle of Ypres.

Gwalla Church, now derelict.

Honour in Kings Park in Perth, dedicated by Jane and Jim King. Jane is the granddaughter of George Senior and Maria Gardener's younger son, John.

George himself lived in Northampton, W.A., until he died of influenza on the 12 May, 1901, just three days short of the 50th anniversary of his arrival in Western Australia. He was seventy-seven years of age and had outlived most of his family; Maria Gardiner who died of natural causes on 2nd February, 1892; his eldest son George who passed away on 4th October, 1893 from blood poisoning; his youngest son, John who succumbed to paralysis on the 18 October, 1898; and his daughter, Mary Ann. He had also outlived most of his family and associates in Bedfordshire.

George's youngest daughter, Georgina, remained living with George to take care of him until his death. She alone inherited his property. The witnesses to the very shaky signature on his will were his near neighbours Gustavus and Anne Varley, the latter being the widow of

John Hosken who had earlier purchased George's land, and had owned the Railway Hotel. The will, dated 29th September, 1900, describes the property as a six roomed cottage, valued at £300. There was never any evidence of George's writing throughout his life, although some records stated that he could do so. The only evidence we have is a signature on his daughter, Maria's birth certificate, and a very feeble signature on his will.

Georgina herself married two years later at the age of thirty-seven and moved away from Northampton. There has been no record found of her having any children. She did not apply for probate of the will until April 1906.

George, together with most of his Australian family, is buried in the little cemetery beside the ruins of the Church at Gwalla, built by Joseph Horrocks for his townsfolk. Horrocks himself is buried alongside them. It is probable that George's children, as with most children of convicts,

The entrance to Gwalla graveyard, where George and most of his family are buried.

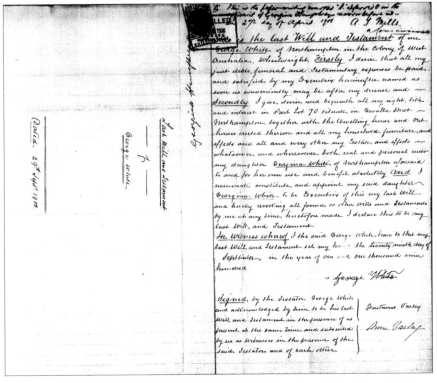

George White's last Will and Testament.

never knew about the circumstances of his arrival there, nor were they sure about were he came from. His death certificate, informant Georgina, shows that he came from Bristol. The name of George's mother was not known, neither were details of Maria Gardiner.

Both the little cottage built on the land at part Lot 70, and the cottage on Lot 130, which is now a part of the Chiverton House museum, still remain. A plaque on the outside wall at the entrance to the museum shows George as the first owner of the cottage, and remains a monument to George's transportation.

It is ironic that Dockerill, who was sentenced to life, was in actual fact able to return to his wife and family. George, who was sentenced to fifteen years, might as well have got life, as there was never any hope of

LAST WILL AND TESTAMENT

In the Supreme Court of Western Australia.
Probate jurisdiction

56 /1906
In the last will of George White late of Northampton in the state of Western Australia Wheelwright deceased

Be it known that on the third day of May one thousand and nine hundred and six the last Will and Testament (a copy whereof is hereto annexed) of George White deceased who died on the twelfth day of May one thousand nine hundred and one at Northampton in the said state of Western Australia was prove approve and registered in the Supreme Court of the said state of Western Australia at Perth and that administration of the real and personal estate of the said deceased was granted by the for said court to Georgina Humphreys of Lake Darlot the sole executrix named in the said will she having been first sworn well and faithfully to administer the same -- given at Perth aforesaid the third day of May one thousand nine hundred and six

By the Court
F S Moseley
Master

This is the last will and testament of me George White of Northampton in the colony of Western Australia Wheelwright Firstly I desire that all my just debts funeral and testamentary expenses be paid and satisfied by my Executrix here in after named as soon as conveniently may be after my decease and secondly I give device and bequeath all my right title and interest in part lot 70 situated in Gwalla Street Northampton together with the dwelling house and out houses erected there on and all my house hold furniture and effects and all and every other my estate and effects whatever and where ever both real and personal unto my daughter Georgina White of Northampton afore said to and for own use and benefit absolutely. And nominate constitute and appoint my said daughter Georgina White to be executive of this my last will and hereby revoking all former or other wills and testaments by me at anytime heretofore made- I declare this to be my last will and testament - In witness wherefore I the said George White have to this very last Will and Testament set my hand the twenty ninth day of September in the year of our Lord one thousand nine hundred - George White

Signed by the testator George White and Acknowledged by him to be his last Will and Testament in the presence of us present at the same time and subscribed by us as witnesses in the presence of the said presence and of each other

Gustavus Varley --- Anne Varley

The plaque on the wall of Chiverton House Museum.

him returning. But there is no doubt that George made something of his enforced migration and his new life in Australia, probably more than if he had remained in Houghton Regis.

On Saturday 28th February, 2004, the Premier announced part of the Government's plans to celebrate the migrant contribution to Western Australia through a Migrant Welcome Wall at the Maritime Museum,

SURNAME, INITIALS	SHIP NAME	DATE
SUTCLIFFE, L & P, Jill, Jenny	Fairsky	1971
TERRIACA, Domenico	Toscana	1948
TONUS, Vanda & Rita	Oceania	1955
TONUS, Vitaliano	Sydney	1954
TRUSTY, George	Britannis	1971
TURNER, WLC & PM & Family	Australia	1966
VACCARO, Lucia	Viminale	1939
VAJDA, Aladar & Eszter	Skaugum	1950
VAJDA, Elemer I	Skaugum	1950
WHITE, Family	Castel Felice	1962
WHITE, George	Mermaid	1851
WILKINSON, Jean & Anne	Strathaird	1953
WOJTCZAK, Adam, Hilda, E, M	Skaugum	1950

The Migrant Welcome Wall at Fremantle.

Victoria Quay, Fremantle, and Australians were invited to sponsor their ancestors. The Wall was unveiled on 19th December 2004, and thanks to his great-granddaughter, Jane King, and her husband Jim, George's name appears forever to be remembered as one of the pioneers, having arrived on the convict ship Mermaid.

Exploring the past

The ruins of the Geraldine Mine.

Lloyd Hasleby shows us the ruins of the mine.

Jane King (née White) at the grave of George White Junior.

Epilogue

George White was my great-great-grandfather and my preoccupation with his life really began in 2001. I am descended from Eliza, the daughter whom he left behind in England when he was transported to Western Australia. Eliza's son, Harry Mead, was my grandfather, and his daughter, Kate, my mother. The fact that George had been transported, this much was known in our family, along with some pre-conceived notions about his part in the crime which, if not glamorised, then certainly lessened the crime and his part in it. Just where he settled in Australia, and what had happened to him, nothing definite had been determined, or had been lost in time and generations.

Although I had gained some basic facts about his transportation and to where and with whom he had supposedly settled, the lack of evidence of a marriage, too many George Whites and several red herrings caused me to shelve the project several times. But I could never totally do so, and every so often I would resurrect George and start poking around in the records once more.

On 4th July, 2002, I embarked upon a journey by car around Australia with members of my family. George came with us in a file, which travelled by my side all the way. At every opportunity I (and George) would dodge into libraries to look for records, but the accessibility of these was very limited in the areas we were travelling. By this stage I was convinced that the line of supposition I was following was the correct one and I determined that I would try and find if there were any descendants from George's Australian family around the town of Northampton, Western Australia, where I believed George had settled. However, I was short of knowledge of the generation required to bring us to the present day.

En route, a lady who had been brought up in Northampton was able to give us some suggestions, starting with a visit to the Lynton convict hiring station. Here I was informed that there was already a file about George in the Chiverton House Museum in Northampton. This was the first of our surprises. But on arrival in Northampton our first visit had to be to the Gwalla cemetery where I now knew that George was buried, along with several other family members, although I had been told not to expect to find any headstones. However, there was a headstone for George White Junior, George's son. In this practically derelict cemetery, the stone had obviously been re-positioned, and the grave tidied. It was quite an eerie feeling.

The following day took us to Chiverton House Museum and the next surprise. A plaque on the wall told us that the very building we were looking at was built for/by George White. Once inside, I was shown the file on George and found almost a duplicate of the information that I had; the newspaper account of his trial in England, and his transportation. It had been lodged by a lady named Jane King, some ten years before. In the file was a telephone number which I lost no time in ringing, not knowing at that stage who Jane was. I shall never forget Jane's words to me when I spoke to her, "I always wondered what happened to Sarah and poor little Eliza whom he left behind".

Jane, too, was a descendant of George and we finally met, forging the two lives of George, and beginning a lasting friendship.

I have mixed emotions about George. Sometimes I admire him for what he achieved. Sometimes I blame him for my faults – saying that it must be in my genes. Mostly I am sad for his forgotten family in England. Certainly I am obsessed with him.

It was meeting Jane, learning of the efforts she and her husband had made to honour George's grandson who was killed in the First World War, the wealth of information that I found about George, and subsequently about Thomas Dockerill, who left on record such a valuable insight into his life, that has determined me to write it down. That George and Dockerill's very colourful lives shall be recorded for our families; the lives of two very ordinary men, but lives which were changed so dramatically by the tragic events of one night.

Simply, George's story...........

APPENDICES

Appendix A

REGULATIONS FOR TICKET-OF-LEAVE HOLDERS

Colonial Secretary's Office, Perth
April, 5, 1851.

His Excellency the Governor has been pleased to direct the publication of the following Regulations for holders of Tickets-of-leave.

By His Excellency's command,
T.N. YULE,
Acting Colonial Secretary.

———

Regulations for Holders of Tickets-of-Leave

I   All tickets-of-leave are issued for particular districts, named in the ticket-of-leave, or passports are allowed to enable the holders to remain in the service of their masters beyond the boundaries of the district.

II   Every man holding a ticket-of-leave is required within seven days after his arrival in his district to report himself, either personally or I writing, to the nearest Resident Magistrate, for the information of the Comptroller-General, giving his name, the ship he arrived in, his master or employer, his trade or calling, or his mode of maintaining himself, and his rate of wages; and also to do so between the 1st and 14th of January, and the 1st and 14th June in each year, to the nearest Resident Magistrate.

III   Every ticket-of-leave holder is required to report to the Comptroller-General every change of service or residence within the district, within 14 days of its taking place, and to obtain the sanction of a magistrate in the meantime.

IV   Immediately after the 14th Jan. and 14th June, the Resident Magistrate will report to the Comptroller-General the names of all absentees who have not duly reported themselves, as directed in paragraph two, with a view to the forfeiture of the ticket-of-leave of such men.

V   The Resident or any other magistrate of the several districts, will, whenever they think necessary, interrogate the holder of a ticket-of-leave as to his manner of means of subsistence, and if not satisfied that the ticket-of-leave man subsists honestly, will report the case forthwith to the Comptroller-General, for the information of the Governor.

VI   No ticket-of-leave holder can change the district assigned to him without permission in writing from the Comptroller-General, to whom all applications for change of district must be made, accompanied by a character for sobriety and good conduct, signed by his last master, or a magistrate of the district he wishes to leave.

VII   The district in which a ticket-of-leave is considered to have effect, is the district within which the authority of the Resident

Magistrate extends, as marked in the official boundary maps.

VIII   No ticket-of-leave holder is to be absent from his district without a pass, except in the exercise of his duty as a constable.

IX   No pass can be granted to a ticket-of-leave holder to be absent from his district except by the Comptroller-General or the Resident Magistrate; if by the Resident Magistrate, it cannot be granted for a longer period than 14 days.

X   Forms of these passes, as well as register books for the ticket-of-leave men within their respective districts, will be furnished to the magistrates by the Comptroller-General.

XI   No ticket-of-leave holder for a country district is allowed to be in either of the towns of Perth or Fremantle without at pass: any man having a pass for this purpose, to produce it immediately on his arrival, if at Perth, to the Colonial Secretary, or at Fremantle to the Comptroller-General, or in their absence, the Resident Magistrate.

XII   No ticket-of-leave holder is allowed to be employed on board whaling or other vessels.

XIII   No ticket-of-leave holder is allowed to have a licence to keep a public house, or retail spirituous or fermented liquors.

XIV   The breach of any of these regulations will subject a ticket-of-leave holder to be deprived of his indulgence, and to be returned to the Penal Establishment.

XV   Any ticket-of-leave holder who shall be guilty of repeated acts of drunkenness, or of any immoral or disorderly conduct, is also liable to forfeiture of his ticket-of-leave.

XVI   Any ticket-of-leave holder forfeiting his ticket-of-leave, returns to the position of ordinary prisoner of the crown, and forfeits all privileges belonging to a ticket-of-leave, and shall be detained until he shall have served the full term of his unexpired sentence or sentences, as well as of the time during which he shall have been absent, if an absconder. The indulgence of a ticket-of-leave can only be restored to him at the pleasure of the Governor.

XVII   Every person having a ticket-of-leave man in his employment, is to report immediately to the nearest magistrate and to the Comptroller-General, in case such ticket-of-leave man shall be absent without leave, or shall abscond from his service, or from the district assigned him; and such magistrate and Comptroller-General will forthwith issue warrants for his apprehension.

XVIII   Such reward as His Excellency the Governor, on the recommendation of the Comptroller-General, may see fit, will be paid for the arrest of any ticket-of-leave holder, absent without leave, or absconding from his district.

XIX   The holder of a ticket-of-leave is liable to be punished in a summary way for all crimes and misdemeanours not punishable with death, by transportation or hard labour, in or without irons, on any of the roads or public works of the colony, for any term not exceeding 3 years, or in case of a male offender by whipping, not exceeding 50 lashes; and such punishment by whipping may be awarded in addition to any sentence of hard labour.

XX   Ticket-of-leave holders are also subject to be punished on summary conviction, before any one or more Justices of the Peace, for the following crimes, viz.

Harbouring a convict illegally at large, – punishment : whipping, not exceeding 100 lashes, or hard labour with or without irons, not exceeding 12 calendar months.

If found on board ship with intent to escape – transportation not exceeding 14 and not less than 7 years.

If found on board ship without lawful authority – hard labour in irons, not exceeding 12 months.

Taking any convict on board ship without lawful authority – hard labour, in or without irons, for any term not exceeding two years, or whipping not exceeding 100 lashes.

14. Vic., No. 6, sec. 29. – "Carrying fire arms without a written permission from the Colonial Secretary, a Justice of the Peace, or the Comptroller-General – imprisonment and hard labour in or without irons for a period not exceeding twelve calendar months."

XXI   Any ticket-of-leave holder sentenced to punishment by magisterial sentence for any of the above offences, will not have his ticket-of-leave restored to him, except at the pleasure of the Governor.

XXII   All sentences to irons, to the roads, to the treadmill, or to hard labour, are to be served in addition to the prisoner's original sentence. Thus, if a prisoner's original sentence is 14 years, and he receives a sentence of 6 months to irons, he will not be free until he has served 14 years and 6 months.

XXIII   Every ticket-of-leave holder is subject to the provisions of the Master's and Servant's Act in Western Australia; and under this act a ticket-of-leave holder can compel his master or employer to perform his part of the contract, in all respects as efficiently as if the prisoner was a free man.

XXIV   Every ticket-of-leave holder by Act of Parliament, is allowed to acquire and hold personal property, and a leasehold and interest in land, and to maintain an action or suit for the recovery of any personal property, or for any debt due to him, or for any damage or injury sustained by him but if he should at any time forfeit his ticket-of-leave from misconduct, the property acquired by him, will become absolutely vested in Her Majesty, and will be disposed of at the discretion of the Governor of the colony.

XXV   Every ticket-of-leave holder is required to pay into the hands of the Comptroller-General of Convicts, the sum of £15, on account of the expenses of his passage to the colony.

XXVI   For the payment of this sum, every employer of a ticket-of-leave holder is required to pay to the Comptroller-General of Convicts, a sum not less than £5 per annum, out of the amount of wages for which the holder of the ticket-of-leave has engaged, and not more than £5 per annum unless at the desire of the ticket-of-leave man; either yearly or half-yearly, as may suit his convenience, or at the termination of any engagement for a shorter period. These payments may be made, either directly to the Comptroller-General or through the Resident Magistrate; but such payments must be notified to the Comptroller-General, who will forward two receipts, one for the employer, and the other for the ticket-of-leave holder.

XXVII No person is allowed to employ a ticket-of-leave man without notifying the same to the Comptroller-General through the Resident Magistrate, together with the rate of wages at which he has been engaged; and the amount of £5 per annum out of wages, if not paid by such employer to the Comptroller-General or Resident Magistrate, will be recoverable in like manner as any other debt.

XXVIII Every ticket-of-leave holder who is allowed to work on his own account will be required to pay such an amount as the Comptroller-General may decide, according to his ability and means of obtaining employment.

XXIX The Comptroller-General has the power of retaining any ticket-of-leave holder he may think fit, or who may not be able to obtain employment, and employ him on the public works, under such regulations as to rations, lodgings, and mode of payment as may from time to time be sanctioned by His Excellency.

XXX No ticket-of-leave holder will, except under special circumstances, be allowed a conditional pardon, until one half of his sentence of transportation, reckoning from date of conviction, has expired, and that he has served without offence which on ticket of leave; nor will receive a conditional pardon until the whole sum of £15 has been paid; but when he has paid the sum of £10 he may apply of a conditional pardon through the Comptroller-General, provided his application be accompanied by a character from his master or employer, for honesty and sobriety, countersigned by a magistrate; he will then be recommended to the Secretary of State for a conditional pardon, so that it may arrive about the period of expiration of his time. If he should commit any serious offence after being recommended for a conditional pardon, he will forfeit that pardon, for such a period as His Excellency the Governor may see fit.

XXXI The wives and families of well conducted ticket of leave men will be sent out to them when half the cost of doing so has been paid by themselves, their friends, or their parishes in the United Kingdom; or the expense of their passage may be assumed as a debt by the ticket-of-leave holder, to be repaid under a bond, by the same means as the expenses of his own passage.

Appendix B

REPORT OF TRIAL FROM BEDFORD TIMES

(sic)

BEDS. LENT ASSIZES,

Saturday, March 10th

Proceedings were resumed in both Courts this morning precisely at nine o'clock.

CROWN COURT.

(Before Mr. Baron Rolfe.)

MURDEROUS ATTACK ON THE POLICE

George White (24) *Thomas Dockerill* (29) and *William White* (22) labourers, Standbridge, were charged with having on the 25 January 1849 at the parish of Standbridge, unlawfully and maliciously wounded James Parrot and William Clough, with the intent to prevent their lawful apprehension, and that the said Thomas Dockerill did unlawfully and maliciously shoot at and wound the afore said James Parrot. The prisoners pleaded "Not guilty".

Mr Prendergast and Mr Tozer prosecuted, and Mr Burcham defended the prisoners.

Wm Clough, Police-constable, stated that he and Parrot were watching the house of Dockerill on the night of the 24th. About 11 o'clock, he saw a man come from the direction of Tilsworth to Dockerill's yard gate, but in consequence of his position he could not see whether he went in or not. In a minute or two after another man came from the same direction, and on that occasion he distinctly heard the gate open. In the course of half an hour he heard several persons leave the house and go towards Eggington. Witness then, with police-constable Parrot went round the field and got into the road leading to the latter village. After remaining concealed under the hedge by the roadside, about 140 yards from Dockerill's house they saw three men coming from the direction of Eggington each carrying a sack. Witness and his companion remained quietly in their place of concealment until the men came up, when

witness sprang out and seized Wm White. The sacks were thrown down and the men prepared themselves to resist. George White had a bludgeon, and Dockerill who had a gun called out "Go in at them;" or words to that effect. George White attempted to strike witness on the head, but he avoided the blow. Dockerill then presented his gun, but witness turned William White round and placed him between, and Dockerill then presented the gun at Parrot and fired. Immediately after, George White struck witness a heavy blow to the head and he fell to the ground. While in that position he felt two or three heavy blows on his head, which he believed from the hollow sound which accompanied them, were given by Dockerill's gun. Witness never let go William White until knocked down, when from repeated heavy blows he became insensible. Had no doubt of the prisoners being the men who attacked them. When he came to himself, the three sacks were lying in the road, and he crawled to the house of Mr. Gadsden at Stanbridge. The witness gave a minute description of the dress of the two Whites, which was the same as that given on a former occasion.

Mr Burcham severely cross-examined the witness, but nothing of moment was elicited.

Police-constable Parrot confirmed the testimony of the last witness up to the time the attack was made upon them, when he proceeded to furnish additional details. At the spot where the affray took place, there were two gates, one on each side of the road, exactly opposite to each other. When Dockerill raised his gun to hit Clough, witness presented his pistol, and said if he offered to hit or harm anybody he would instantly shoot him. Dockerill then passed away a little distance, with the intention apparently to level his gun at Clough; witness repeated his threat when Clough called out, "Look out or you'll be knocked down" and on turning George White was in the act of hitting him, when he fired his pistol but it missed him. On turning to look in the opposite direction, saw Dockerill level his gun at him, and instantly he felt wounded

in the left shoulder. Witness did not fall immediately; he staggered for some distance with the intention to get away, but failed in the attempt and fell down. Dockerill and one of the Whites followed and struck him on different parts of the body. After being struck on the head, one of them said "There, you have done him; he'll not get up again." Witness then became insensible, and on recovering he found himself near Eggington. He knew Dockerill before by his person but was not acquainted with him. He saw George White on the Tuesday following and immediately recognised him. William White was brought to him on the 1st February; he had a clear recollection of his dress, which, however was not the same as the one he had on when brought to him, but thought he was not so tall; he hesitated at first though he had a strong impression on his mind that he was one of the party. The same man was afterwards brought to him in a different dress, when all doubt about him being the man Clough had hold of on the night of the affray was removed. Some of the shots were still in his body.

[During the examination of the last witness, Mr.

Burcham, who had been previously compelled to leave court for a few minutes from indisposition, was again compelled to desist, and transferred the defendant's case to Mr. Power; he, however, remained in court and assisted his learned friend during the remainder of the trial.]

Daniel Billington was in Tilsworth road on the night in question, and met two men whom he thought were the Whites. He wished them "Good night". One of them replied "Good night Daniel". Witness mentioned the circumstance to his brother on the following day.

Thomas Batts deposed that he was called up about two o'clock on the morning of the 25th by Parrot, who presented a sad spectacle; he had been shot, and blood was streaming from his head. In consequence of what he said, witness went to Stanbridge, in company with Mr. Adams. The three sacks were lying in the road, two of which they took with them to Mr. Mead's yard; the third was left against one of the gates before-mentioned. Marks of struggle and blood were found in the road. Afterwards, but before day-light, he went to the house of Dockerill, and found a round frock behind the door; there were marks of blood upon it which appeared to be quite fresh.

John Franklin apprehended Dockerill about four o'clock on the morning of the 25th. Searched his house, but did not find a gun; witness asked him for it, but he said he had not got one. Witness then said. "You had one yesterday; where is it now?" Dockerill replied "I gave it to its owner yesterday afternoon". On asking him the name of the owner he refused to tell witness. Superintendent Young, Jeremiah Boreham, Gains Batchlor, Wm Adams, and Superintendent Jebbutt, also gave evidence to prove several points in the charge against the prisoners, but which more particularly involved Dockerill.

Mr. Wagstaffe, surgeon, stated that he attended Clough, and found him labouring under a concussion of the brain; he remained very slightly sensible for some days. There were two wounds on the right side of the head, about an inch in extent each; and the face was much swollen. The wounds were such as might have been inflicted with the edge of a gun or the tip of a shoe. Clough continued ill for sometime;

and, for nearly a week, there did not appear the least chance of his recovery. Mr Power addressed the jury, at great length, for the prisoners, and contended that the only evidence against the Whites was that of the two policeman who spoke to their identity. After commenting on the meagreness of that part of the case, and that the jury would see the necessity of pausing before they convicted upon such unsatisfactory testimony, he concluded an able address by stating that he should be able to produce evidence to show that the policemen were totally mistaken the persons of the two Whites, who were at their own houses on the night in question.

He then called Ruth King, who deposed she live next door to Geo. White at Houghton Regis. About ten o'clock on the night of the 24th, on finding she had no lucifer matches, she went to the back door of George White's house to borrow some, and opening the door, saw him going upstairs with his child in his arms. The husband of witness was ill at the time, and she sat up nearly the whole of the night. About one o'clock, the wall which separated the two houses being very thin, she heard White talk to the baby.

Sharp, the policeman and Mr Meads went to his house next day to examine White's head, but finding no wound, said he was not the man they wanted. Witness did not mention the circumstance to the police; she went to the Woburn Petty Session, but could not give her evidence.

Wm Scrivenor, fishmonger, of Houghton Regis, said whilst there Geo. White came in with a jug for beer. Witness spoke to him, and asked him to buy the last lot of fish he had left. The witness gave George White a good character. James Rhodes corroborated the above evidence.

Stephen Inns stated, he lived at Chalk Hill, near Wm White. On the night of the 24th, the latter went to his house, and remained talking with him "while" ten. The distance from Chalk Hill to Dockerill's house is three miles. Charles White, brother of William, was at the house of the latter on the night of the January 24th and remained there till he came at ten o'clock.

Samuel Burgess, of Dunstable, gave Wm White a good character.

Mr Prendergast replied for the prosecution. Mr Baron Rolfe went through the evidence very minutely, and was particular in making a distinction between the case of Dockerill and that of the two Whites, and said that the evidence against the former was very conclusive, but as regard the latter there was a great deal of conflicting testimony. His lordship then explained the law of the case: Where several persons concerted together in the dead of night, with arms for the purpose of resistance, should they be detected in the act, if death or any injury occurred to the parties who endeavoured to apprehend the person or prevent the robbery, all the parties engaged in such unlawful practices, and resisted with violence their lawful apprehension, all were responsible in the eye of the law. He then pointed out the circumstances favourable to the Whites, and adverted to the evidence of the witnesses who were called to prove an alibi, and said it was entitled to every consideration. If the testimony of the witnesses for the defence was to be relied upon there was a reasonable probability that the Whites were not the men who took part with Dockerill in the outrage; but if they trusted entirely to the statements of

the policemen to the identity of the men it would be impossible for them to come to any other conclusion that all the prisoners at the bar were guilty to the crime laid to their charge.

The Jury deliberated for some time, and then pronounced a verdict of Guilty against all prisoners, the foreman adding that they considered W. White guilty to a certain degree, but not with the intention of doing bodily harm. This qualification was however withdrawn, on his lordship observing that it could not be received; the Jury must return either a verdict of acquittal, or say he was guilty of the charge. His lordship, in passing sentence, said the prisoners had been convicted of an atrocious crime; it was only by the province of God that the lives of two persons were not sacrificed to their brutal outrage, and their punishment would be most severe. He could conceive nothing more dangerous to life and property than a number of persons going about armed for the purpose of plundering, and to resist to the death should they happen to be interrupted in their nefarious practice. [The Whites here protested

their innocence.] The jury had decided otherwise, and he, as judge, was bound to carry out the law. He should, however, make a difference in the sentence he was about to pass; for though the case for the Whites was bad enough, it was not so bad as that of Dockerill, upon whom would be inflicted the fullest extent of punishment. He then sentenced Dockerill to be transported for life; Geo White and William White for 15 years each. [The latter still protested their innocence, and Dockerill asked the judge to recall the sentence against Wm White, as he was innocent] His lordship said he would be sorry if he had sentenced an innocent person, but the jury had come to a contrary conclusion, and he would not alter it. The younger White then attempted to address the court, but failing to do so, he fell down in a swoon and in that state was conveyed from the dock.

The trial lasted nearly six hours, and excited in the audience, amongst whom there was a great number of persons from the country, the liveliest interest.

Appendix C

SIR JOSHUA JEBB, K.C.B.

Died 26 6 1863

OBITUARY

From Illustrated London Times 4 7 1863 p 19

Major-General Sir Joshua Jebb, K.C.B., Surveyor-General of Convict Prisons and Inspector-General of Military Prisons, whose awfully sudden death occurred on the 26th ult., was the eldest son of Joshua Jebb, Esq., of Walton, in the county of Derby, by his wife Dorothy, daughter of General Henry Gladwin, of Stubbin Court, in the same county. He was born on the 8th of May, 1793, and was educated at the Royal Academy, Woolwich. He received his commission in the Royal Engineers in 1812. He served with that distinguished corps in America in 1812–13, but does not appear to have been subsequently engaged in military matters beyond those of ordinary routine. He became a Lieutenant-Colonel in 1817; a Colonel in 1854; and a Major-General on July 6, 1860. He was made a K.C.B. (for civil services) on March 25, 1859. In 1838 Jebb, then a Major in his corps, turned his mind to civil pursuits; and, after rendering much service to the Home Office, became chairman of the Directors of Convict Prisons, Inspector-General of Military Prisons, and Surveyor-General of Convict Prisons. Of late years Surveyor-General Sir Joshua Jebb has exercised vast influence over our penal system. The ticket-of-leave plan, latterly so much complained of, was adopted before his administration, and Sir Joshua, finding it in existence, but not altogether approving of it, laboured hard to make the most of it, and to mould it into, if not a perfect, at least a useful system. The late frequency, however, of the crime of garrotting created much public alarm, and was attributed to criminals who had too easily obtained tickets of leave. Hence the debates on the subject in Parliament resulting in the Government granting a Commission – which is now sitting – to inquire into the whole

Portrait from a photograph by Mr. Herbert Watkins.
From Illustrated London News 11 7 1863 p 36

system of secondary punishments. Sir Joshua was examined before this commission, but his evidence has not yet been made public.

Among Sir Joshua's various publications may be mentioned, "Notes on the Theory and Practice of Sinking Artesians"; "A Flying Shot at Fergusson and his 'Perils of Portsmouth'"; "A Manual for the Militia"; and a pamphlet on the defence of London. Sir Joshua Jebb married, first, on the 14th of June, 1830, Mary Legh, daughter of William Burtinshaw Thomas, Esq., of Highfield, Derbyshire, by whom (who died in 1850) he had a son, Joshua Gladwyn, and three daughters. He married, secondly, on the 5th of September, 1854, Lady Amelia Rose Pelham, daughter of Thomas, second Earl of Chichester, and sister to Henry Thomas, third and present Earl of Chichester. The family of Jebb, of which that to which Sir Joshua Jebb belonged is a branch, was of very ancient standing at Woodborough, in Notts, and counted among its kindred by marriage the famous Grand Pensionary, John de Witt. Sir Richard Jebb, M.D., of this line (son of the learned Dr. Jebb, editor of "Roger Bacon" and "Aristides"), was physician to George III., and one of the eminent practitioners of his day; he was created a Baronet in 1778. One of his first cousins, the son of the Dean of Cashel, was the learned Dr. John Jebb, Fellow of Peterhouse, Cambridge; and another cousin was Mrs. Radcliffe, the famed author of "The Mysteries of Udolpho". Latterly, the main branch of the family settled in Ireland, and was highly distinguished there, its late representative being the eminent Judge of the Irish Court of the King's Bench, Mr. Justice Richard Jebb, whose brother was the no less eminent Dr. John Jebb, a barrister of Lincoln's Inn, late one of the Jersey Commissioners, and now Vicar-General to the Bishop of Sodor and Man.

Appendix D

THE NEW VICE-CHANCELLOR,
SIR ROBERT MONSEY ROLFE, A.M.
From Illustrated London News 9 11 1850 p357 & 358

This eminent lawyer – one of the most learned of his time – is the elder and only surviving son of the late Rev. Edmund Rolfe, A.B., Rector of Cockley Clay, Norfolk, by Jemima his wife, fourth daughter of William Alexander, Esq., brother of the first Earl of Caledon. His grandfather, the Rev. Robert Rolfe, M.A., and his great-grandfather, the Rev. Waters Rolfe, A.B., were both beneficed clergymen in Norfolk. The former married Alice, daughter of the Rev. Edmund Nelson, Rector of Hilburgh, and thus Sir Robert's father and the great Lord Nelson were cousins-german.

The Vice-Chancellor was born 18th December, 1790. He received his education at Bury St. Edmunds and Cambridge, where he took a Wrangler's degree in 1812; and was called to the Bar in 1816, by the Hon. Society of Lincoln's Inn. In 1832 he obtained a silk gown; and in 1834 was appointed Solicitor-General, which office he continued to hold, with the brief interval of Sir Robert Peel's first Administration, until 1839, when he was raided to the Bench as a Baron of the Exchequer. He sat in Parliament for Penryn from 1832 to 1839; and was Knighted in 1835. Sir Robert married, in 1845, Laura, daughter of the late William Carr, Esq., of Frognall. His Christian name of "Monsey" he derives from his maternal great-grandfather, the celebrated Dr. Monsey, physician to Chelsea College.

As a judge, both in the courts of law and equity, Sir Robert Rolfe enjoys a high and deserved reputation. His perfect temper and courtesy, his thorough knowledge of his art in all its branches, his ready application of it on all occasions, and his wonderful quickness in apprehending the facts and bearings of every case before him, render his services invaluable on the bench. He is indeed a complete impersonation of that intellectual and impartial justice of which we read in the histories of Greece and Rome, but which probably has never so really existed anywhere as in England.

15 August 1868

The Late Lord Cranworth

The death of this esteemed Judge was lately announced. Most of our readers are well acquainted with the facts and dates of his career. He was Robert Monsey Rolfe, son of a clergyman in Norfolk. An equity barrister and M.P. for Penrhyn, he became Solicitor-General under Lord Melbourne's Government, and held that office till 1839, when he was created one of the Barons of the Exchequer. In 1850, when the Great Seal was placed in commission, it was intrusted to him conjointly with Lord Langdale and with Vice-Chancellor Sir Lancelot Shadwell; on whose death, a few weeks afterwards, he was nominated one of the Vice-Chancellors. This post he exchanged in the following year for that of one of the Justices of Appeal in Chancery, which he continued to hold until the Great Seal of the kingdom was intrusted to his hands by Lord Aberdeen, on the formation of the Coalition Cabinet, in December, 1852. He was then raised to the peerage which has now became extinct by his death. He again held the Great Seal in 1865–6, in the interval between Lord Westbury's retirement and the return of Lord Derby to power. The Portrait is engraved from a photograph by Messrs. W. and D. Downey, of Newcastle-on-Tyne.

The Late Lord Cranworth.

Appendix E

OUR PRISON TYRANNY

From Illustrated London News
Saturday 22 October 1842

There is no duty which society more imperatively demands from its administration of public justice than a proper apportionment of punishment to the various criminals who offend against its laws. The scale of retribution should in some measure resemble the quicksilver in a thermometer – ascending or descending, so as to indicate the different degrees of crime; but in all cases the punishment should be abstract – a simple infliction complete in itself, not heightened by accessories of circumstance; not subject to be either mitigated or increased by the prevalence of a bad or good system

There have been within the last few days two of three deaths recorded, of persons committed to prison for minor offences (vagrancy being among them), whom, upon investigation, their imprisonment has been found to have killed. The victims, however, did not die under the natural punishment of the law, but under the illegitimate causes of starvation – low diet, damp cells, and a brutalizing system of inhumanity never contemplated by Christian legislation. This fact is a dreadful one to acknowledge. The lives of prisoners belong as sacredly to the community as the lives of legislators; and, so long as they are fair (?), expiating their crimes or errors, it is the province of justice to see that they be saddled with no extra-judicial tyranny, and, above all, with no unmerciful cruelty or neglect. Yet the public mind has been shocked during the week with the details of a coroner's inquest, in which the sickening account has been adduced of what seems almost like the moral murder of a wretched fellow-being in a prison, to which he had been committed for a crime far less in its enormity than that which its punishers were inflicting upon himself. The poor fellow who gave evidence of the sad cruelty gave it almost in the presence of his God. It was his dying testimony, and he had ceased to bear malice even against those who had brought him to his grave. The inquest upon his own body after death elicited its repetition from a gentlemen of the name of Hollis, to whom he had feebly deposed it. Mr Hollis, one of the guardians at Cheltenham (Charles Beale, the victim in question, died in the Northleach House of Correction), instituted the coroner's inquiry as a matter of duty, and testified thus:

> He appeared sensible that his end was near. I asked him a great number of questions, and he stated, as a dying man, that what he had previously told myself and two other members of the committee was true. He said his death would be caused by his treatment in prison. I asked him if it was true that he had been kept in a cold damp cell? He said it was, he was kept there for fourteen hours a day, and for two successive days. He called it the cellar used for placing the potatoes in, and he said he was employed in picking them. He said he was placed there when he was too ill to work on the treadmill. I then asked him if this was the cold cell he had before told the committee of, as having been forced into when hot from the mill? He said, "No, it was not; that was the one appropriated for taking his meals in, and the cold sustained there was the first cause of his illness." I also then asked him, with reference to the gaoler and surgeon, to whom it was that he attributed blame? He replied, "First and principally to the surgeon, and next to the governor." I asked him why he blamed the surgeon? He replied, that the surgeon, he considered, had the power to prescribe for him medicine and food suitable to the circumstances, but all he did was to allow him half a pound of mutton daily extra, but his stomach was so bad that he could not take it. The governor would not allow him (deceased) to see his father, who had come from Cheltenham for that purpose, but this was accounted for by his not having a visiting magistrate's order.

He said he was quite well when he went to gaol. I did not see him
again until he died.

A fellow prisoner, who declared that he had never been in prison before,
nor charged before a magistrate in his life, and who stated that he and
the deceased were "convicted for selling a stolen board" (we presume
with a supposed guilty knowledge), swore as follows of the deceased:

He was partner-sawyer with me for a long time, and was strong
and healthy. He was kept on the wheel at Northleach for two
months at first. It was not so laborious as sawing, but more
tiresome, as we had no ease or rest, and it was harder to us. I was
weak while there for want of sufficient food, which was brought on
my subsequent illness. I went on the wheel when I was not able;
but I preferred it to being in the cold damp cell, as I was starved
there. The cells are all of cold stones, seat and all, and a brook
runs under them. In one of the cells we had an iron bedstead to sit
on. Deceased and myself got warm on the wheel at first. We were
often removed, with our shirts as wet as dung, to a cold cell. They
were so wet with perspiration that we could wring them so that
it ran on the ground. Deceased was taken ill after we had been
there almost two months. H had a yellow appearance, as if he had
jaundice. He was taken off the wheel, but put on again before he
had recovered. To my knowledge he was then taking medicine.
He walked two turns instead of one, which made it lighter, for
about a fortnight. He was then put on again to his full work, but
was soon taken worse again; he had more medicine, continuing
his full work; but getting worse still worse he was taken off the
wheel and locked up in the cell for some time; after which he was
removed to the hospital. He was employed when ill in the potato-
bin, which is on a level with the brook. That was previous to
his going to the hospital, from which he was discharged in three
weeks, having served his full time of imprisonment. We could

neither of us walk, and our friends sent a cart for us. This was on the 1st of September. The governor, instead of letting us out at six o'clock in the morning, did not do so until eight. He knew we were very weak. Beale told me when I shaved him that he was so famished he had eaten nearly half a peck of raw potatoes while in the cellar. Deceased had applied several times to the two surgeons (who are brothers) for medicine, who made the remark, "You don't get very fat," but gave him none. He coughed very much at nights, and was very ill at those times. I have often made the same application when I have been ill, but they would not attend to it. I have heard him complain to the surgeons of a pain in his chest. He had medicine for his cough. I heard the surgeon tell him to mind and not take cold, and this was just before they put him in the potato-cellar. When he was taken to the hospital he was bled, and had a blister on his chest and side. I went up to shave him, and had then an opportunity of speaking to him. I have known deceased obliged to leave the wheel in consequence of weakness before his proper time. I have seen many faint and fall down in the yard from the wheel. I never was in prison before, or ever charged with any offence before a magistrate in my life. I was convicted with the deceased of selling a stolen board. In rainy weather the wet often runs down the walls.

The evidence of the surgeon went to show that the deceased died of inflammation of the lungs – that, in a predisposed habit, such disease might be initiated by hard labour, aggravated by damp and cold, and brought to a climax by low diet and starvation – in a word, not to mince plain English or compromise the honest truth, that "the man came by his death by the usage he had received in gaol." The coroner, upon the plea of Consulting the authorities (what business had he to consult any other authority than his jury!), postponed his inquiry until this day (Friday), and tomorrow, we presume, we may know the result, though too late to descant upon it in this week's paper.

In the meanwhile, we have thought it right to place the case prominently before our readers, and to preface it with such remarks as may aid the inferences of the charitable and humane upon a subject which is not the less momentous because it refers only to the correction and well-being of the "stray and erring" of the social fold. If a murderer attempts suicide (one has done so latterly with a razor), we sew up his throat, take him to an hospital, and treat him with every care and delicacy that may bring about recovery, in order that we may try and hang him afterwards, as speedily as the law will allow. If a man turns vagrant, or sells a stolen board, we sentence him to a few months' imprisonment, with a particular sort of labour, as sufficient retribution; and, instead of confining ourselves to that retribution, we starve, rheumatise, sweat, chill, and grind him to death. We kill one man for a minor offence, and save the life of another for a major one, by way of setting off the humanity of saving to kill against the humanity of killing to save. Is this question of prison discipline and the inequality of our distribution of justice, one deserving of the strong and earnest observation of the public?

Appendix F

From the Independent Journal, Perth, Western Australia, May 1851
(A letter to the Editor)

"WHY AND BECAUSE"
OR THE GOVERNOR'S FIRST CATECHISM FOR NEW
MEMBERS OF COUNCIL.

Why, does the Governor say, the Chief Commissioner should get £100 more pay?
Because many countrymen and ploughmen, drink more champagne than this gentleman can afford on his salary.

Why should the Colonial Secretary receive £100 a year more?
Because the late Secretary said another paper was wanted; and that the government would take their printing into their own hands, and start a respectable journal.

Why should the Queen's Advocate get £100 more?
Because the Governor thought he would get more than £300 a year by editing a twopenny-halfpenny newspaper.

Why should the Surveyor General get £100 more?
Because it wasn't fair that settlers by honorable industry could drive their wives about in gigs and honorable members could not.

Why should the Collector of Revenue get an increase of £100 a year?
Because there was a wicked West Indian attorney who used to send one cask of sugar to his master and keep two for himself.

Why should the three clerks get an increase?
Because hay had risen, and the clerks should be gentlemen.

Why should the Chaplain get an increase?
Because Everybody else did.

Why should the Colonial Surgeon?
Because it was not his duty to attend to civilians, nor the hospital.

Why should every other official get an increase of pay, and everybody else an increase of taxation?
Because (A lady's reason) THEY SHOULD.

The above is arranged and compiled from the report of the arguments used at the Council last week; the application is, that the increase being granted – the Chief Commissioner must eschew moderation and spend his increased pay in champagne drinking; the Colonial Secretary must start a newspaper which the Advocate General must edit, and which must be sold at two-pence halfpenny; the Surveyor General must drive his wife about in a gig; the Collector of Revenue is put up to the tricks of rascally attornies; the three clerk must eat hay (in default of thistles, their more appropriate food) and become gentlemen; the Chaplain do as everybody else does – and the Surgeon, nothing at all !!!!

RIGDUM FUNNIDOS.

NOTES

Introduction

1 The National Archives (PRO)   ASSI 33/14   223499 Bedford Assizes
2 Bedfordshire and Luton Archives and Records Service QGR 1/29 Dietaries of the Gaol and House of Correction for the County of Bedford
3 Bedfordshire and Luton Archives and Records Service BLARS QGV11/2 Bedford Prison Register
4 Bedford Times, Saturday 10th March 1849
5 Bedfordshire and Luton Archives and Records Service BLARS QGV 10/2 Prison Register
6 Bedfordshire and Luton Archives and Records Service BLARS QGV 10/2 Bedford Prison Register
7 Bedford Times, Saturday 10th March 1849

Chapter 1

1 1841 Census Records HO 107 5 17
2 The History of Bedfordshire by Joyce Godber Chapter 44, Railways, Roads & Waterways, p 516
3 1841 Census Records HO 107 5 17

Chapter 2

1 Britain since 1700, R.J. Cootes, Chapter 5 The Changing Face of the Countryside Agricultural Revolution, p 52
2 English Social History G.M. Trevelyan, Chapter 9, Restoration England, p 236
3 Woburn and the Russells, Gladys Scott Thomson Chapter 4, Grandmother and Grandson, p 40
4 Ibid
5 Woburn and the Russells, Gladys Scott Thomson Chapter 4, Grandmother and Grandson, p 44
6 The English Village by Victor Bonham-Carter, Chapter 5 – The Agrarian Revolution, p 62
7 The Village Labourer Vol 1 J.L. & B. Hammond, Chapter II, Enclosure (1), p 37
8 Ibid
9 The Village Labourer Vol 1 J.L. & B. Hammond, Chapter II, Enclosure (1), p 57
10 The Village Labourer Vol 1 J.L. & B. Hammond, Chapter VI, The Remedies of 1795, p 143
11 The Village Labourer Vol 1 J.L. & B. Hammond, Chapter V, The Labourer in 1795 p 109
12 Reading Mercury, April 20, 1795
13 Trevelyans English Social History Chapter 15, Cobbett's England 1 Social

transformations and tensions p 415

14 Trevelyans English Social History Chapter 15, Cobbett's England 1 Social
transformations and tensions p 414

15 The Village Labourer Vol 1 J.L. & B. Hammond After Speenhamland p 187

16 The English Village Richard Muir. Chapter 6, The good old days?, P 160

17 The Village Labourer Vol 1 J.L. & B. Hammond After Speenhamland p 194

Chapter 3

1 Labouring Life in the Victorian Countryside – Pamela Horn – Chapter 5, Rural
Crafts and Cottage Industries, p 113

2 Village Life and Labour, History Workshop Series – Part 3 Country work girls
in nineteenth century England, Rural Industries, p. 119 – Jennie Kitteringham.
Editor Raphael Samuel

3 Labouring Life in the Victorian Countryside – Pamela Horn – Chapter 5, Rural
Crafts and Cottage Industries, p 114

4 Village Life and Labour, History Workshop Series – Part 3 Country work girls
in nineteenth century England, Rural Industries, p. 120 – Jennie Kitteringham.
Editor Raphael Samuel P.P. 1864 (3414) xxxii, Appendix (d) to the *2nd Report of
the Children's Employment Commission*, p.281

5 Ibid

6 Labouring Life in the Victorian Countryside – Pamela Horn – Chapter 5, Rural
Crafts and Cottage Industries, p 116

Chapter 4

1 Bedfordshire and Luton Archives and Records Service R5/83/1 Russell Rent
Books 1801/1802
Bedfordshire and Luton Archives and Records Service R5/83/2B Russell Rent
Books 1802/1803
Bedfordshire and Luton Archives and Records Service R5/83/3 Russell Rent
Books 1803/1804

2 The Village Labourer Vol.1 J.L. & Barbara Hammond, Chapter 4 The Village after
Enclosure, p. 94

3 Bedfordshire and Luton Archives and Records Service R5/83/2B Russell Rent
Books

4 Bedfordshire and Luton Archives and Records Service R3/2150 18 November
1820

5 Gravestone shows her name as Sally

6 Bedfordshire and Luton Archives and Records Service R5/122 Russell Rentals,

7 Bedfordshire and Luton Archives and Records Service R5/127 1836 R5/595 1832

8 Bedfordshire and Luton Archives and Records Service Land tax assessments
1838/1839

9   Morning Chronicle, 18th January 1850, Supplement, Labour and the Poor: Rural
    Districts, letter xiii.
    Village Life and Labour, Part 3 Country work girls in nineteenth-century England
    by Jennie Ketteringham 5, Moralities, p 130.
10 Bedfordshire and Luton Archives and Records Service BML 10/34/2 Sale
    Particulars 1879
11 Bedfordshire and Luton Archives and Records Service Land tax assessments.
    1850
12 Bedfordshire Times Saturday 21st February 1846
13 Bedfordshire Times Saturday 17th April 1847

Chapter 5

1   Parish Records. Children's baptism and death entries.
2   The English Village by Victor Bonham-Carter, Part 2, Elements of the Village,
    Chapter 3, The Administrative Element, Overseers, p. 140
3   The English Village, by Richard Muir, Chapter 6, The good old days?, p.147
4   The English Village by Victor Bonham-Carter, Part 2, Elements of the Village,
    Chapter 3, The Administrative Element, Overseers, p. 145
5   Ibid, p. 147
6   Ibid, Part 2, Chapter 4, The Religious Element, Account Books, p. 170
7   The English Village by Victor Bonham-Carter, Part 2, Elements of the Village,
    Chapter 3, The Administrative Element, Churchwardens, p. 141
8   Ibid, Chapter 4, The Religious Element, Church, p. 167
9   Bedfordshire and Luton Archives and Records service Churchwardens Accounts,
    P57/5/1
10 Bedfordshire and Luton Archives and Records service Churchwardens Accounts,
    P57/5/1
11 Bedfordshire and Luton Archives and Records service Churchwardens Accounts,
    P57/5/1
12 The English Village by Victor Bonham-Carter, Part 2, Elements of the Village,
    Chapter 3, The Administrative Element, Overseers, p. 147/8
13 Ibid, p.148
14 Ibid.
15 The Village Labourer Vol. 1. by J.L. & Barbara Hammond, Chapter 7, After
    Speenhamland, p 171.
16 The Village Labourer Vol. 2. by J.L. & Barbara Hammond, Chapter 9, The Village
    in 1830 p. 31
17 England in 1815 by Elie Halevy, Chapter 3, Credit and Taxation, p 377
18 Bedfordshire and Luton Archives and Records service Vestry Minutes, P57/8/1
19 Bedfordshire and Luton Archives and Records service Overseers of the Poor,
    1824–1934 (P57/12/1) & 1834–1837 (P57/12/2)

20 Bedfordshire and Luton Archives and Records service Vestry Minutes, P57/8/1

21 Sarah was probably a daughter although no baptism record has been found.

22 Ann was probably a daughter although no baptism record has been found.

23 Ibid

24 A Social History of the English Working Classes, 1815–1945, by Eric Hopkins, Chapter 6, The Problem of Poverty, The Poor Law Commission and the New Poor Law. p, 92

25 Bedfordshire and Luton Archives and Records service Vestry Minutes, P57/8/1

26 Ibid

27 Bedfordshire and Luton Archives and Records service Enclosure Awards MA60

28 Bedfordshire and Luton Archives and Records service Overseers of the Poor, 1824–1934 (P57/12/1) & 1834–1837 (P57/12/2)

29 Bedfordshire and Luton Archives and Records service Vestry Minutes, P57/8/1

30 Bedfordshire and Luton Archives and Records service Enclosure Awards MA61

31 Census records for Stanbridge HO 107 /5 / 26

32 Bedfordshire and Luton Archives and Records service Houghton Regis Land Tax 1839

33 Bedfordshire and Luton Archives and Records service Russell Rent Books R5/127 1836

34 The Bedford Times, Saturday 13th March 1847

35 The Bedford Times, Saturday 13th March 1847

36 The Bedford Times dated Saturday March 20, 1847

37 Ibid

38 Bedfordshire and Luton Archives and Records service BLARS QGV11/2 6887

Chapter 6

1   The Autobiography of William Cobbett, edited by William Reitzel, Chapter 10, 1812–1817 p.141

2   The Village Labourer, Vol 1, J.L. & Barbara Hammond, After Speenhamland p183

3   The Village Labourer, Vol 2, J.L. & Barbara Hammond, Chapter 10 The Last Labourers' Revolt 1 p 43

4   The Village Labourer, Vol 2, J.L. & Barbara Hammond, Chapter 10 The Last Labourers' Revolt 1 p 70

5   Ibid

6   The Village Labourer, Vol , J.L. & Barbara Hammond, After Speenhamland p190

7   Ibid

8   The English Village – Richard Muir Chapter 6 'The Good Old Days?' p. 150

9   The Village Labourer, Vol 2, J.L. & Barbara Hammond, Chapter 10 The Last Labourers' Revolt 1 p 71

10 The Village Labourer, Vol 2, J.L. & Barbara Hammond, Chapter 11 The Last Labourers' Revolt 2 p 74

11 The Village Labourer, Vol 2, J.L. & Barbara Hammond, Chapter 11 The Last
     Labourers' Revolt 2 p 91
12 Ibid, p.92
13 Ibid, p. 110
14 Ibid, p. 127
15 Ibid
16 Bedford Times, Saturday March 20th 1847 Rev. H.J. William sermon Lent Assizes

Chapter 7
1 The Bedford Times, Saturday 17th February, 1849

Chapter 8
1 The Bedford Times, Saturday 10th March 1849
2 TNA (PRO)   ASSI 33/14
3 The Bedford Times, Saturday 10th March 1849
4 The Bedford Times, Saturday 17th March 1849

Chapter 9
1 The National Archives (PRO) HO18 261/43 (Whole chapter – Trial notes of Judge)

Chapter 10
1 1851 census return HO107/1756/183/1 Folio 5
2 The English Village by Richard Muir Chapter 6 – The good old days? p 150
3 Bedford County Records Office. Houghton Regis Land Tax Return. 1850
4 TNA (PRO) HO13/ 96
    All William's appeals HO18/261/43

Chapter 11
1   Bedfordshire and Luton Archives and Records Service   QGR 1/3
2   Bedfordshire and Luton Archives and Records Service   QGR 1/25
3   Bedfordshire and Luton Archives and Records Service   QGR 1/6
4   TNA (PRO)   HO 45 / 1585
5   Bedfordshire and Luton Archives and Records Service   QGR 1/6
6   Bedfordshire and Luton Archives and Records Service   QGR 1/29
7   Bedfordshire and Luton Archives and Records Service   QGV 2/6
8   Bedfordshire and Luton Archives and Records Service   QGR 1/25
9   Bedfordshire and Luton Archives and Records Service   QGR 1/25
10 Bedfordshire and Luton Archives and Records Service   QGR 2/1
11 TNA (PRO)   HO13/97
12 TNA (PRO)   HO18 224/3

Chapter 12

1 TNA (PRO)   HO13/97
2 TNA (PRO)   PCOM2 30   113004
3 The English A Social History 1066–1945, Christopher Hibbert, Chapter 58, Law and Order p 667
4 www.victorianlondon.org Victorian Dictionary by Lee Jackson, Handbook of London, Peter Cunningham 1850
5 TNA (PRO)   PCOM2 30   113004
6 TNA (PRO)   HO45/2545
7 TNA (PRO)   HO45/2545
8 TNA (PRO)   HO45/2545
9 TNA (PRO)   HO45/2545
10 www.victorianlondon.org Victorian Dictionary by Lee Jackson, Communications of Cholera, John Snow. 1855. p. 94
11 TNA (PRO)   HO13/97
12 TNA (PRO)   HO13/97
13 TNA (PRO)   HO 15/1
14 TNA (PRO)   PCOM2 30   113004
15 TNA (PRO)   PCOM2 30   113004

Chapter 13

1 TNA (PRO)   HO 15/1
2 TNA (PRO)   PCOM 2/354   Governors Journals
3 TNA (PRO)   PCOM   30   113004
4 TNA (PRO)   PCOM 2/355   Governors Journals
5 www.victorianlondon.org The Victorian Dictionary, Lee Jackson. Victorian London – Publications – Social Investigation/Journalism – About London, J. Ewing Ritchie, 1860 Chapter 17, Criminal London p 179/180
6 Ibid
7 Ibid p. 179
8 Ibid p. 178
9 Ibid p. 182
10 Ibid p. 181
11 TNA (PRO)   PCOM 2/354   Governor's Journals
12 www.victorianlondon.org Victorian Dictionary by Lee Jackson,The Victorian Dictionary, Lee Jackson. Victorian London – Publications – Social Investigation/ Journalism – About London, by J. Ewing Ritchie, 1860 Chapter 17, Criminal London p. 178
13 States Record Office of Western Australia   Acc 128 / 26

Chapter 14

1   Convicts and the Colonies, by A.G.L. Shaw, Chapter 2, The Beginning of Transportation to Australia, p.43
2   Ibid , Chapter 3, Controversy in England, 1810–1830, p 141
3   Ibid , Chapter 3, Controversy in England, 1810–1830, p 138
4   Illustrated London News, 17. 06. 1848 p 394 Convicts at Bermuda
5   Convicts and the Colonies, by A.G.L. Shaw, Chapter 12, New Projects in Penology, p. 273
6   Ibid, Chapter 12, New Projects in Penology, p. 274
7   Ibid, Chapter 14, Earl Grey's Exiles, p.318
8   Ibid, Chapter 14, Earl Grey's Exiles, p.320
9   Ibid p.323
10 Ibid p.324
11 Ibid p.325
12 Ibid
13 Ibid p.331
14 Ibid p.333
15 Ibid p.342
16 Ibid p.344
17 Illustrated London News. 20th December 1851 p 723
18 The Story of Australia by A.G.L. Shaw, Chapter 7 – Variations on a Theme, p. 117
19 The Penal System in Western Australia by Raymond Gaskin, p. 2
20 Convicts and the Colonies, by A.G.L. Shaw, Chapter 15, The End of Transportation, p. 354
21 Claremont Museum, Western Australia, Expectations of Pensioner Guards as Settlers
22 Website www.convictcentral.com
23 British Library of Political and Economic Science   Jebb 3/14
24 The Independent Journal Friday 28th June, 1850
25 The Independent Journal Friday 14th June, 1850
26 The Independent Journal Friday 12th July, 1850
27 The Independent Journal Friday 12th July, 1850
28 TNA (PRO)   PCOM 2/354   Governors Journals
29 Convicts and the Colonies, by A.G.L. Shaw, Chapter 15, The End of Transportation, p. 348
30 Convicts and the Colonies, by A.G.L. Shaw, Chapter 15, The End of Transportation, p. 357
31 Ibid

Chapter 15

1   Website www.convictcentral.com

2   With Shame Remembered by Bill Beatty, Chapter 1, In the Beginning, p.8
3   The Penal System In Western Australia by Raymond Gaskin p3
4   With Shame Remembered by Bill Beatty, Chapter 1, In the Beginning, p.6 United
    Services Journal, December1846
5   TNA (PRO)   ADM /101/252 Alex Kilroy, Surgeons notes
6   TNA (PRO)   PCOM2/355   Superintendent's Journals
7   Diaries of John Acton Wroth   2816A/3 Battye Library, Perth, Western
    Australia
8   TNA (PRO)   HO 22/3
9   Diaries of John Acton Wroth   2816A/3 Battye Library, Perth, Western
    Australia
10 TNA (PRO)   ADM /101/252 Alex Kilroy, Surgeons notes
11 Ibid
12 Diaries of John Acton Wroth   2816A/3 Battye Library, Perth, Western
    Australia
13 Diaries of John Acton Wroth   2816A/3 Battye Library, Perth, Western
    Australia
14 Diaries of John Acton Wroth   2816A/3 Battye Library, Perth, Western
    Australia
15 Ibid
16 Ibid
17 Ibid
18 Ibid
19 Ibid
20 TNA (PRO)   ADM /101/138 Alex Kilroy, Surgeons notes
21 Diaries of John Acton Wroth   2816A/3 Battye Library, Perth, Western
    Australia

Chapter 16

1   TNA (PRO)   ADM 101/17/10   Surgeon's Notes
2   TNA (PRO)   PCOM2/ 355   Governor's Journals
3   TNA (PRO)   PCOM2/ 355   Governor's Journals
4   TNA (PRO)   ADM 101/17/10   Surgeon's Notes
5   TNA (PRO)   ADM 101/17/10   Surgeon's Notes
6   TNA (PRO)   ADM 101/17/10   Surgeon's Notes
7   TNA (PRO)   ADM 101/17/10   Surgeon's Notes
8   TNA (PRO)   PCOM2 137   113004
9   Convicts and the Colonies by A.G.L. Shaw, Chapter 14, Earl Grey's exiles, p.333
10 Ibid
11 TNA (PRO)   HO 8/116
12 TNA (PRO)   HO 8/122

13 TNA (PRO)   HO18/224/13
14 TNA (PRO)   HO18/224/13
15 TNA (PRO)   HO18/224/13
16 TNA (PRO)   PCOM2 137 113004
17 TNA (PRO)   ADM53/5924
18 TNA (PRO)   AO 19/26/3

Chapter 17

1   Diaries of John Acton Wroth   2816A/3 Battye Library, Perth, Western
    Australia
2   TNA (PRO)   ADM/101/252   Alex Kilroy, Surgeon's notes
3   States Record Office of Western Australia   ACC 1156 / R17 Character Book
4   States Record Office of Western Australia   ACC 1156 / R17
5   States Record Office of Western Australia,   ACC 1386 Vol 1, p.7. Ticket of
    Leave
6   Claremont Museum, Western Australia, Freshwater Bay Depot.
7   Claremont Museum, Western Australia, Reports of Captain Bruce
8   Unwilling Emigrants   Chapter V, Over the Hills, p.100
9   TNA (PRO)   CO 21/4 WA Gov. Gazette Nov. 1852
10 Ibid
11 Claremont Museum, Western Australia, Freshwater Bay Depot
12 States Record Office of Western Australia   WABI Employers of TOL men
13 States Record Office of Western Australia   WABI Employers of TOL men
14 States Record Office of Western Australia   WABI Employers of TOL men
15 States Record Office of Western Australia   AN 358/1 R17 Character Book
16 States Record Office of Western Australia   ACC 1156 / C23 States he is
    reconvicted T.L. Holder
17 Illustrated London News   28th February 1857 p 178
18 Illustrated London News   14th February 1857 p 147
19 Illustrated London News   14th February 1857 p 147
20 TNA (PRO)   CO 21/3   WA Government Gazette 8th April 1851
21 States Record Office of Western Australia   ACC 1156 / C23
22 States Record Office of Western Australia   ACC 1520 Conditional Pardons
23 TNA (PRO)   CO 21/5 WA Government Gazette Apr. 1859

Chapter 18

1   TNA (PRO)   HO 18 224/13 Petitions 2 / 9

Chapter 19

1   Dartmoor Prison A Complete Illustrated History Volume Two by Ron Joy Chapter
    1, Dartmoor Prison Opens, p 14

2   British Library of Political and Economic Science JEBB 7/7

3   TNA (PRO)   HO 18 224/13 Petitions 2 / 9

Chapter 20

1   TNA (PRO)   HO18 224 /13   Petitions 10 / 16

2   TNA (PRO)   HO 13/106   Correspondence and Warrants

3   TNA (PRO)   HO 13/106   Correspondence and Warrants

Chapter 21

1   To Be Heirs Forever, Mary Durack, Chapter 18, p 183

2   The Independent Journal December 1850

3   The Brand on His Coat, Rica Erickson, Chapter 9, Men of Enterprise, Joseph Lucas Horrocks p. 225

4   Ibid, p226

5   Perth Gazette, 2 Oct 1862

6   States Record Office of Western Australia   CONS 5000 SDUR/W4/384

7   Department of Land Information, Western Australia Book V11 67 Memorial 553 Enrolment 2164

INDEX